Insiders' Guide®

to the

Grand Canyon

Help Us Keep This Guide Up to Date

Every effort has been made by the authors and editors to make this guide as accurate and useful as possible. However, many things can change after a guide is published—establishments close, phone numbers change, hiking trails are rerouted, facilities come under new management, etc.

We would love to hear from you concerning your experiences with this guide and how you feel it could be improved and be kept up to date. While we may not be able to respond to all comments and suggestions, we'll take them to heart and we'll also make certain to share them with the authors. Please send your comments and suggestions to the following address:

The Globe Pequot Press
Reader Response/Editorial Department
P.O. Box 480
Guilford, CT 06437

Or you may e-mail us at: editorial@globe-pequot.com

Thanks for your input, and happy travels!

Insiders' Guide® Series

Insiders' Guide®
to the
Grand Canyon

By Tanya Lee
and
Kerri Quinn

Guilford, Connecticut
An imprint of The Globe Pequot Press

Library of Congress Cataloging-in-Publication Data is available

ISBN 1-57380-177-1

Manufactured in the United States of America
First Edition/First Printing

Contents

Directory of Maps

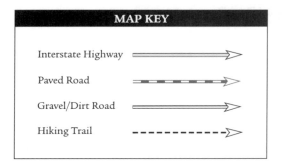

MAP KEY

Interstate Highway

Paved Road

Gravel/Dirt Road

Hiking Trail

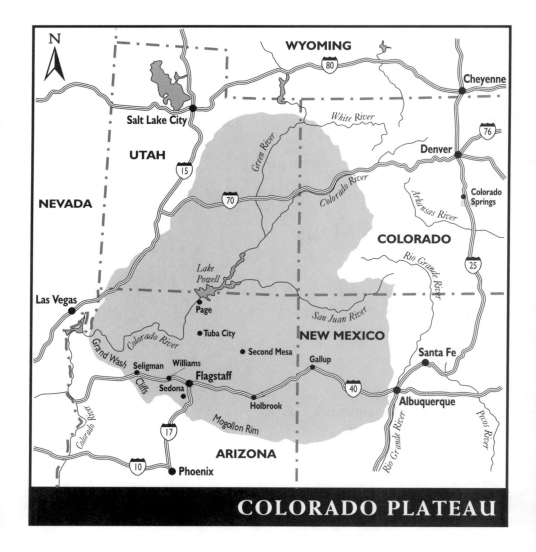

COLORADO PLATEAU

COLORADO PLATEAU TIMELINE

ERA	PERIOD	YEARS AGO IN MILLIONS	ORIGINS OF SOME PLANTS & ANIMALS	EVENTS ON COLORADO PLATEAU
CENOZOIC	Quaternary	1.6	Humans	Grand Canyon formed by uplift and erosion by the Colorado River; San Francisco Mountain and Volcanic field develop.
	Tertiary	66		
MESOZOIC	Cretaceous	138	Flowering plants	Formation of coal deposits on the Black Mesa
	Jurassic	205	Birds	Mountain building and volcanism
	Triassic	240	Mammals	
PALEOZOIC	Permian	290	Gingkos	
	Pennsylvanian	330	Reptiles, pines	
	Mississippian	360		
	Devonian	410	Amphibians, ferns, club mosses,	Western seas cover parts of the Colorado Plateau; erosion
	Silurian	435		No volcanism.
	Ordovician	500		No mountain building.
	Cambrian	570	Shelled animals, fish	Time since Colorado Plateau has been geologically stable: 600 million years
PROTEROZOIC		2500	Single-celled organisms, algae	2 billion years Age of rocks at bottom of Grand Canyon's Inner Gorge
ARCHEAN		3800?	Microscopic single-celled or filament-shaped organisms	
PRE-ARCHEAN		4600	NO RECORD OF LIFE	
FORMATION OF PLANET				

Dinosaurs (spanning Triassic–Jurassic)

Left-hand scale:

- HUMANS
- CENOZOIC
- MESOZOIC
- COLORADO PLATEAU GEOLOGICALLY STABLE
- PALEOZOIC
- 1 BILLION YEARS
- PROTEROZOIC
- 2 BILLION YEARS — AGE OF OLDEST ROCKS AT THE BOTTOM OF THE GRAND CANYON
- 3 BILLION YEARS
- ARCHEAN
- BEGINNING OF LIFE ON EARTH
- 4 BILLION YEARS
- PRE-ARCHEAN
- 4.6 BILLION YEARS

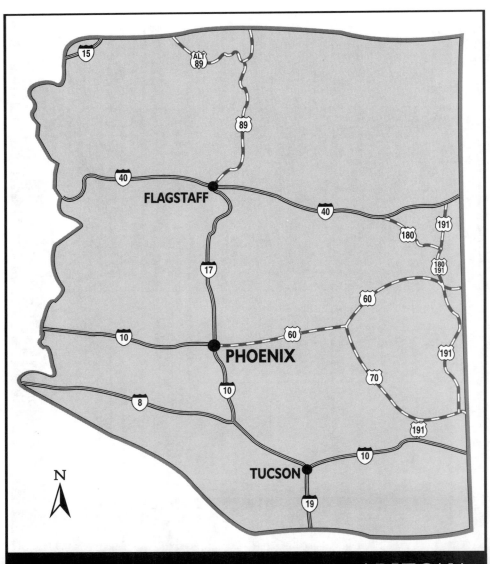

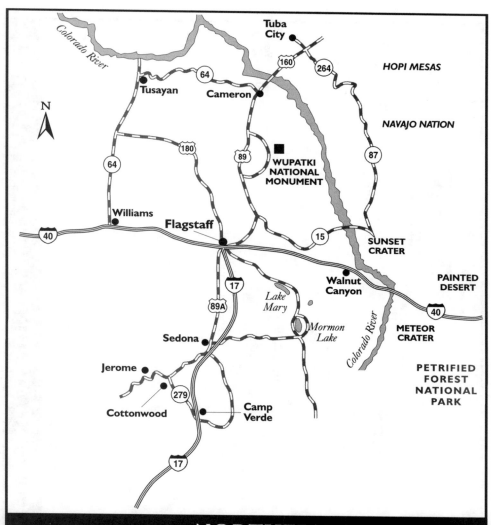

NORTHERN ARIZONA— FLAGSTAFF AND ENVIRONS

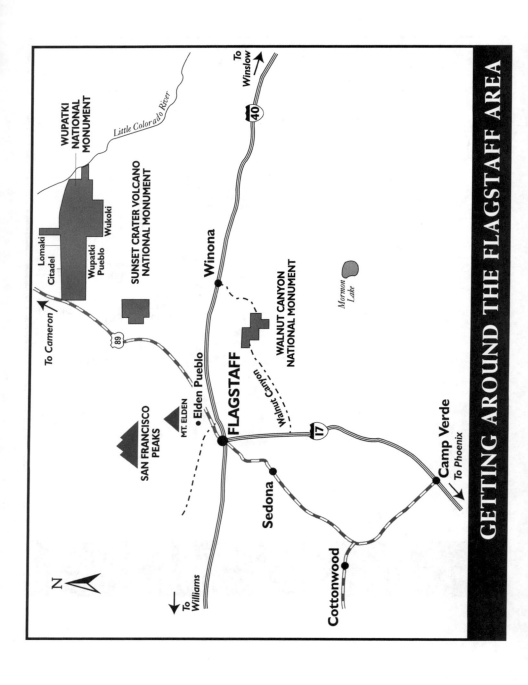

GETTING AROUND THE FLAGSTAFF AREA

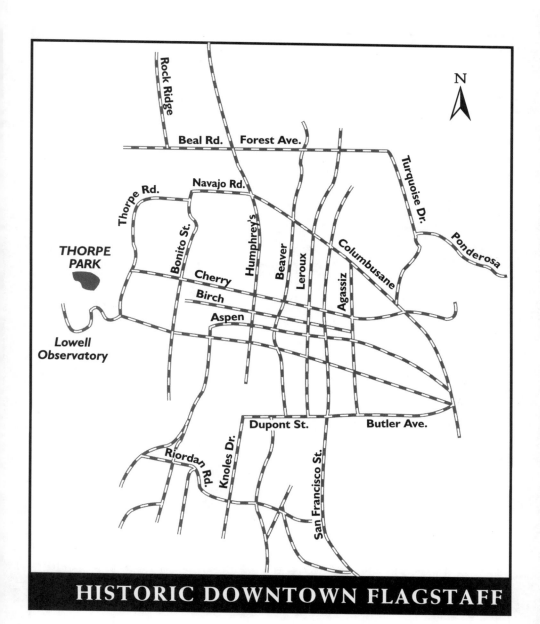

HISTORIC DOWNTOWN FLAGSTAFF

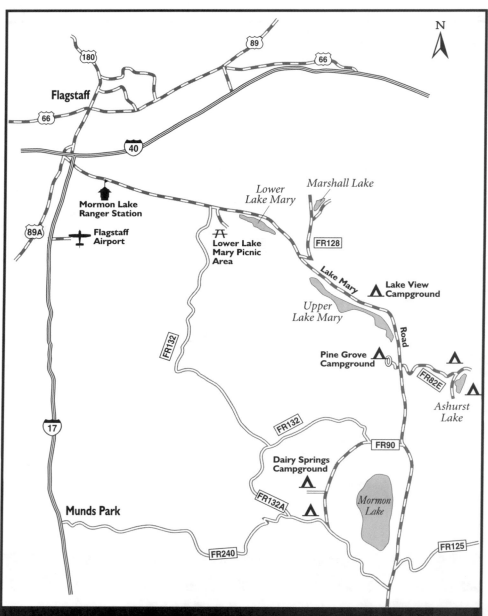

**THE PLATEAU COUNTRY /
FLAGSTAFF LAKES REGION**

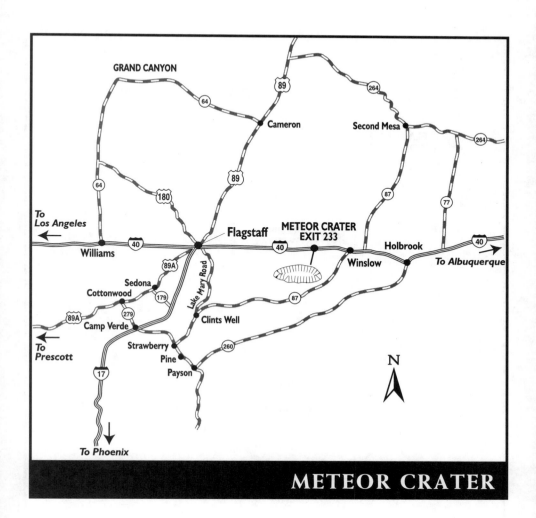

METEOR CRATER

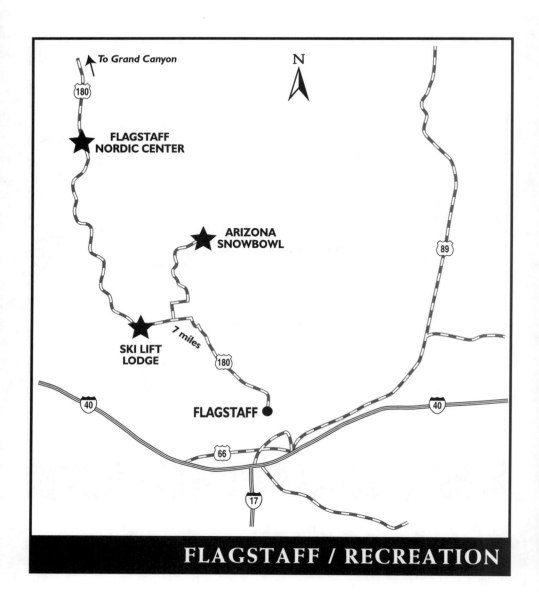

To Grand Canyon

180

N

FLAGSTAFF
NORDIC CENTER

ARIZONA
SNOWBOWL

89

7 miles

SKI LIFT
LODGE

180

40

FLAGSTAFF

40

66

17

FLAGSTAFF / RECREATION

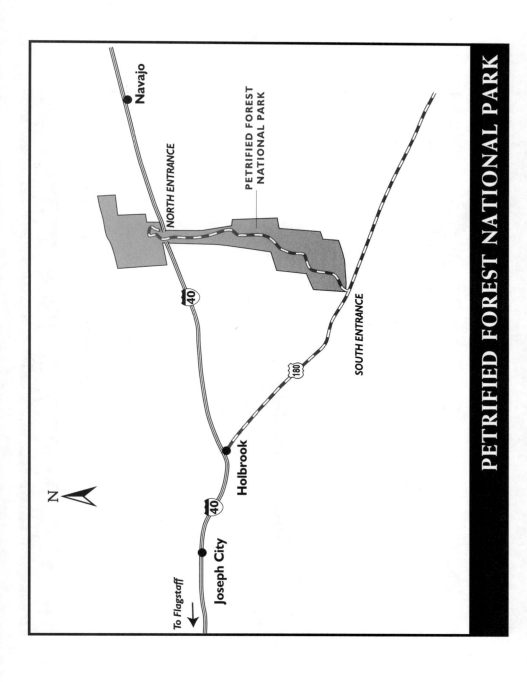

PETRIFIED FOREST NATIONAL PARK

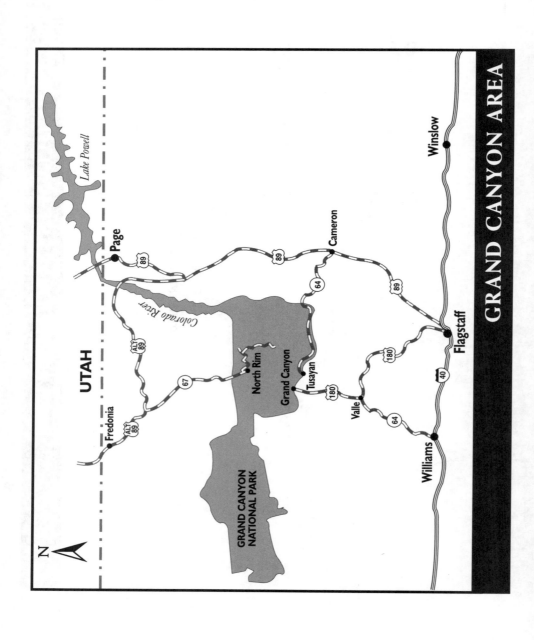

GRAND CANYON

1. Kaibab Plateau Visitors Center
2. Kaibab Lodge
3. House Rock Buffalo Ranch
4. Point Imperial
5. Vista Encantoda
6. Point Sublime
7. Grand Canyon Lodge

8. Visitors Center
9. Walhalla Overlook
10. Cape Royal
11. Phantom Ranch
12. Hermits Rest
13. Pima Point
14. Hepi Point
15. Visitors Center

16. Yavapai Point and Museum
17. Yaki Point
18. Grandview Point
19. Moran Point
20. Lipan Point
21. Tusayan Ruins and Museum
22. Grand Canyon National Airport

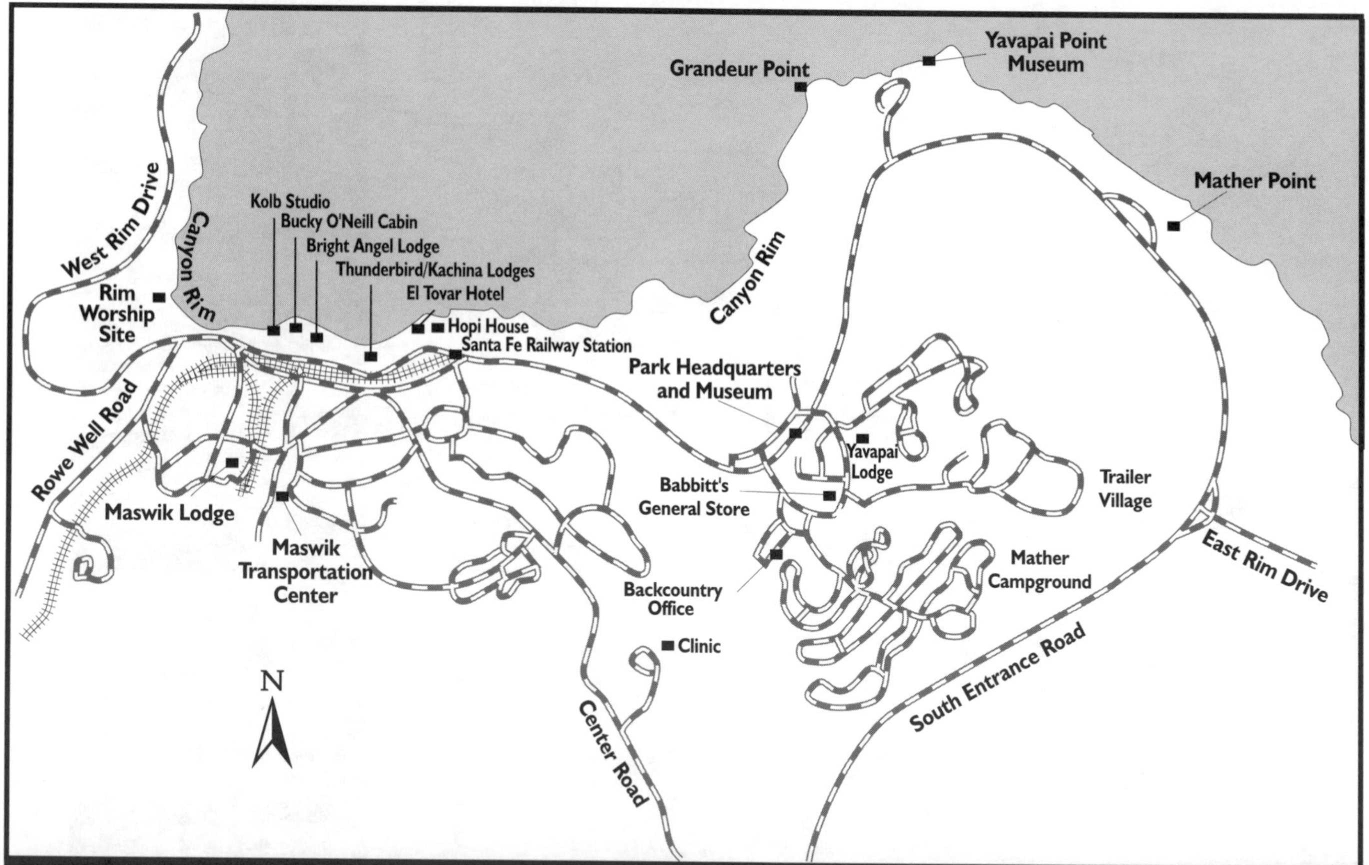

GRAND CANYON VILLAGE

Mather Point

Yavapai Point Museum

Grandeur Point

Canyon Rim

Park Headquarters and Museum

Yavapai Lodge

Trailer Village

Mather Campground

Babbitt's General Store

Backcountry Office

Clinic

Center Road

South Entrance Road

East Rim Drive

Kolb Studio
Bucky O'Neill Cabin
Bright Angel Lodge
Thunderbird/Kachina Lodges
El Tovar Hotel
Hopi House
Santa Fe Railway Station

West Rim Drive

Rim Worship Site

Canyon Rim

Rowe Well Road

Maswik Lodge

Maswik Transportation Center

N

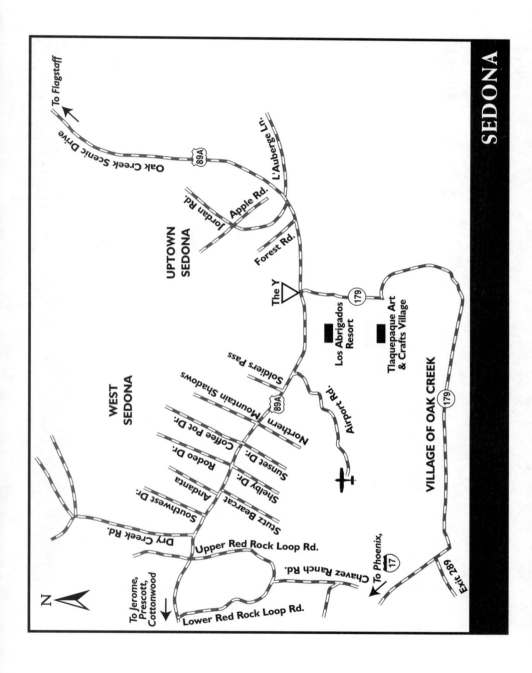

SEDONA

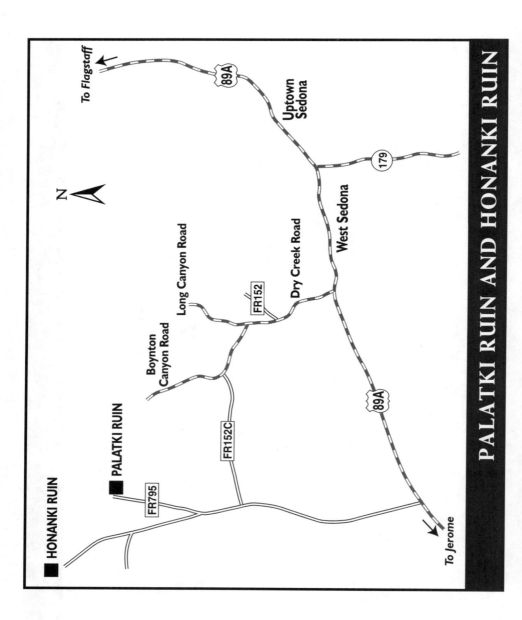

PALATKI RUIN AND HONANKI RUIN

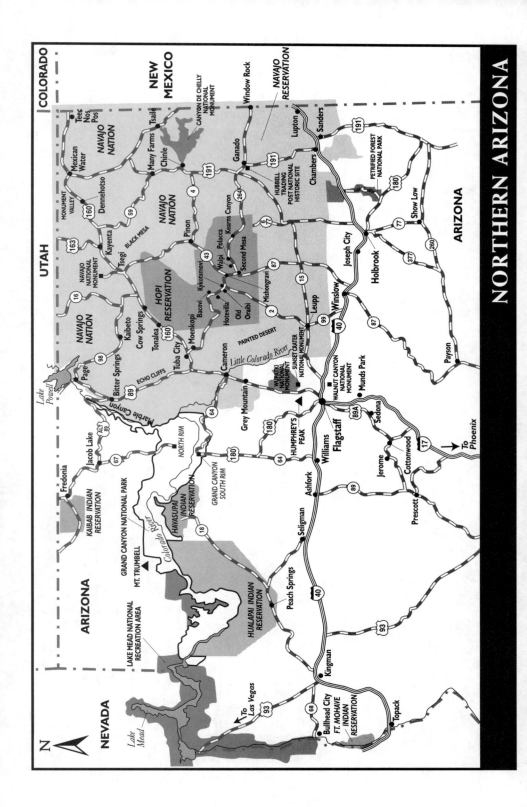

NORTHERN ARIZONA

Preface

We invite you to discover the wonders of Northern Arizona (Flagstaff, Sedona, the Grand Canyon, the Hopi and Navajo Reservations), on the Colorado Plateau in the Southwestern United States. It is a place where tiny railroad camps have grown into vibrant cities in the past hundred years, where land is sacred, and where the scenery is as unique as the people who inhabit the area.

This is a land of geological wonders, of diverse cultures, of sacrifice and betrayal, and of ways of life that have been preserved for thousands of years. The story of this region is complex—historically, economically, socially, and politically—and it is this complexity that makes the land so rich and so rewarding to visit and study and live on.

Here you will marvel at the glory that is the Grand Canyon, at the astounding beauty of the red rocks of Sedona, at the perseverance of the peoples who have developed vibrant cultures—and survived—in a region of high desert, sparse rainfall, and harsh winters.

Considered by Anglo-Europeans just a century ago to be a wild frontier, it is a land that has in fact been inhabited for millennia, and a place where Native American, Hispanic, and European cultures have met to create a human tapestry unlike any other in the world.

We welcome you to this land, ask that you respect its natural and cultural history, and invite you to have the time of your life!

Acknowledgments

For their help, support, and encouragement, we would like to thank all who assisted with this project, particularly Vernon Masayesva for his help with the chapter on the Hopi Reservation, Lynne Brenner for her help with the chapter on Williams, and the staffs of the Flagstaff Chamber of Commerce and Arizona Historical Pioneer Museum.

Kerri Quinn would like to thank Aimee Jackson for her constant support and for her ability to always make her laugh, Stacey Silverness for her keen eye and great photos, and Steve Reynolds who tolerated her, supported her, and loved her even when the deadlines rolled around. Tanya Lee would like to thank her husband, Garret Rosenblatt, for his advice, photos, and unwavering encouragement when she thought she couldn't write another word.

Many thanks also to our editor, Erika Serviss, for her help, advice and understanding.

How to Use This Book

Visiting the Colorado Plateau is a unique experience—few places on earth boast so many rich cultures, such majestic geological formations, and such a variety of activities and sightseeing opportunities in one area. If you come for just a few days, you'll surely want to come back. If you come for a few months, you still will not have exhausted the possibilities for fun, interesting food, adventure, and learning.

In order to fully appreciate your experience here, we feel that you need to know where you are geographically, when you are in geological time, and who you are in reference to the many peoples who live on this sacred land. Therefore, we begin with a chapter on the Colorado Plateau itself, and in the other chapters, we offer specifics about the geology and history of the area you are visiting.

Chapters on the more "urban" areas of northern Arizona—Flagstaff, Williams, Sedona and Grand Canyon—are organized to present our information in a way that makes it as easy as possible to find what you are looking for. Need a place to stay? Our Accommodations sections are full of charming and interesting lodging options from intimate bed-and-breakfasts to upscale resorts. Wondering where to eat? Our Restaurants sections give you a range of tried-and-true options to suit any palate and budget. Don't know what to do? Check out our Recreation and Attractions sections for ideas on activities—there is something for everyone, from the most relaxed to the most adventurous traveler.

The information about the Hopi and Navajo Reservations is organized differently. Here we take you mile-by-mile along routes across the Western Navajo and the Hopi Reservations. These sections are organized geographically because the distances you will travel are so great. From the Grand Canyon or Flagstaff, you can travel to Cameron and Tuba City on the Navajo Reservation. From there you can go eastward across the Hopi Reservation and on to Chinle. Or you might prefer to go northeast from Tuba City to Kayenta, then to Chinle, and follow Highway 264 westward across the Hopi Reservation back to Tuba City. Whichever route you choose and wherever you decide to stop, you will be able to consult the guide to find lodging, food, and advice about what to do.

The *Insiders' Guide to the Grand Canyon* also has an index to help you find exactly what you are looking for, and we have formulated the chapters so that they can be cross-referenced or can stand on their own. We've included addresses, directions, and phone numbers (and in some cases Web sites and e-mail references) for every lodging place, eatery, and attraction we list, so you can plan your itinerary in advance, which is especially important if you are travelling in the busy high season (mid May through mid October). We have also provided maps to help you find your way around. Insiders' Tips offer insight and information important to someone new to the area. Close-ups present very detailed information on special places you might want to visit or things you might want to do—such as purchasing a Navajo weaving.

We want this guide to be as up-to-date as possible. Readers are encouraged to share their opinions and suggestions with us for future editions. You may contact us via our Web site www.insiders.com, or write to us at: *Insiders' Guide to the Grand Canyon*, Globe Pequot Press, P.O. Box 480, Guilford, Connecticut 06473-0480.

The ballcourt at Wupatki National Park is like those found much further south. The red rock is Moenkopi sandstone. PHOTO: TANYA LEE

The Colorado Plateau

The Colorado Plateau stretches, unexpected and magnificent, across the southwestern United States, covering parts of the Four Corners states—Utah, Colorado, New Mexico, and Arizona.

The gorgeous series of red, purple, pink, white, and yellow plateaus extends over 130,000 square miles at elevations of between 2,000 feet at the bottom of the Grand Canyon to 13,000 feet in the LaSal Mountains of Utah. The highest point in Northern Arizona is Humphrey's Peak (12,633 feet), one of the San Francisco Peaks just north of Flagstaff.

The Plateau, really a group of plateaus accentuated by the mesas, buttes, spires, and pinnacles for which the area is justly famous, is part of the Rocky Mountain system. Its western edge is Grand Wash Cliffs along Grand Wash Fault. Two hundred miles of the southern edge is an escarpment known as the Mogollon Rim. In eastern Arizona, the rim is covered by the lava flows of the White Mountains. The Plateau extends north into Utah and east and northeast into New Mexico and Colorado where it meets the edge of the Rocky Mountains.

The main geological force at work in this area of mountains, spectacular river canyons, dry gullies, potentially treacherous washes, steams, deserts, pine forests, and valleys so green one of them is named the Verde, is erosion by the Colorado River system. The unparalleled beauty of the Plateau is being preserved for future generations by conservation areas—National Parks, National Forests, and National Monuments. The first of these was Grand Canyon National Monument created by President Teddy Roosevelt in 1908 as one of the first natural wonders designated for preservation under the Antiquities Act of 1906. Other National Monuments on the Plateau include Canyon de Chelly, Glen Canyon National Recreation Area, Sunset Crater National Monument, and Wupatki National Monument. National Parks include Petrified Forest, Grand Canyon (established in 1919) and Chaco Canyon.

Climate and Animal Life

Winters on the Plateau are cool to cold and the climate is semi-arid, averaging 10 to 25 inches of annual precipitation, much of it in the form of snow in the upper elevations, including Flagstaff and the Grand Canyon. Cold semi-arid desert conditions mean a relatively short growing season. The Hopi, one of the many Native American peoples of the Plateau, are the best dry farmers in the world.

Ponderosa pine forests dominate elevations of 6000 to 7000 feet; higher up are Douglas and other firs, aspens, and spruce. This concentration of tall, straight pine trees created one of Flagstaff's earliest industries—lumbering. At lower elevations, piñon and juniper dominate the Plateau woodlands.

Mammals of the Plateau are incredibly diverse and, because so much of the area is protected, relatively populous. The mammals include black bear, deer, elk, coati, antelope, bobcats, mountain lions, Mexican free-tailed bats, pallid bats, badgers, beaver, coyotes, skunks, porcupines, gray foxes, desert cottontails, mule deer, white-tailed deer, jackrabbits, squirrels, raccoons, wild turkeys, kangaroo rats, long-tailed weasels, white-throated wood rats, deer mice, and chipmunks. Raptors hunt the Plateau in large numbers. Visitors can reasonably expect to sight several different species. They include the turkey vulture, cooper's hawk, goshawk, sharp-shinned hawk, marsh hawk, red-tailed hawk, zone-tailed hawk, bald eagle, golden eagle, osprey, American kestrel, peregrine falcon, barn owl, burrowing owl, common screech owl, great horned owl, pygmy owl, saw-whet owl, short-eared owl, and spotted owl.

Condors are being reintroduced near the Vermillion Cliffs, but the reintroduction program ran into problems when some of the condors ate lead shot and died.

Reptiles and amphibians also abound—tiger salamanders, Arizona tree frogs, Western-banded geckos, collared lizards, desert spiny lizards, Western Whiptail lizards, tree lizards, side-blotched lizards, common kingsnakes, Sonoran Mountain kingsnakes, coachwhips, gopher snakes, ground snakes, wandering garter snakes, Mojave rattlesnakes, and western diamondback rattlesnakes are indigenous to the Plateau.

Animals brought by Europeans in the sixteenth and seventeenth centuries include cattle, sheep, goats, horses, and burros.

Geology

The Colorado Plateau is part of the Cordilleras, the last and greatest system of mountains to rise in North America. These mountains formed mainly in post-Jurassic times, less than 136 million years ago, when the continent, drifting westward from the Atlantic met the floor of the Pacific, which was spreading eastward. These movements created pressure on the west rim of the Laurentian Shield, which is the basic structure of the continent. The shield is made up of the oldest rocks in North America, which can be seen at the bottom of the Grand Canyon. The Colorado Plateau may be a western island remnant of the Laurentian Shield.

The Plateau has been geologically stable for 600,000,000 years, right through the mountain-building Jurassic period. Below the Plateau, the earth's crust is thicker than that in nearby areas, and heat flow from the center of the earth is lower.

The Colorado Plateau is a series of massive flat ridges, made steplike by faulting and intruded by domes of molten rock. The Plateau rose slowly in several stages, while at the same time the Colorado River was cutting the gorge that became the Grand Canyon. The most ancient rocks in Grand Canyon's Inner Gorge are 2 billion years old, roughly half the age of the planet itself.

The awe-inspiring landscape of the entire Plateau results from water and wind erosion of flat-lying or slightly dipping Mesozoic (65 to 225 million years old) sedimentary rocks, including sandstones, limestones, and shales. Mesas, buttes, and pinnacles are created by erosion when a relatively resistant rock unit (such as sandstone) caps relatively weaker rock, such as shales. The semi-arid climate of the Plateau means many areas have little vegetative cover and this factor also influences erosion patterns.

The sedimentary sandstone, shale, and limestone that make up the brilliantly colored layers of the Plateau were created during the Paleozoic Era when what is now Arizona was a shelf immersed in a shallow western sea that advanced and retreated.

The greatest wealth on the Plateau stems from water and fuels—considerable deposits of uranium, colossal fields of oil shale, and high-quality low-sulfur bituminous coal—most of it on Native American-owned land.

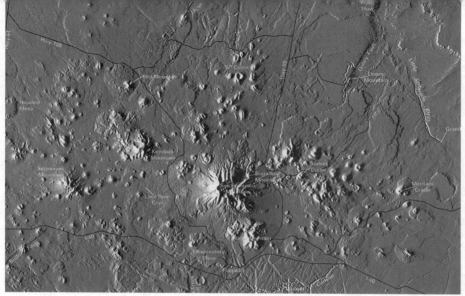

The San Francisco Volcanic Field evolved over thousands of years. PHOTO: IMAGE COURTESY OF U.S. GEOLOGICAL SURVEY, FLAGSTAFF, AZ

Local Cultures

Cultures of the Colorado Plateau today are Native American, European, and Hispanic.

Europeans have been here almost continuously since the late sixteenth century. The Spanish and Mexicans came first and then after 1848, Anglo-American cultures—Southern, Mormon, and Northeastern United States—immigrated in large numbers.

Archaeologists estimate that Native Americans have been on this continent for at least 15,000 years, and possibly for as long as 60,000 years. Today, the Havasupai and Hualapai occupy the Middle Colorado Highlands, including the Grand Canyon. Pueblo (village-dwelling) Indians, highly diverse linguistically, live on the Colorado Plateau and the Middle Rio Grande area. These include the western Pueblo cultures: Hopi, Hano, Zuni, Acoma, Laguna; the central Pueblos: Jemez, Santa Ana, Zia, Cochitii, Santo, Domingo, San Felipe; and the peoples of the eastern Pueblos: San Juan, Santa Clara, San Ildefonso, Nambe, Tesuque, Taos, Picuris, Isleta, and Sandia. The Navajo, Athabascan-speaking Apache, are relative newcomers to the Southwest, having arrived five to seven hundred years ago.

Natural Resources

The main ingredients necessary for the post-war development of the Southwest were fuel, water, and land. The land was here—huge tracts of "worthless" desert, much of which had been allotted to Native Americans when they were restricted to reservations.

The Plateau also had water. In a series of still-on-going court cases, the rights to Colorado River water are being divided among the Western states and Native American tribes.

In addition, the deep, narrow gorges cut by the snow-fed Colorado Plateau rivers were relatively easy to dam, and the Navajo, Hoover, Glen Canyon, and other dams provide an immense amount of hydroelectric power for the build-up of Southwest cities—Denver, Phoenix, Los Angeles, Albuquerque, El Paso.

The Colorado Plateau—high desert, powerlines, and monsoon clouds in August. PHOTO: TANYA LEE

Everyone knew, however, that the dams could not provide enough electricity for the huge urban centers. But that problem could be solved by building coal-burning power plants. Perhaps the world's best source of low-sulfur bituminous coal is Black Mesa, and the federal government's strategies to wrest that resource from the Navajo Nation and the Hopi Tribe for the development of the Southwest cities were an unmitigated success.

On Black Mesa, the one part of the Plateau where Cretaceous rocks remain, there are thick beds of coal formed in ancient near-shore swamps. The coal was formed 136 to 165 million years ago, when dinosaurs roamed the earth and the Colorado Plateau was on the edge of a huge western sea. The land was not desert—the climate was mild and the vegetation prolific. This vegetation, primarily ferns and large conifers, died and was sealed by layers of sediment brought from the mountains by rivers. More and more layers of vegetation and sediment were laid down. The vegetation decomposed to peat and eventually to almost pure carbon—coal. Because this coal was formed in freshwater marshes, rather than in salt marshes, it was low in sulfur (thus complying with modern environmental standards). The coal formed during the Cretaceous period on the Colorado Plateau is possibly the most valuable in the world—and it is on Native American land.

The federal government, motivated both by what they saw as the need to "raise" Native Americans out of "poverty," and by its own interests in developing the Southwest, instituted Western-style governments on the Navajo Nation and Hopi Reservation. By creating tribal councils, the government created entities legally empowered to sign leases with the mining companies that would extract the coal and other minerals—including uranium for Cold War weapons—from the Colorado Plateau, largely by strip-mining.

A particularly disturbing part of this scheme was that the Department of Interior gave a Utah attorney, John Boyden, permission to represent the Hopi Tribe in the mineral lease negotiations. Boyden was at the same time working for the mining company trying to get those leases.

Bear Safety

Black bears in Arizona range in size from 125 to 450 pounds and measure about three feet at the shoulder when they are standing on all four legs. They measure about five feet at the shoulder when standing on their hind legs.

Seeing a black bear is a wonderful experience. Confronting one, however, is an experience worth taking some precautions to avoid, especially since a bear can run at speeds up to 35 miles an hour (much faster than you can).

The Arizona Game and Fish Department makes the following recommendations for avoiding a confrontation with a bear:

A black bear will usually leave the area as soon as it senses a human presence. If, however, the bear has become accustomed to people, it may not fear an encounter and may not leave.

If that should happen, you need to stay calm and make noises to let the bear know that you are there. You should stop and face the bear, moving backwards slowly. If a vehicle or any other safe structure is available, use it. Give the bear plenty of leeway; you do not want it to feel trapped. Do not run or make any sudden movements. Be aware that if the bear has cubs, it will be especially dangerous. Never come between a bear and her cubs. If a bear should attack, fight back any way you can.

Most conflicts between bears and people occur over food. Bears are attracted to human foods, garbage, bird seed, hummingbird feeders, pet foods, livestock feed, tree fruits, and garden vegetables, among other edibles. If you eliminate the availability of food for the bear, you can reduce your chances of encountering one close up. When camping, keep all food out of reach and out of sight. Never take food into your tent or other sleeping area and store food far away from where you will be sleeping. Wash your hands and face before going to bed, and place dirty clothes in your vehicle. Do not leave pet food outside. Clean grills and other cooking utensils thoroughly.

For more information, contact the Arizona Game and Fish Department in Phoenix at (602) 942–3000 or in Flagstaff at (520) 774–5045. In an emergency call the Game and Fish Department, the local law enforcement agency, or 911.

In those negotiations, which eventually resulted in the mining company signing leases with both the Hopi and the Navajo to strip mine Black Mesa (despite the objections of traditional Hopi leaders to the mining and the traditionalists' challenge of the legitimacy of the tribal council that signed the lease), Boyden also sold pristine water from the N-aquifer, the sole source of groundwater for the Hopi Reservation, to the mining company for the supremely ridiculous price of $1.67 per acre foot (the amount of water necessary to cover one acre of land to the depth of one foot). This exceptionally pure water was not sold for drinking, but to slurry coal from Black Mesa to Mohave Generating Plant in Laughlin, Nevada, almost 300 miles away. This is the only coal-slurrying operation in this country, as transporting coal by this means was deemed to be economically inefficient—unless, of course, the water could be purchased for next to nothing. The Hopi Tribe has been able to renegotiate the price of the water, but many Hopis claim that the mining company is using so much water that the springs and seeps they need for farming and sheepherding are drying up. The mining company defends its use of this water by claiming that the aquifer is being depleted by domestic uses. The issue is far from resolved.

The first of the coal-fired plants, Four Corners, went on-line in 1963, fueled by coal strip-mined at Navajo Mine on land once used by traditional Navajo and Hopi for grazing sheep.

During the 1970s, 11 more coal-fired power plants were constructed on the Colorado Plateau. Environmental organizations, including the Grand Canyon Trust, have sued to force the power plant owners—Salt River Project, Arizona Public Service, El Paso Electric, Tucson Electric Power, California Edison, among others—to install scrubbers and other devices to reduce air pollution that they argue is causing haze in the Grand Canyon, in addition to adversely affecting the health of those who live on the Plateau.

Wupatki and Sunset Crater National Monuments

Imagine yourself living nearly one thousand years ago. You are an Indian, a Sinaguan. This name would be given to you in the twentieth century by Harold S. Colton, based on the Spanish phrase for the nearby San Francisco Peaks, Sierra sin Agua or "mountains without water." You live in a village of pit houses dug into the ground and roofed with poles supporting brush. Your ancestors migrated here from the south roughly four hundred years ago. This rock-strewn land at the foot of the mountains has been your home for many generations. You make your living by gathering piñon nuts, hunting squirrels and rabbits, and collecting seeds. You also grow corn, beans, and squash, trying to time your planting to take advantage of the unreliable water cycles of the Colorado Plateau. You build dams across the washes to gather water when the washes run during spring snowmelt and after summer thunderstorms.

One day you begin to feel the ground shudder. You hear a rumbling from far within the earth. Your life is about to change forever.

The Sinagua who lived near Sunset Crater apparently had sufficient warning to move away before the volcano erupted. The remains of their pit houses show that they were abandoned in an orderly way. The Sinagua took with them their stunning redware and brownware pots, the beams so painstakingly cut for roof poles for their houses, and most of the rest of their possessions.

Sunset Crater erupted in the winter of 1064–1065 C.E., spewing black cinders, deadly gases, acid rain, and forest fires across hundreds of square miles of the eastern part of the San Francisco Volcanic Field. Archaeologists know that the area was inhabited before the volcano erupted because they have found a pit house covered by a layer of cinders. The volcano erupted sporadically for 200 years, but a few decades after the first eruption, the Sinagua returned to a vastly different landscape from the one they had left.

Colton theorized that the layer of volcanic cinders and ash acted as a mulch that held in water, so the land was now richer and easier to farm. He argued that many peoples, learning of this new and better farmland, came from miles away. The Pueblo people, or Anasazi, came from the north and the Cohonina from the west. With them came new technologies. It was during the decades after the eruption of Sunset Crater that the great pueblo of Wupatki was built. No longer did the Sinagua live in scattered villages of pit houses. They now built multistory, above-ground pueblos similar to those that can be seen at Hopi today. Colton guessed that the population grew from three thousand people before the volcano erupted to eight thousand after people returned to the area.

Wupatki, a pueblo of rooms for living, ceremonial rooms, and even a ballcourt (showing evidence of contact with peoples far to the south) was a great trading center, one of the many that connected the peoples from south of the Mogollon Rim, perhaps as far south as Central America, to those who lived in the Four Corners area.

The pueblo, ballcourt, and amphitheater have been partially reconstructed and now, along with outliers such as Wukoki and Lomaki, they make up Wupatki National Monument, located about 18 miles from Sunset Crater. Visitors may reach this striking ruin by exiting Interstate 40 at exit 201. Go north toward Page and the Grand Canyon 12 miles and turn right at the entrance to Sunset Crater-Wupatki National Monuments. This is a fee area and the charge is $3 per person (children 16 and under are admitted free). Golden Eagle, Golden Age, and Golden Access passports are sold and accepted at the entrance.

You will drive through Sunset National Monument, then through a wilderness area until you reach Wupatki National Monument. The Wupatki Visitor Center is 21 miles from the intersection with U.S. Highway 89. Along this two-lane road, you will see magnificent vistas of the Painted Desert (there is a pull-out for picture taking) and you will notice that as the elevation drops, ponderosa pine forest gives way to juniper and piñon. Cattle graze on these lands. You may also see deer, antelope, chipmunks, squirrels, red-tailed hawks, and eagles. And the thing that looks like a yardstick flitting across your path is actually a roadrunner.

The Wupatki pueblo is built of red Moenkopi sandstone and Kaibab limestone. The ballcourt incorporates some black volcanic rock. According to Colton's theory, the Pueblo people, or Anasazi, the famed builders of Mesa Verde and Chaco Canyon, taught the Sinagua the masonry techniques for the construction of the pueblo. The purpose of the so-called amphitheater has never been satisfactorily explained. The ballcourt structure resembles known courts for ball games found as far south as Central America. Exactly what game was played there, with what rules, implements, and consequences, remains a mystery.

Evidence that this was a trade center includes archaeological finds of textiles from the Verde Valley 50 miles to the south, turquoise from New Mexico, shells from the Pacific, and copper bells and parrot feathers from Mexico.

According to Colton's "black sand" theory, Wupatki was occupied by Sinagua, Anasazi, and Cohonina until about 1220 C.E. A severe drought that began in 1150—and the wind's removal of the ash that made the land especially fertile—are perhaps the reasons that the people left Wupatki, which would never again be a permanent residence.

Colton's black sand theory has recently been challenged by archaeologist Peter Pilles. He argues that Colton over-emphasized the importance of the ash from Sunset Crater Volcano on the quality of the land for farming. During the same period that Wupatki was built and occupied, the area experienced unusually high rainfall. The rainfall, according to Pilles, may have been a more important factor than the volcanic ash in enticing people to move to the area. Another group, the Hohokam, may also have lived in the area. If so, they may have been the people to bring ballcourts, clay figurines, and shell ornaments to the region. Pilles also maintains that the masonry techniques used at Wupatki were known to the Sinagua before the Anasazi arrived.

That the Anasazi lived here, however, is beyond doubt. Anasazi is a Navajo word that means "enemy ancestors" or "ancient people who are not us." This linguistic evidence, along with archaeological evidence, indicates strongly that the Anasazi were not the ancestors of the Navajo, who are thought to have arrived on the Colorado Plateau 500 to 700 years ago. Further, the Hopi and the Zuni, contemporary pueblo peoples, consider Wupatki and other pueblo and cliff-dweller sites to be the homes of their ancestors. To the Hopi and other pueblo tribes, Wupatki is a place that still has spiritual significance

A self-guided tour through the ruins of the main pueblo at Wupatki National Monument takes about 30 minutes. The ballcourt and amphitheater are just west of the pueblo. PHOTO: TANYA LEE

and that is still vitally important in their religious observances.

The Anasazi, or Pueblo people, are best known for the fabulous cliff dwellings they constructed at Mesa Verde (in Colorado) and Canyon de Chelly (in northeastern Arizona), as well as the incredibly rich pueblo complex in New Mexico known as Chaco Canyon, but these are only a few of the places they lived on the Colorado Plateau. As early as 400 C.E., they lived in pit houses on Black Mesa, around Navajo Mountain and in the Tsegi Canyon area. Anasazi sites all across the Colorado Plateau show evidence of having been inhabited, abandoned, and reoccupied over hundreds of years. When the Indian reservations were created by the United States government, the indigenous peoples of the Colorado Plateau were denied access to the lands on which their ancestors had thrived for hundreds of years.

The origins of the Pueblo people, known also for their black-on-white decorated pottery, are unclear, but archaeologists do know that they emerged as a distinct culture in the first or second century C.E. Their technology included domesticated plants, the digging stick, grinding stones, and storage rooms, all of which are shared by contemporary Hopi.

Also like today's traditional Hopi farmers, the people of the Pueblo culture dry-farmed, taking full advantage of the moisture provided by snow melt and the July-September monsoon rains that soak this area with spectacular afternoon thunderstorms during the late summer. Their primary domesticated plant was maize, or corn, first domesticated in Mexico. They also grew beans and squash. Beans, squash, and corn are the "Three Sisters" of the traditional Hopi diet.

The Pueblo people did not rely entirely on farming for their living. They gathered piñon pine nuts, the fruit of the banana yucca, and the fruit of the prickly pear, and they hunted jackrabbits, prairie dogs, and deer. They also used indigenous plants for many other purposes such as basketmaking and medicine. The addition of the bow and arrow

Wupatki and Sunset Crater National Monuments / 13

to replace the spear or atlatl for hunting and the development of pottery around 500 C.E. contributed to the ability of these people to build and settle in pueblo villages or cliff dwellings. They began building such structures around 700 C.E. and this building technology culminated in the construction Chaco Canyon from about 900–1130 C.E and the cliff dwellings of Mesa Verde, Keet Seel, and Betatakin around 1200 C.E. By the late thirteenth century, all of these sites had been abandoned.

For many years, archaeologists believed that the Pueblo people simply "disappeared." But they did not disappear. They moved—to northern New Mexico and central Arizona, to the upper Rio Grande, Pecos, and Little Colorado River regions. The mesas where the Hopi now live are a mere 60 miles from Wupatki. The Hopi, the Zuni, and the peoples of the Rio Grande pueblos are descendants of the ancient Pueblo cultures.

For two reasons—because it is an archaeological site protected by the United States government and because it is an important site in the religious life of contemporary Native Americans—tourists should think of themselves as invited guests when they visit this and other archaeological sites on the Colorado Plateau. Staying on established trails is important to protect the sites from damage. Sitting or walking on walls damages them, and taking or moving items such as rocks, fossils, animals, plants, or pottery destroys the archaeological record. Needless to say, graffiti scribed or painted on rocks degrades the site. All of these activities are against the law and are punishable by fines.

The Wupatki Trail is one-half mile round-trip and will allow you to see the main pueblo, the ballcourt, and the amphitheater. You can also view the entire complex from the overlook just a few feet from the Visitor Center.

Lomaki Trail is also a half-mile long, and gives views of several other ancient pueblos. There are also trails at Wukoki, Citadel, and Nalakihu. The Doney Mountain Trail takes you from the picnic area to the top of the mountain for unparalleled views of the whole region. Wupatki Trail is wheelchair accessible to the overlook, and wheelchair-accessible restrooms can be found at Doney Mountain picnic area and Lomaki. Hiking is restricted to signed trails, and the backcountry of this national monument is closed to hikers to protect the fragile ecosystem and ruins.

Wupatki National Monument is open year-round except December 25. Generally the hours are from dawn to dusk. The road through Sunset Crater and Wupatki is a loop, and if you follow the loop all the way around you will end up further north on U.S. Highway 89, well on your way to Cameron.

At Wupatki you will find picnic areas, as well as vending machines for snacks and drinks at the Visitor Center, but there are no other services, such as gas, and no food that could be considered lunch.

The closest camping is at Bonito Campground across from the Sunset Crater National Monument Visitor Center. Flagstaff has other campgrounds, as well as many motels and hotels.

For more information, contact Wupatki National Monument, HC33, Box 444A, Flagstaff, AZ 86004; (520) 679-2365; www.nps.gov/wupa.

Sunset Crater National Monument

Some evenings I look out my bedroom window at Sunset Crater and the top of the cinder cone glows such a bright orange-red that I almost wonder if it's about to begin spewing forth hot lava and gases one more time. Then I wonder if my homeowner's insurance covers volcanic eruptions.

Just one of the more than 600 cinder cones of the San Francisco Volcanic Field, Sunset Crater is the most recent to have been active. It began erupting in the winter of 1064-1065 C.E. and continued to explode intermittently for about 200 years, covering the area

The 1-mile Lava Flow Nature Trail gives you a self-guided look at the Bonita Lava Flow at Sunset Crater National Monument. PHOTO: TANYA LEE

with cinder cones and lava flows. Volcanic activity around Flagstaff, which began 6 million years ago, is moving from west to east, so the cinder cones around Williams are older than those east of Flagstaff. The entire volcanic field covers more than 2,200 square miles.

Sunset Crater Volcano National Monument is open year-round except December 25. Drive north from Flagstaff 12 miles on U.S. Highway 89 and turn right on the Sunset Crater-Wupatki Loop Road. The Visitor Center is 2 miles further along the road. The entrance fee of $3 per person covers both Sunset Crater and Wupatki National Monuments. Golden Eagle, Golden Age, and Golden Access Passports are accepted, but wheelchair access to Sunset Crater is limited.

Federal Recreation Passport Program

If you are planning to visit several National Parks (such as Grand Canyon), National Monuments (such as Wupatki) and Historic Sites (such as Hubbell Trading Post), you will probably save money by purchasing a Golden Eagle Passport.

The passport admits the passport owner and any accompanying passengers in a private vehicle to most National Parks, Monuments, Historic Sites, recreation areas, and national wildlife refuges that charge an entrance fee. The passport is good for one year and provides unlimited entries to the fee areas.

Golden Eagle Passports cost $50 and may be purchased at any federal area where fees are charged. This passport does not cover use fees (fees for camping, swimming, boating, parking, and so on).

An even better option for U.S. citizens or permanent residents age 62 or over is the Golden Age Passport, a lifetime pass to most National Parks, Monuments, Historic Sites, recreation areas, and national wildlife refuges. This passport must be purchased in person at any federal area where a fee is charged, and you must show proof of age (a driver's license, a birth certificate, or similar document). A one-time $10 processing fee will allow the passport signee and any accompanying passengers in a private vehicle unlimited access. The Golden Age Passport also gives the holder a 50% reduction for some use fees.

Golden Access Passports are available to people who are blind or permanently disabled. In addition to entrance fees, this passport provides a 50% discount on federal use fees. The Golden Access Passport must be obtained in person at any federal area where a fee is charged. You will be required to show proof of U.S. citizenship or permanent residence status and proof of medically determined eligibility.

For more information on the Federal Recreation Passport Program, write the National Park Service Office of Public Inquiries, Room 1013, U.S. Department of the Interior, 1849 C Street, NW, P.O. Box 37127, Washington, D.C. 20013-7127 or a regional office of the Forest Service. The address of the office for the Southwestern Region is Federal Building, 517 Gold Avenue, SW, Albuquerque, NM 87102.

The Lava Flow Nature Trail is 1.5 miles from the Visitor Center. This one-mile long self-guided hike takes you past a variety of volcanic formations, which are labeled and described for you.

The Lenox Crater Trail is a steep one-mile trail up a cinder cone. Expect to spend about 30 minutes going up and 15 coming down. Sunset Crater Volcano itself is closed to hikers and climbers. Little vegetation grows on this very young cinder cone, so it is too fragile for hiking (much less all-terrain vehicles).

The Sunset Crater cinder cone rises 1,000 feet above the surrounding land. A cinder cone forms when magma (molten rock and compressed gases) rises from its underground source and explodes from a central vent. The magma cools and falls back to the earth as solid rock, forming a mound, or cone, of cinder.

Lava may also flow from the base of the cone. When this liquid rock is exposed to air, the surface cools more quickly than the interior, producing "aa" (pronounced ah-ah). This is the jagged, sharp rock "field" that you see in the Bonita Lava Flow at Bonito Flow Pullout on the north side of the road near Lenox Crater.

Insiders' Tip

Contact the Grand Canyon Association by writing P.O. Box 399, Grand Canyon, AZ 86023, or calling (520) 638-2481. Visit their website at www.thecanyon.com/gca.

Spatter cones are the smaller cones you see around Sunset Crater. The self-guided tour will also help you recognize other volcanic formations such as squeeze-ups, where partly cooled lava pushed through cracks.

Around 1250 C.E., at the end of Sunset Crater's active period, iron- and sulphur-bearing lava erupted from the central vent. These red and yellow particles fell back onto the top surface of the cone, and they are what give Sunset Crater its distinctive color and its name.

Scientists and archaeologists are still working on two fascinating questions. The first concerns the origin of the San Francisco Volcanic Field. One theory is that this area is on top of a "hot spot," an active spot on the earth's surface where the crust is moving over the mantle below. Another "hot spot" in North America is Yellowstone National Park. The second theory is that the southern Colorado Plateau is being cut into by valley and mountain ranges to the south and the west. This kind of collision can cause volcanic activity.

Another question revolves around the people who lived in the area when the volcano erupted. One theory says that the ash from the volcano acted as a sponge, holding rainwater in and making the area much more fertile. Therefore, people moved here to settle. Another theory argues that above-average rainfall in the area between about 1050 and 1130 C.E. is what led ancient peoples to build communities such as Wupatki and the many hundreds of other ruins in the area.

When you visit Sunset Crater, you will find picnic areas at the Visitor Center, Lava Flow Trail, and Painted Desert Vista, and vending machines at the Visitor Center. There are no other services (so make sure you start out with enough gas in your car to see both Sunset Crater and Wupatki National Monument). Bonito Campground is across from the Visitor Center and is open March through October, weather permitting. The largest vehicle that can be accommodated is 35 feet long; there are no hook-ups. For more information on the campground, call (520) 527-1474. Flagstaff has plenty of hotel and motel accommodations, as well as other campgrounds.

For more information, write the Sunset Crater Volcano National Monument, Route 3, Box 149, Flagstaff, AZ 86004, call (520) 526-0502, or visit the website at www.nps.gov/sucr.

The Arizona Lumber and Timber Company stops to pose for a photo in 1885.

PHOTO: COURTESY OF THE ARIZONA HISTORICAL SOCIETY PIONEER MUSEUM

Flagstaff

Surrounded by ponderosa pine trees and delicate aspens, the city of Flagstaff rests at the foot of the San Francisco Peaks. Flagstaff has evolved from a wild west town to a city with small town appeal. Its colorful history is a blend of western legends, courageous settlers, and dedicated citizens who have worked to make this mountain town a family community.

The largest city in northern Arizona, Flagstaff is the county seat for Coconino County. The population as of 1998 climbed to 60,000. By the year 2015, the city estimates the population will grow to 80,000.

A high desert town with alpine weather conditions, Flagstaff is just 146 miles north of Phoenix, and at 7,000 feet in elevation, the climate of the two major Arizona cities differs dramatically. Flagstaff's pleasurable climate with four distinct seasons has an average January temperature of 42 degrees, and in July the daytime highs hover around 80 degrees. Warm summer days, snowy winters, spring wildflowers, and the glowing gold aspens in fall entice visitors to the north country year round to explore the endless recreation possibilities.

A transportation hub since the arrival of the railroad in 1881, Flagstaff was once located along the old wagon road to California. Today the city links I-40 to Interstate 17, U.S. Highway 89 to Page and Utah, and U.S. Highway 180 to the Grand Canyon. Historic Route 66 passes through Flagstaff.

Tourism is a major source of employment and income for Flagstaff. Government institutions, educational facilities, and trucking and the railroad play important roles in the city's economy. Approximately 19,000 students attend Northern Arizona University. Surrounding communities rely on the historic downtown area and shopping centers for their retail and service needs.

The Grand Canyon is just one of the many attractions that bring more than 5 million visitors to the northland every year. Other sites within a short drive of the city limits include the dormant volcanoes of Sunset Crater National Monument, the Indian ruins of Wupatki and Walnut Canyon, Meteor Crater, and the red rocks of Oak Creek Canyon and Sedona.

But Flagstaff holds its own as a destination in and of itself. Intimate shops, art galleries, and unique restaurants, and downtown cafes line the streets. Stop by the recently built Heritage Square to people watch or hear local musicians all year round (depending on the weather).

A variety of local museums and scientific research centers work to preserve the history and culture of the Colorado Plateau and to educate and entertain people of all ages. Flagstaff offers an array of social and recreational activities and hosts many annual events and festivals. Community and professional theaters present live performances year round. The Flagstaff Symphony provides a full concert season from September through May. The San Francisco Peaks, the city's backdrop, offer endless hiking, mountain biking, and cross-country or downhill skiing opportunities.

Flagstaff's motto is: They don't make towns like this any more. Come and experience the spirit and lifestyle that Flagstaff has to offer.

Flagstaff Vital Statistics

Flagstaff Mayor: Joe Donaldson **Arizona Governor:** Jane Dee Hull

Population: Flagstaff: 59,945
State: 4,924,350

Area (sq. miles): 64.1

Nickname/motto : Flagstaff, they don't make towns like this anymore.

Average Temperatures: July (Hi/Lo): 81/50
January (Hi/Lo): 42/15

Average rain / snowfall / days of sunshine: 22.9 inches / 108.8 inches / 300 days

City / State Founded: 1881 / 1912

Major university: Northern Arizona University

Important dates in history:

1881 Post Office established.

1883 On October 21st the Atlantic & Pacific began passenger service from Albuquerque to San Francisco.

1884 Fire destroyed Old Town. "New Town" was relocated to present-day site near the railroad depot.

1886 Another fire ravaged "New Town," but within six months the town was rebuilt and added 40 more buildings.

1912 Arizona became a state.

1930 The planet Pluto was discovered by Clyde W. Tombaugh at the Lowell Observatory.

1966 Arizona State College became Northern Arizona University.

1990s Historic restoration of the downtown area.

Major area Employers:

Coconino County; W.L. Gore Associates; Flagstaff Medical Center; Northern Arizona University; Flagstaff Unified School District

Famous Sons and Daughters:

Eva Marshall—First teacher in Flagstaff; A.E. Douglas—Founder of Lowell Observatory and developer of the science of dendrochronology; Anastasia Frohmiller—First woman to run for governor in Arizona ; Percival Lowell—Famous astronomer; Laura Runke—First female member of Flagstaff's City Council; George Hochderffer—Author of *Flagstaff Whoa!*, a historic account of the town. Dr. Harold Colton—Founder of the Museum of Northern Arizona; Thomas McMillan—One of the area's first settlers and ranchers; The Babbit Family—Economic contributors to Flagstaff's economy.

State/City Holidays:

New Year's Day; Martin Luther King Day; President's Day; Memorial Day; Independence Day; Labor Day; Veteran's Day; Thanksgiving Day; Christmas Day

Chamber of Commerce:

Flagstaff Chamber of Commerce
101 West Rt. 66
Flagstaff, AZ 86001
(520) 774–4505
Fax (520) 779–1209
www.flagstaff.az.us

Major Airports/Interstates:

Sky Harbor International Airport (Phoenix), Pulliam Airport (Flagstaff); Interstate 40; Interstate 17

Public Transportation: Pine Country Transit (bus system)

Military Bases: Fort Tuthill; Bellmont; Camp Navajo

Driving Laws:

Seatbelts must be worn by front seat passengers; right turn on red; speed limit is 55 except where marked; speed limit on Interstates is 75 except in designated areas.

Alcohol Laws:

Legal drinking age is 21 years; blood/alcohol level of 1.0% or higher is DUI in Arizona, but .05% to 1.0% can be designated DUI by the arresting officer.

Daily Newspapers: *Arizona Daily Sun*

Sales Tax:

7.31% City/State taxes on all retail sales; 9.89% City/State accommodations; 9.31% City/State restaurant and bar.

Monsoon clouds roll in with the afternoon train.   PHOTO: STACEY WITTIG

Getting Here, Getting Around: Flagstaff

Since the arrival of the railroad and the earliest pioneers, Flagstaff has been the hub of northern Arizona. Flagstaff sits at the intersection of I–17 (north-south) and I–40 (east-west). U.S. Routes 89 and 180 bring travelers from the Grand Canyon to and from Flagstaff.

Due to weather, northern Arizona is not the easiest place to travel to at times. Mountain weather can strike at any time, so be prepared. If you're looking to escape the heat in the Valley of the Sun, you just need to get "up the hill."

Getting Here by Air

Phoenix Sky Harbor Airport

Travelers must fly into Phoenix Sky Harbor Airport to reach Flagstaff by air. Phoenix is the hub for America West Airlines (800) 235–9292 (reservations). Many of the major airlines have daily flights to Phoenix including Continental Airlines (800) 523–3273 (reservations), United Airlines (800) 241–6522, and American Airlines (800) 433–7300 (reservations). For information about Sky Harbor Airport call (602) 273–3300.

Getting to Sky Harbor from Flagstaff

From Flagstaff take I–17 S to Phoenix. Once you have cleared the outskirts of Phoenix, look for signs for I–10 E. Take I–10 E to exit 149, the Sky Harbor Airport. The exit is clearly marked. It takes approximately 2.5 hours to get to the airport. Remember to take into consideration rush hour traffic and road construction when planning to catch your flight.

Rental Cars/Parking at Sky Harbor

Four national rental car companies serve Sky Harbor Airport: Avis Rent-A-Car, (800) 331–1212; Alamo, (800) 327–9633; Budget, (800) 527–0700; and Dollar (800) 800–4000.

For $15 a day, you can park your car in one of the airport's three covered short-term parking garages. The two long-term parking lots are uncovered, and the airport charges $4 per day. The lots are marked, but the airport has been under construction for the past year. Give yourself plenty of time to get through the construction, park your car, and catch the shuttle to your terminal. For more information about airport parking contact (602) 273-4545.

Bus, Shuttle, and Taxi Services to and from Sky Harbor Airport

Greyhound Bus Lines
399 S. Malpais Ln.
(520) 774–4573, (800) 231–2222

The Greyhound Bus runs five times a day to and from the airport, leaving Sky Harbor from the southwest corner of Terminal 4 at 3 A.M., 8 A.M., noon, 6 P.M., and 10:30 P.M. The Greyhound leaves Flagstaff at 7 A.M., 10 A.M., 3 P.M., and midnight. A one way ticket is $22 and a round-trip ticket is $42.

Nava-Hopi Tours Inc.
114 W. Rt. 66
(520) 774–5003, (800) 892–8687
www.navahopitours.com

An alternative to the Greyhound, this shuttle picks up from the Amtrak Terminal at 6:55 A.M. and then the Nava-Hopi

Insiders' Tip

The state of Arizona does not observe Daylight Savings Time (except on the Navajo Reservation). Arizona does observe Mountain Standard Time.

Terminal at 7:15 A.M. and arrives at Phoenix Sky Harbor Airport at 10 A.M. Passengers may also get off in Camp Verde and at the Metro Center Transit Station in Phoenix. Nava-Hopi departs from Phoenix from Terminal 4 at 11:10 A.M. and Terminal 2 at 11:30 A.M. and arrives at the Nava-Hopi Terminal in Flagstaff at 2:15 P.M., A one way fare is $24 for adults and $12 for children. (See the Flagstaff Recreation chapter for more about the Nava-Hopi Tours.)

Taxis

Cab service usually is waiting curbside at the Greyhound bus station and at Flagstaff Municipal Airport to take travelers to their final destination. In case there isn't a cab on hand, here are a few taxi companies that provide service to the airport: Arizona Taxi & Tours, (520) 779-1111, A Friendly Cab, (520) 774-4444, and Sun Taxi & Tours, (520) 774-7400.

Flagstaff Pulliam Municipal Airport

Located five miles south of Flagstaff off I-17, Pulliam Municipal Airport hosts

America West Express, (800) 235-9292, which serves the region with nine flights a day to and from Phoenix. Flights may be canceled due to high winds and inclement weather. Call America West for reservations and arrival and departure times. Car rental services are available at the airport and in Flagstaff. Local hotel courtesy phones with direct-dial service also are available, and many B&Bs and hotels provide free shuttle service. Please inform your host ahead of time if you will need shuttle service. For further information, contact the airport at (520) 556-1234.

Rental Cars/Parking at Pulliam Airport

Four national companies provide rental service at the airport: Avis Rent-A-Car, (800) 831-2847; Budget and Sears Car and Truck Rental, (800) 527-0700; Hertz Rent-A-Car, (800) 654-3131; and National Car Rental, (800) 227-7386. Parking is open at the airport and there is no fee. If you plan on leaving your car for an extended amount of time please inform the airport by calling (520) 556-1234, ext. 10.

Getting Here by Car

Car rentals are available at the Phoenix Sky Harbor Airport, but due to Phoenix's popularity as a winter destination, it's best to book the rental beforehand. Greyhound Bus service from the airport is available as well as Nava-Hopi Tours, which is based in Flagstaff and offers daily service to the Phoenix airport. Amtrak roars into town two times a day and is a great way to see the country if you have a lot of time.

However, if you are driving here, be forewarned that early fall and late spring storms are common. Flagstaff gets most of its snow during the spring (which makes this a great place for spring skiing). Phoenix could be experiencing balmy weather while Flagstaff is snowed in. Road closures in and out of Flagstaff are common; I-17 and I-40 may be closed due to inclement weather, making northland travel impossible. Call the automated Road Conditions number, (888) 411-7623, for up-to-the-minute traveling information.

Flagstaff via Albuquerque

Take Interstate 40 W passing by Holbrook, Winslow, and Meteor Crater. As you reach the Flagstaff city limits, there are three possible exits to choose from. If you take Exit 204, you will be able to visit Walnut Canyon National Monument. To access U.S. Highway 89 to Utah or High-

way 180 to the Grand Canyon and the east side of Flagstaff, use Exit 201. This exit takes you from east to west Flagstaff and through the downtown area before you get to Hwy. 180 (the road to the Grand Canyon). For the Historic Downtown, take Exit 198 (also marked Butler Ave.). This exit will take you to the south side of the downtown area. To reach the north side of town just cross the railroad tracks. To continue on to Sedona, Phoenix, or the Grand Canyon, look for Exit 195A and B. Exit 195A is the junction for Interstates 17 S and 89A, which will allow access to Sedona and then Phoenix. For the scenic route to Sedona take U.S. Highway 89A. To reach the west side of town take Exit 195B, which will also bring you right into the downtown area and in the direction of the Grand Canyon.

Flagstaff via the Grand Canyon

If you are driving from the south entrance of the Grand Canyon, take Highway 180 to Flagstaff. Grand Canyon Village (south entrance) is 80 miles northwest of Flagstaff. From the North Rim of the Grand Canyon, take Highway 67 to Jacob Lake. At Jacob Lake head east on 89A which will tie into Highway 89 and bring you directly into the east side of town.

Flagstaff via Los Angeles

As you leave L.A., take 15 N to Barstow. At Barstow, you will want to pick up Inter-state 40 and head east bypassing sections of Old Route 66. I–40 takes you straight to Flagstaff. There are three exits for Flagstaff; the second exit will take you to the downtown area.

Flagstaff via Las Vegas

From Las Vegas take Interstate 93 S and cross the Hoover Dam. Continue on I–93 until you reach Kingman. From Kingman, you will head east on Interstate 40. There are three exits for Flagstaff; the second exit will take you to the downtown area. Driving time from Las Vegas to Flagstaff is approximately four hours.

Flagstaff via Phoenix

Take Interstate 10 E and look for the exit marked Interstate 17 N. Once you are on I–17, you will drive straight into the city of Flagstaff. Driving time is approximately 2.5 hours. You will climb to an altitude of 7,000 feet from the desert floor at an altitude of about 1,100 feet.

Getting Here by Alternative Means

Greyhound Bus
399 S. Malpais Ln.
(520) 774–4573, (800) 231–2222

The Greyhound offers bus service to and from Flagstaff, and the station is a routine stop for taxis.

Amtrak Train
1 E. Santa Fe Ave.
(520) 774–8679, (800) 872–7245

Flagstaff's Amtrak station is located in the downtown center. The Amtrak runs on the Burlington Northern Santa Fe Railroad, which travels from Chicago to Los Angeles and back. Eastbound and westbound trains arrive once a day. Call for train schedules and ticket prices.

Getting around Flagstaff

If you have booked a hotel or bed-and-breakfast in the downtown area, the best mode of transportation is your feet. The two-hour parking restriction makes parking on the north side of the tracks a hassle. Visitors can park a few blocks north of downtown with no restrictions. However, there are no parking restrictions on the south side of town and there are even a few parking lots located behind the Chamber of Commerce on South Beaver Street, two lots on Phoenix Avenue, and lots on both sides of the Visitor Center/Amtrak Train Station.

Public transportation is not one of Flagstaff's strongest points, so we have also included local taxi, limousine service, and car rental options. We do have a bus system, but it is not the most efficient way to get around town. It is faster and more efficient to call a taxi.

Walking and biking are also popular ways to get around town. The Flagstaff Urban Trail System is a peaceful way to traverse the city either by foot or on wheels. (For bike rentals, refer to the Flagstaff Recreation Chapter.) A map of the Flagstaff Urban Trail System can be purchased at the Flagstaff City Hall for $2. The Flagstaff Visitor Center has a copy of this map for free, but an original copy of the map is suggested.

Car Rentals

Budget Rent-A-Car
175 W. Aspen Ave.
(520) 779–5255, (800) 527–0700

National Car Rental
2320 E. Lucky Lane (Holiday Inn)
(520) 779–1975, (800) 227–7368

Enterprise Rent-A-Car
100 N. Humphreys St.
3470 E. Rt. 66
(520) 774–9407, (520) 526–1377,
(800) 736–8222

Taxi and Limousine Companies

Some local companies offer special rates to various sights and attractions within the region. Contact the individual company for rates and more information.

A Friendly Cab
(520) 774–4444

Love Limousine
(520) 779–9739

Arizona Taxi & Tours
(520) 779–1111

Sun Taxi & Tours
(520) 774–7400

Harper's Limousine Service & Tours
(520) 779–1234

Accommodations

Price Code

The following price code is for two adults during "high" season, which begins in May and ends Labor Day weekend. Snow attracts many visitors and the season picks up again in December and runs through March. The rates are subject to change and do not include tax, gratuities, or any other guest services.

$	Less than $60
$$	$61-75
$$$	$76-100
$$$$	$101-125
$$$$$	$125 and more

Major motel and hotel chains provide the basics, but if you enjoy getting to know the town and its people and are looking for gourmet food and service with a personal touch, Flagstaff is full of charming and unique accommodations that suit any budget. Bed-and-breakfast inns have warm and comfortable atmospheres that make guests feel like family.

Be sure to fully investigate the inns you are considering before making a reservation. Innkeepers are very proud of their establishments and willingly answer the questions of potential guests to ensure a quality experience. The best part of staying at inns is that they are centrally located and usually within walking distance of shopping and restaurants. Most inns do accept children; however, pets don't seem to be as popular as children, so remember to call ahead to check on this policy. The majority of inns are homes that have been renovated with rooms and suites on the second floor that are not wheelchair accessible, but some may have first floor, wheelchair-accessible rooms. Nonsmoking inns with outside alternative smoking areas do exist, as do non-smoking properties. Transportation is provided to and from the local airport, bus and train stations. Summer and winter are Flagstaff's busiest seasons. Rates fluctuate from season to season. It is important to remember that the local university hosts various weekend events that attract alumni, students' families, and sports and cultural enthusiasts. Make your reservations early.

Bed-and-Breakfasts

Aspen Inn $$-$$$
218 N. Elden Street
(520) 773-0295

The congenial host of this quaint bed-and-breakfast hopes his guests will pick his brain to find out what to do and where to go in Flagstaff. All three rooms include a private bath, cable TV, private phone lines, queen-size beds, and a mini fridge stocked with complimentary beverages and light snacks. "The Wilson Room" is perfect for long visits and comes with a washer and dryer. This house has a common area for guests. Read a book, listen to music, or make yourself at home by the fireplace. A healthy breakfast is served on Spanish china in the dining room from 8 A.M. until 9 A.M. The inn's signature dish is a Spanish "tortilla," potato pie served with a light mushroom sauce and a side of turkey sausage. The innkeeper's wife is from Madrid and her madre taught her how to make this traditional recipe. In September 1999, *Sunset Magazine* recommended the Aspen Inn.

Birch Tree Inn $$-$$$
824 W. Birch Street
(520) 774-1042, (888) 774-1042

If a break from the city is what you need, come to this country style inn, which offers plenty of room for lounging opportunities on the wraparound front porch, back deck, and patio. Take a dip in the Jacuzzi while you gaze at the star filled sky. The five rooms range in price and two come with a shared bath. Comfortable and spacious, the inn was built in 1915 and is registered with the city for historic preservation. You will be treated like family as you curl up by the fire or play a round of billiards in the game room. All rooms are located on the second floor and each room is decorated with a specific theme that pays tribute to the innkeeper's family, the Southwest, or just subtle elegance. Afternoon refreshments are served at 4 P.M. daily. A healthy breakfast is served family style with fresh fruit. The inn caters to dietary restrictions; please inform the innkeepers in advance.

Hilltop Bed & Breakfast
$$-$$$, no credit cards
701 N. Curling Smoke Road
(520) 779-9633, (888) 508-4434

If a secluded cottage off the beaten track is calling to you, look no further. Awake each morning in a king-size bed surrounded by trees, birds chirping, and deer grazing outside your window. Decorated with antiques, leather furniture, and lace baked goodies await guests after a day of exploring. Relax by the fireplace in the common area or step outside to the perennial garden. Breathe in the crisp mountain air while rejuvenating in the gazebo. Can't decide where to go for dinner or which hike to do? The staff or owners are on hand to offer some suggestions. Vegetarian breakfasts are served in the common dining area between 8 A.M. and 9 A.M.. The menu changes daily, but guests can count on exotic juices, fresh baked muffins or breads, and a healthy entree to start their day.

Jeanette's Bed and Breakfast $$-$$$
3380 E. Lockett Road
(520) 527–1912

Resting in the pines with Mt. Elden as its backdrop, this Victorian-style home exudes romance. If you decide to take in the scenery or get a breath of fresh air, take a stroll through pine-covered paths or enjoy the porch swing on a warm summer night. All four rooms have private baths, each with a claw foot bathtub. And what good is a bathtub without home-made soaps and complimentary bubble bath? All rooms have unique features that set them apart, including a private balcony, fireplace, and king-size bed. Enjoy

curtains, the cottage has a charming appeal and plenty of elbow room. The cozy accommodations include a sitting area, a small kitchen with a mini fridge, dishes, coffeemaker, and sink. A Scandinavian sauna was installed to ensure that guests receive the proper amount of relaxation. Designated a backyard wildlife retreat by the National Wildlife Federation, the cottage is located on the top of a ten-mile-long mesa with trails for hiking, biking, and cross-country skiing right outside your cottage door.

Serving only organic ingredients and the highest quality food, the innkeeper believes what you eat is as important as where you stay. A complete breakfast menu is available. Choose from a hearty Southwestern omelet, pancakes, or a fruit parfait smoothie. Can't decide? Mix and match menu items to create the perfect meal.

The Inn at 410 Bed & Breakfast $$$-$$$$
410 N. Leroux Street
(520) 774–0088, (800) 774–2008
www.inn410.com

Built in 1894, this elegant inn offers spacious accommodations guaranteed to soothe the soul. Located two blocks from the historic downtown, the inn has four rooms and five suites with private baths, some with Jacuzzi tubs, fireplaces, and private entrances. The names of the suites are as distinctive as the suites themselves. "Sunflower Room," "Tea Room," and the "Monet Room" give you an idea of what the innkeepers are striving for: an intimate setting for an unforgettable getaway. Two suites are available for families. Complimentary beverages and fresh-

The Inn at 410 B&B creates a peaceful retreat from your busy life.

PHOTO: COURTESY OF THE INN AT 410 BED & BREAKFAST

Nanny's Pound Cake

Just like Lynn's Nanny used to make. Continuing this family tradition, Lynn prepares this family favorite to share with her guests. If the aroma of fresh baked pound cake wakes you from a sound sleep, know that you are in for a treat.

> 1 lb. butter
> 6 eggs
> 2 tablespoons vanilla
> 1 lb. powered sugar (1 box)
> 3 cups of flour

Cream butter very well. Add 1 egg at a time and beat well. Add vanilla. Add sugar in small amounts and beat extra well at this point. Add flour by folding in. Spray Bundt pan with Pam. Bake at 325 degrees for one hour or until a toothpick comes out of the center clean.

This recipe furnished by the innkeeper's at Lynn's Inn Bed & Breakfast

full gourmet breakfasts in the dining room. Guests rave about the Chili Soufflé. No children please.

Lynn's Inn $$-$$$
614 West Santa Fe Avenue
(520) 226–1488, (800) 530–9947

This delightful inn is your home away from home while traveling on business or exploring the wonders of northern Arizona. Pressed tin ceilings, period pieces, and eclectic antiques add to the inn's traditional charm. The three rooms come with private baths; the Franklin Room has its own Jacuzzi tub. The Gibson Suite is perfect for a family or two couples traveling together. The innkeepers think of everything, including the homemade caramels and chocolates they place on your pillow. Guests can help themselves to a cookie jar filled with fresh baked cookies, Nanny's pound cake (find the recipe for this in the close-up in this chapter), seasonal fruit, and hot and cold beverages. Swing on the swing in the lusciously landscaped yard, soak in the outdoor Jacuzzi, or just relax on the couch. Lynn's Inn is conveniently located 5 blocks from the center of downtown, the train and bus station, and Northern Arizona University. Breakfast—an entrée with fresh fruit—is served at 8 A.M. on the back porch.

Atmospheric Places to Stay

Hotel Weatherford $$
23 North Leroux
(520) 779–1919
www.weatherhotel.com

The historic Hotel Weatherford was built at the turn of the century by John Weatherford, who envisioned Flagstaff as the cultural Mecca of the West. Since the opening of the grand hotel, the guest list has been impressive. From President Teddy Roosevelt to novelist Zane Grey to painter

Thomas Moran, these early-twentieth-century legends have contributed a piece of history to the establishment. The hotel was saved from demolition by the previous owner in the early 1970s and has survived several fires and harsh weather. The eight fully restored rooms on the third floor are decorated in the turn-of-the-twentieth-century style, without modern amenities. The refurbished wood floors, light and airy rooms, and in-house bars and restaurant

Relax in turn-of-the-twentieth-century atmosphere of the Old West at the Hotel Weatherford.
PHOTO: BONNIE HOLMES

offer pure relaxation and rejuvenation. Four of the eight rooms come with private baths. Located in the heart of downtown, just one block from the Amtrak station, the hotel is within walking distance of restaurants, art galleries and shopping.

Ski Lift Lodge $$
P.O. Box 40, Flagstaff 86002
(520) 779–1951
www.arizonasnowbowl.com

Located seven miles north of Flagstaff at the base of the San Francisco Peaks, this is the perfect spot for a family vacation or a getaway for two. Whether you like to hike, mountain bike, or ski, The "Peaks" as locals refer to it, is the ideal place for all your outdoor activities.

The lodge has twenty-five cabin units with front porches and fireplaces. The cabins sleep four with two full beds. Some rooms have queen-size beds. Ask for a roll-away bed if needed. The maximum occupancy per room is four. Make reservations early, the lodge—just minutes from the ski lifts—is a popular choice with skiers. A full service restaurant providing breakfast, lunch, and dinner is open seven days a week. The restaurant will prepare snacks for those on the go.

Montezuma Lodge at Mormon Lake
$$-$$$
HC 31 Box 342, Mormon Lake, AZ 86038
(520) 354–2220

Surrounded by oak and pine trees, Montezuma Lodge is 25 miles southeast of Flagstaff at the base of Mormon Mountain. Immerse yourself in the seclusion of the Coconino National Forest, which has plenty of hiking trails, lakes for fishing, and horseback riding trails. The rustic, self-sufficient cabins include stove, fridge, wood-burning fireplaces, linens, bedding, and cooking utensils. Choose from one of sixteen cabins set on sixteen acres of land that range from a cozy cabin for two, a stone cabin, split-level for four, or a hogan-style cabin that accommodates eight people. Pets are welcome. The nearest store and restaurant is seven minutes away. The store has a limited selection, so stock up on supplies before you leave town. This is cushy camping at its best!

Restaurants

Price Code

The costs below represent dinner for two excluding tax, gratuity, and drinks. Menus, times, and prices are subject to change. Please call if you have any questions. Most establishments accept cash, major credit cards, and traveler's checks. Please note that if a restaurant does not accept credit cards, it will be noted in the restaurant listing information.

$ ....Less than $20
$$ ....$21 to $35
$$$ ....$36 to $60
$$$$ ....$60 and more

As you drive into Flagstaff, you will be assaulted by neon lights and fast food restaurants. However, though popular American chain restaurants have invaded Flagstaff, do not despair. Whether you are searching for a fine dining establishment, a casual cafe, or a haven for vegetarians, Flagstaff is home to a variety of eating establishments that will make your taste buds stand at attention. You will find restaurants serving traditional dishes complimented by fresh Southwestern ingredients. If you taste something a little out of the ordinary in your marinara sauce, it's probably some fresh cut cilantro or chipotle chiles.

During the 1800s the number of saloons outnumbered the number of restaurants seven to one. As American tourism increased during the twentieth century, Flagstaff answered the call of supply and demand and built restaurants to accommodate travelers. However, the in-town dining options were still quite limited prior to the renovation of the historic downtown area in the early 1990s, and the subsequent increase in population and tourism. Within the last ten years, dining options have doubled. Flagstaff is made up of health conscious people. Perhaps its the clean air and abundance of outdoor activities that contribute to this healthy attitude. With the recent trend in health awareness and popularity of organic foods, locals expect quality ingredients and healthy alternatives. Restaurants have listened to the requests and needs of their customers by providing vegetarian and ethnic dishes. Cafes and restaurants also serve coffee drinks made with soy milk and yummy vegan pastries and desserts. Don't worry carnivores—there are plenty of free range and hormone-free meat options.

Flagstaff is a town known for its relaxed style and comfortable atmosphere. The dress for restaurants is casual, yet you should feel free to put on a jacket or slip into that little black dress. Don't be surprised if you are sitting next to a table of hikers who have just climbed the San Francisco Peaks on one side, while a well-dressed couple lingering over after-dinner drinks sits at the next table. Self-expression is a way of life in this mountain town. Please remember that all Flagstaff restaurants are non-smoking. While breakfast, lunch, and dinner places are scattered throughout town, most of the restaurants featured in this section are in the downtown area or within a four-mile radius.

Beaver Street Brewery and Whistle Stop Cafe $$
11 S. Beaver St.
(520) 779–0079

Decorated in dark polished wood, this popular eatery is bound to please the pickiest of eaters. Burgers, wood-fire pizzas, and tasty sandwiches are the specialties of the house. Look for the daily soup and chili specials. The lunch and dinner entrees are always a treat. Start off your meal with a savory fondue made with

Beaver Street's own batch of micro-brewed beer. Always busy and consistently good, the lively restaurant atmosphere caters to families and the thirty-something crowd. Be ready to wait on a Friday or Saturday night in the summer or in the dead of winter. Reservations are not taken, thus making patience a virtue. Relax in one of their comfy chairs by the host station or belly up to the bar and try one of the fresh home brews that has made Beaver Street Brewery a household name. The restaurant is wheelchair accessible and is open for lunch and dinner seven days a week.

Brandy's/La Bellavia $
no credit cards
1500 E. Cedar Ave.
18 S. Beaver St.
(520) 779–2187, (520) 774–8301
www.brandysrestaurant.com

La Bellavia has been a Flagstaff institution since 1976. The encore to the popular La Bellavia restaurant was the opening of Brandy's in 1993. Whether you decide to dine at the downtown location or the eastside restaurant you will not be disappointed. Brandy's has won "Best Breakfast in Flagstaff" six years in a row. The menu is a mix of traditional breakfast and lunch items and unique dishes that are made from scratch. All of the recipes are Brandy's own concoctions. Everything from the Hollandaise sauce to the peaches-and-cream danish is homemade. Breakfasts are, to put it simply, huge. Just try and finish a stack of Swedish oat pancakes with hot cinnamon apple topping. Phoenicians (people from Phoenix) drive for two-and-a-half hours just for the award-winning trout and eggs. All breakfasts come with a choice of potatoes or buttermilk pancakes, and toast or English muffin. Both breakfast and lunch menus offer vegetarian options galore. The Reuben with avocado and tomato is a hit. The relaxed casual atmosphere will have you coming back for more. "What's important is not the character of the place, . . . rather the characters in the

place." This is the motto for the friendly and outgoing staff. Open seven days a week.

Buster's Restaurant and Bar $$
1800 S. Milton, Suite 111
(520) 774–5155

Known as the "local eatery," Buster's is an oasis in the desert. Featuring an oyster bar, fresh fish, and certified Angus steak, its contemporary yet comfortable atmosphere assures a top-notch dining experience. Salads, burgers, and steak or chicken fajitas are lunchtime favorites. Dinner entrees come with a choice of homemade soup or crisp salad. Looking for something a little out of the ordinary? Try the halibut poached in pistachio parchment. The Chicken Sonoma smothered with artichoke hearts, tomatoes, and mushrooms simmered in a Chardonnay will make you a regular customer. Reservations are accepted and diners can choose to eat in the bar or restaurant. The beer list is extensive, sporting sixty-six imported and domestic beers. The wine list is traditional and features California whites and reds. If a frozen or umbrella-style drink calls, consult the nearest drink list for an original tasty concoction. Buster's is open seven days a week and is wheelchair accessible. (See Nightlife section for more about Buster's.)

Charly's Pub & Grill in the Historic Hotel Weatherford $
23 N. Leroux St.
(520) 779–1919
www.weatherfordhotel.com

Built in 1900, this casual lunch or dinner institution takes the customer on a historic sojourn back to the early twentieth century. The proprietors of Charly's saved the building from destruction twenty-five years ago. Since the purchase, the building has been under a constant restoration and renovating process. Seasonal outdoor dining is available for lunch and dinner. The lunch menu includes sandwiches, Southwestern dishes, and fresh salads. Dinner at Charly's features traditional

Brandy's Art Gallery

As you enter Brandy's restaurant or La Bellavia you will notice the aroma of fresh roasted coffee, the case of homemade pastries, and the colorful artwork hanging on the walls. Why does the owner of these popular restaurants choose to decorate the walls with artwork? Because amidst the talented and diverse community of Flagstaff, Brandy realized she had the perfect venue to support local artists. By combining food and art, Brandy offers a place for people to come together as a community. The regular clientele come to enjoy good food and to discuss and critique the displayed artwork, which stimulates conversations between staff and customers. Most diners would not expect to walk in and find the work of Navaho artist Shonto Begay hanging above them as they eat their breakfast.

Flagstaff and its surrounding areas have a tremendous number of talented artists who are looking for exposure, and this venue features local and professional artists who clamor to get on the two-year waiting list. Brandy has introduced the work of many artists whose work previously only been exposed in galleries and museums across the country.

As a mother of two, Brandy realizes the importance of introducing art in to the lives of children. Local high schools are invited each year to display the work of their students. The kids enjoy bringing their parents knowing that their work is displayed. Brandy also dedicates a month to the Plein-Air Artists of Northern Arizona and to the Hozhoni Foundation, a foundation for developmentally disabled adults, who produce artwork in pencil, acrylics, and woodwork. Each show lasts for a month and the artist is welcomed with a reception, which is open to the public. Check for reception dates and times in *FlagLive!*. While you're checking out the art, be sure to peruse, mingle, and sample some of Brandy's famous goodies.

pub food and innovative entrees including steak, fish, and chicken. The Salmon Escondido is wrapped in a cornhusk with peppers and onions, and simmered in a teriyaki and prickly pear marinade. All dinner entrees come with homemade soup or salad. The wine list is well-rounded and the beer list is extensive, including locally brewed and imported beers. Reservations are accepted for parties of six or more.

If late afternoon drinks and appetizers are called for, take the stairs up three flights (there is no elevator) to the Zane Grey Ballroom. Decorated in the turn-of-the-century style, with a fully restored bar from Tombstone, Arizona, the room is elegant but casual. Stroll along the restored balcony that wraps around the building for some of the best views of the city and the Peaks. Opened from 5 P.M. until closing, the Zane Grey serves drinks and

yummy appetizers. Try one of their imported beers on tap and piping-hot, baked spinach artichoke dip. (See Nightlife section for more about Charly's Zane Grey Ballroom.)

The Cottage Place Restaurant $$$
126 W. Cottage Ave.
(520) 774–8431
 www.cottageplace.com

This is one of Flagstaff's true fine dining experiences. Set inside a "bungalow" style home that was common during the early twentieth century in Flagstaff, the intimate yet comfortable atmosphere is a favorite among locals and tourists. The service is attentive and friendly without being obtrusive. The fine food and extensive wine list featuring 240 wines compliment a romantic evening for two or an intimate get-together. The Cottage Place proudly serves a traditional Continental/

American menu, with table-side specialties. The Caesar Salad for Two combines crisp romaine lettuce with a classic Caesar dressing and is prepared tableside. Chateaubriand for Two includes rack of lamb with a duet of demi-glace and English mint sauce, and is carved tableside and served with garlic duchess potatoes and fresh vegetables. The menu also includes beef, veal, fresh seafood, and vegetarian dishes. Each entree includes soup, salad, starch, and vegetable. To complete your succulent meal, dessert is a must. Choose one of the many homemade options from the dessert tray. The chocolate decadence, a flourless chocolate cake topped with chantilly creme and served with raspberry puree, is to die for. Reservations are required. The Cottage Place is open Tuesday through Saturday.

Dara Thai $
14 S. San Francisco St.
(520) 774–0047

As you walk into this lively restaurant, you will notice the brightly painted walls with palm trees swaying in the breeze, exotic flowers, and the line of people. The decorated walls will promptly put you in the right frame of mind. Relax and enjoy the experience. Feel free to put your own name on the list. No pretentious wait staff or host here, just busy workers and hungry customers who know that the food is worth waiting for. Try a Singha, a Thai beer, or a refreshing Mai Tai while you wait. You will leave the restaurant full, happy, and smelling like Dara Thai. Specializing in coconut curry sauces, all dishes can be made vegetarian and as spicy as you like. They use the star system to rate the spiciness. Two to two-and-a-half stars is medium; five stars is hot. Then comes Thai hot or extra Thai hot. The kitchen will make it as hot and spicy as you need it. Pad Thai is a house favorite, rice noodles in a sweet sauce topped with ground peanuts, chicken, and shrimp. Another favorite is the Gaeng Kari, a yellow coconut curry sauce with potatoes, carrots, peppers, and your

choice of chicken, beef, pork, or deep-fried tofu. Dara Thai is closed on Sunday but open for lunch and dinner Monday through Saturday. Reservations are accepted for parties of four or more.

The Down Under New Zealand Restaurant
$$$ • 6 E. Aspen Ave.
(520) 774–6677

On the corner of Aspen and Leroux is a taste of the land down under specializing in New Zealand Cervena venison, spring lamb, fresh fish, and Australian kangaroo. Although kangaroo meat is uncommon to most, the taste and texture are comparable to filet mignon. If you are feeling adventurous, the kangaroo is marinated and grilled to medium rare. Only the freshest ingredients and free range and hormone- and steroid-free meats are available on the menu. Yes, the food is exotic, but Down Under offers many traditional choices as well. One of their signature dishes is the Salmon Melissa, which is crusted in pecans and served over an orange ginger glaze. More than one customer has returned at the end of the night requesting this recipe. The wine list features mostly the products of Australian and New Zealand wineries. Ask your wait staff for a suggestion if you are unfamiliar with the choices, or choose from a fully stocked bar. This elegant and airy restaurant is enclosed by windows which makes this an ideal place to people watch or take in the sights of the downtown area. Seasonal outdoor dining is also available. Whether it's a special occasion or a group celebrating the end of a river trip, Down Under is sure to provide the perfect setting. The restaurant is open seven days a week for lunch and dinner; reservations are recommended.

Jitters Gourmet Coffee and Cafe $
no credit cards
3504 E. Route 66
(520) 526–6964

This bright atmosphere is sure to make a morning person out of anyone. Unique gift items (including homemade fudge), local and regional newspapers, and colorful tabletops ensure a morning, afternoon, or evening well spent. The breakfast menu is limited. Choose from pastries, cereal, or a breakfast bagel sandwich with your choice of bagel, scrambled egg, and cheese (ham is optional). The lunch menu is delightful. Jitters is known for their homemade soup, gourmet sandwiches, and personal touch. Have a special request or in a funky mood? Just ask the friendly staff and they will personalize your order. All menu items from the six varieties of quiche, to the sticky buns, to the chocolate walnut fudge are homemade. In addition to the great food and casual atmosphere, Jitters has specialty coffee drinks and a variety of teas. Outdoor seating is available and Jitters is open seven days a week.

Macy's European Coffee House, Bakery, and Restaurant $, no credit cards
14 S. Beaver St.
(520) 774–2243
www.macyscoffee.com

This in-house bakery and restaurant caters to vegetarians, vegans, and anyone who loves good food. All menu items are made on the premises and in the Macy's tradition "baked with love." Breakfast, lunch, and dinner are served daily. Check out the bakery case to see the fresh, homemade specialties of the day. The chalkboard menus include vegetarian sandwiches served on whole wheat molasses bread, salads, and breakfast specials from steamed eggs with the veggies of your choice to oatmeal to breakfast couscous. Don't walk by the daily special board. Try the ever-changing lasagna special prepared with fresh pasta. All items on the specials chalk board come with salad greens, and whole wheat molasses bread. The coffee is roasted in Macy's own roaster every morning. An eclectic blend of people meet here to play chess, chat, and eat delicious home baked goodies. The walls are covered with paintings by local artists. The staff is always friendly and ready to help. People from all walks of life are welcomed here; this place

has a true community spirit.

Main St. Grill and Catering $
no credit cards
16 E. Rt. 66, Suite 103
(520) 774–1519

If you hear the sound of singing voices coming from a restaurant kitchen, go no further. That's just the staff of Main St. Grill, and you know you are in the right place. Gourmet sandwiches, quality ingredients, and lunch items with a twist are the house specialties. Try the Main Street Philly, a half loaf of shepherd's bread stuffed with steak, chicken, or veggies, with cheese, onions, chiles, and a side of marinara, the smoked turkey sandwich piled high with avocado, sprouts, and havarti cheese or the Caesar salad with fresh turkey or portobello mushroom and roasted garlic. All salads are made with organic greens with your choice of a homemade dressing. The specials board has two daily homemade soups. Don't miss Mulligatawny Wednesday. This creamy curry soup is combined with apple and chicken that will delight the senses and entice you to come back for more. Save enough room for dessert. The cappuccino brownie is pure decadence and you won't mind skipping dessert for a week. Place your order at the counter, slide into one of the retro-style booths, and get ready for a mouth-watering experience!

Mamma Luisa Italian Restaurant $$
2710 N. Steves Blvd.
(520) 526–6809

Italian food like your mother (if she were Italian) would make. Walking through the door of this establishment is like walking into Little Italy in New York City. The restaurant is warm and cozy with red checkered table cloths. The recipes come from the original owner's mama who was from Italy. As the restaurant changed hands, the present chef kept the recipes intact, but added vegetarian options. The cuisine is a combination of northern and southern Italian with thick red sauces, tangy pesto, or rich Marsala. Dedicated to serving the finest wine and food, Mamma

Luisa promises all entrees are made to order, including the lasagna. Chicken, veal, and shrimp dishes are the specialties. Ask for the daily special, and if you're lucky zuppa pesce will be featured. Mamma Luisa's is open seven days a week. Reservations are accepted and recommended on the weekend.

Martans Burrito Place $
no credit cards
10 North San Francisco St.
(520) 773–4701

Right in the heart of downtown Flagstaff you'll find a little bit of Mexico. Postcards from locals and tourists alike hang on the walls. These are testimonies of trips taken, hometown greetings, or just a simple "thank you" from customers around the world. The atmosphere is as homemade as the food. Don't forget to say hi to Miss Alice who has been cooking for Martans for the past twenty years. Seat yourself if you can find a table during breakfast or lunch. What better way to start the day off than with an order of homemade chorizo con huevos or the ever popular chilaquiles, scrambled eggs mixed with onions, corn tortillas, enchilada sauce, and topped with cheddar and jack cheese? All breakfasts are served with rice, beans, and hash browns. Lunches are more than generous. Look for the daily special and posole with corn or flour tortilla is always on hand. This is a great place to go before a big hike or if you're on your way to the Grand Canyon.

Pasto Restaurant $$
19 E. Aspen Ave.
(520) 779–1937

As you turn onto Aspen Ave., the smell of garlic will lead you in the right direction. A local favorite, this restaurant's intimate setting, with its crisp white linen tablecloths, is perfect for a first date or a large party. Dark stone walls compliment this affordable yet elegant Italian eatery. Tantalizing dishes await you as your dining experience begins with a plate of drizzled olive oil for dipping chunks of fresh,

Start your day with a cup of Macy's gourmet coffee and a dose of morning sunshine. PHOTO: STACEY WITTIG

crusty bread. For a more than auspicious beginning, the Prince Edward Sound mussels appetizer with chunks of garlic and ripe tomatoes is a must. The entrees include various types of homemade pasta with nine tempting sauces that range in spiciness and flavors. The atomic marinara with crushed red pepper and cayenne is for the adventurous eaters only. Entrees include chicken, veal, and seafood dishes. The Balsamic Salmon is poached and simmered with artichoke hearts, mushrooms, and fresh basil, and served over orecchiette (an ear-shaped pasta). The attentive and friendly servers are well-educated in wine. The wine selection is sure to please the toughest of palettes. Or you can choose from a selection of imported and local micro-brewed beers. All desserts are homemade. The tiramisu, made especially by the owner, is a must. Reservations are recommended. Ask for a table for two by the window. A great view of the downtown area gives you a feel for the local scene. Pasto Restaurant is open seven days a week for dinner. Call for times as winter approaches.

Sakura Restaurant $$-$$$
Radisson Hotel
1175 W. Route 66
(520) 773–9118

If an entertaining and exotic evening is planned, try the Japanese menu at Sakura, which was recently nominated by *Food & Wine Magazine* as one of the top one hundred restaurants in the Southwest. Customers may either dine at a table or sit at a Teppanyaki grill. (Pick the grill!) A trained Teppan chef prepares teriyaki or hibachi style chicken, beef, and seafood dishes in traditional Japanese fashion. The New York steak and lobster combination is a favorite among regulars. All dinner entrees come with soup, steamed rice, and fresh vegetables. Any sushi lover will devour the made-to-order specialties. Ask for the daily sushi specials and current market prices. Wine list, Japanese beers, and sake are available. Sakura is open for lunch (except on Sunday) and dinner. Reservations are highly recommended.

Woodlands Cafe $$-$$$
Radisson Hotel,
1175 W. Route 66
(520) 773–9118

Woodland's Cafe is the best-kept secret in Flagstaff. Serving breakfast, lunch, and dinner, this cafe's menu will easily accommodate anyone in your party. Don't forget about the Sunday Brunch from 10 A.M. to 2 P.M. The brunch includes made-to-order omelets, fresh sushi, seasonal fruits, imported cheeses. The casual atmosphere and atrium-style windows offering views of the San Francisco Peaks make this a perfect spot for a business meeting, lunch with a friend, or a leisurely dinner. The lunch menu is a mixture of salads, sandwiches, and extravagant dishes. Dinner entrees range from beef and lamb to fresh seafood dishes. The daily dinner specials will certainly impress. The restaurant is open seven days a week and reservations are suggested.

Attractions

Mingling Native American influences and western tradition, Flagstaff is a city that is surrounded by natural wonders and a diverse cultural history.

While you visit local museums, ancient ruins, and historic homes, you will glimpse the lives of the pioneers and Native Americans who have cultivated this land and made this area their home. Visitors will learn about native plant life, hike to ancient pueblos, and admire turn-of-the-century architecture. As you take time to understand past generations, you will discover a rich heritage that is continuing into the future. Flagstaff is proud to hold onto its identity by preserving natural and popular attractions for locals and visitors to share. It is not only one strand that defines this city, but rather a multitude of fibers that have been woven together to produce a thriving community.

The Arboretum at Flagstaff
(520) 774–1442
www.thearb.org

The arboretum is dedicated to helping visitors understand the native plants of the Colorado Plateau. At 7,150 feet in elevation, the arboretum is an educational adventure. Sample one of the 250 types of herbs in the herb garden, or view the San Francisco Peaks from the 1.2-mile nature trail. Visit the constructed wetlands or the solar greenhouse. Bring your binoculars; there are guided birdwalks. Educational outings and programs are offered for children and adults. The arboretum is open April 1–December 15 from 9 A.M–5 P.M. and is located 3.8 miles south of West Rt. 66 on Woody Mountain Rd. Admission is $4 for adults, $3 for seniors, $1 for children 6–12, and kids under 6 are admitted free. (See the Flagstaff Kidstuff chapter for more on educational programs.)

Arizona Historical Society Pioneer Museum
2340 N. Fort Valley Rd.
(520) 774–6272

The Pioneer Museum was first a hospital, then a boarding home before it was bought by the Historical Society in 1960 and turned into a museum. The museum specializes in exhibits that are representative of the history of Flagstaff and northern Arizona. In addition to the museum's extensive collection of artifacts, photographs, and memorabilia, they also sponsor two annual exhibits: Playthings of the Past, and the Wool Festival. (Please refer to Flagstaff Annual Events chapter for more information.) Admission is free to the Pioneer Museum, but donations are greatly appreciated. The museum is open Monday through Saturday 9 A.M.–5 P.M. and is closed on Sunday.

Elden Pueblo Indian Ruins
(520) 527–3475

Elden Pueblo, which is still being excavated, offers a unique opportunity to understand the archaeology of the native peoples of northern Arizona. The ruins are located just past the Mt. Elden Lookout trailhead on the left side of U.S. 89. Visitors have a choice between the self-guided tour that allows you to observe the ruins without disturbing them or to participate in a group dig coordinated by The Elden Pueblo Archaeology Program. This educational program teaches archaeological skills, concepts, and laws. For more information on the Elden Pueblo Archaeology Program contact the Northern Arizona University Science and Mathematics Learning Center at (520) 523–7953.

Lowell Observatory
1400 W. Mars Hill Rd.
(520) 774–3358
www.lowell.edu

Learn about the wonders of the sky at Lowell Observatory. The public is invited to view the daytime sky through specially filtered telescopes; this daily viewing begins at 9 A.M. Other tours begin at 10 A.M. and are spread throughout the day. The tours include a presentation explaining the beginnings and history of Lowell Observatory. Preceding the presentation, the public is invited to tour the telescopes. There is also a hands-on exhibit for children and adults of all ages. The observatory is located 1 mile west of downtown Flagstaff. Call the observatory for special events and evening hours. Please remember that the observatory tours and events are weather permitting. (For more information about viewing the night sky see the Flagstaff Nightlife chapter.)

Northern Arizona University
North Campus
(520) 523–9011
www.nau.org

With its sandstone buildings and white pillars, the 100-year-old North campus of NAU is a testimonial to Flagstaff at the turn of the twentieth century. Old Main was built in 1894 and was originally proposed to be a home for juvenile delinquents. The town objected and the building eventually became the Northern Arizona Normal School in 1899. Other buildings of interest on North Campus include the Blome Building and North Morton Hall, which is believed to be haunted. (Old Main is now home to the Old Main Gallery; see the Flagstaff Arts chapter.)

Elden Pueblo

Join professional archaeologists as they reconstruct Elden Pueblo during Public Dig Days held throughout the summer and fall. PHOTO: TANYA LEE

Introduce yourself and your children to the wonders of archaeology and to the indigenous peoples who once lived in the area around Flagstaff with a quick tour of Elden Pueblo, just a few minutes north of downtown on U.S. Highway 89.

This partially excavated archaeological site was inhabited by the Sinagua (see-na-wa) who lived in the Flagstaff area from about 700 to 1400 C.E. The word Sinagua means "without water" and refers to the semi-arid high desert conditions of this area.

The Sinagua at Elden Pueblo built aboveground stone houses like those some of the Pueblo tribes occupy today. They made brownware and redware pottery and traded their pots for items such as shells, jewelry, macaws, minerals, and copper bells. Some of the trade items came from as far away as Mexico. You can learn more about the Sinagua by visiting the Museum of Northern Arizona, Wupatki National Monument, and Walnut Canyon.

The 70 rooms that make up Elden Pueblo, which is named for the mountain behind the site, were inhabited from about 1070 to 1275 C.E. A large "dormitory" room suggests that Elden Pueblo may have been a center of trade, as was Wupatki.

In 1926, Dr. Jesse Walter Fewkes, an archaeologist for the Smithsonian Institution, excavated some of the rooms at Elden Pueblo. While the site was not made into a national monument as he had hoped, it is nonetheless open to the public year round. Modern-day Hopi, a Pueblo people who now live on three mesas northeast of Flagstaff, consider Elden Pueblo to be a place important in their ancestral history. They call it "Pasiovi" or "Pavasioki."

To get to the pueblo, drive north on Highway 89 past the Flagstaff Mall on your right. The sign for the pueblo is on your left, just before the traffic light at Townsend-Winona Road. Parking is plentiful, and there is no entrance fee.

Self-guided tours are available at this site, which is used to train archaeologists. The Forest Service holds several Public Dig Days, usually on weekends, in the summer and the fall, during which adults and children can help professional archaeologists excavate the site and look for treasures—pottery sherds, feathers, bones of animals used for food, and the remains of tools.

As at all archaeological sites you visit, please do not remove anything, however insignificant it may seem. Vegetation, pot shards, stones, pebbles—everything here is part of the archaeological record.

For more information and a schedule of educational activities held at Elden Pueblo, write Coconino National Forest, Archaeology Section, 2323 East Greenlaw Lane, Flagstaff, AZ 86004 or visit the Coconino National Forest office on Highway 89 just about a mile south of the pueblo.

Museum of Northern Arizona
3101 N. Fort Valley Rd.
(520) 774–5213
www.musnaz.org

Founded in 1928, the Museum of Northern Arizona has over 5 million pieces in its permanent collections and is home to a life-size skeletal model of Dilophosaurus, a carnivorous dinosaur of the Plateau. Dedicated to preserving the natural and cultural history of the Colorado Plateau, the museum sponsors year-round events, exhibits, and seminars for children and adults including the Heritage Program, a summer long celebration of Native American art. The museum is open daily from 9 A.M–5 P.M. and is located on Hwy 180 on the way to the Grand Canyon. Admission is $5 adults; $4 seniors; $3 college students; and $2 for children ages 7 to 17.

Riordan Mansion State Historic Park
409 Riordan Rd.
(520) 779–4395
www.pr.state.az.us/parkhtml/riordan.html

This historic building was built in 1904 and has 40 rooms with over 13,000 square feet of living area. Interesting features of the Riordan home are the rustic log-slab siding exterior, volcanic stone arches, and hand-split wooden shingles. The Park's Visitor Center offers a slide program, exhibit area, and a children's "touch table." A guided tour of the interior of the mansion is the only way to see it. Don't miss the Holidays Tours at the Mansion during the month of December (See Flagstaff Annual Events chapter for more information.) The park is surrounded by six acres of pine and has picnic tables for visitors. The park is open 7 days a week from 8:30 A.M. to 5 P.M. and is located next to Northern Arizona University. Reservations are recommended for tours.

Sunset Crater and Wupatki National Monument are located on a 26-mile loop that showcases lava craters and Indian ruins. Take Hwy. 89 north from Flagstaff to access both monuments. The $3 admission fee (17 and older) for Sunset Crater gets you into Wupatki too. The monuments are opened every day except for Christmas from 8 A.M. to 5 P.M.

Sunset Crater Volcano National Monument
Route 3 Box 149
(520) 526–0502
www.nps.gov/sucr

Located 15 miles north of Flagstaff off Hwy. 180, Sunset Crater was formed as ash and cinders spewed from an opening in the ground. Lava flowed from the crater, creating rivers of hardened lava. Today, trails and viewpoints allow visitors to view this natural wonder. John Wesley Powell, leader of many Grand Canyon expeditions, named the crater for the red-orange hue around its rim.

Walnut Canyon National Monument
Walnut Canyon Rd. #3
(520) 526–3367
www.nps.gov/waca

As you hike down a paved trail into this pristine canyon, you will be transported back in time to a thousand years. The ancient cliff dwellings were built into the walls of the canyon and to this day are well preserved. The Visitor Center Museum has artifacts on display. The monument is located seven miles east of Flagstaff and open seven days a week. The admission fee is $3 for adults 17 and older. Everyone else is free.

Wupatki National Monument
H.C. 33 Box 444A
(520) 679–2365
www.nps.gov/wupa

Once the home of the Anasazi, Sinagua, and Hopi, Wupatki National Monument has preserved Indian pueblos that allow visitors to see how ancient people lived. Wupatki National Monument is located 39 miles north of Flagstaff on Hwy. 89.

The San Francisco Peaks is Flagstaff's playground. PHOTO: STACEY WITTIG

Recreation

The state of Arizona boasts almost 300 days of sunshine a year throughout its four distinct seasons. The diverse terrain of the Colorado Plateau insures plentiful outdoor recreational activities any time of the year. Whether you are a hardcore outdoor enthusiast or a first-time skier, people of all fitness levels will agree that the scenery is beautiful and the outdoor recreational activities are endless.

Bike Rentals

Pedal your way through the streets of downtown, coast along the Flagstaff Urban Trail System, or plan a mountain bike excursion for the whole family with the help of the following bike shops. Suggested mountain bike rides can be found in the Coconino National Forest chapter. (Please refer to the Flagstaff Shopping chapter for more information on bike shops.)

Absolute Bikes
18 N. San Francisco St.
(520) 779–5969

This shop located in historic downtown Flagstaff meets your mountain bike rental needs with front- or full-suspension mountain bikes. Absolute Bikes is open 9 A.M. to 7 P.M. Monday through Friday, Saturday 10 A.M. to 6 P.M., Sunday 10 A.M. to 4 P.M. Rentals start at $25 for front suspension and $45 for full-suspension mountain bikes.

Cosmic Cycles
901 N. Beaver St.
(520) 779–1092

This shop can get you up and riding with their selection of rigid-, front-, or full-suspension mountain bikes ($25 for front suspension and $45 for full suspension mountain bikes). Look for it near the Flagstaff Medical Center. Cosmic Cycles is open 10 A.M. to 5:30 P.M. Monday to Saturday and is closed on Sunday.

Single Track
575 W. Riordan Rd.
(520) 773–1862

Single track can outfit the entire family with state-of-the-art mountain bike rentals. Front suspension rentals (only) are $25 for the first day, after which the price decreases $5 each day. So second day would be $20 and so on. . . . Single Track is open 9 A.M. to 6 P.M. Monday through Saturday and Sunday 10 A.M. to 4 P.M.

Bowling

Starlite Lanes
3406 E. Route 66
(520) 526–1138

Starlite Lanes has 16 lanes with automatic scoring. Starlite Lanes opens daily at 11 A.M. Open bowling is available to the public every Saturday. They even have

Bumper Bowling for kids. Starlite Lanes has a cocktail lounge, satellite dish, and a full service Pro Shop. The cost per game to bowl is $2 until 6 P.M.; after 6 P.M. the price is $2.25. Prices are the same for kids and adults.

Camping and RV Parks

These accommodations make camping and roughing it in the outdoors a little bit easier. For National Forest campgrounds, please refer to Coconino Forest chapter.

Black Barts RV Park
2760 E. Butler Ave.
(520) 774–1912

Black Barts offers all the necessary amenities for camping, including an antique store, full hookups, general store, shower, laundry, and steakhouse with saloon. RV spaces with full hookups are $20 per night.

Flagstaff KOA
5803 N. Highway 89
(520) 526–9926, (800) KOA–FLAG
www.koakampgrounds.com

Flagstaff KOA is conveniently located on U.S. Highway 89 as you enter Flagstaff from Page or Utah. The KOA is close to the Flagstaff Mall and other shopping conveniences. Flagstaff KOA also offers showers, laundry, general store, and camp kitchen for breakfast. The campground is open all night with night drop or morning payment options. Tent sites are $19 per night and RV spaces with full hookups are $25 per night.

Fort Tuthill Campground
AZ Hwy. 89 A
(520) 774–3464   co.coconino.az.us/tmp/

This campground is close to town, the Flagstaff Urban Trail System, shopping, and restaurants. It also offers the seclusion of the ponderosa pines for those who want to commune with nature without giving up store and shower amenities. The campground is three miles south of Flagstaff at exit 337 off Interstate 17. Tent and RV sites with partial hookups are available. Sites without hookups are $9 per night, and partial hookups are $13 per night.

Woody Mountain Campground and RV Park
2727 W. Route 66
(520) 774–7727, (800) 732–7986

This is luxury camping at its best! Woody Mountain Campground has a heated outdoor swimming pool, store, laundry, playground, propane, and tent and RV camping spaces with full hookups. Tent sites are $16 per night; RV sites are $21 per night.

City Parks and Recreation

For general information on Flagstaff's city parks and recreations departments, call (520) 779–7690, or visit the website at www.flagstaff.az.gov.

Bark Park
600 N. Thorpe Rd.

Dog lovers and their dogs can roam freely inside this enclosed park, which is divided into areas for large and small dogs. From May through October, dogs can refresh themselves at a hose bib. Humans have their own sitting area.

Buffalo Park
West of Gemini Dr. off Cedar Hill

Buffalo Park has 163 acres of natural plateau and hills. Known for its breathtaking views of the San Francisco Peaks and Mt. Elden, the park has a two-mile walking/jogging course with exercise stations. Runners, walkers, and cross-country skiers enjoy this expansive acreage. Buffalo Park is adjacent to McPherson Park; both parks have great views of the San Francisco Peaks.

Bushmaster Park
Alta Vista & Lockett Rds.

Bushmaster Park is Flagstaff's most popular park because it offers a plethora of outdoor amenities for the whole family, including picnic facilities, footpaths, playgrounds, tennis and basketball courts, and a BMX skate park.

McPherson Park
N. Turquoise Dr.

McPherson Park is made up of 43 acres and connects with Buffalo Park by various hiking trails. The park has outdoor tennis courts, playground equipment, and is home to the Jay Lively Activity Center, the seasonal ice and roller skating rink. (Check out the Jay Lively listing later in this chapter.)

Thorpe Park
245 N. Thorpe Rd.

The recreational opportunities are endless at this community park. Playgrounds, hiking and running trails, tennis and basketball courts, and lighted ballfields offer year-round family entertainment. Thorpe Park is home to Northern Arizona's premier disc golf course.

Urban Trail System
Flagstaff Visitor Center, 1 E. Rte. 66
(520) 774–9541, (800) 842–7293

This citywide network of trails is closed off to motorized transportation. Twenty miles of trails connect neighborhoods, schools, and community activity centers, while providing alternative methods of transportation and exercise. Open year round, this trail system offers bicycling, running, cross-country skiing and walking opportunities for both visitors and residents. A map for the Flagstaff Urban Trail System can be purchased for $1 at the Flagstaff City Hall in the Parks and Recreation office, 211 W Aspen Ave., (520) 774-5281.

Cross-Country Skiing and Snowshoeing

Flagstaff Nordic Center
on AZ Hwy. 180, past Arizona Snowbowl
(520) 779–1951 ext. 195
www.arizonasnowbowl.com

The Flagstaff Nordic Center is just 8 miles north of Snowbowl Road on Arizona Highway 180. The Nordic Center has more than 40 kilometers of groomed ski trails and 15 kilometers of snowshoe trails. Equipment rentals and private and group lessons are available. An all day pass (9 A.M. to 4 P.M.) is $10. Kids seven and under are admitted free. The day snowshoe pass is $5.

Discovery Programs

Museum of Northern Arizona Discovery Programs
3101 N. Fort Valley Rd.
(520) 774–5211   www.musnaz.org

For students of all ages, the Discovery Programs offer a variety of field studies, workshops, and intergenerational excursions designed to promote the arts, sciences, history, and cultures of the Colorado Plateau. Call to make reservations. The program runs June through September. (For more information about the Museum of Northern Arizona, see the Flagstaff Attractions chapter.)

Golf

Elden Hills Public Golf Course
2380 Oakmont Dr.
(520) 527–7997 (information)
(520) 527–7999 (tee times)

Although Flagstaff does not have as many golf courses as the Phoenix area, it makes up for the lack of quantity with Elden Hills Public Golf Course, home to the Northern Arizona University women's golf team. The 6029-yard course is considered one of the state's finest. The course is open until November, weather permitting, and offers tee times up to 14 days in advance. Summer rates are $30 to walk and $42 to ride during the week. Call for weekday and weekend rates.

Hayrides and Cookouts

Arizona Snowbowl
AZ Hwy. 180 and Snowbowl Rd.
(520) 774–4481
www.arizonasnowbowl.com

Get a true taste for the West with a hayride and an outdoor meal. Day or evening cookouts are available. Reservations are required; please make your reservations in advance.

Horseback Riding

Arizona Snowbowl
(520) 779–1951
www.arizonasnowbowl.com

Take a one hour or two hour ride through the Coconino National Forest with experienced wranglers. Enjoy the quiet and solitude of northern Arizona on horseback. All rides begin and end at the Fort Valley Barn on Arizona Highway 180 and Snowbowl Road. Guided horseback rides start at 8 A.M. and the last ride leaves at 5 P.M.. Call for reservations and rates.

Flying Heart
(520) 526–2788

Let experienced wranglers show you the ropes and the scenery as you ride along the trails of Coconino Forest. Day-long sightseeing trips along well-maintained trails are available, as are one- and two-hour trail rides. Contact Flying Heart for current rates and times.

Hitchin' Post Stables
Lake Mary Rd.
(520) 774–1719

Hitchin' Post Stables offers a variety of rides for all levels of riders. Explore Indian ruins and caves in Walnut Canyon or take the sunset ride to an authentic western campsite with cowboys cooking over an open fire and live entertainment. Hayrides and pack trips are available. Call for current rates.

Ice/Roller Skating

Jay Lively Activity Center
1650 N. Turquoise Dr.
(520) 774–1051

Skating is fun exercise for kids of all ages (and adults too!). Roller skating begins in June and ends in the beginning of August. Ice skating season runs mid September through the end of April. Lessons, public skating, and hockey are offered. Contact the Activity Center for admission prices and open skating hours.

River Trips

Whether you want to white water raft down the Colorado River, escape civilization, or sea kayak in Baja, Mexico, Arizona River companies will organize, and plan your trip down to the most minute detail; all you need to do is show up and bring your own toothbrush.

Arizona Raft Adventures
4050 E. Huntington Dr.
(520) 526–8200
www.azraft.com

Venture down the mighty Colorado River or paddle your way down the San Juan River with Arizona Raft Adventure. AZRA has a reputation for providing experienced guides, gourmet food, and trips to please the whole family. Call AZRA for dates, prices, and reservations.

Canyoneers, Inc.
7195 N. AZ Hwy. 89
(520) 526–8200, (800) 525–0924
www.canyoneers.com

Specializing in white water trips down the Colorado River, Canyoneers also operates Kaibab Lodge and Kaibab Camper Village. Both are located near the North Rim of the Grand Canyon. Contact Canyoneers for trip availability, rates, and reservations for their river trips and North Rim accommodations.

Rivers & Oceans
12620 N. Copeland Ln.
(520) 526–4575, (800) 473–4576
www.rivers-oceans.com

Rivers & Oceans is unique because it offers one-stop trip planning for travelers and will check availability with other rafting and outdoor water adventure companies for you. So if you are planning a (water) trip to Arizona, Colorado, Utah, the Caribbean, or Mexico, contacting Rivers & Oceans is your first step. Call for locations, dates, and prices.

Skiing/Snowboarding

The Arizona Snowbowl has a vertical drop of 2,300 feet and 32 trails for beginners and experts. Arizona gets most of its snowfall during the spring, and the mountain may be open as late as April or even early May. Snowbowl offers ski and snowboard packages and daily private, group, and children's lessons. The packages include a ski lift ticket, rentals, and a two-hour lesson. You can purchase half- and full-day passes for children and adults. Full day passes are $37 for adults; $20 for children ages 8 to 12; and $17 for seniors.

Snowbowl also has a full-service equipment rental and repair shop, two restaurants (each with its own bar). The Agassiz Lodge features live music on weekends.

Rock Climbing

Vertical Relief
205 S. San Francisco St.
(520) 556–9909, (877) 265–5984
www.verticalrelief.com

With over 6,500 square feet of climbing space and 40 foot walls, Vertical Relief offers quality rock climbing lessons and equipment for locals and travelers. Indoor climbing allows people of all ages and abilities to experience rock climbing in a safe and managed atmosphere. Day passes are $14. Vertical Relief is open seven days a week. Call for more information.

Flagstaff Mountain Guides
(520) 635–0145

Looking for an interesting way to see the sights in Flagstaff? Try rock climbing. Flagstaff Mountain Guides can accommodate all levels of climbers from beginner to advanced. Call for more information and special group rates.

Skyrides

The Scenic Skyride at Arizona Snowbowl
P.O. Box 40, Flagstaff
(520) 779–1951
www.arizonasnowbowl.com

This is truly a wonderful way to experience the breathtaking views of northern Arizona. The skyride will take you to an elevation of 11,500 feet with over 70 miles of amazing scenery. The trip is 25 minutes one way in an open chair lift. The lift is opened daily 10 A.M. to 4 P.M. from Memorial Day through Labor Day. After Labor Day, the lift operates on Friday, Saturday, and Sunday only through mid October. The cost for adults 13 and up is $9; seniors pay $6.50; and the cost for kids ages 8 to 12 is $5; kids seven and under are admitted free. Group rates are available.

> ## Insiders' Tip
>
> If you are visiting northern Arizona from July through September, be prepared for monsoon season. These sometimes-wicked afternoon storms will roll in with dark clouds and heavy winds. During monsoon season, try to plan your outdoor recreational activities for early morning, and don't forget to bring your rain jacket.

Shopping

Flagstaff is the retail center for northern Arizona with numerous strip malls and shopping centers. The Flagstaff Mall features national stores and is located on the east side of town. However, in this chapter we will direct you to the quaint boutiques, shops, and trading posts that reflect the true feel of the city.

The downtown area has a concentration of shops, restaurants, and unique gift stores where you will find the perfect souvenir for yourself and anyone on your list. From hand-crafted jewelry to quality outdoor gear to gourmet chocolate, you will find it here. Park your car, stroll through the streets, window shop, and enjoy the sunshine on your face and the crowd-free streets.

Antiques

Carriage House Antique Mall
413 N. San Francisco St.
(520) 774–1337

Voted best antiques shop in the "Best of Flagstaff" for the past eight years, Carriage House Antique Mall is an antiques lovers' dream. From furniture, to vintage clothing, to china and silver, you will find a little bit of everything here. This antiques haven is open Monday through Saturday 10 A.M. to 5 P.M. and Sunday 11 A.M. to 4 P.M.

The Dragon's Plunder
217 S. San Francisco St.
(520) 774–1708

The Dragon's Plunder houses antiques reminiscent of treasures you would find in your grandmother's attic, including collectibles, furniture, and used books. The Dragon's Plunder can be found on the northwest corner of S. San Francisco Street and Butler Avenue. The store is open Monday through Saturday 10 A.M. to 5:30 P.M. and is closed on Sunday.

Monsoon clouds collect over downtown Flagstaff.   PHOTO: STACY WITTIG

Books

McGaugh's Newsstand
24 N. San Francisco St.
(520) 774–2131

McGaugh's has the most extensive international and national magazine selection in town. With over 3,500 choices, including alternative health, fashion, and sports magazines, you could get lost among the titles. McGaugh's has books for children, NY Times bestseller's, cigars and cigarettes, cards, and gift items. McGaugh's is open Monday through Saturday from 7:30 A.M. to 9 P.M. and Sunday from 8 A.M. to 7 P.M.

Starrlight Books
15 N. Leroux St.
(520) 774–6813

Find high quality new, used, and rare books at Starrlight Books. This quiet bookstore encourages people to browse through their small but particular selection of titles, which includes a children's book area. Starrlight Books focuses on science, Native American, and Southwestern titles. Starrlight is open Monday through Saturday from 10 A.M. to 7 P.M. and from noon to 5 P.M. on Sunday.

Convenience Store/Market

New Frontiers
1000 S. Milton Rd.
(520) 774–5747

This "healthier kind of supermarket" has all natural and preservative free food. From hemp products to hormone free meat to "large" bulk selections, New Frontiers is a healthy alternative for the conscientious eater. Check out the deli with their great salads, fresh baked goods, and homemade soups. New Frontiers is open from 8 A.M. to 8 P.M. Monday through Saturday and 10 A.M. to 7 P.M. on Sunday. The deli closes a half an hour before the store.

Pay-N-Take Downtown Market
12 W. Aspen Ave.
(520) 226–8595

If you forgot film for your camera, Advil, or need snacks for the road, Pay-N-Take will have it. A full espresso bar and tasty homemade pastries are available in case you are in a hurry to catch the next Amtrak train. The espresso bar can also serve a draft beer or a glass of wine if the mood strikes you. This place is a favorite local haunt from happy hour to close Thursday through Saturday. (See the Flagstaff Nightlife chapter for more information.) Hours are Monday through Wednesday 7 A.M. to 10 P.M.; Thursday through Saturday 7 A.M. to 1 A.M.; and Sunday 9:30 A.M. to 5 P.M.

Gifts

All That Jazz
19 E. Aspen Ave.
(520) 774–6234

Whatever you are looking for, you will find it here. This small shop is packed with sterling silver jewelry and bath and body products that will make you smile and smell good too. They have t-shirts, journals, candles, toys, frames….must I go on? The owners have done a fine job of stocking their store with eclectic and contemporary gifts for everyone on your souvenir list (even yourself!). All That Jazz is open six days a week from 10 A.M. to 6 P.M. and from 11 A.M. to 4 P.M. on Sunday.

Black Hound Gallerie
Old Town Shops, 120 N. Leroux St.
(520) 774–2323, (800) 96 Hound

One of the most intriguing things about this store is the window display. There is always something hanging in the window that will make a passerby do a double take or help initiate a conversation between total strangers. Black Hound has eclectic and mostly off-the-wall gifts, posters, and prints from the great masters of art to the great legends of jazz. You will enjoy the journals, cards, refrigerator magnets, and pasta that resembles human body parts. Hmmm…

Black Hound Gallerie is open Monday through Thursday 9:30 A.M. to 8 P.M., Friday and Saturday from 9:30 A.M. to 9 P.M., and Sunday 10:30 A.M. to 6 P.M.

The Kitchen Source
112 E. Rt. 66
(520) 779–2302

The Kitchen Source makes cooking fun with its supply of kitchen gadgets, quality cookware, and gourmet foods. Stock your kitchen or someone else's with the necessary olive oil spray, garlic crusher, or colorful pot holders. The Kitchen Source is open seven days a week from 10 A.M. to 6 P.M.

Mountain Candy
Old Town Shops, 120 N. Leroux St.
(520) 779–5611

The owner's philosophy is that everyone who has visited Mountain Candy leaves a little bit happier. If candy is what you want, candy is what you will get! Specializing in fine chocolates, Mountain Candy has a little bit of everything to satisfy the pickiest of sweet tooths, from gourmet jellybeans, to salt water taffy, to fudge and sugar-free chocolates. Don't forget the assorted flavors of truffles. Mountain Candy is open Monday through Saturday 10 A.M. to 6 P.M. and is closed on Sunday.

> ## Insiders' Tip
> Black Hound Gallerie will frame your new print and ship it to your home (anywhere in the continental United States).

Mountain Christmas
14 N. San Francisco St.
(520) 774–4054

It is Christmas every day on San Francisco Street. How could you be a Scrooge with the delightful smell of seasonal spices and selection of hot chocolates to warm even the meanest Scrooge's heart? Mountain Christmas sells ornaments, decorations, and seasonal collectibles, including Matchbox and Department 56 items. Get ahead of your Christmas shopping Monday through Saturday 10 A.M. to 6 P.M. and from 10 A.M. to 4 P.M. on Sunday.

P.J. Chilcottage
Old Town Shops, 120 N. Leroux St.
(520) 774–0009

At P.J. Chilcottage, you will learn the art of pampering yourself with bath salts, lotions, and massage oils. Rejuvenation is a must as you choose among quality bedding, robes, and P.J.s. Try the "soap bar." Don't worry you don't have to be 21 years old to spoil yourself with a piece of "Mango Madness" or "Cinnabun." The whole family can be clean, relaxed, and happy with the help of this store. P.J. Chilcottage is open Monday through Thursday 9 A.M. to 7 P.M. and from 9 A.M. to 8 P.M. on Saturday; Sunday the store is open from 10:30 A.M. to 5 P.M.

Vino Loco
Old Town Shops, 120 N. Leroux St.
(520) 226–1764

Wine, wine, and more wine. Vino Loco carries hard to find imported and domestic wines. Did I say wine? The store also specializes in champagnes, ports, and sherries. And if you think you had enough options to choose from, how about deciding among the wine accessories, gourmet snacks, and gift baskets? Vino Loco can ship gift items to selected locations. Tucked away in the Old Town Shops, this wonderful little wine shop is open seven days a week from 10 A.M. to 6 P.M. Sunday hours vary.

Zani Futons & Frames
9 N. Leroux St.
(520) 774–9409, (800) 294–9409

As you walk into this store you will feel as if you walked into someone's house. That's because the owners have used the entire space to display their wonderful selection of jewelry, bedding, furniture, cards, journals, and unique gifts. The word is that Zani may be haunted, so don't be surprised if you notice something move out of the corner of your eye. Zani can ship your purchases anywhere, and is open Monday through Saturday from 10 A.M. to 6 P.M.; Sunday hours are 10 A.M. to 4 P.M.

Clothing

Gene's Western Wear & Shoe Hospital
111 N. Leroux St.
(520) 774–3543
www.geneswesternwear.com

Do the clear blue skies and open range make you want to wear a Stetson hat? Do you hear the call of the wide-open spaces and suddenly need a pair of Tony Lama boots? Gene's can outfit the entire family from head to toe in full western apparel. They have a full line of felt and straw hats, shoe laces, boots, and more. This is your cowboy and Native American jewelry headquarters. Gene's is open Monday through Saturday 9 A.M. to 6 P.M.; Sunday hours are 9 A.M. to 4 P.M.

Favorites to Wear
10 N. Leroux St.
(520) 774–7516

Favorites offers one of the finest selections of ladies' fashions in northern Arizona. Whether you are looking for that special outfit or a comfortable sweater, Favorites has it. They also have accessories to complete any outfit, including jewelry, hair clips, and lingerie. Favorites is open Monday through Saturday from 10 A.M. to 5 P.M. and closed on Sunday.

Incahoots
9 E. Aspen Ave.
(520) 773-9447

This vintage clothing and costume rental shop is busting at the seams with retro wear from the disco dancing days of the 70s, the groovy 60s, the rocking 50s, and the swinging 40s. You will find classic Levis, albums, and rare turn-of-the-century clothes. Incahoots is open weekdays 10 A.M. to 6 P.M. and weekends 10 A.M. to 7 P.M.

Sage Brush Trading Co.
Old Town Shops, 120 N. Leroux St.
(520) 773-1625

Specializing in stylish and comfortable clothes for men, women, and kids, Sage Brush knows that quality counts. That's why there is a lifetime warranty on every item sold in the store. Sage Brush has a complete line of leather accessories including shoes, hats, and briefcases. Sage Brush is open from 9 A.M. to 8 P.M. Monday through Saturday and from 10 A.M. to 5 P.M. on Sunday.

THREDZ
18 N. Leroux St.
(520) 779-0862

Supplying Flagstaff with fun, hip, and trendy clothes for the young at heart, THREDZ has junior and petite sizes, shoes, accessories, and a great selection of swimsuits that make you wish you were closer to the beach, even if it's just for a day. THREDZ is open seven days a week; hours of operation vary.

Jewelry

Jeff Karl Jewelers
204 B E. Rt. 66
(520) 773-8914

With over 20 years of experience, Jeff Karl Jewelers is a full service (repairs are done on the premises) fine jewelry store that specializes in wedding sets and has an extensive selection of Bulova and Seiko watches for men and women. Jeff Karl is known for his uniquely designed custom jewelry. The store is open Tuesday through Friday 10 A.M. to 6 P.M., Saturday 10 A.M. to 5 P.M., and is closed on Sunday.

Native American Trading Companies

Puchteca Indian Art
20 N. San Francisco St.
(520) 774-2414

This store features Native American paintings, pottery, jewelry, and Hopi Katsinas. From the Navajo pottery of Alice Cling, to the Hopi pottery of James Nampeyo, to the paintings of the famous painter Harrison Begaye, Puchteca Indian Art is the only store in town that hosts an exclusive list of artists. Puchteca is open Monday through Saturday 9 A.M. to 5:30 P.M., and Sunday 10 A.M. to 4 P.M.

Thunder Mountain Traders
20 E. Rt. 66
(520) 779-5291, (888) 886-6205

This trading company features an extensive collection of cowboy and Indian art, Navajo, Hopi, and Zuni jewelry, books, pottery, and paintings. Thunder Mountain Traders is open seven days a week from 10 A.M. to 6 P.M.

Winter Sun Trading Co.
107 N. San Francisco St.
(520) 774-2884
www.wintersun.com

A Flagstaff institution since 1976, Winter Sun Trading Company is part gallery and part herb shop. The art gallery features local and Native American artists and has an extensive collection of authentic Hopi Katsina carvings. Winter Sun has a large selection of herbs, natural beauty products, teas, and tinctures for optimum health. Winter Sun is open Monday through Thursday 9 A.M. to 5 P.M.; Friday and Saturday 9 A.M. to 6 P.M.; and is closed on Sunday.

Outdoor Clothing/Gear/Equipment

Absolute Bikes
18 N. San Francisco St.
(520) 779–5969

Absolute Bikes is your downtown full-service bike store with quality mountain, road, and recreational bikes and cycling apparel. Absolute rents mountain bikes and can accommodate all sizes. Group rentals are available. Professionally trained mechanics are on duty. Absolute Bikes is open Monday through Friday 9 A.M. to 7 P.M.; Saturday 10 A.M. to 6 P.M.; Sunday 10 A.M. to 4 P.M.

Aspen Sports
15 N. San Francisco St.
(520) 779–1935

Specializing in quality outdoor gear, clothes, and equipment that will help you breeze from one season to the next, Aspen Sports also rents everything for the outdoor enthusiast from cross-country skis, to snowboards, to telemark skis. It is the only shop in town where you can rent white water rafts and sea kayaks. Aspen Sports is open from 8 A.M. to 8 P.M. Monday through Saturday and from 9 A.M. to 6 P.M. on Sunday.

Babbitt's Backcountry Outfitters
12 E. Aspen Ave.
(520) 774–4775

Babbitt's is stocked with outdoor equipment, apparel, and clothing for all your outdoor needs. With a full-service rental shop, books, maps, and technical gear Babbitt's is located on the corner of Aspen Avenue and North San Francisco Street. Babbitt's is open Monday through

Saturday 9 A.M. to 7 P.M. and Sunday 10 A.M. to 6 P.M.

Babbitt's Fly Fishing Specialist
15 E. Aspen Ave.
(520) 779–3253

Specializing in everything that makes the ideal fly fishing experience, Babbitt's is an angler's haven for equipment, clothing, books, maps, and that hard-to-find gift for your favorite angler. Call for the latest fly fishing classes. Babbitt's also sells Arizona State Fishing Licenses.

Cosmic Cycles
901 N. Beaver St.
(520) 779–1092

"If you don't like it, bring it back." This motto has been echoed by this full-service bike shop since 1971. Cosmic Cycles guarantees their products and ensures all customers will receive prompt, friendly service. A mechanic is on duty at all times. Check out their cycling apparel, equipment, and hydration systems. Cosmic Cycles is open Monday through Saturday from 9 A.M. to 6 P.M. and is closed on Sunday.

Peace Surplus
14 W. Rt. 66
(520) 779–4521
www.peacesurplus.com

Providing northern Arizona with quality outdoor gear since 1976, Peace Surplus has something for everyone. They carry low, medium, and high end products that are affordable by anyone's standards. They stand by their ever popular slogan:

"If it's outdoors—It's us." Peace Surplus is open Monday through Friday from 8 A.M. to 9 P.M. and on Friday and Saturday from 8 A.M. to 6 P.M.

SingleTrack
575 W. Riordan Rd.
(520) 773–1862

For the past 11 years, Single Track has provided more than bikes to the Flagstaff community. A full-service bike shop known for its efficient and friendly service, Single Track features a complete line of bike accessories, apparel, and equipment, including hydration systems. Professional mechanics are on duty at all times. Single Track has mountain bike rentals for the whole family, and is open Monday through Saturday 9 A.M. to 6 P.M. and Sunday from 10 A.M. to 4 P.M.

Nightlife

When the sun goes down on this small mountain town put on your dancing shoes! Live entertainment is found on almost every downtown street corner ranging from funky jazz to hip hop to toe-tapping bluegrass. Strolling the streets on a starry evening promises to be just as entertaining as the clubs themselves. Street performers provide outdoor entertainment even on the coldest Flagstaff nights. Donations are accepted and always appreciated. Flagstaff is home to Northern Arizona University's 19,000 students, which means there are quite a few college bars with long waiting lines.

Don't worry, bar hopping isn't the only thing to do in town. Many of the downtown restaurants serve dinner until 10 P.M., but there are a few late night options mentioned in this section. Special art gallery shows and functions are scheduled throughout the year; check the local arts and entertainment newspaper *FlagLive!* for a complete listing of events and times. Flagstaff has community theater, a symphony, and a university offering top notch entertainment. Please contact the organization for a schedule of events and ticket prices.

Bars and Nightclubs

Flagstaff police are aggressive about enforcing the state's drinking and driving laws. If you are pulled over with a blood level of .10% or more you will spend the night in jail. The best advice is don't drink and drive, and ask a bartender to call a taxi for you. The legal drinking age in the state of Arizona is 21. Supermarkets, liquor stores, and bars serve alcohol until 1 A.M. Most bars turn into nightclubs at 9 P.M. and charge a small cover to enter. All bars are smoking establishments unless otherwise noted. If you look 35 years of age or younger be prepared to show your ID. If you aren't carrying a U.S. driver's license, passport, or military ID, you will be turned away at the door. Dancing alone or in a group is encouraged and the "shake dem bones" attitude is prevalent among the young and old. The thing about Flagstaff is that the locals like and know how to have fun.

The Alley
22 E. Route 66
(520) 774–7929

The Alley is preserving the tradition of its previous owners by continuing to supply "the best music in northern Arizona." Within the Alley's walls, you will find the hottest local, regional, and national bands any day of the week. The stage is in the back of the club and the rustic wooden floor is great for dancing. The down-home atmosphere welcomes both locals and visitors. Pictures of locals and employees hang from the stone walls. Look for the daily drink specials to wet your whistle. On a quiet night, the Alley has a foosball table and two pool tables for entertainment. This building was once home to one of the original bars in town. There is a cover charge for the great music, ranging from $1 and up.

Beaver Street Whistle Stop Cafe & Brewery
11 S. Beaver St.
(520) 779–0079

This upbeat and energetic meeting place for the thirty-something and over crowd invites great conversation and good times with friends. Serving wine, specialty drinks, and handcrafted ales and lagers brewed on the premises, Beaver Street is a great place for Sunday Bloody Marys, after the movie munchies, and just plain socializing. Open seven days a week, Beaver Street serves food in the bar (from a limited menu) until 11 P.M. (For more information about Beaver St. Brewery, refer to the Flagstaff Restaurants chapter.)

Buster's Restaurant & Bar
1800 S. Milton
(520) 774–5155

A big screen TV, plenty of tall round tables, and a fireplace are welcoming features on a cold Flagstaff night or for a Sunday afternoon football game. The beer list is extensive, sporting sixty-six imported and domestic beers. Happy hour begins at 4 P.M. and continues until closing with great drink and appetizer specials. If you are not in the mood to watch the game, slide into a comfortable booth, sip on a Margarita, and nosh on some of the tasty appetizers from the only oyster bar in town. If you're in the mood for something different and decadent, consult the nearest drink menu for either a fruity frozen or creamy concoction. Open seven days a week, Buster's serves appetizers in the bar until 11 P.M. (See our Flagstaff Restaurants chapter.)

Charly's Bar & Pub in the Historic Hotel Weatherford/Zane Grey Ballroom
23 N. Leroux St.
(520) 779–1919

The band starts at 9 P.M. and so do your feet. Dance the night away in Charly's Bar with the local and regional bands who have made this place a local institution. If the dance floor gets too crowded, climb the stairs to the third floor and relax in the turn-of-the-century style Zane Grey Ballroom. Completely renovated with a restored wraparound balcony and an antique bar from Tombstone, Arizona, this dark and intimate room also boasts a fireplace and quaint tables for two. If you have a larger party, feel free to pull a few tables together. The balcony has outside seating and is an interesting way to view the nightlife scene down below. (Refer to our Flagstaff Restaurants chapter.)

Flagstaff Brewing Company
16 E. Route 66
(520) 773–1442

The crowd that congregates at the Flagstaff Brewing Company is a mixture of young and old people who just want to have a good time. Brewing beer since 1994, the brewery features seasonal home-cooked ales and lagers on tap.

Enjoy the simple elegance of the restored Zane Grey Ballroom located on the third floor of the Hotel Weatherford. PHOTO: COURTESY OF PAULA JENSEN

Happy hour is Monday through Friday from 4:30 to 6:30 P.M., and all FBC pints are $2. The full bar is stocked with premium liquors and offers one of the finest scotch and bourbon selections in town with over fifty-two single malts to choose from. Just ask your bartender or server for a suggestion. Live entertainment fills the place Thursday through Saturday, and Wednesday night is "Dead Night," when you can hear the best live tapes and recordings from fellow Grateful Dead aficionados. The outside patio is open year round, so you can soak up the sun, watch the clouds roll in, or the snow fall from the sky while you enjoy your beer. Every Saturday night from Memorial Day until late September, FBC hosts their "Party on the Patio" with live music, drink specials, and lots of dancing under the stars.

Mogollon Brewing Company
15 N. Agassiz St.
(520) 773–8950

Old-town rustic and comfortable, this bar and nightclub makes you feel right at home—probably because over 95% of the bar was rebuilt using recycled materials mostly from torn down Flagstaff buildings. Even the wooden bar is made from an old chicken coop, but don't worry, there are no feathers here, just good beer. Mogollon makes its own handcrafted beer on the premises. Amber, stout, pale, wheat, and seasonal ales are available on tap. The Sampler Platter is a taste for those who can't decide. Growlers and Mogollon bottled beer are for those who can't stay, but are happy to take a brew home. There is live entertainment six nights a week. Happy Hour is from 4 to 7 P.M. Monday through Friday. Mogollon now serves food. The menu includes pizza, subs, calzones, and apps! Food is served until midnight.

Museum Club
3404 E. Rt. 66
(520) 526–9434

Built in 1931, the Museum Club is the largest log cabin in the state of Arizona.

Insiders' Tip
If the late night munchies hit, head on over to Beaver Street Whistle Stop Cafe & Brewery. The late night menu includes wood-fired pizzas, appetizers, and desserts available in the bar area until 11 P.M.

Put your cowboy boots on and get your country fix here. Every Thursday, Friday, and Saturday live music starts at 9 P.M. Learn how to two-step on Thursday; dance lessons are free and start at 6 P.M. A DJ spins your favorite dance tunes Tuesday and Wednesday nights. Ask the bartender for the weekend drink specials. Expect to pay a $4 cover charge on nights with music (live or DJ). The Museum Club opens daily at 11 A.M.

Pay-N-Take Downtown Market
12 W. Aspen St.
(520) 226–8595

This small market also doubles as a happy haunt for locals. The bar area is intimate and the crowd is large on Thursdays, Fridays, and Saturdays when it's open until 1 A.M. Pay-N-Take features local breweries on tap and wine by the glass. (For more information about the Market see the Flagstaff Shopping chapter.)

Uptown Billiards
114 N. Leroux Street
(520) 773–0551

There are many places to play pool in Flagstaff, but Uptown Billiards is the classiest pool hall in northern Arizona, and it's nonsmoking. A haven for pool sharks, novices, and anyone who wants to have a good time, Uptown is home to ten full-size tournament tables, fine house cues, and pool balls. If the tables are full get on the waiting list and enjoy one of the thirty-five imported and specialty beers on tap. The martini menu features over 106 tempting mixes for your drinking pleasure. Slip some money into the CD jukebox and listen to a few of the local musicians crooning their love for coffee and the beloved Colorado River. Uptown Billiards opens daily at 1 P.M.

The Wine Loft
17 N. San Francisco St. (2nd Floor)
(520) 773–WINE

Tucked away on the second floor, high above the main drag, this is one of Flagstaff's best kept secrets. Don't be intimidated if you don't know the difference between a White Zin and a Red Zin, this place is warm and inviting. Slide into one of the large comfortable bar chairs and ask your own personal wine expert or bartender for his or her suggestion. The well-educated and attentive staff is passionate and knowledgeable about their wines and will assist you in your wine-making decisions. The Wine Loft has over 300 wines to choose from. Grab a table by the window to view the passersby or chat at the long spacious bar. A baby grand sits next to the polished dance floor. Check *Flaglive!* for nightly entertainment, wine tastings, and special events.

Different Things to Do

Macy's European Coffee House & Bakery
14 S. Beaver St.
(520) 774–2243

If the smoky bar scene doesn't appeal to you maybe a late night game of chess at Macy's will? People come here to converse, meet friends, or just to read. Open until midnight Thursday through Saturday, Macy's serves homemade pastries and sandwiches until 9 P.M. Specialty coffee drinks and a large assortment of teas are served until midnight. Macy's has live entertainment too! Thursday is Open Mic night. Bring your guitar or recite your favorite poetry. Friday is Jazz night and Saturday's entertainment is usually a surprise. (See the Flagstaff Restaurant chapter for more about Macy's.)

The Art Walk
The Artists Gallery
17 N. San Francisco St.
(520) 773–0958

The Art Walk, an open gallery tour and reception, takes place the first Friday of every month. Participating galleries are open from 6 to 8 P.M. to celebrate the work of new and local artists. This "Gallery Hop" offers lively conversation, complimentary hors d'oeuvres, and the best artwork that northern Arizona has to offer. Pick up a map at any of the participating galleries. Participating galleries are: Aspen Fine Gallery, Father Wolf Gallery, Old Town Gallery, Starrlight Books, West of the Moon, Arizona Handmade Gallery, and High Desert Gallery. This event is free and open to the public. (See the Flagstaff Arts chapter for more information.)

Lowell Observatory
1400 West Mars Hill Rd.
(520) 774-3358
www.lowell.edu

View the constellations and learn about the wonders of the night sky at Lowell Observatory. Weather permitting, Lowell offers nightly tours Wednesday, Friday, and Saturday. The tour includes a presentation describing the history and campus of the Observatory, followed by telescope viewing. Please call for the current tour times and special events.

Music and Theater Performances

Flagstaff Symphony Orchestra
113 E. Aspen Ave.
(520) 774-5107
www.flagstaffsymphony.com

The symphony's seasonal programs blend international influences and talented performers, and promise to dazzle audiences. Call the symphony office for a calendar of events and ticket information. (See the Flagstaff Arts chapter for more information.)

Northern Arizona University Spectrum Series
(520) 523-5661
(888) 520-721
www.nau.edu

Some of the nation's top acts have graced the stage at the University's Ardrey Auditorium. (See the Flagstaff Arts chapter for more information.)

Northern Arizona's Summer Arts 2000
(520) 523-4780
www.nau.edu

Flagstaff Symphony Orchestra and Northern Arizona University have joined forces to provide a summer of professional theater and music concerts. All performances take place in The Clifford White Theater and Ardrey Auditorium. Call for ticket information and a schedule of performances.

Northern Arizona University Theater
(520) 523-5661, (800) 520-7214
www.nau.edu/spa

Enjoy a night at the theater with the talented NAU School of Performing Arts. The 2000-2001 season includes *A View from the Bridge, Angels in America, Crimes of the Heart,* and *Medea.* Contact the University Theater for ticket prices and performance times.

Magic Theater Productions Youth Cultural Center
2575 E. 7th Ave.
(520) 526-3787

Enjoy a night at the theater performed by a cast made up of children. Come out and support the budding performers of the Flagstaff community. (For more about Magic Theater, see the Flagstaff Kidstuff chapter.)

Theatrikos Theater Company
11 W. Cherry Ave.
(520) 774-1662

Music isn't the only kind of live entertainment to be found in Flagstaff. Theatrikos is known for its memorable performances and talented cast of amateur and professional actors. If dinner and a show are on your agenda, contact the Theatrikos Box Office for a performance schedule and ticket information.

It may be sunny in the Valley, but there's snow elsewhere in Arizona during the winter. This snowman came to life near Flagstaff. PHOTO: COURTESTY OF THE FLAGSTAFF CONVENTION AND VISITORS BUREAU

Kidstuff

Flagstaff's cultural and recreational activities welcome people of all ages, including kids and adults who still think they are kids. Most Flagstaff residents bring their children to the symphony, art gallery openings, or outdoor concerts. There aren't many age restrictions enforced, except of course in bars and nightclubs. Children are allowed in establishments that serve food and alcohol until 9 P.M. If you're traveling through Flagstaff with your kids, they will surely be interested in the following Kidstuff options.

Bowling

Starlite Lanes
3406 E. Rt. 66
(520) 526–1138

Bowling can provide hours of family fun on a rainy vacation day. Starlite has Bumper Bowling for kids. The cost per game for children and adults is $2 on weekdays and $2.25 on the weekends. Shoe rental is $1.25. (For more information about Starlite Lanes, please refer to the Flagstaff Recreation section.)

Horseback Riding

Flying Heart
U.S. Hwy. 89
(520) 526–2788

Let an experienced wrangler guide you through the Coconino National Forest. One- and two-hour or day trips are available. Call for seasonal rates. (See the Flagstaff Recreation section for more information.)

Hitchin' Post Stables
Lake Mary Rd.
(520) 774–1719

Discover Walnut Canyon's Indian ruins and caves on horse with guided tours. Hitchin' Post Stables also offers pack trips, hayrides, and a sunset ride to a 1880s wagon train campsite. Call for rates. (For more information, refer to the Flagstaff Recreation section)

MacDonald's Ranch at Arizona Snowbowl
6355 U.S. Hwy. 180
(520) 774–4481
www.arizonasnowball.com

Horseback ride through the pristine Coconino National Forest. The ranch offers one and two hour rides. Group hayrides and cowboy cookouts also are available. (See Flagstaff Recreation section for more information.)

Ice/Roller Skating

Jay Lively Activity Center, McPherson Park
N. Turquoise
(520) 774–1051

Kids and adults will enjoy indoor ice skating from September through April and indoor roller skating during June, July, and August. Call the rink for public session times and prices.

> ## Insiders' Tip
> Looking for a place to picnic? Grab a blanket and go to Wheeler Park, between Aspen Avenue and Birch Street on Humphreys. They have sturdy trees for climbing.

Parks, Plants, and Recreation

For more information on the area's parks, call the Flagstaff City Parks and Recreation Department at (520) 779-7690, or visit www.flagstaff.az.gov.

The Arboretum at Flagstaff
(520) 774-1442
www.flagguide.com/arboretum

Introduce your child to the native plants of the Colorado Plateau. Fun-filled educational programs for kids are scheduled throughout the season; please call for an updated events listing. See the arboretum in one of their guided tours, beginning at 11 A.M. and 1 P.M. daily. Admission is $4 for adults; $3 for seniors; $1 for children 6 to 12; and free for children under six. The arboretum is closed from December 16 until March 30.

Bark Park
600 N. Thorpe Rd.

Families traveling with kids and dogs will enjoy this park. Dog lovers of all ages and dogs can roam freely inside this fenced area. The park is divided into a smaller area for small dogs and a larger area for large dogs. Water is available from a hose bib May through October and humans have their own sitting area.

Bushmaster Park
Alta Vista & Lockett Rd.

This park has its own BMX skate park, plenty of playground facilities, and a spacious picnic area. (For more information, see the Flagstaff Recreation section.)

Buffalo Park
West of Gemini Dr., off Cedar Hill

Buffalo Park has 163 acres of natural plateau and hills. The two-mile walking/jogging course gives kids plenty of room to roam. A good place for strollers, big kids, and toddlers. (See the Flagstaff Recreation section for more information.)

McPherson Park
N. Turquoise Dr.

McPherson Park connects with Buffalo by various hiking trails. Children will enjoy the outdoor tennis courts and playground equipment. (For more information, see the Flagstaff Recreation section.)

Thorpe Park
245 N. Thorpe Rd.

This community park offers endless recreational opportunities, including playgrounds, trails, tennis and basketball courts, and lighted ballfields. (Please refer to the Flagstaff Recreation section for more information on Thorpe Park.)

Museums

Museum of Northern Arizona
3101 N. Fort Valley Rd.
(520) 774-5213   www.musnaz.org

The museum welcomes children with a variety of activities scheduled throughout the summer. During the summer-long Heritage Program, kids will learn about Native American culture. Please call for a more detailed schedule. The museum sponsors Discovery Programs, which are designed for the whole family, and emphasize the science, art, and culture of the plateau region. River trips, campouts, and bike excursions are only a few examples of the family trips offered. The Discovery Programs include day and weekend trips. Call (520) 774-5211, ext. 20 to find out more. The museum is open 7 days a week from 9 A.M. to 5 P.M. (For more about the Museum of Northern Arizona, see the Flagstaff Attractions section.)

Pioneer Museum Arizona Historical Society
2340 N. Fort Valley Rd.
(520) 774-6272

The popular exhibit "Playthings of the Past" will appeal to children of all ages.

The exhibit showcases toys, dolls, games, and children's books from the past, and gives children an interesting way to learn about the pioneer history of the West and particularly of Flagstaff. The museum is open Monday through Saturday 9 A.M. to 5 P.M. and is closed on Sunday. There is no admission fee, but donations are appreciated. (For more information about the Pioneer Museum, refer to Flagstaff Attractions and Annual Events sections.)

One of the many ruins at Wupatki National Monument. PHOTO: STACY WITTIG

National Monuments

Sunset Crater Volcano National Monument
Rte. 3, Box 149
(520) 526–0502
www.nps.gov/sucr

Sunset Crater erupted more than 900 years ago leaving fascinating volcanic features for you to explore. The park is open daily. If you visit Wupatki National Monument, your admission is free. (See the Flagstaff Attractions section for more about Sunset Crater.)

Walnut Canyon National Monument
Walnut Canyon Rd. # 3
(520) 526–3367
www.nps.gov/waca

Hike down a paved path and view prehistoric cliff dwellings of the Sinagua Indians. The National Park Service is recruiting Junior Rangers. Ask at the Visitor Center for a *Junior Ranger* booklet. Complete as much of the booklet as you can to join the Ranger team. The entry fee is $3 for people 17 and older. For children

under 17, there is no entry fee. (For more information about Walnut Canyon, see our Flagstaff Attractions section.)

Wupatki National Monument
H.C. 33 Box 444A
(520) 679–2365
www.nps.gov/wupa

Wupatki was once home to the farmers and traders of the Anasazi and Sinagua peoples. Don't miss the Wupatki Pueblo Trail, a self-guided tour of the largest pueblo and its unusual geological feature: a blowhole. The National Park Service is recruiting Junior Rangers. Get your copy of the *Junior Ranger* booklet from the Visitor Center. It takes about 1.5 hours to complete the Wupatki Trail and answer the questions. The entry fee is $3 for individuals 17 and older. Admission is free for children under 17. The fee also allows admission into Sunset Crater. (For more information, see our Flagstaff Attractions section.)

Rock Climbing

Vertical Relief
205 S. San Francisco St.
(520) 556–9909, (877) 265–5984

Let your kids' minds reach new heights at Vertical Relief. Climbing builds muscles, increases flexibility, and improves coordi-

nation for all ages. Vertical Relief offers a variety of programs for kids 5 to 18 and full-guided outdoor services as well. Purchase a day pass for $12 for students K through grad school. A "belay" lesson for $6 is required before using the facility.

Vertical Relief is open Monday through Friday 10 A.M. to 11 P.M. and Saturday and Sunday 12 P.M. to 8 P.M. Call for more details. (For more information about Vertical Relief, see the Flagstaff Recreation chapter.)

Theater

Magic Curtain Productions
2575 E. 7 Ave.
(520) 526–3787

The only children's theater in Flagstaff, Magic Curtain Productions is a unique organization where children are the stars of the show. Plays, activities, and workshops are scheduled throughout the year. Previous performances include: *Annie, Winnie the Pooh,* and *Cinderella*. Call for dates and times of the productions.

The Arts

Flagstaff's art community has undergone many changes within the past ten years; however, the dedicated artists' community and concerned citizens have banded together to enhance the quality of art in Flagstaff. Art galleries have persevered and are full to the brim with creations by local artists. Music has experienced a resurgence with the help of the Spectrum Series sponsored by Northern Arizona University in conjunction with its 100th anniversary. This series has brought national acts to town and put Flagstaff on the map. Entering its 51st season, The Flagstaff Symphony entertains audiences with eight concerts and special guest performances throughout the year. The symphony has also joined forces with NAU to implement the Summer Arts Program. The program includes concerts and live theater performed on the NAU campus. Local community and children's theater have survived changes and challenges as well. The recent inception of Flagstaff Cultural Partners, an arts and science agency, will play a major role within the arts, culture, and science communities.

During the Wild West days, the community of Flagstaff encouraged and appreciated different forms of art. Flagstaff was once a major stop along the transcontinental route to California which brought with it filmmakers, writers, and famous painters, including Thomas Moran, who brought the wonders of the West to the world on canvas. His paintings immortalized the Grand Canyon and Indian cliff dwellings of the region. The popularity of Southwestern art declined between the 1930s and the 1960s, but the art world of the 1960s witnessed a Western revitalization, which was found in the popularization of cowboy art.

Women artists have played an important, but sometimes silent, role within the art world, as earlier historians did not recognize or record many of their contributions. Mary Colton, who founded the Museum of Northern Arizona with her husband Harold, instituted programs designed to rejuvenate the interest and quality of Native American art. An artist originally from Philadelphia, Colton was intrigued by the enigmatic Colorado Plateau and many of her paintings are of Southwestern landscapes.

A longtime painter of Arizona landscapes, Lillian Wilhelm Smith gained further recognition as the first and only woman to illustrate the Western novels of Zane Grey.

In this chapter, we explore the artistic happenings that bring forth the area's newest stars and shape Flagstaff's art scene. While the number of options may not break any records, visitors and locals alike can count on seeing memorable performances, meeting members of the passionate artistic community, and viewing quality craftsmanship in intimate and unique venues.

Galleries

Downtown Flagstaff boasts a gallery on almost every street corner. With intimate settings and diverse media selections, you'll welcome the chance to browse around Flagstaff's galleries and acquaint yourself with local artists and their work any day of the week. Mark your calendars for the first Friday of each month and head downtown for the Artwalk. This "Gallery Hop" offers lively conversation, complimentary hors d'oeuvres, and the best artwork that northern Arizona has to offer. Stroll through the downtown area, browse in the participating galleries, and meet local artists. Participating galleries are open from 6 to 8 P.M. Pick up a map at any of the participating galleries.

Arizona Handmade Gallery
13 N. San Francisco St.
(520) 779–3790

The name of this gallery fits. Everything in the gallery is handcrafted by Arizona artists. Enjoy the vast array of jewelry, ornaments, clothing, and ceramics by local artisans. The gallery is open Monday through Saturday from 9:30 A.M. to 7 P.M. and on Sunday from 9:30 A.M. to 6 P.M.

The Artists Gallery
17 N. San Francisco St.
(520) 773–0958
www.theartistsgallery.net

Since 1992, The Artists Gallery has showcased the finest arts and crafts from over forty northern Arizona artists. From blown glass to woodworking to sculpture, this contemporary cooperative features quality craftsmanship and is a favorite among locals and visitors. The Artists Gallery is open 7 days a week, Monday through Saturday 9:30 A.M. to 7:30 P.M. and Sunday 9:30 A.M. to 6:30 P.M., and is located in the historic downtown.

Father Wolf Designs and Gallery
17 N. Leroux St. Suite 102
(520) 226–8495
www.fatherwolf.com

Featuring the art and jewelry of Native Americans from across the country, the Father Wolf Gallery educates and increases public awareness by introducing cultural and artistic elements of Native American artists. The gallery hosts special events, including storytelling, dancing, and art demonstrations. The gallery is open weekdays from 10 A.M. to 7 P.M. and 11 A.M. to 9 P.M. on weekends.

Old Main Gallery
NAU, North Campus, Old Main Building
(520) 523–3471

Displaying nationally acclaimed contemporary art, Old Main Gallery offers a variety of workshops and scheduled lectures throughout the year. The gallery is open Tuesday through Friday 8 A.M. to 5 P.M. and Saturday 10 A.M. to 2 P.M. Old Main Gallery is located on north campus in the Old Main building on the corner of Knoles and McMullen Circle. Admission is free to the public.

Old Town Gallery
2 W. Santa Fe Ave.
(520) 774–7770   www.flagstaff.az.us/otg

From woven Navajo rugs to Darien rain forest baskets to Pueblo pottery, the Old Town Gallery carries the work of well-known Native American artists as well as Southwest landscape painters. The gallery specializes in contemporary jewelry and paintings; customized jewelry can be made on the premises. The gallery is open Tuesday through Saturday 10 A.M. to 5 P.M.

Insiders' Tip

Don't forget the First Friday Art Walk which takes place—you guessed it—the first Friday of every month from 6 P.M. to 8 P.M. Call (520) 774-0465 for more information.

This fine art exhibit at the Beasley Gallery compliments the work of NAU students.

Richard E. Beasley Gallery
NAU, Central Campus, Performing and
Fine Arts Building
(520) 523–3549

One of the university's two galleries, the Beasley Gallery's exhibits reflect the School of Fine Arts' current academic year. The gallery's highlights include a Faculty Art Show, juried exhibits for students, and a Bachelor of Fine Arts exhibit from graduating seniors. Beasley Gallery is open Monday through Friday 10 A.M. to 4 P.M. Admission is free to the public.

West of the Moon
111 E. Aspen Ave.
(520) 774–0465

Named for a Norwegian folktale, the gallery's primary focus is to support local artists. The smallest gallery in northern Arizona (the room is 11 x 15), West of the Moon has instituted the philosophy that quality, not quantity, is what defines them. You will find an eclectic mixture of photography, beadwork, jewelry, and sculptures. West of the Moon is open from 10 A.M. to 3 P.M. Tuesday through Friday. Weekend hours are Saturday 10 A.M. to 5 P.M. and Sunday 10 A.M. to 3 P.M.

Concerts/Festivals

The warm summer days and brilliant blue sky make a perfect backdrop for outdoor concerts and arts and crafts festivals. People come for miles to buy the wares of local artisans, to listen to local music, and enjoy the weather.

A Celebration of Native American
Art/Heritage Program
Museum of Northern Arizona
3101 Fort Valley Rd.
(520) 774–5213
www.musnaz.org

Featuring the arts and crafts of the Hopi, Navajo, Pai, and Zuni, this summer long event sponsored by the museum cele-brates Native American arts and culture with artist demonstrations, dances, music, and exhibits. The Heritage Program runs from the end of May through September. (For more on the Heritage Program and the Museum of Northern Arizona, see the Flagstaff Attractions chapter.)

Concerts in the Park
Wheeler Park across from the City Hall,
211 W. Aspen Ave.

Dance the summer away every Wednesday in June from 6 P.M. to 8 P.M. A family event appropriate for music lovers of all ages, Concerts in the Park primarily feature acoustic, folk music. (See the Flagstaff Annual Events chapter for more information.)

Labor Day Arts and Crafts Festival
Wheeler Park across from the City Hall,
211 W. Aspen Ave.
(520) 779–6176

A family-oriented event featuring local and regional artists, live music, and food. (For more on the Labor Day Festival, refer to the Flagstaff Annual Events chapter.)

Music and Theater

Whether you enjoy community theater, the symphony, or a night of jazz, you will be delighted by the variety of performances around town. Recently the Flagstaff Symphony and Northern Arizona University have joined forces to provide a Summer Music and Theater program. Event schedules and tickets can be purchased at the organization's box office or by phone. For Flagstaff Symphony Orchestra tickets, call (520) 774–5107. The NAU Central Ticketing Office is located on Central Campus in the Central Union (building #30) across from the Information Desk; for tickets or events information call (520) 523–5661 or (888) 520–7214.

Flagstaff Symphony Orchestra
113 E. Aspen Ave.
(520) 774–5107
www.flagstaffsymphony.com

Welcome to the 51st season of the Flagstaff Symphony. The symphony is composed of seventy-five professional and community members. From Chabier's *Espana* to Moussorgsky/Ravel's *Pictures at an Exhibition*, this season's program is a blend of international influences and talented performers that will dazzle audiences. Call the symphony office for a calendar of events and ticket information.

Magic Theater Productions Youth Cultural Center
2575 E. 7th Ave.
(520) 526–3787

Enjoy a night at the theater performed by an all children cast. Come out and support the budding performers of the Flagstaff community. (For more about Magic Theater, see the Flagstaff Kidstuff chapter.) Previous performances include *Annie*, *Winnie the Pooh*, and *Cinderella*.

NAU Spectrum Series
(520) 523–5661, (888) 520–7214
www.nau.edu

Some of the nation's top acts have graced the stage at the University's Ardrey Auditorium (located on central campus). The NAU Spectrum Series brings innovative performances to the campus year round, and proceeds help introduce children to the arts.

Northern Arizona's Summer Arts 2000
(520) 523–4780
www.nau.edu

Flagstaff Symphony Orchestra and Northern Arizona University have joined forces to provide a summer of professional theater and music concerts. All performances take place in the Clifford White Theater and Ardrey Auditorium (located on Central Campus).

Northern Arizona University Theater
(520) 523–5661,
(800) 520–7214
www.nau.edu/spa

Enjoy a night at the theater with the talented NAU School of Performing Arts. The 2000-2001 season includes *A View from the Bridge*, *Angels in America*, *Crimes of the Heart*, and *Medea*. Performances are held in the Clifford White Theater and Ardrey Auditorium on Central Campus.

Theatrikos Theater Company
11 W. Cherry Ave.
(520) 774–1662

In May of 1972, a small group gathered in the basement of the Historic Hotel Weatherford to discuss the possibility of forming a community theater group. Today, Theatrikos thrives as Flagstaff's premier community theater group and produces six shows a season. Previous performances include Neil Simon's *Jakes' Women*, *Diary of Anne Frank*, and *True West* by Sam Shepard. Look for performance schedules, previews and reviews in *FlagLive!* or call the Theatrikos Box Office for more information.

Annual Events

The ideal weather, friendly atmosphere, and beautiful scenery make Flagstaff a prime destination for year round events. Residents are proud of their roots and enjoy reminiscing about the past. Stop any old-timer on the street and you will see how sentimental the locals are. Many of Flagstaff's annual events blend together the history, traditions, and industries that have contributed to the making of the town. This section will provide the month-to-month coverage for the happenings in northern Arizona. Most of the events are sponsored by local organizations and the Flagstaff Chamber of Commerce, 101 W. Route 66, (520) 774–4505; the Flagstaff Visitors Center, 1 E Route 66, (800) 842–7293; and Flagstaff Convention and Visitors Bureau, 323 W. Aspen Ave., (520) 779–7611.

January is a quiet month in northern Arizona, but if the town is blessed with snowy weather, outdoor activities abound. (Refer to the Flagstaff Recreation chapter.) Also consult the calendar events listing in the *Arizona Daily Sun* and the weekly arts and entertainment rag, *Flagstaff Live!*, for your up-to-the-minute schedule for musical, cultural, and family-oriented events. Keep in mind that times and dates are subject to change. However, in order to help you plan your vacation, we've provided phone numbers and, if available, website addresses.

February

Flagstaff Winterfest
Flagstaff Chamber of Commerce,
101 W. Rte. 66   (520) 774–4504

Winterfest is a celebration of snow. Restaurants, local accommodations, and businesses partake in the fun as well. The weekend highlights include dogsled races, nordic and alpine skiing competitions, snowboard and snowshoe events, stargazing, children's activities, cultural events, and other fun-filled entertainment. Winterfest takes place during the month of February.

Ski Events
Arizona Snowbowl, P.O. Box 40, Flagstaff
(520) 779–1951
www.arizonasnowbowl.com

Throughout February, the Arizona Snowbowl and the Flagstaff Nordic Center offer a variety of winter events for all levels of skiers, including the Mountain Sports Cup, Arizona Citizens' Cup, Arizona Special Olympics Winter Games, and the Grand Canyon State Winter Games competitions. Contact the Arizona Snowbowl for times and dates.

March

Arizona Ski and Golf Classic
Arizona Snowbowl, P.O. Box 40, Flagstaff
(520) 779–1951
www.arizonasnowbowl.com

The weekend event begins in sunny and warm Phoenix with four person teams competing in a golf tournament on Saturday. Sunday, the teams travel north to the high country of Flagstaff for a modified slalom ski race at the Arizona Snowbowl. Spectators are welcome. This event is for those who like extremes.

Voices of the Past
Lowell Observatory, 1400 W. Mars Hill Rd.
(520) 774–2096
www.lowell.com

Combining astronomy, history, and theater, Voices of the Past is a unique program that introduces visitors to famous astronomers and scientists from the past.

This program, performed by the observatory staff, recreates the lives of such astronomers as Galileo, Copernicus, Caroline Herschel, Maria Mitchell, and Percival Lowell himself. A tour of the night sky follows. The series usually runs Friday and Saturday nights with at least two performances each night. Please call ahead for times and to ensure night time visibility.

Archaeology Day
Museum of Northern Arizona, 3101 Fort Valley Rd., Flagstaff
(520) 774–5213
www.musnaz.org.

The museum focuses on the indigenous peoples that inhabit the Colorado Plateau. This fun-filled day for children and adults includes special activities and events about Southwestern archaeology.

May

The Scenic Skyride at Arizona Snowbowl
P.O. Box 40, Flagstaff
(520) 779–1951
www.arizonasnowbowl.com

This is truly a wonderful way to experience the breathtaking views of northern Arizona. The skyride takes you to an elevation of 11,500 feet, with over 70 miles of amazing scenery. The trip is 25 minutes one way in an open chair lift. At the top, a U.S Forest Ranger will be on hand to answer questions about the biology and geology of the region. After the scenic skyride, enjoy an afternoon hike and lunch on the deck. The lift is open daily 10 A.M. to 4 P.M. from Memorial Day through Labor Day. After Labor Day the lift operates on Friday, Saturday, and Sunday only through mid October.

A Celebration of Native American Art
Museum of Northern Arizona,
3101 Fort Valley Rd.
(520) 774–5213   www.musnaz.org

From Memorial Day to Labor Day, the Museum of Northern Arizona honors the creativity of Native American and Hispanic artists of the Colorado Plateau. The weekend-long family-oriented events include exhibits featuring the arts and crafts of the Hopi, Navajo, Zuni, and Pai. Children's activities are scheduled throughout the weekend. Representatives from Native American and Hispanic groups perform traditional dances. Please contact the museum for a schedule of events.

Insiders' Tip

The Snowbowl skyride offers scenic views of northern Arizona and the Grand Canyon, but be prepared for the change in elevation and in weather. Bring a jacket and wear sneakers or hiking boots to ensure a safe and enjoyable trip.

Flagstaff's Historic Walks
(520) 774–8800

Join Flagstaff historians Richard and Sherry Magnum, dressed in turn-of-the-century costumes, as they lead educational and entertaining tours through Flagstaff's historic downtown area. The guides offer unique information, anecdotes about downtown's buildings and inhabitants. The tours begin at the Visitor Center and are scheduled every other Sunday beginning in May at 10 A.M. until the end of September. A special tour is available on July 4th. All tours are free, but please call for reservations.

June

Concerts in the Park
Wheeler Park
(520) 779–7690

Flagstaff Parks and Recreation host this concert series every Wednesday during the month of June, between 6 P.M. and 8 P.M. in Wheeler Park, located across from the City Hall, 211 West Aspen Avenue. The series features local and regional musicians. Bring a blanket or chair to this toe-tapping event.

Wool Festival
Arizona Historical Society Pioneer
Museum, 2340 N. Fort Valley Rd.
(520) 774–6272

The earliest European settlers introduced sheep to the Flagstaff area and began an industry that played an important economic role in Flagstaff until the mid 1900s. Paying tribute to these settlers and their flocks, this festival features a sheep wagon from the museum's collection; sheep, goat, and llama shearing; and livestock and fleece judging. Food is prepared in Dutch ovens and on griddles, just as it was in the sheep herding days. Felting, spinning, dyeing, and weaving demonstrations are held throughout the first weekend in June.

Gem and Mineral Show
Little America Hotel, 2515 E. Butler Ave
(520) 779–2741

Held in the second week in June, the Gem and Mineral Show features displays of everything from rough rocks to gemstones, minerals, jewelry, beads, crystals, tools, and equipment.

Flagstaff Heritage Days
Flagstaff Visitor Center, 1 E. Rte. 66
(520) 774–9541

Heritage Days is a celebration of the heart and soul of the American West. A variety of events take place during twelve action-packed days. During the Pine Country Rodeo, top rodeo contenders compete in roping and riding events. The Great Fiesta Del Barrio and Fajita Cook-off pays homage to the culture and customs of the Hispanic community. The popular Route 66 Festival and car show drives into Flagstaff in all their glory. Other events include the Arizona Dream Cruise and Route 66 Car Rally, dances, mixers, and kids' carnival rides.

In the heart of historic Flagstaff, Heritage Square hosts musical entertainment during the summer months. PHOTO: STACEY WITTIG

Coconino County Horse Races
Fort Tuthill Coconino County Park,
S. U.S. Hwy. 89A
(520) 774–5130

Featuring thoroughbred and quarter horse races, the Coconino County Horse

Races are held annually over the Fourth of July weekend at Fort Tuthill Downs. Distances range from 350-yard sprints to one-mile endurance races. This event draws a large crowd, so be sure to arrive early.

July

Festival of Arts and Crafts Extraordinaire
Northland Hospice,
P.O. Box 997, Flagstaff
(520) 779–1227

Held over the Fourth of July weekend, this fund-raiser benefits the Northland Hospice and features a variety of entertainment, food, children's activities, and arts and crafts from artisans around the country.

Flagstaff's Fabulous 4th Festivities
Flagstaff Visitor Center, 1 E. Rte. 66
(520) 774–9541

Celebrate Flagstaff's favorite holiday and the Fourth of July with an old-fashioned community parade. Citizens go all out as they dress in turn-of-the-century costumes. The parade takes place in the historic downtown area. Get there early to see decorated floats, live music, and locals doing their thing.

August

Flagstaff Summerfest
Fort Tuthill Coconino County Fairground,
S. U.S. Hwy. 89A
(480) 968–5353

Held the first week of August, Flagstaff Summerfest is the coolest place to be in the summer. This three-day celebration of fine arts and crafts features 200 juried artists from across the country. Over forty musicians from throughout the West perform on three stages, while an array of delectable fine foods tempts your senses. A hands-on activity area for children provides entertainment for the whole family.

Coconino County Fair
Fort Tuthill Coconino County Fairgrounds,
S. U.S. Hwy. 89A, Flagstaff
(520) 774–5130

For the past fifty years, Coconino County Fair has been the largest county fair in

northern Arizona. Enjoy live music performed on outdoor stages, a demolition derby, livestock auction, and arts and crafts festival. The kids will love the petting zoo, carnival rides, and all the hot dogs, popcorn, and cotton candy. For ticket prices and information on this Labor Day weekend event, contact the Fort Tuthill Coconino County Fairgrounds.

Labor Day Arts and Crafts Festival
(520) 779–6176

Looking for something to do over the Labor Day weekend? Take the family to this arts and crafts festival and enjoy the food, entertainment and regional artists' displays. Local musicians perform throughout the festival. Admission is free. This is an alcohol free event.

September

Annual Bed Race
(520) 523–1642

The bed race includes a parade, banquet, silent auction, and hilarious racing com-

petition. Come join the fun the second week in September as teams from businesses and community groups push "beds" down Aspen Avenue.

Shoot-Out-In-The-Pines
(520) 556–9573

Held on the third weekend in September, this sports festival features a 3-on-3 basketball tournament involving over 100 teams for all ages and skill levels. The Shoot-Out-In-The-Pines benefits Toys for Tots, an organization that provides toys at the holiday season for the children of northern Arizona.

Flagstaff Festival of Science
P.O. Box 22402, Flagstaff 86002
(800) 842-7293   www.scifest.org

A great educational experience for the whole family, this ten-day event is filled with fun and family-oriented learning activities, including field trips and interactive exhibits. Local museums, observatories, and other scientific facilities offer open houses. Events take place at various locations throughout the Flagstaff area at the end of September and beginning of October. For more information, contact the festival coordinator at the address above.

October

Flagstaff Symphony Guild's
"Elegant Affair"
(520) 522–0549

To benefit the Flagstaff Symphony Guild, this grand event includes a luncheon, silent auction, and champagne served butler style. Support for the silent auction comes from the donations made by Arizona sports teams and local businesses. Auctioned items include great vacation giveaways, antique jewelry, and gift certificates. Dillard's Department store presents their famous "Elegant Affair" fashion show, which features fall and holiday fashions perfect for a night on the town, cruises, or any social function. Reservations are required. The "Elegant Affair" is held the last Saturday in October.

November

Voices of the Past
Lowell Observatory,
1400 W. Mars Hill Rd.
(520) 774-2096   www.lowell.edu

Combining astronomy, history, and theater, Voices of the Past is a unique program that introduces visitors to famous astronomers and scientists from the past. This program, performed by the observatory staff, recreates the lives of such astronomers as Galileo, Copernicus, Caroline Herschel, Maria Mitchell, and Percival Lowell himself. A tour of the night sky follows. The series usually runs Friday and Saturday nights with at least two performances each night. Please call ahead for times and nighttime visibility.

Handel's "Messiah"
Northern Arizona University
(520) 523–5661

A Flagstaff holiday gem, this performance showcases the talents of NAU's student soloists, chamber orchestra, and chorus. The concert is normally held in late November, however, the date varies, so contact the university for further information.

Playthings of the Past
Arizona Historical Society Pioneer
Museum, 2340 Fort Valley Rd.
(520) 774-6272

Children and adults will enjoy learning about toys that came before computers and handheld games. The toy exhibit runs November through January, and features dolls, trains, cars, and other playthings from the 1880s through the 1960s.

December

Annual Holiday Lights Festival
Little America Hotel, 2515 E. Butler Ave.
(520) 779–7979, (800) 435–2493

Forget the hustle and bustle of the holidays! The Little American Hotel kicks off the holiday season with more than 2 million decorative lights. This sight, and the celebration that surrounds it, are sure to start your holiday season off right. The ceremony takes place on the Saturday after Thanksgiving with a visit from Santa, live entertainment, caroling, and complimentary cookies and warm beverages. Local high school choirs sing Christmas favorites.

Holiday Tours at Riordan Mansion
Riordan Mansion State Historic Park,
1300 Riordan Ranch St.
(520) 779–4395

Experience the joys of Christmas past with a guided tour of the historic Riordan Family Mansion. Well-informed guides lead tours of this living piece of Flagstaff history and share Christmas folklore and traditions both past and present. The mansion is decorated in turn-of-the-century style with wreaths, garland, and a tree trimmed with old-fashioned ornaments. The staff recommends making reservations.

Daytrips

Drive in any direction from Flagstaff and you will encounter new sights, dramatic altitude changes, and magnificent scenery. The 300 days of sunshine are reason enough to immerse yourself in the tranquility of the great outdoors. Along with a variety of secluded outdoor day or weekend trips, northern Arizona offers a plethora of natural wonders that are popular among tourists, but don't let that stop you. The endless sky, fresh air, and monolith rock formations will help you forget any crowds as you observe the ancient ruins, pueblos, and natural wonders of the area.

Mogollon Rim

If you are looking for a quiet escape from noise and people, a visit to the Mogollon Rim (an approximate 40-minute drive from Flagstaff) promises lush forest, amazing views, and solitude among the pines. Miles of trails await the hiker, mountain bike rider, and sightseer. Even during the peak season, you could spend a whole day exploring the rim and not see one person.

The expansive Mogollon Rim, a 1,000-foot cliff, runs for miles across central Arizona and forms the southern edge of the Colorado Plateau. The rim provides excellent views of this area and the Plateau country (the San Francisco Peaks area) and drops 2,000 feet in some areas. The region also boasts some of the most picturesque lakes in the state for boating and fishing. Hiking and sightseeing along the Rim are other favorite activities. Come to the

Mogollon Rim during the fall to watch the leaves change to gold and crimson. This is one of the most striking geologic features in Arizona.

Blue Ridge Reservoir
Blue Ridge District, HC 31, Box 300,
Happy Jack, AZ 86024 (520) 477–2255

This extensive body of water, nestled between tree-covered canyon walls, provides lush scenery and water recreation possibilities in a secluded setting. This spot is out of the way and worth every mile you travel to get here. The Arizona Game and Fish Department stocks the Reservoir with rainbow, brown, and brook trout. If fishing doesn't interest you, the Rim Country is a haven for sightseeing, wildlife watching, hiking, and mountain biking along the Mogollon Plateau.

Blue Ridge Reservoir is 63 miles south of Flagstaff, and part of the driving is on

Boaters enjoy the solitude and beautiful scenery of Blue Ridge Reservoir. PHOTO: STACEY WITTIG

graveled forest road. Take Lake Mary Road (Forest Highway 3) for 55 miles to Clints Well. Turn northeast (left) about 4 miles on Arizona Highway 87 to Forest Road 751. Then head southeast about six more miles to the reservoir. With the exception of FR 751, all roads are paved and accessible by passenger cars in most weather. The reservoir and FR 751 are closed during the winter. The boat ramp is accessible from the reservoir and boat motors are limited to a maximum of eight horsepower.

If you decide that a daytrip is not enough, Blue Ridge and Rock Crossing Campgrounds are open from Memorial Day through mid-fall. Rock Crossing is only 4 miles from the reservoir on FR 751. Blue Ridge Campground is located on FR 138. To get to the Blue Ridge Campground, turn northeast on AZ Highway 87, go about 7.5 miles to FR 138, and then 1 mile to the campground. (FR 138 and 751 are closed during the winter.) Rock Crossing has 35 single unit campsites and Blue Ridge has 10 sites. Both campgrounds have tables, fire rings, grills, and drinking water.

Arizona Trail
Moderate

The 8-mile Blue Ridge section of the Arizona Trail runs through meadows, forests, and canyons and takes between three and four hours to complete. The trail begins at General Springs Cabin, which is across from the Blue Ridge Ranger District. This Forest Service station was named after a nearby water source discovered by General George Crook, who was famous for his campaigns against the Apaches in this area.

From the old cabin, the trail winds down General Springs Canyon to the Fred Haught Trail, named after another historic resident. This part of the Cabin Loop System leads the Arizona Trail to the top of Battleground Ridge. The trail descends into East Clear Creek Canyon and crosses the small stream that flows into Blue Ridge Reservoir. To access the trailhead, take Lake Mary Road (Forest Road 3) for 55 miles until you reach Clints Well. Go southwest for 9 miles on Arizona Highway 87 to FR 300 (the General Crook Trail). Turn east and drive about 6 miles to the General Springs trailhead, or turn north from Clints Well and go about 7.5 miles to the Blue Ridge Trailhead. FR 300 is closed in winter.

Barbershop Trail # 91
Moderate

The 4.5-mile-long Barbershop Trail leads hikers through forests and shallow canyons, which are home to mule deer, elk, wild turkey, and black bear. The forest's maple, aspen, and oak make this trail a must during the fall. This hike should take approximately three hours to complete.

The Barbershop Trail is approximately 77 miles southeast of Flagstaff. Take Lake Mary Road (Forest Road 3) about 55 miles. Turn north 9 miles on Arizona Highway 87 to FR 95 and then south (right) 8 miles to FR 139 and continue 7 miles to the trailhead. FR 3 and Arizona Highway 87 are paved.

Willow Crossing # 38
Easy

Beginning at the end of Forest Road 122A, this trail is set in a rugged canyon surrounded by lush forest. The 1.3-mile trail offers a brief yet secluded hike through the woods, following the west side of a small drainage before it drops into Willow Valley. Surrounded by ponderosa pine, locust, and gamble oak, you descend into Willow Valley (watch for poison ivy along side the drainage area). The secluded canyon of Willow Valley is the ideal habitat for wildlife, including black bear. The trail gradually ascends out of the canyon through ponderosa pine as it follows the south side of the fence line to the trailhead on FR 9366M. Watch for the rock cairns that mark the trail through this stretch. Hiking time is approximately one hour.

To access the south trailhead, take Lake Mary (Forest Road 3) to Clints Well. From Clints Well (junction of Arizona Highway 87 and the Forest Road 3) drive north on FR 3 approximately 4 miles to FR 196. Turn left (west) and proceed approximately 2 miles to FR 122A. Follow 122A to the trailhead at the end of the road.

To access the north trailhead from Happy Jack Ranger Station, follow Lake Mary Road (Forest Road 3) south 7.5 miles to FR 81. Go right (west) on FR 81 and continue for approximately 5 miles to the FR 9366M. Go 0.3 mile to the trailhead, which is located on the left. High-clearance vehicles are recommended and the road may not be passable during wet weather.

Insiders' Tip

Trails may be closed during times of high fire danger, usually beginning in late June and running into July.

Rim Road and General Crook Trail Loop

Take a scenic drive along the Mogollon Rim as it winds through lush forest, rugged canyons, impressive views, and wildlife habitat. The cliffs along the rim make this a drive worth taking. Part of this drive traverses the rim's edge across the Coconino National Forest. In so doing, it follows the General Crook Trail, which was blazed by the famous general as he tried to fight off the Apache Indians.

To explore the rim by car, drive 50 miles south from Flagstaff to Clints Well. The scenic drive starts here. Head 9 miles north on Arizona Highway 87 to Forest Road 95. Follow FRs 95, 96, and 321 a total of 19 miles to FR 300, and then 17 miles west (right) to Arizona Highway 87 and 9 miles back to Clints Well. The scenic drive is a 154-mile round-trip from Flagstaff, and is a 54-mile round-trip from Clints Well. FR 3 and Arizona Highway 87 are paved. All Forest Roads are graveled and suitable for cars, but are closed in the winter.

Oak Creek Canyon
Sedona Ranger District, P.O. Box 300, Sedona, AZ 86336
(520) 282–4119

Drive south from Flagstaff on U.S. Highway 89A. Just 14 miles south of Flagstaff, the road drops nearly a thousand feet down a series of switchbacks and continues for 13 more miles beside tranquil Oak Creek.

This clear canyon stream may be one of the most scenic fishing and swimming holes in the world, and is known for its vibrant red rocks, unique formations, and spectacular scenery. Oak Creek flows through a narrow gorge, the smaller cousin of the world-famous Grand Canyon. As you wind your way through the canyon, crystal pools and lush vegetation await you. Travelers can take in the view from outside their cars at the many overlooks, picnic areas, swimming holes, and hiking trails along U.S. Highway 89A. Oak Creek Canyon is a photographer's paradise; bring plenty of film, and don't forget your bathing suit, hiking boots, and fishing pole.

Before you drive into the canyon you'll want to stop at Oak Creek Canyon Vista. Here you can view the canyon and shop for crafts and jewelry made by local Native American artists.

As you leave Oak Creek Canyon and continue past Sedona through Red Rock Country, watch for familiar shapes among the rock formations. Most likely you will be able to make out Snoopy Rock, Bell Rock, and many more.

You can continue down this scenic road to Interstate 17 and then drive north back to Flagstaff. Or perhaps you would like to turn around and do it all over again. An alternative and scenic route is to return to I–17 via Schnebley Hill Road. The road is rocky, but the panoramic views are worth the bumpy ride. Drive south from Flagstaff on Arizona Highway 89A 14 miles to Oak Creek Canyon and then 13 miles more to Sedona. Turn east on Arizona Highway 179 and go 11 miles to I–17 and then drive 40 miles back to Flagstaff.

Hiking through Oak Creek Canyon affords views of stunning rock formations and magnificent scenery, but remember this is one of the most popular tourist vacations spot in the world.

Sterling Pass Trail #46
Moderate to Strenuous

Sterling Pass Trail begins with a steep climb at the trailhead. This 2.4-mile trail takes hikers from Oak Creek Canyon into nearby Sterling Canyon. The trail ascends an unnamed drainage and passes through a forest of ponderosa pines and dwarf canyon maples. This spot makes a great destination if you're looking to view the changing leaves during the fall months.

Take the steep climb, but don't forget to look up at the gigantic red rock formations towering above you. As you descend into Sterling Canyon, you will walk between huge red rock masses. The best views of the canyon are along the climb. Remember to take a well-deserved rest to enjoy them because the view from the top is partially blocked by trees. Please, no mountain bikes on the trail. Sterling Pass Trail can be hot and dry in summer; it takes two hours to complete.

To access Sterling Pass Trail, take U.S. Highway 89A for 22 miles from Flagstaff (5.5 miles north of Sedona) through scenic Oak Creek Canyon. The trailhead is hard to see from the road; it's located on the west side of the highway, near mile marker 380, about a hundred yards north of the entrance to Manzanita Campground. The only parking that is available is on the east side of U.S. Highway 89A.

West Fork Oak Creek #108
Easy to Strenuous

This trail is one of the most popular in the Coconino National Forest and has the most foot traffic. Don't let that stop you; plan your hikes for mornings and weekdays during the peak season. The trail traverses the creek and is enclosed by towering, dramatic cliffs. This hike is a must for all seasons. In the spring, colorful birds migrate to the area. Come enjoy the leaves changing color in the fall, and in the winter icicles hang from rugged red cliffs above.

The trail is marked for the first three miles. Remember that the trail crisscrosses the stream; hikers can walk through the shallow water or use strategically placed stones to help maneuver across. The trail does end at the three-mile mark. It will take approximately two hours to complete the trail round-trip. If you choose to continue into Secret Mountain/Red Rocks Wilderness, plan to take advantage of the opportunities to swim, climb large boulders, and wade through the water along the way. The journey from one end of the Canyon to the other is 14 miles round-trip.

To access the West Fork trailhead, drive south on U.S. Highway 89A for 17.5 miles from Flagstaff or north 9.5 miles from Sedona to about halfway between mileposts 385 and 384. The trailhead is on the west side of the highway down a paved lane. Don't park on the side of U.S. Highway 89A, as cars drive fast on this curvy road. The best place to park is at the Call O' The Canyon day area, which is about a quarter mile north of the trailhead.

Meteor Crater
P.O. Box 70, Flagstaff, AZ, 86002
(520) 289–2362, (800) 289–5898
www.meteorcrater.com

Fifty thousand years ago, a meteorite struck the terrain in this part of eastern Arizona leaving behind a 550-foot deep chasm that is more than 4,000 feet in diameter. Theories surmise that the meteorite was approximately 150 feet across and weighed several hundred tons. Pieces of limestone—some the size of small houses—were thrown onto the rim. Beds of rock within the crater walls were overturned in a matter of seconds and moved about 150 feet.

Today Meteor Crater is a popular attraction with an elaborate Visitors Center. It is also home to the Museum of Astrogeology, a newly remodeled, state-of-the-art facility, which includes interactive computer displays providing information and high-tech graphics on the solar system, meteorites, and asteroids. The museum also has exhibits on meteoritics and the mechanics of impact cratering.

The Astronaut Hall of Fame commemorates the Mercury, Gemini, and Apollo crews and also displays a spacesuit worn by astronaut Charles Duke and an Apollo test capsule that was used for studies and retrieval practice. The newest addition to the facilities is an eighty-seat movie theater that features "Collisions and Impacts," shown twice an hour.

Behind the museum, you'll find four observation areas that provide plenty of room to view the Crater. Observation telescopes are available for your convenience and allow greater visibility of points of interest inside the crater. Daily guided tours, beginning at the Visitors Center, leave hourly from 9:15 A.M. until 2:15 P.M. for those who would like to get a closeup view. The tours last approximately one hour. Proper walking shoes are recommended for the 0.3-mile hike around the rim.

Astronaut Memorial Park provides a

place for visitors to picnic or just relax. A snack bar is available for your convenience. The facilities are wheelchair accessible.

To get to Meteor Crater from Flagstaff, take Interstate 40 East heading toward Albuquerque. Take the exit marked 233. Meteor Crater's summer hours (May 15 through September 15) are 6 A.M. to 6 P.M. Winter hours (September 16 through May 14) are 8 A.M. to 5 P.M.

Petrified Forest National Park/Painted Desert
1 Park Rd.
(520) 524–6228
www.nps.gov/pefo.

The Petrified Forest National Park was first established as a National Monument on December 8, 1906. A bill passed by Congress in 1962 turned the monument into a National Park.

The park is one of the world's largest and most colorful areas of petrified wood. Located in eastern Arizona, the Petrified Forest is also home to the 93,533 acres known as the Painted Desert, archeological sites that date back to 1400 C.E., and 225-million-year-old fossils.

A visit to this park will take you back to the Triassic Period, a time when ancient amphibians, reptiles, and early dinosaurs roamed the earth. During this geological period, the area was flooded, trees were washed away and covered by mud, volcanic ash, and silt, cutting off the oxygen to the logs which slowed down their decay. Even-

tually water seeped through the logs, encasing the wood with silica deposits. The silica crystallized into mineral quartz and the logs were preserved as petrified wood.

As erosion removed the sediment and exposed petrified logs and animal and plant fossils, the multi-colored badlands of the Painted Desert were formed. Artifacts testify to human occupation, but fade away around 1400 C.E.

The mid-1800s brought Army explorers who returned home with stories of this wondrous landscape. After the explorers came, farmers and settlers made their way west and settled in the area, using petrified wood at an alarming rate. Land was set aside for preserving the area, and in 1932 more land was added.

The park exists for the purpose of preserving the land and the petrified wood. Visitors are not allowed to take wood from the park or use it for any reason. Petrified wood can be bought from dealers who collect it from outside the park. Large and small pieces are made into jewelry, clocks, and other souvenirs.

Hiking in the Petrified Forest National Park is encouraged. Day hikes are the most popular way to explore the park. There are no marked or developed trails, and hikers can park the car and blaze their own trail. The lack of vegetation and the variety of landmarks make for excellent hiking conditions. Overnight camping is permitted in designated areas only. Apply for your wilderness permit and purchase maps at the Visitor Center, located at the north end of the park. First-time visitors are encouraged to watch a 20-minute park orientation film at the center.

The Painted Desert Inn offers great views and has exhibits and a gift shop.

The Rainbow Forest Museum is located at the south end of the park and hosts petrified wood exhibits and 20-minute ranger talks. Park hours are from 8 A.M. to 5 P.M. The museum is open year round except for Christmas.

The Petrified Forest is located 116 miles east of Flagstaff off Interstate 40. Take exit 311 off the highway.

Petroglyphs adorn rocks at the Petrified Forest National Park. PHOTO: STACEY WITTIG

Tours

If you would like someone else to do the driving, take a guided tour of the most popular attractions in northern Arizona. Reservations are required and can usually be made 24 hours in advance.

The Gray Line of Flagstaff
114 W. Rt. 66
(520) 774–5003, (877) 467–3329
Gray Line offers five-day tour packages. **The Grand Canyon National Park South Rim Tour** will first take passengers to the Navajo Indian Reservation. The second leg of the trip takes you to the Grand Canyon's east entrance, which offer fewer crowds and more enjoyment. The journey continues to the south entrance of the park where passengers break for lunch at the Bright Angel Lodge. (The meal price is not included in the price of the tour.) Before leaving from the south gate, visitors will have the chance to view the Canyon one last time at Mather Point. After leaving the park, the tour will attend *The Grand Canyon–Hidden Secrets* at the IMAX Theater in Tusayan (also not included in the price of the tour). The tour returns to

Flagstaff through the Coconino Forest and takes approximately nine hours. The cost for children 5 to 15 years is $21; those 16 and older pay $42.

The Oak Creek Canyon, Sedona, Jerome, Montezuma Castle National Monument Tour begins in Oak Creek Canyon. The tour continues to Sedona for lunch (not included in price of the tour) and also a brief shopping and gallery excursion. After Sedona, the tour heads to Jerome, a ghost town that was once a "billion dollar copper camp." Next on the list is Montezuma Castle National Monument, prehistoric Sinagua Indian dwellings that lie in the heart of the Verde Valley. The entry fee to the castle is not included in the price of the tour. The tour is approximately eight hours. Ages 5 to 15 pay $20; people 16 and over pay $40.

The Navajo Indian Reservation, Monument Valley Tribal Park Tour

How It All Began

In 1902, Daniel Moreau Barringer, a Philadelphia mining engineer, heard about a crater in Arizona and felt it offered great potential for mining iron. After visiting the site, Barringer was convinced the crater was formed by the impact of a large iron meteorite and that the meteorite was buried beneath the floor of the crater. Barringer's assumptions were correct in that the crater was formed by the impact from a meteor, but he did not know that the meteorite disintegrated from the intense heat caused by the impact.

In 1903, Barringer filed four mining claims with the federal government. He was later granted the patents and ownership of the two miles that encompass the crater. Barringer spent the next 26 years trying to uncover the iron meteorite that he thought was buried within the crater.

After years of research, Barringer never found the supposed meteorite, but he did prove to the scientific community that the site was created by the impact of a meteor.

At present, the site is still owned by the Barringer family and the crater is leased to Meteor Crater Enterprises. This organization operates the Visitors Center, Astronaut Hall of Fame, and Museum of Astrogeology, which has played a significant role in the study of earth and space sciences.

begins at the heart of the Navajo Indian Reservation. Along the tour route, visitors will be able to enjoy the diverse geographic features of northern Arizona. Once the tour arrives at Monument Valley, another vehicle will give visitors a unique view of the area. The tour begins by bus and then tourists take jeeps through off-road areas. The tour takes approximately 11 hours and covers 315 miles. The cost for children ages 5 to 15 is $ 37; people 16 and over pay $74.

For an overview of the city and the history of Flagstaff, try the Flagstaff City Tour. The tour begins at the Museum of Northern Arizona, "The Gateway to the Colorado Plateau."

The tour also stops at the Pioneer Historical Museum and the Riordan State Historic Park. Both museums offer keen insight to the early settlers of Flagstaff. The last stop is at Old Town Springs, the city's original site and the location of the "first flagpole" for which Flagstaff was named. This tour takes approximately three hours. The cost for children 5 to 15 is $9.50; ages 16 and over pay $19.50.

Grand Canyon

Area Overview

When Spanish explorers first saw the Grand Canyon from the South Rim, probably somewhere between Moran and Lipan Points, they estimated the river was only six feet across. Since their Hopi guides "didn't know" the way down into the Canyon, the Spanish sent three explorers to find a way to the river. They only made it a third of the way down, discovering as they went that boulders that appeared to be only five or six feet high were in fact almost two hundred feet tall.

Even today, looking into the Grand Canyon from the rim, it is hard to appreciate its true vastness—the Canyon is 217 miles long, 8 to 14 miles across, and 5,300 feet deep! It is rightly considered one of the seven natural wonders of the world, a place to be cherished and protected for future generations.

Geology and Wildlife

Like so many of the spectacular geological sites on the Colorado Plateau, the Grand Canyon was created by erosion. The Colorado River cut the canyon as the plateau itself rose. Though you can see at the bottom of the Canyon rocks half as old as the planet itself, the Canyon was created only over the last 6 to 10 million years.

Each layer or group of layers of rock in the Canyon has its own color, and these are the muted pastel horizontal "stripes" you see.

The oldest rocks can be seen near the river at the eastern end of the canyon. These are the Vishnu schist and Zoroaster granite, formed two billion years ago during Precambrian times when layers of sandstone, shale, and limestone interspersed with ancient lava flows were laid down. These rocks were overlaid by 12 vertical miles of new rocks. Heat and pressure crushed, folded, and melted the older rocks before the overlying rock eroded away at the end of the Precambrian Era. The resulting gap in the geological record between the oldest rocks in the Inner Gorge and the much younger Paleozoic rocks directly above them is called the Great Unconformity. Other, smaller unconformities, probably also caused by erosion, can also be seen in the Grand Canyon.

After the Precambrian erosion ended, the land was covered by an ancient tropical sea. Sandstone, shale, and limestone layers of rock were laid down. When the sea retreated, erosion began again, followed by another period of sedimentary rock formation. Later, a Permian desert covered the region and winds deposited sand dunes. Twice more, the area was covered by shallow seas that laid down layers of limestone. At the end of Permian times, the most recent sea retreated. The sedimentary rock that had been deposited since the end of the Paleozoic Era eroded away on the Kaibab and Coconino Plateaus, but those rocks are the ones you see in the Painted Desert and other areas east, southeast, and north of the Grand Canyon.

The river cut the Canyon to a depth of almost a mile. What widened it was erosion from rain and snow, which flowed over the rims, "melting" the soft sandstone and limestone layers and causing major rockfalls.

Erosion by the Colorado has been slowed by the building of the Glen Canyon Dam, but horizontal rain and snow erosion continue unabated. Just two summers ago, a huge rockfall closed some of the hiking trails and broke the water pipeline that crosses the Canyon.

The geological record in the Canyon is only part of the historical story. The layers of rocks also contain a fossil record, from primitive algae in the lowest Precambrian layers to trees, dinosaurs, camels, and elephants in the upper layers.

Today, the flora and fauna of the Grand Canyon are representative of three "life zones." Nearest the rim is the Transition Zone. Here you will see piñon pine, juniper, ponderosa pine, and gambel oak. The Abert squirrel, mule deer, and coyote roam the forests. Overhead, look for red-tailed hawks, golden eagles, and jet black ravens.

The middle zone is called the Upper Sonoran. Cliff rose, mountain mahogany, and prickly pear cactus (long a food source for the indigenous peoples of this area and available to visitors as jam in most gift shops) inhabit this zone. Here you may be lucky enough to see bighorn sheep (and to avoid seeing rattlesnakes!).

The lowest zone, through which the river flows, is the Lower Sonoran Zone (below 3,500 feet). This is essentially a desert zone, and here you will see yucca, tamarisk, and Russian olive.

Before the Glen Canyon Dam was built in the early 1960s, rushing floods scoured the riverbanks clean every spring and created sandbars along the river's shores. The river was high and muddy during these floods, warm in the summer and low, muddy, and cold during the winter. When the river was dammed, these natural cycles were interrupted; the river flowed cold and clear all year long. Changing the river's flow changed the habitat for fish, wildlife, and plants that once lived here. Four native species of fish have been lost from the river, and non-native vegetation such as salt cedar has invaded the river's beaches. In 1996, the Bureau of Reclamation instituted major releases of water from the dam to simulate the historic floods, but since the amount of water released was much less than flowed during a normal flood, the effects on the ecology of the river were minimal, and the goal of restoring habitat for the fish and plants that once thrived in and near the river was not achieved.

History

Hundreds of ancient Indian ruins have been found within the Grand Canyon. The recent discovery of a Folsom point preform (the first step in flaking an arrowhead) dates the earliest known human habitation of the Grand Canyon at roughly 8500 B.C.E.

Artifacts made by the people of the Desert Culture indicate that the canyon was inhabited by cave dwellers at least 4,000 years ago. Among these artifacts are split twig figurines of animals. Today, jewelers and other artists create modern interpretations of these distinctive sculptures in silver, gold, bronze, and paint.

The Pueblo peoples also left their mark here by building the Tusayan Ruins on the South Rim, a village of approximately 30 people that dates from the late 1100s. Walhalla Glades was built between 1050 and 1150 C.E. The inhabitants of these 100 farm sites built one-room structures and terraced gardens where they grew squash, beans, and corn, the staples of the diet of the indigenous peoples of the Southwest. Unkar Delta was occupied from about 850 to 1100 C.E. The fertile delta was an excellent spot for an agricultural people to settle, but eventually drought and deforestation drove them out. The Pueblo peoples are called the Hisatsenom by today's Hopi, who live in villages on Black

Mesa. The Hopi are among the descendants of the Pueblo people, and they identify a site in the Grand Canyon as the sipapu from which the people emerged into this, the Fourth World. Hopis still make pilgrimages to their shrines within the Canyon. The Navajo word that identifies the Pueblo peoples is Anasazi, which means "ancient enemy." But because the descendants of the Pueblo peoples, such as the Hopi, and Navajos have intermarried, some Navajo also claim descent from peoples of the Pueblo culture.

Today the Hualapai and the Havasupai Indians live on reservations within the canyon and on its South Rim.

The first Europeans to see the South Rim of the Grand Canyon were part of the Coronado expedition of 1540 that set out in search of the Seven Cities of Cibola. The expedition, led by García López de Cárdenas, was guided by Hopis who "didn't know" how to get to the bottom of the Canyon.

For the next two centuries, European explorers pretty much ignored the impassable chasm. In 1776, the Spanish priest who had been appointed to oversee San Xavier Mission south of Tucson began to explore the Canyon from the west. On June 20, 1776, Francisco Tómas Garcés reached Cataract Creek, a tributary of the Colorado and home to the Havasupai. Five days later, he left to follow the river east, crossing the Little Colorado and going on to Moencopi and then to the Hopi pueblos.

The "discovery" of the North Rim is credited to two Franciscan priests, Francisco Atanasio Domíngez and Silvestre Vélez de Escalante in 1776.

From 1821 to 1848, the Grand Canyon belonged to independent Mexico and no record remains of any Mexican exploration of the Canyon, though American trappers, including Bill Williams, explored the Canyon in search of beaver in the early 1800s. In 1825 fur trader William Henry Ashley (of the Rocky Mountain Fur Company) and six others attempted to run the river in two canoes. They started down the Green River in Wyoming and found the beginning of the trip so arduous that he never actually made it to the Grand Canyon.

The Grand Canyon became part of the United States in 1848, ceded by Mexico in the Treaty of Guadalupe Hidalgo. Two years later, the Territory of New Mexico, including the Grand Canyon, was created. The federal government began to map the new territory, sending soldiers to find routes across it and to build military strongholds.

In the late 1850s, Lieutenant Joseph Chrismas Ives attempted to travel upstream from the mouth of the Colorado in a steamboat that had been manufactured in Philadelphia and shipped, piece by piece, to Ives' starting point. Three hundred and fifty miles, two months, and a great deal of trouble later, the boat struck a submerged rock near what is now the site of Hoover Dam. A competitor, George Alonzo Johnson, who had been operating steamboats on the lower Colorado, had, in the meantime, chugged up the river nearly as far as the mouth of the Virgin River. In the same year, F.W. von Egloffstein, an artist with the Ives' expedition, fell into Havasu Canyon and became the first European to visit the Havasupai in 80 years.

The Grand Canyon was wrested away from New Mexico when President Abraham Lincoln established the Arizona Territory in 1863. During the roundup of Navajos for the Long Walk to Bosque Redondo, some may have escaped capture by hiding in remote parts of the Grand Canyon. The Treaty of 1868 established a Navajo Reservation to which those who survived the incarceration at Fort Sumner were allowed to return. The reservation was expanded in 1884, 1900, and 1930 to include the eastern rim of the Grand Canyon and Marble Canyon north of the Little Colorado.

The Mormon missionary Jacob Hamblin crossed the Colorado several times on his way to visit the Hopi, and in 1862, he made a trip around the entire canyon. The following year he visited the Hualapai and Havasupai. Jacob Lake is named for him.

James B. White, arriving half-drowned at a small frontier town in Nevada below the

Grand Canyon, claimed to have made the first trip on the river through the length of the canyon, but many believe that he started his trip at Pierce's Ferry and had never even been in the Grand Canyon.

The man credited with the first successful trip down the Colorado River is Major John Wesley Powell, who, near the end of May 1869, descended Green River in Wyoming and traveled with ten companions in four wooden boats the length of the Canyon, arriving at mouth of Little Colorado River three months later. Powell was a veteran explorer and a geologist, and this was the first scientific exploration of the Canyon. The men were forced to portage their boats frequently, their provisions often ran low, and the rapids presented a formidable challenge. By the end of the trip, only two boats and six men remained. The other boats had been destroyed; the other men had left the expedition along the way. In May 1871, better prepared, Powell led a second Colorado River expedition, this time taking with him amateur scientists, an artist, and a photographer. This expedition made winter camp at Kanab Creek in October and started down the river again in August 1972, leaving the river at Kanab Creek in early September. One of the people with Powell on the North Rim in the early 1870s was Thomas Moran, a young artist, whose paintings of the Grand Canyon helped make it known worldwide. His illustrations accompanied Powell's 1875 report, "The Exploration of the Colorado River." Moran Point is named for him.

Between 1870 and 1880, the non-Indian population of the Arizona Territory quadrupled and ranchers, settlers, and colonists arrived on the new frontier. The population increase, along with cattle grazing, mining, and lumbering, put pressure on the Native peoples already here, and conflict often ensued. A reservation for the Hualapai Indians was set up on the Lower Colorado in 1874 after they were defeated in a three-year war with the U.S. military. They escaped from the reservation and returned to their traditional lands near Kingman and Peach Springs. In 1883, President Chester A. Arthur ordered that a reservation of 1 million acres south of the southern bend of the Colorado be established for the Hualapai, and this is the reservation that exists today. In 1880, President Rutherford B. Hayes created the Havasupai Indian Reservation, which two years later was reduced to just over 500 acres of land including only the village and fields.

In 1871, Mormon John Doyle Lee established a ferry at the Colorado River that crossed near the mouth of the Paria River. Lee was something of an outcast, having had a part in a massacre of pioneers by Mormons and Paiutes several years earlier. Lee was arrested in 1874 and executed in 1877 for his part in the atrocity. No one else was ever tried. After Lee was arrested, his wife, Emma, took over the ferry until it was purchased by the Latter Day Saints in 1879. The Grand Canyon Cattle Company owned it briefly, and then sold it to Coconino County. The ferry was in operation until an accident killed three men in 1928. The ferry did not reopen after the accident, and Navajo Bridge replaced it as the river crossing. Lee's Ferry is the place from which distances on the Colorado River are measured.

The late-nineteenth century saw an invasion of prospectors in the Grand Canyon; the mining claims did not pay off until much later, and some of the prospectors turned into tourist guides. Seth B. Tanner was one such. He used an old Indian trail to get to his claims, and the trail eventually became known as the Tanner Trail. Legend has it that John D. Lee buried his gold somewhere below the Tanner Trail. It became part of the trail used by horse thieves and later the site where bootlegged liquor was made and then sold in Grand Canyon Village during Prohibition.

As the railroad came through northern Arizona, more people came to know about the wonders of the Grand Canyon. In 1901, the Santa Fe Railroad reached the Grand Canyon's South Rim, saving tourists an arduous stage coach or horseback ride. Grand Canyon Village soon spread out from the train depot.

Emery Kolb lived at his studio until his death in 1976. The historic building is now a bookstore run by the Grand Canyon Natural History Association. PHOTO: TANYA LEE

The first-class, quarter-million-dollar El Tovar Hotel opened in 1905 to accommodate visitors. All the water needed at the El Tovar and at Grand Canyon Village was brought by train 120 miles from Del Rio.

Hermits Rest is named for Louis Boucher, who arrived in the Canyon in 1891 and stayed for 21 years tending his mining claims in Boucher Canyon and living at Dripping Springs. He planted an orchard and a garden, and he too took advantage of the growing popular interest in the Canyon by renting out cabins to tourists.

The first automobile arrived on the South Rim on January 12, 1902. It had been driven from Flagstaff and, because it broke down frequently, the trip had taken five days. But by the early 1920s, the automobile was the preferred way for tourists to come to the Canyon. No later than 2004, private cars will not be allowed on the South Rim. A public transportation system will take as many as 4,200 visitors an hour from a transportation center on the north side of Tusayan into the park, where quiet, non-polluting electric or electric-hybrid buses will run the entire 40-mile length of the West Rim and East Rim Drives, from Hermits Rest to Desert View.

Also in 1902, Ellsworth and Emery Kolb built the Kolb Studio for photographing travelers as they started down the Bright Angel Trail. Ten years later, the Kolb brothers made the first moving picture of a river trip on the Colorado.

Grand Canyon National Monument was created by President Theodore Roosevelt in 1908 under the Antiquities Act of 1906. In 1912 Arizona became a state, and in 1917 bills were introduced in the House and Senate to make Grand Canyon a national park, which was done in 1919 by President Woodrow Wilson. The newly formed National Park Service, headed by Stephen Tyng Mather, for whom Mather Point is named, had the challenging task of administering the park and managing and preserving the natural and cultural resources there. In 1927, Congress added 51 square miles to the park, and in 1932, President Herbert Hoover created a new Grand Canyon National Monument of 300 square miles on the west, an area that includes Toroweap viewpoint and Vulcan's Throne.

Former President Clinton and Interior Secretary Bruce Babbit announced the creation of the Parashant National Monument on January 11, 2000 at Hopi Point. PHOTO: TANYA LEE

From the beginning of the twentieth century, water used at Grand Canyon was brought by rail to the South Rim. In 1926, when the demand for water had increased dramatically because more and more tourists were visiting the Canyon, M. R. Tillotson, a park engineer, built a plant to recycle waste water for use in steam locomotives, in boilers, to flush toilets, and to irrigate landscaping. In 1931, construction began on a pipeline for pumping water from Indian Gardens 3,200 feet down in the Canyon up to the rim. By 1932, the water train was no longer in operation. In 1960, the available water supply was inadequate. A pipeline was built from Roaring Springs below the North Rim down Bright Angel Canyon, across the suspension bridge, and up to the pumping station at Indian Garden. The pipeline was operational in 1970.

Fred Harvey was given the contract as the principal concessionaire at the South Rim of Grand Canyon in 1920, though he had been operating tourist services there for many years prior. In 1922 he built Phantom Ranch as an overnight stopping place for tourists on mule trips down the Bright Angel Trail. The ranch, like Desert View Watchtower and Hermits Rest, was designed by Mary Jane Colter.

Copper, gold, and silver mining in the Canyon had been unprofitable, but in 1951, the U.S. Geological Survey found that the Orphan Mine was a rich source of uranium. In 1954, the Golden Crown Mining Company reopened the mine and sent the ore to Tuba City for processing. Not only did Native American tribes consider all mining in the Canyon a desecration of sacred land, but uranium was mined to build Cold War weapons here and elsewhere on the Colorado Plateau by a government and by companies who did not provide the miners (mostly Navajos) with adequate information about the dangers of mining uranium or adequate protective equipment. Recently declassified papers show that the federal government knew of the dangers to miners but concealed those dangers from the workers. People started dying in the 1960s, and the Uranium Radiation Victims Committee estimates that so far more than 400 uranium workers and members of their families have died from diseases resulting from exposure to radiation. The 1990 Radiation Exposure Compensation Act, recently amended by Congress, recognized the government's role in this tragedy, but in practice, it does little to compensate the uranium workers and their families.

The first dam on the Colorado was the Hoover Dam, built at the west end of the Canyon in 1936, forming Lake Mead. As the Big Buildup to provide power to the new urban centers of the Southwest continued, more dams and power plants were built on the Colorado Plateau. The last dam to be constructed was Glen Canyon Dam in 1964. The reservoir behind the dam, Lake Powell, flooded many historic and prehistoric cultural sites, as well as geological wonders. Other dams were proposed for the Colorado River, but pressure from the public and environmentalists kept the proposed dams at Marble Canyon and Bridge Canyon from being built.

Today, Lake Powell is a major Arizona water recreation site. A proposal to drain the lake has been on the table for several years, as has been a proposal to build a pipeline from Lake Powell to supply water to the Navajo and Hopi Reservations as well as the cities of Flagstaff and Williams.

The most recent efforts to protect the Grand Canyon area were the creation of the one-million acre Parashant National Monument on the North Rim on January 11, 2000 and the establishment of Vermilion Cliffs National Monument on November 9, 2000 by President Clinton. Parashant National Monument includes most of the Arizona Strip and nearly doubled the number of acres protected as part of the greater Grand Canyon. The Vermilion Cliffs National Monument on the Paria Plateau northeast of Grand Canyon protects an additional 293,000 acres just west of the Colorado River.

Getting Here, Getting Around

Today, about five million visitors a year come to see the Grand Canyon. They come by car and bus from the gateway communities of Flagstaff and Williams, as well as by plane from Las Vegas (which we here in Arizona decline to recognize as a gateway city).

Nava-Hopi Tours provides bus service between Grand Canyon National Park and Flagstaff. Buses leave Flagstaff at 7:30 A.M. and 2:30 P.M. arriving at Maswik Transportation Center at the South Rim at 9:45 A.M. and 4:15 P.M. respectively. You can return from the canyon from Maswik at 10 A.M. (arrives Flagstaff 12:01 P.M.) or 4:30 P.M. (arrives Flagstaff 6:30 P.M.). For reservations, call (800) 892–8687. South Rim Travel offers a shuttle service between the park and Flagstaff; call (520) 638–2748 or (877) 638–2257.

If you want a more exotic trip to the Canyon, take the train. Grand Canyon Railway runs a round-trip service once a day from Williams. Call (800) THE–TRAIN for reservations. For more information about the train, see the Williams chapter.

Airplanes from Las Vegas and other points land at Grand Canyon Airport. A shuttle leaves the airport every half hour. The shuttle stops in Tusayan and at Maswik Transportation Center. Call (520) 638–0821 for more information. Twenty-four hour taxi service is also available; call (520) 638–2822 or 2631. You can rent a car from Enterprise at the airport terminal. To reserve a car, call (520) 638–2871 or (800) 736–8222.

Grand Canyon via Williams and Flagstaff

Most people drive to the Grand Canyon from Williams or Flagstaff.

Your drive north on U.S. Highway 180 from Flagstaff to the South Rim of the Grand Canyon will take you through part of the San Francisco Volcanic Field. Some of the small cinder cones you see still have craters, and there are several lava caves in this area. Further north the highway passes just north of Red Mountain, Slate Mountain, and Kendricks Peak, mountains formed by volcanic activity. Highway 180 climbs to 8,000 feet through ponderosa pine and aspen forest, then descends into a piñon, juniper, and sagebrush landscape. The highway joins Arizona Highway 64 near Valle and here you begin a thousand-foot climb onto the Kaibab limestone (about 250 million years old) that forms both rims of the Grand Canyon.

North Rim via the South Rim

To get from the South Rim to the North Rim by car, expect a five-hour, 215-mile drive. Take Arizona Highway 64 east to Cameron, where the road meets U.S. Highway 89. Go north on U.S. 89 and then west at U.S. 89A. At Arizona Highway 67 (Jacob Lake), turn south and that road will take you past the Kaibab Lodge to the Grand Canyon Lodge, where the road dead ends. If you want to go to the North Rim directly from Flagstaff, take U.S. Highway 89 north to Cameron and follow the preceding directions. Rim to rim bus service is available daily from Transcanyon Shuttle. The bus departs the North Rim at 7 A.M. and arrives at the South Rim at noon, leaving for the return trip at 1:30 P.M. arriving at 6:30 P.M.. Call (520) 638-2820 or write Transcanyon Shuttle, P.O. Box 348, Grand Canyon, AZ 86023 for more information. Bear in mind that the North Rim is open mid May through mid October only.

Weather Considerations

Summer temperatures on the South Rim range from the mid 80s during the day to the low 50s at night. Winter temperatures average in the mid 50s during the day and in the mid 20s at night. Temperatures on the North Rim are about 10 degrees cooler because the elevation of the North Rim is 1,200 feet higher than that of the South Rim. The North Rim is open from mid May until mid October, depending on weather. Up to 25 feet of snow during the winter make the roads impassable.

Temperatures in the Canyon itself are much higher than on the rims, and in the summer you can expect temperatures of 110 degrees or more.

Plan to dress in layers, and pack a heavy sweater even for summer trips—you'll need it at night on the rims.

The Colorado Plateau is subject to heavy thunderstorms during the monsoon season (roughly July and August), and hikers need to be aware that extremely dangerous flash flooding and lightning storms can occur. Heavy rain or snow may also loosen boulders and cause rock slides in the Canyon. You can get current weather conditions by calling (520) 638-7888.

Where to Start

Okay, so you've finally reached Grand Canyon National Park, paid your $20 per vehicle entrance fee (Golden Eagle, Golden Access, and Golden Age Passports are sold and accepted, as is an Annual Grand Canyon Passport for $40), and you have your sunscreen, plenty of water, snacks for the kids, and a camera with several rolls of film. What now? Most visitors to the Canyon spend only 15 minutes here! With a little thought and preparation, you can do a lot better, planning a truly unique experience that you and your family will treasure forever.

Begin your visit by stopping at the new Canyon View Information Center, opened last October as the first step in the implementation of the 1995 General Management Plan, which will eventually include a public transportation system and the removal of several motels from the Canyon rim. To get to Canyon View Information Plaza, continue past the entrance station and turn left at the first (and so far only) stoplight in the Park. You're now on Center Road. Turn right on Market Plaza Road and continue on to Market Plaza and Yavapai Lodge. Between the two is one of the five parking lots on the South Rim. Park your car and board the free Village Loop (blue) shuttle in front of Yavapai Lodge. The bus will stop at Yavapai Rooms and then take you to the new information plaza, about six minutes from Yavapai Lodge. This is the only way to get to the information plaza and to the Kaibab Trail Route shuttle. Stop at the huge information building (open 8 A.M. to 5 P.M.) to get oriented before you decide what to do first (Notice that you haven't seen the Canyon yet!). The Canyon View Information Plaza, which also has restrooms and a bookstore (open 8 A.M. to 5 P.M.) in separate buildings, is open every day from one hour before sunrise to 10 P.M. from March 1 through November. From December 1 through February, it is open until 9 P.M.

Accessibility

Some programs and facilities on the South Rim are wheelchair accessible with assistance, and wheelchair-accessible tours can be arranged with prior notice. Check at the lodges' transportation desks or call (520) 638–2531. The Park Service provides wheelchairs for temporary day use at no fee. You can usually find a wheelchair at the Visitor Center. Inquire there to get a temporary parking permit for designated parking. TDD phones are available at hotels. You may obtain The Grand Canyon National Park Accessibility Guide at the Visitor Center, Yavapai Observation Station, Kolb Studio, Tusayan Museum, and Desert View Information Center.

On the North Rim, wheelchair-accessible restrooms can be found at the Visitor Center, General Store, and Ranger Station. The Grand Canyon Lodge dining room and patios can be reached by a lift. The Cape Royal Nature Trail is a 0.6-mile paved path with Canyon views from several places. A wheelchair is available for temporary day use at the Visitor Center; there is no fee. Parking permits may also be obtained at the Visitor Center. TDD phones are available to hotel guests. You can obtain a copy of the Accessibility Guide at the Visitor Center.

If you can't wait another minute to see the Canyon, Mather Point is just a few feet from the information plaza, or board the Village Loop or Kaibab Trail Loop shuttle bus to take you to other viewpoints (see below for shuttle bus routes).

From now until 2004, when the public transportation system will be in place, five parking lots (labeled A-E) are available to you in the park; they are located at Yavapai Lodge (A), Shrine of the Ages (B), Center Road (C and D), and Backcountry Information Center (E). The Village Loop bus stops at all of these parking lots.

The National Park Service offers a variety of ranger-led activities. At 12:30 P.M., meet at the El Tovar flagpole for a cultural and natural history one-hour walk along the rim. A Geology Walk (one hour) departs from Yavapai Observation Station daily at 2 P.M.. At 3:30, a fireside chat in the El Tovar lobby reveals the Canyon's geology and human history. A one-hour presentation on the park is offered at 7:30 P.M. nightly at Shrine of the Ages. "Glimpses of the Past" is a wheelchair-accessible (with assistance) 0.1-mile, ranger-led walk that explores questions about the Pueblo people who lived here 800 years ago. Meet at the Tusayan Museum for the walks, which begin at 9:30 A.M. and 1:30 P.M. daily. The walk takes about 45 minutes.

The South Rim by Car

The East Rim or Desert View Drive begins at Grand Canyon Village and takes you to the East Entrance at Desert View, a 25-mile one way trip. Along the way, you can stop at Yaki Point, Grandview Point, Moran Point, Lipan Point, and Navajo Point for views of the Canyon. At Desert View, you can climb the 70-foot Watchtower for a spectacular vista. Tusayan Ruins Museum is also along this route between Moran and Lipan Points. You'll find picnic tables at Yaki Point and just west of Grandview Point. Wheelchair-accessible restrooms, an information center, and an interpretive trail are located at Tusayan Museum and Ruins. A 0.5 mile, ranger-led sunset walk begins every day an hour before sunset at Desert View Point. Wear warm clothes and sturdy shoes.

The Grandview Trail begins at Grandview Point. This is a steep, unmaintained trail recommended for experienced desert hikers only. The round-trip to Coconino Saddle is

Canyon View Center is part of the new information plaza on the South Rim. PHOTO: TANYA LEE

1.5 miles with a 1600-foot drop in elevation; allow two hours. It is 6-mile round-trip, with a 2600-foot drop in elevation, to Horseshoe Mesa; the trip takes from four to eleven hours. Once you're there, you'll see the remains of one of Pete Berry's cabins. Berry was a miner who worked his claims about a hundred years ago. There is a toilet and designated campground at Horseshoe Mesa, but there are no other facilities or services on this trail.

At Desert View, the Watchtower is open from 8 A.M. to 7:30 P.M. and the Information Center and Grand Canyon Association Bookstore are open from 9 A.M. to 7 P.M.. Wheelchair-accessible restrooms are just south of the General Store, which is open from 9 A.M. to 7 P.M. The Trading Post Snack Bar is open from 8 A.M. to 7 P.M. year round and the gift shop is open from 8 A.M. to 8 P.M. during the winter and from 8 A.M. to sunset in the summer. The Watchtower Gift Shop has the same hours as the Trading Post Gift Shop. A Chevron Service Station, located just before the East Entrance, is open from 7 A.M. to 7 P.M.

Desert View Campground has fifty sites and is open during the summer (roughly May through October) on a first-come first-served basis. There are no hookups or dump stations here. Note that camping is allowed in Grand Canyon National Park only at designated campgrounds.

From the East Entrance Ranger Station, you can exit the park along Arizona Highway 64, which leads to Cameron.

From December 1 through the end of February, you may drive the West Rim Drive from Grand Canyon Village to Hermits Rest. During the rest of the year, this route is open to shuttle buses only.

The North Rim by Car

Point Imperial Drive

Take the 11-mile drive from the Visitor Center to Point Imperial, which, at 8,800 feet, is the highest point on either rim of the Canyon. From here you will have unparalleled views of Mt. Hayden, the Little Colorado River Gorge, Saddle Mountain, and Marble

Canyon. Picnic tables and restrooms are available at Point Imperial, but you need to bring your own food and water. Allow 20 minutes driving time each way.

From Point Imperial you can hike the 10-mile Ken Patrick Trail through the forest and along the North Rim to the North Kaibab parking area. Allow six hours one way.

Cape Royal Drive

This 23-mile drives takes you from the North Rim Visitor Center past Point Imperial, and south across the Walhalla Plateau. You can stop at Vista Encantada (picnic tables available), Roosevelt Point, and Cape Final on your way to Walhalla Overlook, where you'll find an interpretive trail. The drive all the way to the overlook takes about 45 minutes.

The Cape Final Trail

This two-mile plateau-top walk begins at the parking area to Cape Final and affords amazing views of the Canyon along the way. The round-trip takes about two hours.

Cliff Springs Trail

Just past the Walhalla Overlook is the Cliff Springs Trail, a one-mile walk down a ravine that begins directly across from a small pullout .3 miles from Cape Royal. About 100 yards down the trail you'll see a well-preserved Pueblo granary. The trail ends at a large boulder and the spring is on the cliff side of the boulder. Do not drink the water. Allow one hour for this walk.

Cape Royal Trail

The Cape Royal Trail is wheelchair accessible. The 0.6 mile trail is flat and offers views of Angels Window and the Colorado River. The interpretive trail begins at the southeast side of the Cape Royal parking area, where you will find picnic tables and restrooms. Allow about 30 minutes for this walk.

Widforss Trail

The Widforss Trail is a 10-mile (round-trip) walk offering forest and canyon views. The first half of this plateau-top trail takes you on a self-guided hike through spruce, aspen, and ponderosa pine forest. The second half will take you to Widforss Point above Haunted Canyon. The trail starts just west of the North Kaibab Trail parking area. Take the dirt road that is one quarter mile south of Cape Royal Road one mile to the Widforss Trail parking lot. Allow 6 hours for this hike.

Remember that there is no food or water available along the Cape Royal drive or at any of the trailheads, and even the shortest hike will require that you have water. Plan your hikes so you will not overexert yourself—it will take you twice as much time to get back to where you started as it took you to get wherever you are.

The South Rim by Shuttle Bus

Hermits Rest Route: The free shuttle buses run every 30 minutes from one hour before sunrise to 7:30 A.M. From 7:30 till sunset, they run every 10 to 15 minutes and after sunset they run every 30 minutes for another hour. The round-trip takes 90 minutes if you don't get off the bus. Bus service may be stopped during thunderstorms. Pets, except for service animals, are not allowed on the bus. The only place you will be able to get water is at the end of the 8-mile, one-way trip to Hermits Rest at the end of the road. A snack bar is open daily from 9 A.M. to 4 P.M.

The West Rim Drive shuttle stops at Trailview Overlook, Maricopa Point, Powell Point and Memorial, Hopi Point (restrooms available), Mohave Point, The Abyss, Pima Point, and Hermits Rest, where there are restrooms and water available. You may get off the shuttle at any stop and walk along the Rim Trail to another stop and get on another bus. West of Maricopa Point, the trail is unpaved.

Hermit Trail begins 500 feet west of Hermits Rest, a historic landmark and the westernmost point on the West Rim Drive. This is an unmaintained, steep trail recommended for experienced desert hikers only. The hike to Santa Maria Springs is 4.5 miles round-trip and descends 1,680 feet into the Canyon. The water here must be treated before you drink it. The round trip to Dripping Springs is 7 miles, and the trail descends to 1,700 feet below the rim. Here too, you must treat the water before drinking it. Narrow sections of this trail require extreme caution. The round trip to Santa Maria Springs will take five to eight hours. Allow another hour to get to and from Dripping Springs.

Village Loop: The Village Loop shuttle bus takes you (beginning at Canyon View Information Center) to Yavapai Rooms, Market Plaza, and Yavapai Lodge (parking lot A), Shrine of the Ages (parking lot B), Train Depot (which is the stop for El Tovar, Hopi House, and Verkamp's), Bright Angel Lodge (the stop for Lookout Studio and Kolb Studio), Hermits Rest Transfer, Maswik Lodge, Backcountry Information Center (parking lot E), Center Road (parking lots B and C), Village East (auto repair), Shrine of the Ages, Mather Campground, Trailer Village, Market Plaza (Yavapai Lodge), and back to Canyon View Information Center. Buses run every thirty minutes from one hour before sunrise to 6:30 A.M. and every ten to fifteen minutes from 6:30 A.M. until 10:30 P.M. (9 P.M. December through February).

Kaibab Trail Route: The Kaibab Trail (green) shuttle bus loop stops at Canyon View Information Plaza and stops at the South Kaibab Trailhead, Yaki Point, Mather Point, Yavapai Observation Center, and back to the information plaza. This is the only way to access Yaki Point and the South Kaibab trailhead. Buses run every thirty minutes from one hour before sunrise to one hour after sunset year round. Private vehicles are allowed on Yaki Point from December 1 through February.

Most shuttle buses are not wheelchair accessible. Accessible shuttles are available with 48 hours' notice, or you may get an accessibility permit at the Visitor Center to allow your private vehicle into shuttle-only areas.

The North Rim by Shuttle Bus

A hikers' shuttle to the North Kaibab trailhead leaves Grand Canyon Lodge at 5:30 A.M. and 7:45 A.M. daily. You must schedule the shuttle in advance, and you may purchase tickets at the Grand Canyon Lodge front desk.

Rim to rim shuttle bus service is available daily from Transcanyon Shuttle. The bus departs the North Rim at 7 A.M. and arrives at the South Rim at noon, leaving for the return trip at 1:30 P.M. arriving at 6:30 P.M. Call (520) 638–2820 or write Transcanyon Shuttle, P.O. Box 348, Grand Canyon, AZ 86023 for more information.

Hiking

Hiking the South Rim

There is a hiking experience for people of all ages and skill levels here at the Grand Canyon—from a few minutes' walk along the Rim Trail to an arduous journey into the depths of the Canyon.

The South Rim Trail runs from Hermits Rest west of Grand Canyon Village to Mather Point east of the village. You can access the trail from many points and walk along the rim for as long or short a distance as you wish. The path is paved between Maricopa Point west of the village to Yavapai Point on the east. Along the way, stop and visit the historic Mary Colter structure at Hermits Rest, have a look at Kolb Studio, stop for a cool drink at the El Tovar, shop at Hopi House, and rest at Yavapai Point while enjoying the spectacular scenery, which changes every moment. You'll even have time to enjoy part of the South Rim Trail if you've come on the Grand Canyon Railway from Williams and plan on spending only a few hours at the Canyon.

For longer hikes from the South Rim, you need to be prepared—carry water and food and wear sturdy shoes or boots and sunscreen. Remember that you will spend about one third of your time hiking down into the Canyon and about two thirds of your time getting back out.

From the rim, you cannot anticipate how hot it will become as you descend into the Canyon. The Park Service recommends that you hike during the cooler times of day, eat salty foods, drink one-half to one liter of water or sports drinks for every hour you are hiking, go slowly, rest often, and plan your hike before you go. They suggest that while hiking the Canyon you consume twice the number of calories as you usually would, starting with a large breakfast, followed by a full lunch and a snack every time you take a drink. The best times for hiking into the Canyon are spring and fall, though the most people do so in the summer.

The Grandview Trail

The Grandview Trail begins at Grandview Point east of Grand Canyon Village along Desert Rim Drive. This is a steep, unmaintained trail recommended for experienced desert hikers only. The round trip to Coconino Saddle is 1.5 miles with a 1,600 foot drop in elevation; allow two hours. It is 6 miles round-trip, with a 2,600-foot drop in elevation, to Horseshoe Mesa; the trip takes from four to eleven hours. There is a toilet and a designated campsite at Horseshoe Mesa, but there are no other facilities or services on this trail.

Hermit Trail

Hermit Trail begins 500 feet west of Hermits Rest, a historic landmark at the westernmost point on the West Rim Drive. You can get to Hermits Rest by walking along the South Rim Trail or by taking the free shuttle bus. Hermit Trail is an unmaintained, steep trail recommended only for experienced desert hikers. The hike to Santa Maria Springs is 5 miles round-trip and descends 1,680 feet into the Canyon. The water here must be treated before you drink it. The round-trip to Dripping Springs is 7 miles and the trail descends to 1,700 feet below the rim. Here too, you must treat the water before drinking it. Narrow sections of this trail require extreme caution. The round-trip to Santa Maria Springs will take five to eight hours. Allow another hour to get to Dripping Springs.

Bright Angel and South Kaibab Trails are Corridor Trails, and they are maintained and patrolled by the National Park Service.

Bright Angel Trail

Bright Angel Trail begins just west of Bright Angel Lodge, the westernmost motel on the rim. This steep trail is 9.4 miles to Bright Angel Campground and descends 4,360 feet into the Canyon. The trailhead is near the Kolb Studio in Grand Canyon Village. One and a half miles down you'll find the One-and-a-Half-Mile Resthouse, which provides restrooms and water from May through September. If this is your destination, the round-trip will take between two-and-a-half and four hours. A mile-and-a-half further on is Three-Mile Resthouse, where you will find water during the summer. At this point, you have descended over 2,000 feet into the Canyon; if you turn back now, the round-trip should take you four to six hours. At Indian Garden, about 4.5 miles from the rim, you will have descended over 3,000 feet. You will find restrooms and water here. The round-trip from the rim to Indian Garden and back takes six to nine hours. You may camp overnight at Indian Garden (a backcountry permit is required).

There is a hiking experience at Grand Canyon for people of all ages and skill levels. PHOTO: COURTESY OF THE PHOENIX CONVENTION AND VISITORS' BUREAU

The trail splits here and going to the left, you can continue on to Plateau Point, 6.1 miles from the rim. This stopping place has water from May through September. The round-trip takes eight to twelve hours. Inexperienced hikers should note that the trail to Plateau Point is not a maintained or patrolled trail.

If you go to the right, you will reach the River Resthouse 3 miles further on. The Silver Bridge across the Colorado River is another 1.2 miles. One half mile further, you'll find the entrance of Bright Angel Campground. The campground has water, restrooms, a ranger station, and picnic tables. Another half mile takes you to Phantom Ranch. All of the stopping places along this trail except Plateau Point have emergency phones.

During the hottest part of the summer, park rangers recommend that you end your day hike at Three-Mile Resthouse and begin your return to the rim, which will take you twice as long as your descent. If you go as far as Bright Angel Campground, park rangers recommend that you stay there for at least one night. Hiking to the river and back in one day is strongly discouraged.

To camp overnight in the Canyon, you will need a permit from the Backcountry Office (see Hiking in the Backcountry section). Overnight hikers may lodge and eat at Phantom Ranch; reservations are required well in advance. Call (303) 297-2757.

From Bright Angel Campground, you can return to the South Rim via the Bright Angel or South Kaibab Trail or continue back up the canyon on the North Kaibab Trail to the North Rim (see Hiking the North Rim). The Bright Angel Trail is the route taken by mule trains into the canyon. If you meet the mules on the trail, they have the right of way.

South Kaibab Trail

The very steep South Kaibab Trail begins near Yaki Point on Desert View Drive. The only access to the trailhead is via shuttle bus. The first 1.5 miles of this trail to Cedar Ridge is the most popular day hike from the South Rim, offering spectacular views of the main river gorge. The first stopping point on this trail, however, is Ooh Aah Point (we're not kidding!), about three quarters of a mile from the rim. There is no water here.

At Cedar Ridge you will have descended over 1,100 feet into the Canyon. There is a toilet, but no water. The round-trip from the rim to Cedar Ridge and back takes two-and-a-half to four hours.

Skeleton Point is 3 miles from the rim and 2,040 feet down. The round-trip will take six hours. There is no water here either. Tonto Trail Junction is another 1.4 miles; toilets are available here. From the junction you can take the Tonto Trail 4.1 miles to Indian Garden, where there is a campground. The Tonto Trail is not maintained or patrolled; it is recommended for experienced desert hikers only.

River Trail Junction is 6 miles from the rim and another 2 miles further on you can cross the Colorado River at Black Bridge and continue on to the entrance of Bright Angel Campground (about one-half mile from the bridge) or Phantom Ranch (0.9 miles from River Trail Junction).

Park rangers strongly recommend that you do not attempt to hike to the river and back up to the rim in one day. They recommend spending at least one night near the river. To camp overnight in the Canyon at Bright Angel Campground, you will need a permit from the Backcountry Office (see Hiking in the Backcountry section). Overnight hikers may lodge and eat at Phantom Ranch; reservations are required well in advance. Call (303) 297-2757.

Emergency phones on the South Kaibab Trail are available at Tonto Trail Junction, Bright Angel Campground, and Phantom Ranch.

Hiking the North Rim

The Transept Trail goes along the canyon rim from Grand Canyon Lodge to the North Rim Campground. The 3-mile round-trip takes about an hour and a half.

Bright Angel Point Trail is a 0.5-mile walk south from the Grand Canyon Lodge parking lot to Bright Angel Point where you will have an amazing view of the Canyon. The path is paved. Nature trail pamphlets are available for a self-guided walk. This short hike should take about thirty minutes round-trip.

The Ken Patrick Trail also begins at the North Kaibab Trail Parking Lot from which it meanders east through the forest to Imperial Point, ten miles away. The first 3 miles of the trail follows the Canyon rim. The hike will take six hours one way. One mile east of the trailhead the Uncle Jim Trail branches off to the south. This easy, 4-mile loop takes you through the forest to an outlook, Uncle Jim Point, over the North Kaibab Trail and should take about three hours. This trail is also used by mule trains, and the mules have the right of way.

The Widforss Trail is a 10-mile walk offering forest and canyon views. The first half of the trail takes you on a self-guided hike through spruce, aspen, and ponderosa pine forest. The second half will take you to Widforss Point above Haunted Canyon. The trail starts just west of the North Kaibab Trail parking area. Take the dirt road that is one quarter mile south of Cape Royal Road one mile to the Widforss Trail parking lot. Allow six hours for this hike.

Cape Royal Road will take you to several other trails to consider for day hiking. The Cape Final Trail is an easy 2-mile plateau-top walk (one way) from the parking area to Cape Final, with amazing views of the Canyon along the way. The round-trip takes about two hours.

Just past the Walhalla Overlook at the end of Cape Royal Drive is the Cliff Springs Trail, a 1-mile walk down a ravine that begins directly across from a small pullout 0.3 miles from Cape Royal. The trail ends at a large boulder and the spring is on the cliff side of the boulder. Do not drink the water. Allow one hour for this walk.

The Cape Royal Trail is wheelchair accessible. The 0.6-mile walk over an easy, flat trail offers views of Angels Window and the Colorado River. This interpretive trail begins at the southeast side of the Cape Royal parking area, where you will find picnic tables and restrooms. Allow about thirty minutes for this walk.

The North Kaibab Trail is the only North Rim Corridor Trail; it is maintained and patrolled by the National Park Service. The trailhead is on the North Entrance Road two miles north of Grand Canyon Lodge. You can take a short hike along this trail for spectacular canyon views. Coconino Overlook is a 1.5-mile round-trip and Supai Tunnel is 4 miles round-trip. There are restrooms and seasonal water at Supai Tunnel.

The most common day trip destination for North Rim hikers is Roaring Springs, a full-day, 9.4-mile, extremely arduous hike to a spot 3,050 feet below the rim. Drinking water is available at Roaring Springs from May through September. Park rangers recommend that you begin this hike before 7 A.M. and that you do not attempt a one-day round-trip hike to any point beyond Roaring Springs. If you want to continue, you can camp at Cottonwood Campground 6.9 miles from the rim (a backcountry permit is required), which is open only during the summer. Water is available at the campground.

Ribbon Falls is 8.4 miles from the rim at an elevation of 3,720 feet above sea level. Another 5.6 miles takes you to Phantom Ranch, one half mile north of Bright Angel Campground. The campground has water, restrooms, a Ranger station, and picnic tables. To camp overnight in the at Bright Angel, you will need a permit from the Backcountry Office (see Hiking in the Backcountry section). Hikers may also stay and eat at Phantom Ranch; reservations are required well in advance. Call (303) 297–2757.

On the North Kaibab Trail, emergency phones are available at Cottonwood Campground and Bright Angel Campground.

Hiking in the Backcountry

Backcountry trails are not maintained or patrolled. Trails include the South Bass, Grandview, Hermit, and Tanner Trails from the South Rim, the Thunder River, North Bass, and Nankoweap Trails from the North Rim and the Tonto Trail in the Canyon. Only experienced Grand Canyon hikers should attempt these trails.

You will need a backcountry permit for all overnight hiking, overnight horseback riding, overnight cross-country ski trips, off-river overnight hikes, and overnight camping in the backcountry, including camping at Cottonwood and Bright Angel Campgrounds. Permits are not required to stay at Phantom Ranch (but you do need reservations). Nor are permits required for day hikes. You should request your backcountry permit on the first of the month four months prior to your trip. A non-refundable (if you cancel your trip after your permit has been issued) fee of $20 per permit plus a $4 per person per night impact fee are charged. Payment by VISA or MasterCard is preferred.

You may obtain a Backcountry Permit Request Form at the Backcountry Office on the South Rim, on the Internet at www.thecanyon.com/nps, by faxing (520) 638-2125, or by writing Backcountry Office/GCNP. P.O. Box 129, Grand Canyon, AZ 86023. Telephone requests are not accepted. Once you have filled out your Permit Request Form, you may submit it, along with your itinerary and other required information in person at the Backcountry Office, by mail or by fax. All written requests are answered through the mail, never by fax. It will take at

> **Insiders' Tip**
>
> If you meet mules while hiking in the Grand Canyon, remember that they have the right of way.

least three weeks to process your request. If you arrive at the Canyon without a permit, you may be able to get one by applying in person at the Backcountry Office; expect to be put on a waiting list and to wait one to three days or longer before your permit is issued.

Backcountry Guides and Tours

Discovery Treks
8135 North Fran Drive,
Flagstaff, AZ 86003
(888) 256–8731
www.discoverytreks.com

For a Grand Canyon adventure, join Discovery Treks for a guided hike into the Grand Canyon. The company provides pick up from Flagstaff or Grand Canyon, transportation to and from the trailheads, tents, backpacks, sleeping bags, sleeping mats, food, and backcountry park permits. Choose from one of several hikes: Havasu Canyon, 20 miles round-trip, three to six days, starting at $645; Grandview Trail, 20 miles round-trip, one to seven days, starting at $125; South Bass Trail, 14 miles round-trip, three to eight days, starting at $645; Hermit Trail, 17 miles round-trip, one to seven days, from $125; Kanab Creek, 22 miles round-trip, five to ten days, starting at $1,045; Thunder River Trail, 24 miles round-trip, six to ten days, starting at $1,045; and Bright Angel Trail, 19 miles round-trip, one to seven days, starting at $125. Except for the Bright Angel Trail hike, which is

available year round, hiking treks are scheduled for spring through fall.

Grand Country Trail Guides
P.O. Box 87, Grand Canyon, AZ 86923
(520) 638–3194, (888) 283–3194
www.grandcanyontrailguides.com

Grand Canyon Trail Guides offers custom guided hikes into the backcountry of Grand Canyon National Park, as well as guided day hikes of the Grandview, Tanner, Hance, Bright Angel, Kaibab, and Hermit Trails. They also offer National Park Service permits, impact fees, food, trail munchies, electrolyte supplements, first-aid supplies, water treatment systems, toiletries, day packs, water bottles, and a backcountry kitchen. Children are welcome. For overnight hikes, plan to make your reservations four to six months in advance. For trips that include river rafting, plan to schedule two years ahead of time. This company is licensed to operate in the backcountry by the U.S. government, National Park Service, Department of the Interior.

Don't let heat ruin your trip!

Hiking the Grand Canyon during the summer months can be a wonderful adventure that you and the kids will always remember. But to prevent it from being an experience you don't want to recall, you need to be aware of some cautions. One of the most important of these is to remember that temperatures in the Grand Canyon can exceed 100 degrees, and fatigue, insufficient water and food, and excessively strenuous hiking can lead to life-threatening illnesses.

Heat exhaustion is caused by dehydration. Hikers can sweat out as much as two liters of water per hour. Symptoms of heat exhaustion are pale face, nausea, cool and moist skin, headache, and cramps. Treat heat exhaustion by drinking water, eating high-energy foods (grains, crackers, fruit, non-fat energy bars), resting, and cooling the body. Remember that there is little water and no food available along the Canyon's hiking trails. You must carry enough of both for everyone in your party.

Hyponatremia, or water intoxication, is caused by drinking too much water and losing too much sodium from the body through sweating. The symptoms of water intoxication include nausea, vomiting, altered mental states, and frequent urination. Treat this condition by eating salty foods. If the person seems drowsy, you need to find medical help immediately.

Heatstroke can be fatal—the body can no longer regulate its temperature. Symptoms of heatstroke are flushed face, dry skin, weak and rapid pulse, high body temperature, poor judgment or inability to cope, and unconsciousness. Cool the victim immediately by pouring water on his or her head and trunk, moving him or her into a shady area, fanning, and removing excess clothing. Send someone for help—the victim needs immediate hospitalization and will be airlifted out of the Canyon.

Hypothermia is not limited to just cold weather. It can occur as a result of exhaustion and exposure to cold, wet weather (as during a summer rain storm). The symptoms of hypothermia are uncontrolled shivering, poor muscle control, and a careless mood. To treat this condition, put dry, warm clothes on the victim, provide warm liquids to drink, warm the person by body contact with another person, and find shelter. To help prevent this condition, carry layers of clothing, eat frequently, drink before you feel thirsty and avoid wet weather if you can. You can get weather information at the Visitors Center or Backcountry Office or by calling (520) 638–7888.

Camping

Camping in the Canyon

Bright Angel Campground and Cottonwood Campground are designated camping areas within the canyon. A backcountry permit is required, and demand usually exceeds supply for overnight camping permits.

Camping on the South Rim

Mather Campground

To find this campground, located just southwest of Grand Canyon Village, take Center Road off Arizona Highway 64 and turn right on Market Plaza Road. This large, year-round campground operated by the National Park Service has 350 family sites and seven group sites. No hookups are available, but a dump station, laundry, showers, and restrooms are just north of the campground. Reservations are strongly recommended. For more information, call Biospherics at (800) 365-2267.

Desert View Campground

Desert View Campground is 25 miles east of Grand Canyon Village on Desert View Drive. The campground has fifty sites and is open during the summer (roughly May through October) on a first-come first-served basis. There are no hookups or dump stations here.

Trailer Village

Trailer Village, adjacent to Mather Campground, has eighty-four RV sites with hookups. This campground is open year-round. Register at the entrance to Trailer Village.

Grand Canyon Camper Village
P.O. Box 490, Grand Canyon, AZ 86023
(520) 638–2887

Grand Canyon Camper Village is a commercial campground seven miles south of Grand Canyon Village on Highway 64 in Tusayan. It offers full hookups, tent sites, teepee rentals, and coin-operated showers.

Ten-X Campground

This campground is operated by the Forest Service. It is two miles south of Tusayan in the Kaibab National Forest. Seventy sites are open on a first-come first-served basis from May through October.

Grand Canyon National Park
P.O. Box 129, Grand Canyon, AZ 86023
(800) 365-2267
www.thecanyon.com/nps.

Camping in Grand Canyon National Park is permitted only at designated campgrounds. For information on campgrounds within the park, contact Grand Canyon National Park Campgrounds. Call (520) 638-7888 for recorded park information or to receive a "Trip Planner."

Dispersed camping is permitted in the national forest outside the park. Call (520) 638-2443 for further information.

Camping on the North Rim

North Rim Campground

This campground, operated by the National Park Service, is located on the rim just above the Transept Trail north of Grand Canyon Lodge on Arizona Highway 67. There are no hookups, but a dump station is available and showers and a laundry are nearby. Camping here is limited to seven days per season and reservations for one of the eighty-two sites are strongly recommended. Call Biospherics at (800) 365-2267. You may check at the campground for last-minute cancellations. If the weather is good, the campground may stay open past October 15.

DeMotte Campground

You can find this U.S. Forest Service-operated campground 16 miles north of the North Rim. DeMotte has twenty-three sites (no hookups) and is open during the summer beginning June 1. Reservations are not accepted.

Jacob Lake Campground

Also operated by the U.S. Forest Service, this campground is just 45 miles north of the North Rim. Fifty-four sites are available, but there are no hookups and no reservations are accepted.

Kaibab National Forest

Dispersed camping is permitted in the Kaibab National Forest outside the park. For more information about dispersed camping or campgrounds run by the Forest Service, contact the North Rim Visitor Center or the Kaibab Plateau Visitor Center at Jacob Lake (520) 643-7298.

In the off-season, contact the North Kaibab Ranger District, Kaibab National Forest, P.O. Box 248, Fredonia, AZ 86022; (520) 643-7395.

Kaibab Camper Village at Jacob Lake

This commercial campground—located one quarter mile south of Jacob Lake on Arizona Highway 67—offers full hookups for sixty RV sites. The campground also has fifty tent sites. Call (520) 643-7804 during the summer from mid May through mid October. During the winter, call (520) 526-0924 or (800) 525-0924.

Grand Canyon National Park

Camping at Grand Canyon National Park is permitted only at designated campgrounds. For more information on campgrounds within the park, contact Grand Canyon National Park Campgrounds, P.O. Box 129, Grand Canyon, AZ 86023; (800) 365-2267; www.thecanyon.com.nps.

Camping Ethics

Whether you're camping in the national forests or below the rim in Grand Canyon, the phrase to keep in mind is "zero impact." By respecting the land and resources you use when camping, you help to preserve these natural wonderlands for your friends, your children, and your grandchildren.

Be well-prepared. Know the route and area in which you're planning to hike.
Good campsites are found, not made. Altering a campsite is prohibited.
Stay on the main trails; do not shortcut switchbacks.
Pack out what you bring in—this includes toilet paper and all trash.
Fires are prohibited below the rim. Do not burn toilet paper—pack it out.
Bury solid human waste at least 200' away from water in a shallow cathole 4-6" deep and 4-6" in diameter.
To wash yourself or your dishes, carry water 200' away from creeks and potholes. Scatter strained dish water.
Keep loud voices and noises to a minimum.
Leave what you find—this includes natural resources and cultural resources both.
To get more information about zero impact outdoor recreation, visit the Leave No Trace Website at www.lnt.org.

Tours

The South Rim by Motorcoach, Van, or Jeep

The Gray Line of Flagstaff
Nava-Hopi Tours, Inc.
114 West Route 66, P.O. Box 339,
Flagstaff, AZ 86002
(520) 774–5003, (877) 467–3329;
fax (520) 774–7715
www.navahopitours.com;
navahopi@aol.com

Depart Flagstaff at 8:30 A.M. and travel past Sunset Crater and on to the Navajo Reservation. The tour stops at the Cameron Trading Post (where there is a restaurant and snacks), then enters the Canyon at the East Gate, stopping at Desert View Overlook where you can climb the Watchtower. Driving along the East Rim, you'll pass rock features such as Duck-On-A-Rock, Brahma Temple, Zoroaster Temple, and Wotans Throne. Lunch (not included in the fare) is at Bright Angel Lodge in Grand Canyon Village, where you can shop at Hopi House. The tour leaves through the South Gate with a last stop at Mather Point. Stopping in Tusayan, you will have time to see *The Grand Canyon–Hidden Secrets* at the IMAX (not included in tour fare). The adult fare for this nine-hour tour is $42; children 5 to 15 pay $21; children under four sitting on a parent's lap tour free. The tour operates every day except Thanksgiving, Christmas, and New Year's Day. The Grand Canyon National Park entry fee is additional. Reservations may be made up until departure time. Transportation from your Flagstaff hotel or the Amtrak station is available with advanced reservations. Two- and three-night package tours are also available; two weeks' advance registration is required. Call for details.

American Dream Tours
P.O. Box 2822, Flagstaff, AZ 86003
(520) 527–3369, (800) 203–1212
www.infomagic.com/~amdream

This full-day tour of the East and South Rim of the Grand Canyon leaves Flagstaff at 9:15 A.M. and returns at 6 or 6:30 P.M. Pick up service from your hotel or RV park is available. Small, friendly groups and knowledgeable guides travel in 15-passenger club vans. The fare ($70 for adults, $40 for children under 10) includes round-trip transportation, a picnic at the Canyon under the pines (in good weather), drinks, snacks, and a champagne toast. IMAX tickets available at a discount. Tours are given in English and German.

Blue Feather Tours
P.O. Box 3474, Sedona, AZ 86340
(520) 284–3343, (877) 733–6621
www.azgrandcanyontours.com;
aztran@sedona.net

This tour begins with your being picked up at your Sedona resort or hotel. You'll travel up through Oak Creek Canyon to Route 66 in Flagstaff. The tour stops at many viewpoints at the Canyon, and you'll have time for a walk along the rim or a short hike down into the Canyon. Lunch and a stop at the IMAX theater in Tusayan (both included in tour price) will complete your tour. The adult fare is $92 plus the Grand Canyon entrance fee; children 12 and under pay $68 and kids do not pay the entrance fee at the Canyon. The company also offers a two-day excursion including the Hopi mesas and the Grand Canyon. Call for rates and details.

Grand Canyon Jeep Tours & Safaris
P.O. Box 1772, Grand Canyon, AZ 86023
(520) 638–5337, (800) 320–5337;
fax (520) 638–8245
www.grandcanyonjeeptours.com

Experience the back roads of the Grand Canyon National Park and the Kaibab National Forest in an open-air, four-wheel drive safari vehicle with a guide who knows the geology, history, wildlife, and Native American tribes of the region. The Grand Sunset Tour, about three hours, departs two hours before sunset and takes you through the Kaibab National Forest to overlooks of the Painted Desert, the San Francisco Peaks, and finally, the Grand Canyon. Adults pay $53 and children under 12 pay $40. The Canyon Pines Tour follows an 1880s stagecoach trail through the forest to the edge of the Grand Canyon. The two-hour tour, which departs at noon, is $48 for adults and $35 for children. The hour-and-a-half Indian Cave Paintings Tour takes you to a petroglyph site in the forest. The trip departs in the morning and in the afternoon and is $35 for adults and $25 for children. The Deluxe Combo Tour includes the Grand Sunset Tour or the Canyon Pines Tour with the Indian Cave Paintings Tour. The Sunset Combo departs three-and-a-half hours before sunset; the price is $83 for adults and $65 for children. The Canyon Pines Deluxe Tour departs at 10:30 A.M. and takes about three-and-a-half hours; adults pay $78 and children $60. There is a two-adult minimum for these tours. Last-minute reservations are honored, depending on availability.

The Grand Canyon by Air

Most of the air tour companies at Grand Canyon follow routes specified by the National Park Service and the FAA. Exceptions are Papillon Air Tours, which is authorized by the Havasupai Tribe to fly helicopters into Supai Village, in addition to flying the two routes that the other companies offer, and AirStar Helicopters, which offers a 40- to 45-minute flight.

The 45- to 50-minute air tour begins at the airport, flies over the East Rim of the Canyon to the confluence of the Little Colorado and Colorado Rivers, turns north and flies over Nankoweap Mesa and Point Imperial, and then turns west to fly over the eastern portion of the North Rim as far as Dragon Head. The flight then turns south and flies back over the Canyon to return to the airport.

The 25- to 30-minute tour leaves the airport and flies west to Hermits Rest on the South Rim. The tour then turns north, flying over the Canyon to Dragon Head where it makes a U-turn and flies back over the Canyon to return to the airport.

All of the companies listed below are at the Grand Canyon National Park Airport on Arizona Highway 64, just south of Tusayan (P.O. Box 3188, Grand Canyon, AZ 86023, (520) 638-2446). Reservations may be made through your hotel or at the air tour company's building. During the winter, it is better to schedule your air tour in advance, as each company requires a minimum number of passengers for each flight. During the summer, you can just walk in and probably find that a tour will be ready to leave fairly soon.

The National Park Service, the FAA, and the air tour operators at Grand Canyon are currently in negotiations to revise these air routes in order to reduce noise pollution over the Canyon. The argument pits environmentalists and hikers, who want to restore a natural quiet to the Canyon, against the air tour companies who maintain that noise pollution is not a problem and that for many people—especially the elderly, young children, and people unaccustomed to the 7,000 altitude at the South Rim—this is the only way to see the Canyon from anywhere but the rim. When these negotiations will be complete, and when the court challenges by the operators will be exhausted, is not known, so it is imperative that you check with the air tour company about routes and prices prior to booking your flight over the Canyon.

Flights operate between 8 A.M. and 6 P.M. in the summer and 9 A.M. and 5 P.M. in the winter. Flights may be cancelled or routes changed without notice due to weather or other safety concerns.

Kenai Helicopter, Inc.
P.O. Box 1429, Grand Canyon, AZ 86023
(520) 638–2764, (800) 541–4537;
fax (520) 638–9588
www.flykenai.com; info@flykenai.com

Kenai Helicopters is smaller than some of the other air tour companies and therefore their operators have more time to talk to people. They charge $99 for the shorter flight, and $155 for the longer, with $10 off for children. A minimum of three passengers is needed for each tour. Credit cards and traveler's checks are accepted. In-flight multi-lingual narration is available.

Grand Canyon Airlines
P.O. Box 3038, Grand Canyon, AZ 86023
(520) 638–2407, (800) 528–2413;
fax (520) 638–9461
www.grandcanyonairlines.com

This company flies 19-passenger twin-engine Vistaliners, with quiet, climate-controlled cabins and all forward-facing seats. The minimum number of passengers per flight is six. They charge $75 for the longer tour. Children ages 2 to 12 are charged $45. French, Dutch, Italian, Spanish, and Japanese narration are available. Reservations are recommended but not required.

AirStar Helicopters
P.O. Box 3379, Grand Canyon, AZ 86023
(520) 638–2622, (800) 962–3869;
fax (520) 638–2607
www.airstar.com

Flying the Aerospatiale 350B Astar, AirStar Helicopters offers a smooth, quiet, air-conditioned ride, with all passengers in forward-facing seats. This is the smallest of the air tour companies at the Canyon, and it is owner-operated. Narration is offered in seven languages, and customers receive a free souvenir photograph of their party boarding the aircraft. The 25- to 30-minute tour is $94; the 50- to 55-minute flight is $161; and the 40- to 45-minute tour is $141. A minimum of six passengers per flight is required. This company also offers a 50-minute flight in a Cessna 207 Turbo Air-

craft. Window seats are guaranteed. The prices are $71 for adults and $51 for children 14 and under.

Air Grand Canyon
P.O. Box 3399, Grand Canyon, AZ 86023
(520) 638–2686, (800) 247–4726
www.airgrandcanyon.com

Air Grand Canyon flies high wing Cessna 207s, which hold six or seven passengers who all sit facing forward; the pilot provides live narration. This company's 30- to 40-minute flight takes you along the east side of the South Rim, past the confluence of the Little Colorado and Colorado Rivers and back to the airport along the same route. The cost is $74 for adults and $44 for children. The 50- to 60-minute tour is the same as other airlines' longer flight; the price is $89 for adults and $49 for children. A longer flight, 90 to 100 minutes, includes the same route as the 50- to 60-minute tour, but extends your flight northward along Marble Canyon all the way to Lake Powell. The cost is $174 for adults and $94 for children. You might also be interested in a combination air tour and river rafting experience. You'll fly to Lake Powell, land in Page, and take a river-rafting trip down the Colorado to Lee's Ferry. From there, ground transport will take you to the Cameron Trading Post and back to the airport. This tour leaves the airport at 8:30 a.m. and returns at 4:30 P.M. The cost is $260 for adults and $240 for children under 13; lunch is included.

Papillon Grand Canyon Helicopters
P.O. Box 455, Grand Canyon, AZ 86023
(520) 638–2419, (800) 528–2418;
fax (520) 638–0349
www.papillon.com

Papillon operates a fleet of Bell jet-powered helicopters from its own heliport at the Grand Canyon National Airport. The largest air tour company, Papillon serves 800 to 1,200 people during the summer; reservations are definitely recommended. The 25- to 30-minute North Canyon Tour is $99 for adults and $80 for children. The 40- to 50-minute Imperial Tour is $159 for adults and $123 for children. Papillon is the only commercial air tour company authorized to fly into Supai Village on the Havasupai Reservation. They offer a Havasupai Daytime Excursion, with round-trip airfare with tour, landing and entrance fees at Supai Village, and a guided horseback tour to Havasu Falls. The cost is $440. There is no children's rate on this tour, and meals are not included. A Havasupai Overnight Excursion includes everything the daytime excursion does, with the addition of a night's stay at Havasupai Lodge in Supai Village. The cost is $482, with no children's rate and no meals included. Papillon also offers air tours over the Canyon from Las Vegas. Write 245 E. Tropicana Avenue, Suite 121, Las Vegas, NV 89109, or contact (702) 736–7243, (888) 635–7272, or www.papillon.com for further information.

The Grand Canyon by River Raft

Arizona River Runners
P.O. Box 47788, Phoenix, AZ 85068
(602) 867–4866, (800) 477–7238;
fax (602) 867–2174
www.raftarizona.com

Arizona River Runners offers adventures on the Colorado from three-day excursions to two-week odysseys. Everything is included in the cost of the trip—river equipment, meals, sodas, transportation, sleeping gear, tent, portable toilet facilities, eating utensils, waterproof bags and containers, life vests, and expert guides; you just bring your personal items, a camera, and a yen for adventure. Six- and seven-day motor trips cover 190 miles in the heart of the Grand Canyon from Lee's Ferry to Whitmore Wash. From Marble Canyon, the fare for the six-day raft trip is $1,605; add $160 if you want to leave from and return to Las Vegas by air. The eight-day Grand Canyon Adventure travels the full 280-mile length of the Canyon, starting at Lee's Ferry and ending at Lake Mead. The fare is $1,625; add $55 for round-trip bus transportation to and from Las Vegas. The three-day escape starts in Las Vegas and includes a scenic airplane flight, a day at the Bar Ten Ranch (including horseback riding), a helicopter ride to the Canyon floor, 100 miles of adventure on the river, a jet boat ride to Pearce Ferry, and your optional return by motorcoach to Las Vegas. The cost is $725 with an additional $20 for transportation back to Las Vegas. If you're ready for an oar powered adventure, try the 13-day journey 225 miles from Lee's Ferry to Diamond Creek with ground transportation to Peach Springs. You'll have plenty of time for exploring side canyons on this trip. The fare is $2,335, with an additional $75 for optional bus transportation to and from Las Vegas. A nine-day oar powered trip starts with a hike from the South Rim to Phantom Ranch where you'll board your craft and travel 138 miles to Diamond Creek. You can opt for ground transportation back to Las Vegas, or end your trip at Peach Springs. The fare is $1,690 plus an additional $35 to get back to Las Vegas. The five-day oar trip begins at Lee's Ferry and ends at Phantom Ranch, where you will hike out of the Canyon. The fare is $930; add $40 for ground transportation from Las Vegas the first day. The hike into and out of the Canyon is a strenuous 9.5 miles, so you need to be in good shape if you choose either of the last two trips. People with sensory or mobility impairments are encouraged to contact the office to make arrangements for their trip.

Arizona Raft Adventures
4050 E. Huntington Drive,
Flagstaff, AZ 86004
(520) 526–8200, (800) 786–7238;
fax (520) 526–8246
www.azraft.com

Explore the Colorado on a motorized, oar and paddle (hybrid), or all-paddle river raft.

People say running the whitewater rapids on the Colorado River is a life-changing experience. Give it a try—and let us know! PHOTO: ARIZONA RIVER RUNNERS

Trips range from six to fifteen days. The company supplies meals, two waterproof bags, a life vest, a sleeping unit (sleeping bag, pad, and ground cloth), and eating utensils. You bring your clothes, camera, and extra beverages (if you wish). On motor trips, the minimum age is 10 and the maximum number of guests is 15; on hybrid trips, guests must be at least 12 years old, and the maximum number is 15; and on all-paddle rafts, the minimum age is 16 and the maximum group size is 18. Arizona Raft Adventures will make every effort to accommodate people with disabilities and those who require special diets; contact the company with your specifics. A six-day motorized river trip runs $1,350 and a fifteen-day trip is $2,750.

Rivers & Oceans
12620 N. Campbell Lane,
Flagstaff, AZ 86004
(520) 526–4575, (800) 473–4576;
fax (520) 526–8268
www.rivers-oceans.com;
whitney@infomagic.com

This travel company can arrange white water rafting trips on the Colorado River with several outfitters. All outfitters provide meals, boats, life jackets, and group kitchen gear, and most also provide waterproof bags for your personal stuff and sleeping gear. The minimum age for motorized tours is usually 8 and for oar-powered trips 12. No one is too old, assuming they are in general good health. Special dietary requirements can be accommodated. You may decide to explore the river in a 35-foot pontoon raft powered by an outboard motor (accommodates 12 to 18 passengers); an oar-powered 18-foot raft for 4 to 8 passengers; an 18-foot raft paddled by a team of 6 participants, or an 18-foot wooden boat rowed by your guide (4 to 5 passengers). Full-length trips are available from Lee's Ferry to Lake Mead, from Lee's Ferry to Diamond Creek, and from Lee's Ferry to Whitmore Wash. Oar, paddle, and dory trips range from eleven to nineteen days and prices start at $1,950. Motorized trips are six to eight days and start at $1,350. Partial trips are also available. These allow you to see the upper or lower section of the Colorado and they require a 9-mile hike into or out of the Canyon. The

Upper Canyon trip is 88 miles from Lee's Ferry to Phantom Ranch. Beautiful side canyons, Indian ruins, and some of the largest rapids on the river will make this trip unforgettable. Five- to seven-day oar, paddle, and dory trips start at $1,000. Four-day motorized trips begin at $650. The Lower Canyon trips begin at Phantom Ranch and go to Whitmore Wash, Diamond Creek, or Lake Mead (100, 137, and 190 miles respectively). After hiking into the Canyon, you begin this trip by running huge white-water rapids. Hiking opportunities, side streams, and waterfalls will add to your adventure. Oar, paddle, and dory trips (seven to nine days) start at $1,350. Motorized trips (three to four days) start at $650. A deposit is required to confirm your reservation, and cancellation penalties are charged. June, July, and August are the most popular months. Spring and fall are less busy (and cooler). Plan to make your reservations as far in advance as you can.

Grand Canyon Expeditions Company
P.O. Box O, Kanab, UT 94741
(435) 644–2691, (800) 544–2691;
fax (435) 644–2699   www.gcec.com

Eight-day motorized trips from Lee's Ferry to Lake Mead on a self-bailing, 37-foot specially-designed raft cover 280 miles of rapids and exploration. The company provides transportation to and from Las Vegas, professional guides, all camping equipment, waterproof river bags, deluxe meals, non-alcoholic beverages, and portable toilet facilities. The price is $1,933. Eight-day special interest expeditions cover the same territory but focus on ecology, history, photography, archeology, or geology. Private charter trips for 1 to 28 people may also be arranged. Dory trips offer a leisurely paced journey aboard a five-passenger, 18-foot hard-hulled wooden boat with lots of time for exploring. The 14-day trip takes you from Lee's Ferry to Lake Mead, and the price is $2,705. This company suggests a minimum age of 8, and they will try to accommodate special diets.

Moki Mac River Expeditions, Inc.
P.O. Box 71242, Salt Lake City, UT 84171
(801) 268–6667, (800) 284–7280;
fax (801) 262–0935   www.mokimac.com,
mokimac@mokimac.com

"You have to experience it," says the Quist family, owners of Moki Mac, about rafting the Grand Canyon. Moki Mac offers the opportunity to float the entire length of the Canyon. The company provides food, eating utensils, waterproof bags, meals, and sanitation facilities; you bring a sleeping bag, tent, toiletries, and clothes. Special dietary needs can be accommodated, and "differently abled" folks are encouraged to contact the office for pre-trip planning. Grand Canyon trips are suggested for people over 12. Moki Mac offers a 280-mile, eight-day motorized trip for $1,785 and a 14-day rowing trip for $2,615. The six-day rowing trip is $1,325, and the nine-day rowing trip is $1,775. The six-day trip travels the upper canyon from Lee's Ferry to Phantom Ranch. The nine-day trip covers the river from Phantom Ranch to Pearce Ferry. Motorized 33- and 37-foot rafts carry up to 12 guests, and 18-foot rafts (rowed by your guides) carry up to 5 passengers. Optional pre- and post-trip transportation and accommodation packages are available for an extra fee. A deposit is required to make your reservation. Moki Mac also offers rafting trips on the Green River through

Desolation Canyon and Gray Canyon (where a one-day trip is available). Their Cataract Canyon trip takes you from Mineral Canyon to Hite Marina on Lake Powell, and you might opt for a six-day canoe combo trip during which you get to paddle a 17-foot, two-person canoe down the Green River to the confluence with the Colorado. The Westwater Canyon trips are one or two days on a 17-mile stretch of the Colorado.

Colorado River & Trail Expeditions
P.O. Box 57575, Salt Lake City, UT 84157
(801) 261–1789, (800) 253–7238;
fax (801) 268–1193
www.crateinc.com, crate@crateinc.com

Dutch-oven dinners, salad bar lunches, and hearty breakfasts will keep you going on these exciting river trips through the Grand Canyon on a motorized 22-, 33- or 37-foot pontoon raft propelled by a 30-HP outboard motor or an 18-foot, oar-powered rowing rig. The company provides you with a sleeping bag, foam pad, ground cloth, waterproof bags, waterproof camera bag, meals, plates, cups and utensils, life preserver, and round-trip transportation from the designated meeting place. The minimum age for Grand Canyon trips is 12. The company is happy to accommodate special needs. The full-canyon, eight- or nine-day motorized trip travels 280 miles from Lee's Ferry to Lake Mead and costs $1,850. A nine-day natural history trip 280 miles from Lee's Ferry to Pearce Ferry is also $1,850 and focuses on the geology, biology, prehistory, and ecology of the Colorado River in Grand Canyon. You can row and paddle eleven days and 190 miles from Lee's Ferry to Whitmore Wash in an 18-foot rowing rig supplemented by an eight-person paddle raft for $2,550. The upper canyon four-day motor trip from Lee's Ferry to Phantom Ranch is $895. A five-day rowing and paddling trip following the same route is $1,095. The lower canyon six-day motor trip from Phantom Ranch to Lake Mead is $1,295 and the seven-day rowing and paddle trip 100 miles from Phantom Ranch to

Whitmore Wash is $1,795. All of these trip prices include a $25 to $100 fee for optional pre- or post-trip transportation. A 10% youth discount is offered on all but the lower Grand Canyon trips. Pre-season (April) rafting and hiking trips that emphasize river hiking and exploration start at $850 for the five-day upper canyon trip; an eleven-day and a seven-day trip are also offered. Colorado River & Trail Expeditions also offers rafting trips on the Green River (Gray Canyon, Desolation Canyon) and other trips on the Colorado. The truly intrepid adventurer can consider the Tatshenshini-Alsek River Trip in Alaska or the twenty-one-day Everest walking tour in Nepal.

Canyoneers, Inc.
P.O. Box 2997, Flagstaff, AZ 86003
(520) 526–0924, (800) 525–0924;
fax (520) 527–9398
www.canyoneers.com;
answers@canyoneers.com

From a thirteen-day full river run in a row boat to a three-day introduction to the wonders of the Colorado River, Canyoneers offers a variety of trips to meet anyone's needs and schedule. While the recommended minimum age is 10, Canyoneers has taken passengers from ages 6 to 84 on their trips. The company provides the meals, rain shelters, inflatable sleeping pads, and life vests; you may bring your own or rent a bedroll (on seven- and thirteen-day trips), which includes a sleeping bag and ground cover. On three- and five-day trips, the boat will carry your bedroll so you do not have to hike into the Canyon with it. The "All the Grand" trip is seven days and 280 miles from Lee's Ferry to Pearce Ferry. The $1,600 (peak season) fare covers pre- and post-trip transportation to Flagstaff. "Best of the Grand" is a five-day, 193-mile trip from Bright Angel Beach to Pearce Ferry aboard a powered pontoon boat. The fare is $1,200, which includes one night's lodging at Grand Canyon and a guided nine-mile hike to Bright Angel Beach to begin your trip. "Best of the Grand with Phantom Ranch," at $1,325, is the same as the "Best of the Grand," except that you hike on your own down to Phantom Ranch (9.5 miles with a 5,000-foot change in elevation) and stay at Phantom Ranch the night before you begin your river trip. Travelers who want to spend less time on the river may opt for the "Upper Grand"—two days and two nights on the river from Lee's Ferry to Bright Angel Beach (87 miles) on a powered pontoon boat and a one-day hike out of the Canyon. The fare for this trip is $650. Finally, the "Upper Grand with Phantom Ranch" trip ($770) is two days and two nights on the river on a powered pontoon boat from Lee's Ferry to Bright Angel Beach (87 miles), and one day and night at Phantom Ranch at the end of your trip before you hike out of the Canyon.

Diamond River Adventures
916 Vista, P.O. Box 1300, Page, AZ 86040
(520) 645–8866, (800) 343–3121;
fax (520) 645–9536
www.diamondriver.com;
info@diamondriver.com

A women-owned and -operated enterprise, Diamond River Adventures offers four to thirteen-day motorized and oar trips with guides who have more than 5,000 river miles before they graduate from the company's training program. The company provides life vests, a waterproof tarp, tent, sanitized sleeping bags, mattress pad, eating utensils, and a watertight metal box for cameras and other personal items. Three meals, snacks, and non-alcoholic drinks are included in the price. Physically challenged adventurers are welcome; call for details. On oar-powered trips, the minimum age is 8; on motorized tours, the minimum age is 12. Full-length trips leave Lee's Ferry and travel 226 river miles to Diamond Creek. The eight-day motorized trip runs $1,812, while the twelve-day oar trip is $2,397 and the thirteen-day oar trip $2,507. Rafting on the Upper Colorado takes you from Lee's Ferry to Phantom Ranch (87.5 miles), where you will begin your 9.5-mile hike or mule ride out of the

Canyon. The four-day motorized trip is $780 and the five-day oar trip is $1,140; the six-day oar trip is $1,255. The Lower Colorado River trip is 138.5 miles from Phantom Ranch to Diamond Creek. You hike or ride a mule into the Canyon to Phantom Ranch (9.5 miles) in time for lunch, then board your boat to begin your trip. The five-day motorized trip is $1,137 and the eight-day oar trip is $1,847. Mules for packing gear in or out must be arranged separately. Call Grand Canyon Lodges at (303) 297–2757 or fax (303) 297–3175. A deposit is required to schedule your trip and the company will book by phone with your credit card number.

Wilderness River Adventures
50 South Lake Powell Blvd.
P.O. Box 717, Page, AZ 86040
(520) 645–3279, (800) 528–6154
www.riveradventures.com

Not up to white-water rapids? These float trips from Page to Lee's Ferry cover 15 miles of calm river waters in a motorized raft. Sit back and enjoy the spectacular canyon walls, and keep your eyes open— you may be lucky enough to spot one of the California condors recently reintroduced in the Colorado River area. After your river trip, you'll travel by motorcoach back to Page. Full-day trips (which include a riverside picnic lunch of sandwiches, cookies, and beverages) are $75 for adults and $45 for children. Half-day trips (early morning or early afternoon) are $53 for adults and $45 for children. Prior to this year, float trips have been scheduled from March through October. This year, Wilderness River Adventures is experimenting with offering these trips year-round.

This outfitter also offers oar trips in the Canyon. From Lee's Ferry to Bar Ten Ranch (Whitmore Wash), the eight-day motorized trip on a 15-foot x 37-foot boat powered by a 25 HP motor is $2,094; the seven-day trip is $1,845. The minimum age for these trips is eight. The twelve-day oar trip in an 18-foot, traditionally designed rowing rig, is $2,655 and the fourteen-day trip is $2,873. The minimum age for oar trips is 12. A five-and-a half day oar trip from Lee's Ferry to Phantom Ranch (86 miles) is $1,391 and the Hiker Special, a six-and-a-half day oar trip from Phantom Ranch to Bar Ten Ranch is $2,133. The trips to and from Phantom Ranch require a 9.5-mile hike into or out of the Canyon. All the other trips include a charter flight at the end of the trip to Las Vegas or Page. The Hiker Special Lower Canyon trip from Phantom Ranch to Bar Ten Ranch is 102 miles and begins with a hike into the Canyon. The cost is $850 for the three-and-a-half-day motorized trip. A four-and-a-half day motorized trip from Phantom Ranch to Bar Ten Ranch (102 miles) also begins after you hike 9.5 miles into the Canyon. The price of $1,603 includes a charter flight to Las Vegas or the South Rim at the end of your trip. The

Insiders' Tip

The Grand Canyon is beautiful, but you don't want to fall into it. Several people do each year. Do not go beyond the guardrails, and be particularly careful where there are no barriers.

three-and-a-half day motorized trip from Lee's Ferry to Phantom Ranch is 86 miles and costs $850. Wilderness trip prices include meals, a waterproof bag, sleeping bag, foam pad and ground tarp, waterproof container for camera, a Colorado River guidebook, and life jacket. People with special needs are encouraged to contact the company so that appropriate arrangements can be made.

The Grand Canyon by Mule or Horse

The best way to see the Canyon, in our opinion, is aboard some animal that will do the walking for you.

Grand Canyon Lodges
P.O. Box 699, Grand Canyon, AZ 86023
(303) 297–2757
www.grandcanyonlodges.com

Mule trips into the Canyon from the South Rim can be arranged through Amfac, which manages in-park lodging and activities. For reservations, which you usually need to make well in advance (up to 23 months in advance is possible), contact Amfac at (303) 297–2757, or write Amfac Parks and Resorts, 14001 East Iliff, Suite 600, Aurora Colorado 80014, or visit the website at www.grandcanyonlodges.com. For same-day reservations, which may be available due to cancellations, call (520) 638–2631. Riders must be at least four feet, seven inches tall and weigh less than 200 pounds. Overnight accommodations are available at Phantom Ranch, about a mile past the river crossing in the bottom of the Canyon. Rates include a cabin, meals, and the mule. The cost is about $300 for one person, $500 for two people, and $230 for

each additional person. Children pay the same rate as adults here.

Apache Stables
P.O. Box 158, Grand Canyon, AZ 86023
(520) 638–2891/2424
www.apachestables.com

Guided horse and muleback tours along the South Rim depart from Moqui Lodge during the summer months. One- and two-hour trail rides stroll through the pines of the Kaibab National Forest. Prices are about $30 and $55 respectively. The East Rim Ride goes through Long Jim Canyon to a Grand Canyon viewpoint on the East Rim. This $100, four-hour ride is physically demanding and not recommended for everyone. A one-hour evening trail ride ($40) joins a horse-drawn wagon ride at a campfire in the forest where you can roast the hot dogs and marshmallows you have brought along. The wagon ride is $12.50, with special rate for children under 5.

Waitress Tanya Reed awaits diners in the formal El Tovar dining room overlooking the canyon.

Restaurants

El Tovar Dining Room at El Tovar Hotel
$$$ • P.O. Box 699,
Grand Canyon, AZ 86023
(520) 638–2631; fax (520) 638–2154

This is dining at its finest! The formal dining room is adorned with murals by Hopi artist Bruce Timeche. Created in the early 1960s, and just recently restored, the four oil paint murals depict activities of the Hopi, Apache, Mohave, and Navajo Tribes. The Hopi painting is "Praying to Hahay'imana, Mother of all Kachinas" and shows a central figure asking Hahay'imana for a good harvest. The Katsina on the left will carry the message to the gods. The boy holds a melon, representing good crops, and a water jug holds water to bless the people. In the Apache painting, "Sun Rise Dance," two young girls will dance all night as part of their puberty ceremony. The painting also shows four mountain spirit dancers on the right and on the left a drummer and a singer. "Bird Dance or Harvest Dance" is the Mohave picture. Here a bird dancer and singer are on the right, with two girls on the left giving thanks for the harvest, and birds clean the fields. The Navajo painting, "Feather Dance," shows a Navajo Yeh-bits-hi as an old man in a mask. A singer occupies the center of the picture and the two kneeling figures are making an offering while a spectator on the left looks on. The spectacular murals are equaled by the food here. For lunch, how about Prickly Pear Grilled Chicken Breast, Smoked Corn Chowder with Asiago Cheese, or Roasted Tortellini Primavera in a Roasted Garlic Tomato Sauce? Ready for dinner? Start perhaps with an appetizer of Grilled Garlic Bruschetta with Black Bean Purée and Charbroiled Corn Salsa. You may choose among several dinner entrées, including Flame-Broiled Peppercorn Crusted Ribeye Steak with Blue Cheese Butter or Pan-Seared Salmon Tostada with Organic Greens. For dessert, you'll have trouble choosing among the offerings, which include Gingered Crème Brulée and a Semi-Sweet Chocolate Mousse served in a Chocolate Taco. Service is friendly and professional without being overbearing; a full bar and a wine list are available. Reservations are not taken for breakfast or lunch, but are required for dinner. Call (520) 638–2526, ext. 6431.

The Coronado Room
Best Western Grand Canyon Squire Inn
$$$ • P.O. Box 130,
Grand Canyon, AZ 86023
(520) 638–2681, (800) 622–6966;
fax (520) 638–2782
gbryan@grandcanyonsquire.com

The Coronado Room offers excellent food in this somewhat formal dining room (casual clothes are fine). Serving appetizers such as oysters on the half shell, escargot, and boursin cheese, and entrees including steak, prime rib, game hen, elk, and lobster thermidor, this restaurant also has house specialties including chicken marsala and veal picata. Or you can select from several Mexican entrees. A full bar and extensive wine list will add to your leisurely dinner enjoyment.

Canyon Star
$$$ • P.O. Box 3319,
Grand Canyon, AZ 86023
(520) 638–3333; fax (520) 638–3131
www.gcanyon.com,
thegrand@gcanyon.com

Located in the Grand Hotel, Canyon Star, with its rustic Western décor, including wall paintings by James King Woolenshirt, and long wooden tables for large groups, serves Southwestern cuisine and barbecue ribs and steaks. The adjacent saloon-style room where lunch is served has a full bar. A lunch buffet is available until 2 P.M. during the winter; in the summer months, the restaurant also serves a breakfast and a dinner buffet. Reservations are not required; major credit cards and traveler's checks are accepted. Open seven days a week, the restaurant offers free nightly entertainment with cowboy singers and Native American dancers.

Accommodations

South Rim

Accommodations at the South Rim fall into two categories—those within the park itself, which are run by Amfac, and those in Tusayan (seven miles south of the park entrance) or in Valle (25 miles south). All accommodations within the park are reserved by calling Amfac at (303) 297–2757 or writing Amfac Parks & Resorts, 14001 East Iliff, Ste. 600, Aurora, CO 80014; the local number for Amfac is (520) 638–2631; the website is www.grandcanyonlodges.com. Accommodations outside the park can be reserved by calling the individual hotels.

In-Park Accommodations

All in-park South Rim motel rooms have phones and televisions. Motels offer smoking and non-smoking rooms and some wheelchair-accessible rooms. No pets are allowed, but there is a kennel on the South Rim, (520) 638–0534. Children under 16 are admitted free. These accommodations accept major credit cards and traveler's checks, but no personal checks. Room rates given below do not include taxes. During the season, these rooms fill up quickly, so call well in advance for your reservations.

The El Tovar

The oldest hotel in the park, the El Tovar is located right in the center of Grand Canyon Village on the South Rim. Opened in 1905 to accommodate the influx of tourists at the Canyon resulting from the opening of a rail line from Williams to the South Rim, the El Tovar was designed in the alpine style and built at the exorbitant cost of a quarter million dollars. The 78-room hotel has been updated several times. The rooms are small and decorated in a rustic Western style. Room rates range from about $115

Call Bright Angel Lodge to reserve a rustic cabin just feet from the rim. PHOTO: TANYA LEE

to $130 per night. This is where the rich and famous stay, including presidents. President Clinton stayed here in January 2000 when he came to the Canyon to announce the formation of Parashant National Monument. There is a gift shop in the lobby, a lounge, and a very good restaurant (see listing under Restaurants).

Yavapai Lodge

Yavapai Lodge has 358 rooms and a cafeteria serving breakfast, lunch, and dinner. Room rates range from $88 to $102. The cafeteria is closed from January 2 to February 16.

Maswik Lodge

Maswik Lodge offers 250 rooms, ranging in price from $73 to $118. A cafeteria here is open for breakfast, lunch, and dinner. A sports lounge is open daily from 5 p.m. to midnight.

Kachina Lodge

Kachina Lodge offers Canyon-side rooms for $124, with other rooms going for about $10 less. The facility has a total of forty-nine rooms.

Thunderbird Lodge

Thunderbird Lodge, a mirror image of Kachina, has fifty-five rooms, some with Canyon views. Rates range from $114 to $124.

Bright Angel Lodge

Bright Angel Lodge offers eighty-nine cabins. Historic cabins do not have baths; guests use the central bath in the Lodge. Regular cabins go for $46; historic cabins are $73. The lodge has a restaurant that serves breakfast, lunch, and dinner, a lounge, and a fountain for ice cream and snacks, open daily if weather permits. The Arizona Steakhouse is located next to Bright Angel Lodge and is open daily for dinner only, and closed January 2 to February 16.

Moqui Lodge

Moqui Lodge, located at the park entrance six miles from the South Rim, has 136 rooms priced at $94. This lodge offers a complimentary breakfast.

Phantom Ranch

Designed by Mary Jane Colter, Phantom

Ranch is located in the Canyon and is accessible by mule train or by hiking Bright Angel or the South Kaibab Trail. Overnight accommodations include a cabin, meals, and the mule you rode in on. Rates are about $300 for one person, $500 for two people, and $230 for each additional person. (Children pay the same rate as adults here.) Hikers may stay in the dormitory at Phantom Ranch for $21.50 per person. Meals are additional: $12 for breakfast; $7.50 for a box lunch; and $16.75 for a stew dinner or $26.75 for a steak dinner. Phantom Ranch fills up quickly, so make your reservations early. You may reserve a cabin here up to 23 months in advance.

Out-of-Park Accommodations

Grand Canyon Inn
$$$ • P.O. Box 702, Williams, AZ 86046
(520) 635–9203, (800) 635–9203

The Grand Canyon Inn is located at the intersection of U.S. Highway 180 and Arizona Highway 64 in Valle. If you want a low-key place to stay away from the crowds at Grand Canyon, this 101-room, family-owned motel should be perfect. A seasonal swimming pool and children's pool, restaurant, and souvenir shop are right on the premises. Children 12 and under stay for free. Credit cards and traveler's checks are accepted, but not personal checks; smoking and non-smoking rooms are available, and most rooms are wheelchair accessible. Pets are not allowed. Reservations are recommended during the high season. The Valle Travel Stop is just next door, with fuel, dump services, and restrooms, as well as a food court open for breakfast, lunch, and dinner, a convenience store, an ATM, and a Chevron gas station. The Planes of Fame air museum and Flintstones Bedrock City are just across the highway, and several souvenir shops are nearby.

The Grand Hotel
$$$$$ • P.O. Box 3319,
Grand Canyon, AZ 86023
(520) 638–3333; fax (520) 638–3131
www.gcanyon.com,
thegrand@gcanyon.com

The newest hotel in Tusayan is an architectural marvel, with a huge, comfortable lobby featuring a central fireplace and a large gift shop with the usual souvenir items, as well as a conference room that accommodates up to fifty people. Ask which items of Southwest-style jewelry in the gift shop are authentic Indian work and which are machine made. The hotel also has the only indoor pool and Jacuzzi in town. The rooms are smallish, with rustic furnishings, televisions, and phones. Balcony rooms (more expensive than standard) have coffeemakers, irons, ironing boards, and hair dryers. Smoking and non-smoking rooms are available, as are wheelchair-accessible rooms. There is a charge for more than two adults in a room; children under 19 stay for free. Pets are not welcome. Major credit card and traveler's checks are accepted. The Canyon Star restaurant on the premises (see listing above) is open for breakfast, lunch, and dinner.

Best Western Grand Canyon Squire Inn
$$$$$ • P.O. Box 130,
Grand Canyon, AZ 86023
(520) 638–2681, (800) 622–6966;
fax (520) 638–2782
gbryan@grandcanyonsquire.com

There's lots to do here other than sleep and eat. This 250-room hotel has a fitness room with a sauna and Jacuzzi, a sports bar, a six-lane bowling alley, a beauty salon for haircuts and manicures, a tanning booth, and a masseur on weekends. The pleasant waterfall lobby with adjacent gift shop has a display of the tools of the working cowboy. Rooms have coffeemakers, hair dryers, TVs, and phones. Non-smoking rooms are available, as are three (two deluxe and one standard) wheelchair-accessible rooms. A coffee and refrigerator. Sixty rooms have mini-bars, and all rooms have coffeemakers, hairdryers, irons, and ironing boards. This full-service, family-owned motel has smoking and non-smoking rooms and wheelchair-accessible rooms; credit cards and traveler's checks are accepted. There is an extra charge for more than two adults in a room; children under 18 are not charged, and pets are not allowed.

A large souvenir shop off the lobby offers some original art and a selection of authentic Navajo jewelry as well as the usual tourist items. The casual restaurant serves American food for breakfast, lunch, and dinner, with a full bar. Dinners run around $40 for two and feature chicken, prime rib, burgers, sandwiches, and T-bone steaks. A reasonably price dinner buffet is available. Reservations are not required.

shop serves breakfast and lunch (with buffets available during the summer). The Coronado Room is open for dinner (see listing under Restaurants). Children under 18 stay free in their parents' room. No pets are allowed. Credit cards and traveler's checks are accepted.

Grand Canyon Quality Inn & Suites
$$$$ • P.O. Box 520,
Grand Canyon, AZ 86023
(520) 638–2673; fax (520) 638–9537

Enter this hotel behind the IMAX to the soothing sounds of a waterfall in its well-designed lobby with a cathedral ceiling. The hotel has 232 rooms, a seasonal swimming pool with a whirlpool, and an 18-foot indoor spa. Suites have a microwave

Holiday Inn Express Grand Canyon
$$$$ • P.O. Box 3245,
Grand Canyon, AZ 86023
(520) 638–3000, (800) HOLIDAY;
fax (520) 638–0123
www.gcanyon.com/holiday

All 197 rooms here have cable color TV and phones; suites have refrigerators, microwaves, and coffeemakers. A complimentary continental breakfast will get you on your way for a day of sightseeing. Kids 18 and under stay free. Wheelchair-accessible and non-smoking rooms are available.

North Rim

Jacob Lake Inn
$$$ • Jacob Lake, AZ 86022
(520) 643–7232
jacob@jacoblake.com

Located 30 miles north of the Park boundary on the North Rim, Jacob Lake Inn offers thirty-nine cabins and motel rooms without phones or televisions. Some rooms are wheelchair accessible and some are non-smoking. An adjacent

restaurant serves breakfast, lunch, and dinner. A café, a gift shop, and a convenience store are also nearby. The inn is completely booked during the summer and during the fall hunting season, so call well in advance for your reservations. A 48-hour cancellation fee applies, except during hunting season when you must cancel more than two weeks in advance to avoid the fee.

Kaibab Lodge
$$$$ • P.O. Box 2997, Flagstaff, AZ 86003
(520) 638–2389 (mid May through Oct.);
(520) 526–0924 (Nov. through mid May);
fax (520) 527–9398
www.canyoneers.com

Twenty-nine rustic rooms with no phones will make this lodge a retreat from the hustle bustle of everyday life. Only two rooms have TVs; one of those also has a microwave and refrigerator. Limited non-smoking rooms and one wheelchair-accessible room are available. Rooms are priced per person, with no charge for children under three. All except the newest rooms will accommodate pets, but animals cannot be left in the room while you go sightseeing. Major credit cards and traveler's checks are accepted. The Kaibab Lodge is open from mid May through October; call well in advance for your reservations.

Grand Canyon Lodge
General Delivery, North Rim, AZ 86052
(303) 297–2757
www.amfac.com

The largest accommodation at the North Rim, located at the end of Arizona Highway 67 on Bright Angel Point, Grand Canyon Lodge offers 203 Western Cabins, Frontier Cabins, and motel rooms. Western Cabins have full baths, two double beds, and a fireplace; Frontier Cabins and motel rooms have 3/4 baths. Open from May 15 through October 15, all rooms have phones, but no TVs.

Amfac advises that more than half of the calls to their reservations desk are to cancel rooms or change dates; therefore, if you cannot be accommodated on the dates you need, it is worth calling back frequently to find out what rooms have become available. For reservations, contact Grand Canyon Lodges, P.O. Box 699, Grand Canyon, AZ 86023; (303) 297-2757; www.grandcanyonlodges.com.

Amfac manages in-park lodging and activities. For reservations, which you usually need to make well in advance (up to 23 months in advance is possible), contact Amfac at (303) 297-2757, write Amfac Parks & Resorts, 14001 East Iliff, Ste. 600, Aurora, CO 80014, or visit the website at www.grandcanyonlodges.com. For same-day reservations, which may be available due to cancellations, call (520) 638-2631.

Every Grand Canyon Park visitor receives a map at the South and East entrances of the park. This map directs visitors to all in-park accommodations. As you cannot access some of the lodges by car, many of the accommodations listed here do not have addresses. However, this map will help you find them.

Attractions

If the Canyon itself isn't attraction enough, you'll find lots to do and see in the surrounding area, including shops filled with creations by local artists, fun for the whole family at the IMAX, music festivals, and an old general store.

Grand Canyon Music Festival
P.O. Box 1332, Grand Canyon, AZ 86023
(800) 997–8285; fax (520) 638-3373
www.grandcanyonmusicfest.org

Sponsored by the National Park Service, the Grand Canyon Music Festival features concerts at the Shrine of the Ages on the South Rim in July and September. Season

and individual tickets are available. Call for schedule information.

Planes of Fame
HRC 34 Box B, Valle Williams, AZ 86046
(520) 635–1000

Located at the intersections of U.S. Highway 180 and Arizona Highway 64 in Valle,

Veterans particularly enjoy Planes of Fame, an aircraft museum in Valle. PHOTO: TANYA LEE

this aviation museum, unique to Northern Arizona, features twenty-two historic airplanes, including General Douglas MacArthur's authentically refurbished command plane, *Bataan*. This Lockheed Constellation is kept in airworthy condition. Among the aeronautical museum's other rare aircraft are a 1928 Ford Trimotor, a Cessna L-19 Bird Dog observation plane, and a Grumman F-1 Tiger supersonic Navy jet fighter. The museum's director, Robert Reid, himself a pilot, conducts educational guided tours. A pictorial history and memorabilia of women in aviation from hot air balloons to the space shuttle will encourage little girls who hope to become pilots. The museum is open seven days a week from 9 A.M. to 5 P.M. in the winter and 9 A.M. to 6 P.M. in the summer, except Thanksgiving and Christmas. A nominal admission fee is charged; children under four are admitted free. The museum is located just next to the Valle airport, which has a souvenir shop and a gallery of original art.

Flintstones Bedrock City
HRC 34, Box A, Williams, AZ 86046
(520) 635–2600
Located at the intersection of U.S. Highway 180 and Arizona Highway 64 in Valle, this stop is guaranteed to be a hit with the kids! Prehistoric cartoons and a ride on the Bedrock City train through the city will make up for all the scenery you've made them look at. The gift shop sells officially licensed merchandise, t-shirts, hats, and other souvenirs. Fred's Diner serves breakfast, lunch, and dinner, including Fred's famous Bronto Burgers, Dino Dogs, and Chickasaurus in a Basket. Or try a Mammoth Milkshake with Gravelberry Pie or a Pebbles' Ice Cream Cone. The adjacent campground has pull-through campsites with full hookups, modern restrooms, hot showers, a laundry, and a TV and game room. Call for advanced reservations.

Grand Canyon IMAX Theater
P.O. Box 1397, Grand Canyon, AZ 86023
(520) 638–2468; fax (520) 638–2807
www.grandcanyonimaxtheater.com;
imax@thecanyon.com
"Grand Canyon–The Hidden Secrets" will take you on a spectacular 34-minute adventure through 4,000 years of human history on the Colorado River. State-of-the-art 70-mm film technology projects the movie onto a screen 82 feet wide and six stories high. The image area encompasses the viewer's entire field of vision, and this, combined with six-track Dolby stereo surround sound will make you feel like you're right there with the first explorers of the Grand Canyon. The film shows hourly on the half hour every day, from 8:30 A.M. to 8:30 P.M. in the summer and 10:30 A.M. to 6:30 P.M. November 1 through February 28. The IMAX complex includes a National Geographic Bookstore, a kiosk for public internet access, a gift shop, a tour desk, an Official National Park Service Pay Station, and several fast food outlets. For the history buff, there is a replica of the wooden canoe used by John Wesley Powell on the first navigation of the Colorado River through the Grand Canyon. The IMAX complex is easy to find right in the middle of Tusayan on Arizona Highway 64.

Shopping

Hopi House
P.O. Box 97, Grand Canyon, AZ 86023
(520) 638–2526, ext. 6383;
fax (520) 638–2394

Located just east of El Tovar, Hopi House, Mary Colter's first building at the Grand Canyon, was opened a little before the hotel and served not only as a salesroom but also as living quarters for the Hopis who worked there as artists and dancers. Downstairs you'll find Hopi overlay, Navajo silver and turquoise, and Zuni inlay jewelry, including some gorgeous modern pieces. Also have a look at the alabaster stone carvings, the Katsina carvings, the Acoma and Navajo pottery, and the genuine Navajo weavings. One room is set aside for media—books, videos, CDs, and calendars, and another small room offers T-shirts and Western hats and belts. The really good stuff is in the upstairs art gallery. Stunning Hopi and Acoma pots, large alabaster carvings, excellent Katsina carvings, and sumptuous Navajo weavings will take your breath away, but don't get so involved looking at the beautiful art for sale that you forget to look at the building's design and construction. It was built by Hopi stonemasons using rock and timber indigenous to the area. The current salespeople disavow any knowledge of the Hopi ceremonial altar that is recorded to have been placed in the original building, but they do admit that there is a kiva, though it is not open to the public. Hopi House is open from 8 A.M. to 6 P.M.

Verkamp's
P.O. Box 96, Grand Canyon, AZ 86023
(602) 638–2242
www.verkamps.com

Located on the South Rim east of Hopi House this historic building was designed by John Verkamp and opened in 1906. A glowing fire greets you as you walk into this store, much of which is devoted to souvenir items. You will, however, find some good Hopi, Zia, Acoma, Navajo, and San Juan pottery as well as Zuni inlay and Navajo jewelry, and Hopi, Paiute, and Santa Domingo basketry. This is the only shop where we've seen jewelry by Colorado Congressman Ben Nighthorse Campbell, who creates lovely bracelets, both inlay and sandcast silver and gold. Don't miss the excellent silverwork by Bryon, Lynol, and Alvin Yellowhorse in the same case. The store is open from 9 a.m. to 6 p.m. every day except Christmas, and the staff is friendly and helpful.

El Tovar Gift Shop
P.O. Box 97, Grand Canyon, AZ 86023
(520) 638–2526, ext. 6413;
fax (520) 638–2394

Located in the El Tovar lobby and open 365 days a year from 7 A.M. till 10 P.M., the El Tovar Gift Shop sells fine Navajo, Hopi, and Zuni jewelry, Acoma and Santa Clara pottery, and classy souvenir T-shirts, sweatshirts, and other clothing, including reversible blanket vests. Here you can also buy salsa, jalapeño jelly, and desert hot

This corner of Hopi House displays paintings, carvings, and weavings. Notice the adobe wall and wooden roof beams. PHOTO: TANYA LEE

A warm fire and a buffalo greet you at Verkamp's on the South Rim. PHOTO: TANYA LEE

chocolate offered under the Fred Harvey Desert Trading Company label and items designed by Robert Shields. This is the only shop where you can order reproductions of Mimbreno dinnerware, the service designed by Mary Colter for the El Tovar based on ancient Indian pottery decoration.

**Tusayan General Store
P.O. Box 159,
Grand Canyon, AZ 86023
(520) 638–2854/9228;
fax (520) 638–9828**

If you haven't stocked up on food for your camping trip or hiking snacks in Flagstaff, Williams, or Tuba City, this is where you'll need to shop. The store's inventory includes fresh produce, canned and packaged goods, drinks, and lots of frozen foods. This is one of the few places to get food at the Canyon (except at restaurants), and prices are high. A souvenir shop with the usual t-shirts, hats, books, videos, and post cards fills the other half of the store. You'll also find a Bank of America ATM, a UPS drop box, ice, and phones outside. The U.S. Post Office is located in the back of the store; it is open weekdays from 9:30 A.M. to 4 P.M. from April to October and from 10 A.M. to 3 P.M. during the winter months.

Kidstuff

Grand Canyon National Park has a Junior Ranger Program for kids ages 4-14. You can pick up a *Junior Ranger* newspaper at Canyon View Center, Yaqui Observation Center, or at the Tusayan Museum, and find out which activities are suitable for your kids. IMAX and Flintsones Bedrock City are also hits with the kids.

Kaibab National Forest Wilderness Areas

The 1.5 million acre Kaibab National Forest borders both the North and South Rims of the Grand Canyon at elevations from 5,500 to 10,418 feet. At higher elevations, the forest is mostly ponderosa pine with alpine meadows and mixed conifers, such as aspens, which are particularly beautiful in the autumn. At lower elevations, expect to see mostly juniper and piñon.

Two Kaibab National Forest wilderness areas—Kanab Creek and Saddle Mountain—are accessible from the North Rim of the Grand Canyon.

Kanab Creek is the largest northern tributary of the Colorado River, originating in southern Utah. The creek has cut a network of deep gorges into the Kanab and Kaibab Plateaus. Water and wind erosion have sculpted an array of fantastic geological features in this land of little vegetation, except in the creek bottom, and few reliable water sources. The Kaibab mule deer winters in the upper parts of the canyons. Elevations in this wilderness area range from 2,000 to 6,000 feet. Many trails cross this region for the intrepid hiker, but they are neither well-marked nor maintained. Access is limited and difficult, and hikers should know that they are hours or days from medical help should they need it.

Saddle Mountain Wilderness is in the far southeastern portion of the North Kaibab Ranger District. The steep, rocky terrain of this wilderness area is bounded on three sides by canyons. Elevations range from 6,000 to 8,000 feet.

A 1960 fire destroyed 8,000 acres here, creating prime habitat for mule deer and the only herd of bison in a National Forest wilderness. The Nankoweap Trail follows the main ridge and offers views of Grand Canyon, Marble Canyon Gorge, Cocks Combs, House Rock Valley and the Vermillion Cliffs.

The Wilderness Act of 1964 created the National Wilderness Preservation System. The act defines a wilderness as "an area where the earth and its community of life are untrammeled by man, where man himself is a visitor who does not remain." Wilderness areas have no piped water, no prepared shelters, no toilets, no tables, and no grills. Signs mark some of the trails, but the user is on his or her own. "Leave No Trace" camping is critical in wilderness areas in order to protect and preserve them.

The natural and cultural resources of the forest are protected and regulated by the stewardship of Forest Service. You are asked to report illegal excavations, collecting and other insults to the natural and cultural resources of wilderness areas.

The Forest Service will provide maps of wilderness areas for a fee. They will also provide names of outfitters and guides who are authorized to conduct trips through the areas.

For more information, contact North Kaibab Ranger District, P.O. Box 248, Fredonia, AZ 86022; (520) 643–7295.

Cathedral Rock rests high above Red Rock Country. PHOTO: STACEY WITTIG

Sedona

Though its population hovers around 16,000, Sedona welcomes an estimated 3.5 million visitors a year, making it the second most popular visitor destination in the state of Arizona next to the Grand Canyon. A tourist, recreation, resort, and art mecca, Sedona rests at the center of Red Rock Country, an area that affords panoramic views, monolith rock formations, and a mild climate that appeals to visitors of all ages.

Located 120 miles north of Phoenix and 30 miles south of Flagstaff, Sedona was established in 1902, but not incorporated until 1988. Sedona sits at an elevation of 4,500 feet and spreads across two bordering counties: Coconino and Yavapai.

Visitors often ask, "When is the best time of year to visit Sedona?" By far, the best answer to this question is any time of year. Each season offers its own special nuances. Come in the fall and camp among Oak Creek Canyon's explosion of autumn color. Take refuge from the snow and ice of other locations in Sedona's mild winter. Watch wildflowers bloom during the spring, and every month is an ideal to participate in the area's endless outdoor activities. The Forest Service stocks Oak Creek with trout from Memorial Day through Labor Day. Highway 89A, which runs through Oak Creek Canyon, was named one of the most beautiful drives in America by Rand McNally.

Tourism is Sedona's main economic force, and the city prides itself on its locally owned businesses that strive to preserve Sedona's small town character. Though you can find a four star hotel, Sedona is also home to quaint bed-and-breakfasts, accommodations for the whole family, and a variety of camping possibilities.

A major cultural center for the arts in the west, Sedona is home to over 40 galleries and a multitude of artists and writers. Spend a few days here to shop, dine, and to explore other attractions in northern Arizona—visit Jerome's old mining town, dance the night away on Prescott's Whiskey Row, or take a daytrip to the Grand Canyon.

Ancient ruins and geological evidence dating back to 700 C.E. surround the area and add to its cultural mystic. This land is sacred to Native Americans. People of all walks of life come to Sedona every year to explore the power of the world-renowned vortexes. Pioneers, surveyors, and trappers came to the area in the early 1800s. In the early 1920s author Zane Grey wrote *Call of the Canyon* and later convinced producers to film the silent movie in Sedona. Since then hundreds of movies, TV commercials, and music videos have been filmed in Sedona.

Still a well-kept secret among visitors to northern Arizona, Sedona is an unforgettable experience, and we hope you enjoy every minute of it.

Sedona Vital Statistics

Mayor: Alan Everett   **Arizona Governor:** Jane Dee Hull

Population: Sedona: 16,000
                     Arizona: 4,924,350

Area (sq. miles): 15

Nickname/motto: Arizona's scenic sensation.

Average Temperatures (Hi/Lo):   July: 95 degrees F/65 degrees F
                                       January: 55 degrees F/32 degrees F

Average rain/snowfall: combined: 8.8 inches
Average days of sunshine: 300

City founded: 1902; incorporated in 1988

Important Dates in History:

1863	President Abraham Lincoln signed the Congressional bill that established the Territory of Arizona. Resting at the center of the new territory was the area that would become the Sedona region.
1872-73	General Crook began his offensive against the Yavapai and Tonto Apache Tribes.
1875	Native Americans were moved from the Camp Verde Reservation to the San Carlos Reservation in eastern Arizona. More than 200 Native Americans died on this walk. The Yavapai call this forced relocation the "March of Tears."
1879	The Abraham James family became the first residents of what is today known as Sedona.
1895	A school was established in Oak Creek Canyon.
1900	Yavapai and Tonto Apache Indians were granted permission by the federal government to return to the Verde Valley area and Sedona region.
1902	Sedona was named by Ellsworth Schnebly for his sister-in-law, Sedona.
1910	The first school was established in Sedona.
1914	The first road through Oak Creek Canyon was completed.
1923	Western author Zane Grey published *Call of the Canyon*. Oak Creek Canyon is one of the settings for the novel.
1939	W.W. Midgley Bridge was dedicated in Oak Creek Canyon.
1956	Chapel of the Holy Cross was completed.
1970	Population of Sedona reached 2,000.
1975	Honanki Cliff Dwellings, built by the Southern Sinagua 800 years ago, was listed on the National Register of Historic Places.
1987	Sedona's population reached 9,000.

Major Area Employers:

Double Tree Sedona; Enchantment Resort & Spa; Los Abrigados Resort & Spa; Sedona/Oak Creek Unified School District

Famous Sons and Daughters:

John James "Jim" Thompson became the first settler at Indian Gardens in Oak Creek Canyon.
Sedona Schnebly: The town was named after this woman in 1902.
The Abraham Jones Family: This family became the first residents of what is today known as Sedona.

Jesse Jefferson "Bear" Howard: An escaped convict from California, he used the alias "Charles Smith Howard" and hunted bear in the Sedona region. He sold the meat in Flagstaff. His great size and imposing demeanor earned him the nickname "Bear."

Ellsworth Schnebly: Brother of Theodore Schnebly, he was the person who suggested that the town be named after his sister-in-law, Sedona.

Theodore Schnebly: Husband of Sedona Schnebly, Theodore was made Sedona's first postmaster in 1902.

William W. Midgley: A grocer, state senator, and county supervisor, Midgley actively promoted road development in the Oak Creek/Sedona area. He passed away in 1949.

State/City Holidays:

New Year's Day; Martin Luther King Day; President's Day; Memorial Day; Independence Day; Labor Day; Veteran's Day; Thanksgiving Day; Christmas Day.

Chamber of Commerce:

Sedona-Oak Creek Chamber of Commerce and Visitors Center
Forest Rd. & N. U.S. Highway 89A
(520) 282-7722

Major Airport:

Sky Harbor International Airport (Phoenix)

Driving Laws:

Seatbelts must be worn by front seat passengers; right turn on red; speed limit is 55, except where marked; speed limit on Interstates is 75, except in designated areas.

Alcohol Laws:

Legal drinking age is 21 years; blood/alcohol level of 1.0% or higher is DUI in Arizona, but .05% to 1.0% can be designated DUI by the arresting officer.

Newspaper:

Sedona Red Rock News, a biweekly.

Sales Tax:

8.8% city/state taxes on all retail sales; 9.89% city/state accommodations; 8.7% city/state restaurant & bar.

Visitors come to Sedona year-round to enjoy the majestic Red Rocks. PHOTO: STACEY WITTIG

Getting Here, Getting Around

Sedona was once the home of the Sinagua Indians and then to the pioneers and settlers of the West. Today it rivals the Grand Canyon as one of Arizona's most popular attractions. Its remote location deters some visitors while others enjoy the quiet isolation.

The region is divided into three major sections: Oak Creek Canyon, Red Rock Country, and the three communities of Sedona (Uptown Sedona, West Sedona, and the Village of Oak Creek.) Tourist activity centers mainly within Uptown and West Sedona. The quintessential "Y" intersection connects U.S. Highway 89A and Arizona Highway 179. U.S. 89A, the "Main Street" for both Uptown and West Sedona, connects the Sedona region with the city of Prescott (63 miles southwest of Sedona) and Flagstaff (28 miles north). Travelers looking to access the intersection of Interstate 17 and Interstate 40 will take U.S. 89A north to Flagstaff. Visitors are encouraged to take the 14-mile scenic U.S. 89A from Flagstaff. The trip down the switchbacks of Oak Creek Canyon is considered the most beautiful scenic road in the country.

Sedona Airport only deals with charter and private planes. For more information about the facilities at the airport call (520) 282-1993. Travelers can fly into Phoenix and rent a car or take a shuttle to Sedona. It takes about two hours to drive from Phoenix (except during rush hour) and seems to be the least complicated of the options.

Walking along Oak Creek Canyon can be precarious, as cars tend to drive fast along the narrow road. Uptown Sedona is pedestrian friendly. Shops, galleries, and restaurants line both sides of the street. However, while on narrow AZ Highway 179, and busy West U.S. 89A, stick to driving. Remember: visitors are looking at the outrageous rock formations and are not always watching the road. The trick is to use defensive tactics; we suggest keeping bikes to the designated mountain bike trails surrounding the area.

Sedona via Albuquerque

Take Interstate 40 W past Holbrook, Winslow, and Meteor Crater. As you reach the Flagstaff city limits, Sedona visitors will look for Exit 195A, the junction of Interstate 17 S and U.S. Highway 89A, which will allow access to Sedona and to Phoenix. Travelers are encouraged to take scenic Highway 89A to Sedona. You will only be on I-17 for a few minutes before you take the exit marked Pulliam Airport, U.S. 89A. As you are exiting the off ramp make a right. Go to the stop sign and turn left. You will be on U.S. 89A.

Sedona via the Grand Canyon

If you are driving from the south entrance of the Grand Canyon take U.S. Highway 180 to Flagstaff. Grand Canyon Village (south entrance) is 80 miles northwest of Flagstaff. Once you are in Flagstaff follow U.S. 180 until you reach Humphrey's Street. Make a right on Humphrey's and follow it until you meet Milton Road.

Turn right on to Milton Road, which will take you directly out of town to Interstate 17 S. From I-17 S, take the exit marked Pulliam Airport and take scenic U.S. 89A to Sedona or take I-17 S to the Sedona exit. Travel time is approximately two hours.

From the North Rim of the Grand Canyon, take Arizona Highway 64 to Jacob Lake. At Jacob Lake head east on U.S. 89A which will tie into U.S. 89 and bring you directly into the east side of town. Instead of driving through Flagstaff, travelers can bypass the traffic

Insider's Tip

Road conditions change rapidly at higher elevations during snowy and icy weather. Call the automated road conditions number, (888) 411-7623, for up-to-the-minute traveling information.

and take the exit marked I–40 and I–17 S (Phoenix). Once you have exited, you will be on I–40. Take the exit marked I–17 S (Phoenix). Now you will have two choices: to take scenic U.S. 89A (look for the exit off of I–17 S marked Pulliam Airport, U.S. 89A) or take I–17 S to the Sedona exit. It takes approximately five hours to get to Sedona from the North Rim.

Sedona via the Los Angeles area

As you leave L.A., take U.S. 15 N to Barstow. At Barstow, pick up Interstate 40 and head east bypassing sections of Old Rt. 66. To reach Sedona, take the exit marked I–17 S (Phoenix.) Visitors can take I–17 S straight to the Sedona exit or from I–17 S visitors can access scenic U.S. 89A. Look for the exit marked Pulliam Airport, U.S. 89A. Driving time to Sedona is approximately nine hours from the Los Angeles area.

Sedona via Las Vegas

From Las Vegas take Interstate 93 S across the Hoover Dam. Continue on I–93 S until you reach Kingman. From Kingman, you will head east on Interstate 40. As you reach the city limits of Flagstaff, look for the exit marked I–17 S Phoenix. Visitors can take I–17 S straight to the Sedona exit or from I–17 S visitors can access scenic U.S. 89A. Look for the exit marked Pullium Airport, U.S. 89A. Driving time from Las Vegas to Sedona is approximately five hours.

Scenic Highway 89A traverses Oak Creek Canyon.
PHOTO: STACEY WITTIG

Sedona via Phoenix

Take Interstate 10 E and look for the exit marked Interstate 17 N. Take I–17 north to Arizona Highway 179 (Exit 298) and continue 15 miles to Sedona. This exit allows visitors access to Arizona Highway 179 and to the Village of Oak Creek. Driving time is approximately two hours.

Getting Here by Airplane

Travelers will fly into Phoenix Sky Harbor Airport to reach Sedona. Phoenix is the hub for America West Airlines (800) 235-9292 (reservations). Many of the major airlines have daily flights to Phoenix including Continental Airlines (800) 523-3273 (reservations), United Airlines (800) 241-6522, and American Airlines (800) 433-7300 (reservations). For information about Sky Harbor Airport call (602) 273-3300.

Rental Cars/Parking

These are the four national companies that serve Sky Harbor Airport: Avis Rent A Car, (800) 331–1212; Alamo, (800) 327–9633; Budget, (800) 527–0700; and Dollar, (800) 800–4000. There are three covered garages for short-term parking for $15 a day. The two long-term parking lots are uncovered and cost $4 a day. The lots are marked, but the airport has been under construction for the past year. Give yourself plenty of time to get through the construction, park your car, and catch the shuttle to your terminal. For more information about airport parking, contact (602) 273–4545.

Getting to Sky Harbor Airport

From Sedona take Interstate 17 S to Phoenix. Once you have cleared the outskirts of Phoenix, look for signs for Intersate 10 E. Take I-10 E to exit 149, Sky Harbor Airport. The exit is clearly marked. It takes approximately two hours to get to the airport. Remember to take rush hour traffic and Phoenix's constant construction into consideration when planning your travel itinerary.

Getting Here by Shuttle

Ace Xpress
(520) 639–3357, (800) 336–2239
www.acexpress.com

Ace Xpress provides door-to-door service to and from the airport by reservation only. A one-way trip is $47 and round-trip is $78. Ace Xpress does not provide service on Thanksgiving and Christmas Day.

Sedona Phoenix Shuttle Service, INC.
P.O. Box 3342, Sedona, AZ 86340
(520) 282-2066, (800) 448-7988

This service provides six daily shuttles to and from the Phoenix airport (except for Thanksgiving and Christmas). The 10-passenger van is comfortable and air-conditioned. Shuttles pick up at the Super 8 Motel in West Sedona and at the Bell Rock Inn in the Village of Oak Creek. Advance reservations are required. Fares fluctuate; call for current rates.

Getting around Sedona

Limousine Service

Red Rock Limo
(520) 282–0175, (877) 282–0175

Sedona Limousines
(520) 282–204-1383, (800) 775–6739

Taxis

Bell Rock Taxi—A Sedona Taxi & Tour Company   (520) 282–4222

Bob's Sedona Taxi
(520) 282–1234

Accommodations

Sedona is one of the most popular tourist destinations in the world. Surrounded by rugged red rocks, acres of national forest land, and ancient Indian ruins, visitors can spend the day hiking along famous rock formations or riding in a jeep on dirt roads and then return to their top-notch accommodations with first-class amenities. This paradoxical community appeals to many vacationers who want the best of both worlds: to play hard all day and relax in luxury at night.

Whether you like to stay at an inn, resort, or bed-and-breakfast, we have covered the spectrum with our selection. The resorts are renowned, the inns charming, and the bed-and-breakfasts are quiet retreats away from the hectic world. Some of the accommodations listed below do not have telephones or TVs, but we've balanced these listings with those establishments that have cable and VCRs.

Wherever you decide to stay, hosts or resort staff will point you in the right direction to find a particular piece of art, gourmet coffee, or an ideal spot to watch the sunset. Each of the accommodations listed has a reputation for providing excellent customer service and the "extras" that make the difference: plush robes, afternoon goodies, and gourmet breakfasts are just a few of the perks you can expect when staying in Sedona.

Sedona's peak season is from February through June and from September through the end of December. It is common for accommodations to offer special winter rates from the end of December to the beginning of February. Most guests are return guests and make their reservations a year in advance, so plan your trip early. However, if you find yourself driving into Sedona during the high season without reservations, do not hesitate to check with establishments, especially during the week. Midweek cancellations are more common that weekend ones; plus weekday rates are cheaper.

Most of the accommodations are non-smoking and pets are not allowed. Please call and check if the accommodation accepts pets. If they don't, many establishments will happily put guests in touch with a kennel service or take care of the arrangements themselves.

We have divided this chapter geographically: U.S. Highway 179, Oak Creek Canyon, Uptown Sedona, and West Sedona. We have also combined resorts, inns, and bed-and-breakfasts in each section.

Price code

Prices are based on two-person occupancy and are subject to change. Prices do not include gratuity, room service, or an extra person in the room. (The average fee for an extra person is $5, but some accommodations charge up to $45.)

$ . . . .$65 or less
$$ . . . .$66 to $95
$$$ . . . .$96 to $150
$$$$ . . . .$151 to $200
$$$$$ . . . .$201 or more

AZ Highway 179

Canyon Villa Bed-and-Breakfast Inn
$$$-$$$$ • 125 Canyon Circle Dr.
(520) 284–1226, (800) 453–1166
www.canyonvilla.com

Majestic views of red rock country are as close as your own balcony or patio. This 11-room inn with private baths is elegantly furnished, intimate, and quiet. Guestrooms include individual climate control, whirlpool tubs, remote color TV, telephone, and ceiling fans. Breakfast is served in the dining room between 8 and

9 A.M. and includes fresh fruit, breakfast entree, and homemade cinnamon rolls. A continental breakfast is available for early and late risers.

The Inn on Oak Creek $$$$-$$$$$
556 AZ Hwy. 179
(520) 282–7896, (800) 499–7896

The elegant rooms have spa tubs, gas fireplaces, private baths, plush robes, and make for a romantic getaway any day of the week. A gourmet breakfast is served from 8 to 9:30 A.M. Guests are treated to complimentary hors d'oeuvres each day at 5 P.M. The inn is in walking distance to shops, galleries, and restaurants.

Los Abrigados Resort & Spa $$-$$$$
160 Portal Ln.
(520) 282-1777, (800) 521-3131
www.ilxinc.com

Adjacent to Tlaquepaque arts and crafts village, Los Abrigados Resort & Spa's 175 luxurious suites rest in the heart of Sedona. Guests will enjoy strolling through the 22 acres of lush landscaping and Spanish-style plazas and walkways. Suites have a separate living area, bedroom, and balcony, and many come with a fireplace and patio spa. Los Abrigados is home to the Sedona Spa. Guests will enjoy luxurious pleasures like facials, manicures, and a eucalyptus steam room. The resort has three restaurants on the grounds. On the Rocks Bar & Grill offers casual dining, Steak & Sticks has prime beef at its best, and for fine Italian dining try Joey Bistro. For more information on these restaurants, see the Sedona Restaurant section.

The Penrose Bed-and-Breakfast $$$$
250 Red Butte Dr.
(520) 284-3030, (888) 678-3030
www.thepenrose.com

The Penrose features five guest rooms and is tucked away in a residential neighborhood one-half mile from AZ Highway 179. Each room has a private bath with either a two-person shower or a double Jacuzzi with separate shower. All rooms have east facing windows offering majestic views of red rock formations and private balconies or patios. A complete breakfast is served from 8 to 9 AM in the

> ## Insiders' Tip
> Within the Los Abrigados Resort and Spa is the Red Rock Spring Farmer's Market. The Market has fresh seasonal fruits and vegetables and the hottest to the mildest salsa. The market is open daily 9 A.M. to 6 P.M., weather permitting.

breakfast room or outside on the deck. Vegetarian and low-fat meals are available upon request. The Penrose offers complimentary afternoon hors d'oeuvres, nighttime snacks, and refreshments any time of the day.

Poco Diablo Resort $$-$$$$$
1752 S. AZ Hwy. 179
(520) 282-7333, (800) 528-4275
www.pocodiablo.com

Poco Diablo Resort is great for a weekend getaway or family vacation. The resort has a 9-hole par 3 golf course, heated pool and spa, and tennis and racquetball courts. The rooms are spacious and include wet bar, refrigerator, and Nintendo. You won't have to leave the resort if you don't want to. Enjoy your meals indoors or outdoors at the resort's two restaurants, T-Carl's and Jersey's Bar & Grill. (See the Sedona Restaurant section for more information.)

Oak Creek Canyon

Briar Patch Inn $$$-$$$$$
3190 N. U.S. Hwy. 89A
520) 282-2342, (888) 809-3030
www.briarpatchinn.com

These romantic cottages, furnished with Native American art, have wood-burning fireplaces and private patios. Designed for comfort and relaxation, Briar Patch Inn is a secluded getaway on over eight acres along Oak Creek. Guests start the day with a homemade breakfast in the privacy of their cottage, fireside in the lounge, or creekside.

The Canyon Wren $$$
6425 N. U.S. Hwy. 89A
(520) 282–6900, (800) 437–9736
www.canyonwrencabins.com

Looking for that special place to celebrate a birthday, anniversary, or just looking for an intimate escape? The Canyon Wren exudes romance with its private accommodations. The three chalet-styled cedar cabins have an open loft bedroom with queen bed and outside deck, complete kitchen with dining area, private bath with whirlpool bathtub, wood-burning fireplace, and patio or deck with gas grill. Continental breakfast is served daily.

Don Hoel's Cabins $$-$$$$
9440 N. U.S. Hwy. 89A
(520) 282–3560, (800) 292–4635
www.hoels.com

In the heart of the Oak Creek Canyon's pines, you will find eighteen quaint and charming cabins that can accommodate a family or are cozy enough for two. Family cabins come with full kitchens and some cabins have gas log fireplaces. A continental breakfast is served each morning in the "Parlor," a community cabin with TV and telephone for guests to utilize.

Garland's Oak Creek Lodge $$$-$$$$
8067 N. U.S. Hwy. 89A
(520) 282–3343
www.garlandslodge.com

Guests have to ford Oak Creek (with the help of a paved road) to enjoy the secluded and intimate Garland's Oak Creek Lodge. The lodge's sixteen cabins are hidden on nine acres, with four cozy cabins that overlook the creek. The larger cabins have a spacious sitting area and wood-burning fireplace. Full breakfasts and dinners are included with lodging. A

light snack is served with afternoon tea daily. The lodge is open April 1 through November 15. For more about Garland's restaurant, see the Sedona Restaurants section.

Oak Creek Terrace Resort $$-$$$
4548 N. U.S. Hwy. 89A
(520) 282–3562, (800) 224–2229
www.oakcreekterrace.com

Casual and comfortable, Oak Creek Terrace Resort is an oasis along the banks of Oak Creek. The resort has suites, bungalows, and family units. Bungalow and family units include fireplace, mini-kitchenette, and private deck with outdoor barbecue. Relax by the creek in a hammock or in a swing built for two. Small pets are allowed. There is a $25 non-refundable fee for animals.

Sedona Reál Inn $$$ -$$$$
Hwy. 89A at 95 Arroyo Piñon Dr.
(520) 282–1414, (800) 353–1239
www.sedonareal.com

Don't let the hotel amenities fool you. Behind the luxurious accommodations, you'll find an all-suites inn with a friendly atmosphere and an attentive staff. Suites come with private decks, fireplaces, Jacuzzis, refrigerators, and microwaves. Continental breakfast is served daily.

> ## Insiders' Tip
> Garland's Oak Creek Lodge is surrounded by organic fruit orchards. A greenhouse is located in the orchard where Garland's grows organic vegetables and herbs.

Uptown Sedona

Apple Orchard Inn $$$-$$$$$
656 Jordan Rd.
(520) 282–5328, (800) 663–6968
www.appleorchardbb.com

Just minutes away from Uptown Sedona,

Apple Orchard Inn is secluded among the pines. Each of the seven rooms is custom designed with Jacuzzi tubs. Spend the day by the pool or have an invigorating massage in the massage room. Start your day with a gourmet breakfast on the red rock patio or in the dining room. Afternoon snacks and evening hors d'oeuvres are served daily.

L'Auberge de Sedona $$$-$$$$$
301 L'Auberge Ln.
(520) 282–1661, (800) 272–6777
www.lauberge.com

Choose from an intimate cottage with fireplace that sits along the banks of Oak Creek, the European lodge with canopied king-size bed, or the charming rooms at the Orchards at L'Auberge, which offers spectacular views from the private balconies or patios. After a morning walk by the creek spend the afternoon soaking in the Jacuzzi or sipping a drink poolside. Enjoy the gourmet cuisine of L'Auberge, an elegant French restaurant, or the relaxed atmosphere of the Orchards. For more information about L'Auberge and the Orchards, see the Sedona Restaurant section.

Sedona's Matterhorn Lodge $$-$$$
230 Apple Ave.
(520) 282–7176
www.arizonaguide.com/matterhorn/

The Matterhorn Lodge sits perched high above Uptown Sedona. Each room has a picture window looking out on the beauty of the surrounding red rocks, plus a balcony or patio near the room. The lodge has an outdoor whirlpool spa and heated pool, in-room refrigerator and complimentary coffee, and cable TV. If you're bringing your pet, ask about designated pet rooms.

West Sedona

Boots & Saddles $$$-$$$$
2900 Hopi Dr.
(520) 282–1944, (800) 201–1944
www.oldwestbb.sedona.net

For a true Western experience with spectacular views of the red rocks, Boots & Saddles has four custom designed rooms that will bring out the cowboy or cowgirl in any guest. This casual yet romantic B & B offers in-room spa tubs, homemade and hearty breakfasts, and afternoon appetizers. Some rooms come with fireplaces; all rooms have a TV/VCR, telephone, and refrigerator.

Casa Sedona Bed & Breakfast Inn
$$-$$$$ • 55 Hozoni Dr.
(520) 284–1226, (800) 525–3756
www.casasedona.com

Nestled in a tranquil setting surrounded by stunning red rocks, this secluded inn's private guest rooms come with fireplaces, spa tubs, and refrigerators. A healthy, gourmet breakfast is served outside (weather permitting) each morning between 8 and 9:30 A.M. Breakfast includes entree, fresh fruit, and baked goods. A "side bar" is always available with homemade granola, cereal, and yogurt.

Afternoon appetizers are served from 5 to 6 P.M.

Enchantment Resort $$-$$$$$
525 Boynton Canyon Rd.
(520) 282–2900, (800) 826–4180

Tucked away among Boynton Canyon's red rocks and cedar forests, Enchantment Resort's spacious suites can be joined together to create one- or two-bedroom casitas or haciendas. All guest accommodations have private decks. The resort offers a wide variety of activities, including nature walks, yoga, T'ai Chi, swimming, and tennis. Enchantment has two 18-hole championship golf courses for guests. World-renowned spa services are also available.

The Yavapai Room is open for breakfast, lunch, and dinner. For more about the resort's restaurant, see the Sedona Restaurant section.

Sky Ranch Lodge $$-$$$$
Airport Rd.
(520) 282–6400, (888) 708–6400
www.skyranchlodge.com

These cozy, secluded rooms and cottages have fireplaces and kitchenettes. The lodge offers 75-mile panoramic views in every direction. You will feel close to heaven here. Guests enjoy six acres of lush gardens, year-round pool and spa facilities, and relaxing by the streams and ponds.

A Territorial House Bed & Breakfast
$$$-$$$$ • 65 Piki Dr.
(520) 204-2732, (800) 801-2737
www.oldwestbb.com

Experience Western hospitality at this friendly bed-and-breakfast. The spacious rooms include stone fireplaces, whirlpool tubs, and private decks. All rooms come with private baths. The hearty, home-made breakfasts provide plenty of energy for tourists looking to tackle the highlights of Sedona. Families are welcome.

Insiders' Tip

Enchantment Resort has facilities just for kids ages 8 to 12. Camp Coyote is dedicated to arts, crafts, and outdoor activities. Trained counselors will introduce campers to the wonders of Boynton Canyon. Call the resort for registration.

Restaurants

Price code

This reference guide is based on the average price for two people, minus cocktails and gratuity.

$	Less than $20
$$	$21 to $35
$$$	$36 to $60
$$$$	$61 and more

Casual eateries, four star restaurants, and steak houses await you in Sedona. The relaxed atmosphere of the town permeates the restaurants. The dress code is casual, but if you want to dress up feel free. Only a few of the upscale eating establishments require dinner jackets for men, but be sure to ask when you call to make your reservations. As for reservations, make them. This is a busy resort town, if you don't want to wait more than an hour for dinner, you will heed this warning.

Since this is a resort town, restaurants accept all major credit cards with the exception of Diner's Club. But ask as you make your reservation, not as you are paying your bill. There is no law in Sedona that prohibits smoking in restaurants; however, most establishments only allow smoking in the bar area and don't have a smoking section in the restaurant. In researching this chapter, we did not notice any offensive smoky restaurants, but if smoking does offend you, outside dining is available at most restaurants. The mild climate and beautiful scenery entice visitors to dine outdoors during the summer, fall, and spring months. Once the sun goes down, even during the summer, the nights cool off, so be prepared and bring a sweater or jacket.

In this chapter, we have divided the restaurants geographically: Arizona Highway 179 (which includes Hillside Sedona and Tlaquepaque Arts and Crafts Village), Oak Creek Canyon, Uptown Sedona, and West Sedona. We've included a price guide to help you stick to your budget or plan ahead for that special evening. Hours, menus, and forms of payment are subject to change. If you have any questions or concerns call ahead.

Joey Bistro/Los Abrigados Resort & Spa
$$ • 160 Portal Ln.
(520) 282-1777
www.ilxresorts.com

This fun, classic-Italian eatery's menu features homemade pasta, seafood, and chicken dishes. The desserts are "ta die for." The decadent Italian specialties include tiramisu, cannoli, and cheesecake. The crisp, white linen tablecloths add to the casual elegance of the bistro-style restaurant. Joey's is open daily for dinner 5 P.M. to 10 P.M.

On the Rocks Bar and Grill $$
Los Abrigados Resort & Spa, 160 Portal Ln.
(520) 204-7849
www.ilxresorts.com

Sports enthusiasts, locals, and visitors agree that this bar and grille's relaxed atmosphere and tasty menu items are a winning combination. The ribs, rotisserie chicken, and wood-fired pizzas are local favorites. On the Rocks has the only 10-foot TV screen in Sedona, and is open for lunch and dinner from 11 A.M. to 10 P.M.

The bar is open until 1 A.M. See the Sedona Nightlife section for more information.

Steak & Sticks $$
Los Abrigados Resort & Spa, 160 Portal Ln.
(520) 204-7849
www.ilxresorts.com

Featuring steak, chops, seafood, and grilled specialties, Steak & Sticks tempts their guests with their open kitchen and custom-made brass accouterments. Dining guests are invited to sit at the tiled counter facing the cooking area to watch the chef create. Choose from a full bar with imported beer, spirits, and Los Abrigados Resort & Spa's private-label wine. The restaurant is open for breakfast 7 A.M. to 11 A.M. The Sunday omelet bar—available 7 A.M. until noon—has received rave reviews. Dinner is served daily 5 P.M. to 10 P.M. Reservations are recommended. A billiards room is adjacent to the restaurant. For more information about the Billiards Club see Sedona Nightlife section.

Hillside Sedona

Javelina Cantina $
671 AZ Hwy. 179
(520) 203-9514
www.sed-biz/javelinacantina

This popular eating establishment serves Sonoran-style Mexican cuisine with Southwestern flair. The menu has traditional south of the border favorites, fresh salads, and seafood dishes. The margarita menu is extensive. Don't forget to specify frozen or on the rocks and add the salt. Javelina Cantina is open for lunch and dinner 11:30 to 9:30 P.M. daily.

Jersey's Bar and Grill/ Poco Diablo Resort
$ • 1752 S. AZ Hwy. 179
(520) 282-7333   www.pocodiablo.com

Try Jersey's "quick and casual" menu with gourmet sandwiches, tasty appetizers, and crisp salads as you play a game of pool or watch the game on the big screen TV. For more on Jersey's see the Sedona Nightlife section. Jersey's Bar and Grill is open daily.

Shugrue's Hillside Grill $$
671 AZ Hwy. 179
(520) 282-5300
www.sed-biz/javelinacantina

Shugrue's Hillside has spectacular views of the red rocks and a continental menu that will knock your socks off. The seafood is so fresh it makes you wonder how close Sedona really is to the ocean. The chef uses fresh ingredients and Cajun spices to create dishes featuring chicken, seafood, and veal. Shugrue's Hillside Grill is open daily for lunch 11:30 A.M. to 3 P.M. and for dinner 5 P.M. to 9 P.M.

T. Carl's at Poco Diablo Resort $-$$
1752 S. AZ Hwy. 179
(520) 282–7333
www.pocodiablo.com

T. Carl's is open daily for breakfast, lunch, and dinner. The breakfast menu served from 7 A.M. to 11 P.M. includes traditional dishes from French toast to waffles to Southwestern favorites like the Breakfast Burrito with fresh chiles. Lunch is served from 11 A.M. to 2 P.M. and features grilled sandwiches, Southwestern dishes, and salads. The restaurant closes between 2 and 5 P.M. to prepare for dinner. The dinner menu is continental with seafood, steak, and chicken dishes. T. Carl's has a full bar and serves dinner from 5 P.M. to 9 P.M.

Tlaquepaque Arts and Crafts Village

El Rincon $
Ste. A112
(520) 282–4648
www.rinconrestaurants.com

Guests will enjoy the "Arizona-style" Mexican cuisine. Locals come back for the Green Chile and Shrimp Rellenos and the Spinach Cream Cheese Enchiladas. Sit inside by the fireplace or outside under the sycamore trees. El Rincon has the number 1 rated Margaritas in Sedona. The restaurant is open for lunch and dinner 11 A.M. to 9 P.M. Tuesday through Sunday, and is closed on Monday.

René at Tlaquepaque $$-$$$
Ste. 118
(520) 282–9225
www.rene-sedona.com

Nestled in the Mexican courtyard of Tlaquepaque is René at Tlaquepaque, an exquisite and elegant dining experience. The continental menu has traditional and intriguing seafood, vegetarian, pasta, and game dishes. The country French ambiance—with delicate lace curtains combined with the superb service—ensures that you will want to make reservations. Outdoor seating in the courtyard is available, weather permitting. Don't forget to ask for the dessert tray. It changes daily, and if you're fortunate, flourless chocolate cake will be a dessert option. René is open daily. Lunch is served from 11:30 A.M., dinner from 5:30 P.M.

The Secret Garden at Tlaquepaque $
Ste. 66
(520) 203–9564

Bright yellow walls and lush plants invite customers to bring a book and stay for a while. The outdoor seating provides a private getaway for one or two. The quiche bar and selection of homemade pastries offer a light reprieve from the traditional American breakfast. The lunch menu features grilled veggie and meat sandwiches, fresh salads, and soups. All menu items are homemade. The Secret Garden is open daily 10:30 A.M. to 4 P.M.

Guests will enjoy the exquisite food under the blue Sedona skies. PHOTO: COURTESY OF RENÉ AT TLAQUEPAQUE

Oak Creek Canyon

Garland's Oak Creek Lodge
$$-$$$ • 8067 N. U.S. Hwy. 89A
(520) 282-3343

Dinner at Garland's is a treat. Cocktails start at six, the dinner bell rings at seven. The one entree special menu begins with homemade bread, soup, and garden salad. Entrees range from beef filet and rack of lamb, to fresh fish and breast of duckling.

Specify beforehand if you are vegetarian or have other dietary restrictions. Choose from a fine selection of wines to complement your dinner. Exquisite desserts and coffee or teas top off the meal. Limited dinner reservations are available for those not staying at the lodge. See the Sedona Accommodations section for more about Garland's Oak Creek Lodge.

Uptown Sedona

Black Cow Cafe $
229 N. U.S. Hwy. 89A
(520) 203-9868

Kids and adults will enjoy the homemade ice cream, home-baked goodies (including breakfast items and pastries), and gourmet sandwiches. There is also a full espresso bar for the much-needed afternoon pick-me-up. Black Cow Cafe is open daily 7 A.M. to 9 P.M. The lunch menu is served until closing.

The Cowboy Club/Silver Saddle Room
$-$$ • 241 N. U.S. Hwy. 89A
(520) 282-4200
www.cowboyclub.com

The Cowboy Club is open for lunch and dinner serving Southwestern delicacies. The menu has unique and tasty options including buffalo, rattlesnake, certified Angus beef, and fresh seafood dishes. Decorated in dark wood with Western detail, Cowboy Club offers casual dining, perfect for families and large parties. Silver Saddle Room is open for dinner and serves the same menu as Cowboy Club, but offers a romantic atmosphere. The menu in the Silver Saddle Room also includes sorbet intermezzo, appetizers, and dessert amusé. All menu items are made from scratch. Breads, pastries, and desserts are made in the restaurant's own bakery. The Cowboy Club is open for lunch 11 A.M. to 4 P.M. daily. Dinner is served in both dining rooms from 5 P.M. until 10 P.M. Reservations are recommended.

L'Auberge De Sedona Restaurant
$$-$$$$ • 301 L'Auberge Ln.
(520) 282-1667
www.lauberge.com

Featuring gourmet French cuisine, L'Auberge serves an award-winning á la carte or prix fixe menu by European-trained master chefs. Step inside and enjoy the ambiance of this country French inn with imported fabrics, fine china, and excellent service. The wine list is extensive and will please the most discriminating of palettes. L'Auberge serves breakfast, lunch, and dinner 7 A.M. to 9 P.M. Try the gourmet Sunday Brunch. The buffet is served 11 A.M. to 3 P.M. and includes omelets, international cheese and pâtés, fresh baked breads, and more. Outdoor dining is available along the banks of Oak Creek. Reservations are recommended.

Orchard's $$
254 N. U.S. Hwy. 89A
(520) 282-7200
www.lauberge.com

Influenced by its French cousin, L'Auberge, this American grill offers a casual setting and can accommodate large parties or an intimate party of two. The menu features chicken, beef, and seafood dishes, traditional and Southwestern breakfast items, and fresh salads and homemade soup for lunch. Look for the nightly dinner specials. Orchard's serves breakfast, lunch, and dinner 7 A.M.

to 9 P.M. daily. Reservations are suggested. For more about Orchard's, see the Sedona Nightlife section.

Takashi Japanese Restaurant $
465 Jordan Rd.
(520) 282–2334
www.takashisedona.com

The extensive menu features teriyaki, tempura, sukiyaki, teppan yaki, and sushi.

Dinner entrees include vegetarian, chicken, beef, and seafood options, and include salad, miso soup, rice, and tea. Takashi is open daily for lunch and dinner. In good weather, enjoy your meal in the restaurant's outdoor seating. Reservations are suggested.

> ## Insiders' Tip
> Orchard's has live entertainment Thursday, Friday, and Saturday during Sedona's high season. Kick back, have an after-dinner cordial, and listen to the acoustic music of some of the region's most talented musicians.

West Sedona

Casa Rincon & Tapas Cantina $
2620 W. U.S. Hwy. 89A
(520) 282–4849
www.rinconrestaurants.com

Casa Rincon offers a variety of tapas (appetizers), soups, salads, and traditional Southwest dishes including tamales, tacos, enchiladas, and burritos. A kids' menu is also available. Casa Rincon is open Tuesday through Sunday for lunch 11:30 A.M. to 4 P.M. Dinner is served 5 A.M. to 9 P.M. For more about Casa Rincon & Tapas Cantina see Sedona Nightlife section.

Dahl & DiLuca $$
2321 W. U.S. Hwy. 89A
(520) 282–5219

Guests will feel like they stepped into an authentic Italian restaurant in Italy. Dark tiled floor, cherub fountains, and Italian paintings decorate the long, intimate room. The menu is filled with northern and southern Italian dishes. All ingredients are fresh and the pasta is homemade. The chef specializes in seafood and veal dishes. The desserts are as delightful as the dinner menu. Dinner begins at 5 P.M. Reservations are required.

Heartline Cafe $$-$$$
1610 W. U.S. Hwy. 89A
(520) 282–0785

For a casual evening or an elegant affair, experience the original creations at Heartline Cafe. Using only the freshest ingredients, all menu items are made from scratch. The menu features seasonal dishes, but you can always count on quality and healthy seafood and vegetarian entrees. Heartline Cafe has a full bar and an extensive wine list. Reservations are suggested. Lunch is served Friday, Saturday, Sunday, and Monday beginning at 11 A.M. Dinner is served daily 5 to 9 P.M.

Judi's Restaurant $$
40 Soldier Pass Rd.
(520) 282–4449   www.brand-x.net

Tucked away in La Posada Shopping Plaza, this local eatery continues to deliver great food in an intimate setting. Known as "Sedona's best kept secret," Judi's Restaurant serves a continental menu. Guests will have a hard time deciding between the baby back ribs, fresh seafood, and hearty pasta dishes. Judi herself makes all the desserts from scratch, including the ice cream. Lunch is served from 11:30 A.M. to 5 P.M. Dinner begins at 5 P.M. Dinner reservations are suggested.

Keiser's West $
2920 W. U.S. Hwy. 89A
(520) 204–2088
www.brand-x.net
This is food like your mother would make—the breakfasts are big, and your coffee cup is bottomless. Locals agree that Keiser's serves the tastiest French toast in town. Lunch is a delight with hickory-smoked sandwiches. Dinner is a tradition, with chicken, ribs, and pork basted in Keiser's secret sauce. Early bird dinner specials are from 4:30 to 6:30 P.M. The atmosphere is casual, so roll up your sleeves and dig in. Keiser's West is open Monday through Saturday 7 A.M. to 9 P.M and Sunday 7 A.M. to 2 P.M.

Rainbow's End Steakhouse and Saloon
$-$$ • 3235 W. U.S. Hwy. 89A
(520) 282–1593
If you are searching for good steaks, ribs, and chicken, look no further. Rainbow's End serves large portions of homemade "grub" that will fill your stomach and warm your heart. The service is friendly and attentive. You'll feel like a local after spending an evening here. After dinner, the band starts, so put your cowboy boots on. For more information about the Rainbow's End weekend entertainment, see the Sedona Nightlife section. The restaurant is open for lunch and dinner from 11 A.M. 'til the kitchen closes.

Yavapai Room at the Enchantment Resort
$$-$$$ • 525 Boynton Canyon Rd.
(520) 282–2900
www.enchantment.com
Plan an intimate evening dinner, a relaxing lunch, or start your day with the breakfast buffet at the Yavapai Room. The menus incorporate local, regional, and traditional ingredients and the outcome is memorable. Guests will love the food and enjoy the breathtaking views of Boynton Canyon. Breakfast is 6:30 to 11 A.M. Lunch is served 11:30 A.M. to 2:15 P.M. Dinner is 5:30 P.M. to 9:15 P.M. Reservations are required for all menus.

Attractions

While exploring red rock country, be sure to break away from the souvenir shops that line the streets of Uptown Sedona and immerse yourself in the history of the area. Besides the picturesque landscape, Sedona and the surrounding region have a story to tell. Ancient ruins and historic monuments provide insight to the past

Visitors will be introduced to the ancient Sinagua Indian who lived in the region from 650 C.E. to about 1400 C.E., when the culture mysteriously vanished. While some Sedona residents believe extraterrestrials abducted the ancient culture, there is no evidence to support this theory, and scientists remain perplexed as to why the people left as they were tending to tasks such as preparing a meal. Tuzigoot and Montezuma Monuments and Palatki and Honanki sites are silent testaments to this lost culture and other Native American tribes.

Fort Verde State Historic Park is the site of several major battles between the U.S. Calvary and Yavapai and Apache Indians. Jordan Historical Park is a tribute to the earliest settlers of Sedona.

In this chapter, we will direct you to the historic and ancient monuments, museums, Native American sites, an arts and crafts village, area parks, a chapel, a theater, and one of the best places to watch the sunset.

Insiders' Tip

For up-to-the-minute weather conditions call (520) 774-3301.

Parks and Museums

Fort Verde State Historic Park
(520) 567–3275
www.arizonaguide.com

During the late 1880s, this site was the base for General Crook's U.S. Army scouts and soldiers as they fought against the Apache and Yavapai Indians. Visitors will be intrigued by the military history of the park. Located southwest of Sedona, three miles east of Interstate 17 in Camp Verde, Fort Verde is open every day except for Christmas. The entrance fee is $2 for adults and $1 for children ages 7 through 13. (For more about Fort Verde State Historic Park, see the Sedona Kidstuff section.) The park is open 8 A.M. to 5 P.M. daily.

Jordan Historical Park/Sedona Heritage Museum
735 Jordan Rd.
(520) 282–7038
www.sedonamuseum.org

This museum is a tribute to Sedona's earliest settlers. The four acres were once home to Jordan Orchards. The grounds include exhibits on antique farm equipment, an apple processing shed, and the Jordan house, now home to the Sedona Heritage Society. Located in Uptown Sedona, the museum is open September through May, 11 A.M. to 4 P.M. During June, July, and August, hours are noon to 4 P.M. Admission is $3 for adults and children over 12. Children under 12 years of age are admitted free.

National Monuments

Montezuma Castle National Monument
(520) 567–3322
www.nps.gov/moca

An ancient, five-story cliff dwelling, Montezuma Castle has 20 well-preserved rooms. Early settlers were awestruck by the dwelling, which was built by Sinagua Indians in the twelfth and thirteenth centuries, and named it after the Aztec king, Montezuma. The monument is open from 8 A.M. to 5 P.M. every day except for Christmas. Extended summer hours run from Memorial Day until Labor Day. Children under 16 are admitted free. There is a $2 entrance fee for adults.

Tuzigoot National Monument
P.O. Box 219
(520) 634–5564
www.nps.gov/tuzi

Tuzigoot Monument, which encompasses 43 acres, was built by the Sinagua Indians in the thirteenth century. The original pueblo had 110 rooms and second and third stories. Talks and guided tours are offered daily (depending upon the availability of the staff). The monument is open Monday through Sunday except for Christmas. Summer hours are 8 AM to 7 PM. Winter hours are 8 AM to 5 PM.

Montezuma Castle National Monument is one of the most well-preserved structures built by Arizona's ancient settlers the Sinagua Indians.

PHOTO: PETER PFEIFFER

Other Native American Ruins

Honanki
Sedona Ranger District
(520) 282–3854
www.visionsofheaven.com

These 700-year-old ruins are a sacred place, once home to three different cultures: the Sinagua Indians and the Yavapai and Apache Nations. Many of the pictographs have been destroyed by weather and by vandals, but much of the rock art covering the walls is still well preserved. As you approach the site, the main room is to the left, and it has a circular clan symbol painted on the ceiling. As visitors proceed to the right of the site, they will find smaller rooms with preserved rock art. The site is open 9:30 A.M. to 4:30 P.M. Entrance fee is $5 for adults. Children 16 and under are admitted free.

Palatki Ruins
Sedona Ranger District
(520) 282–3854
www.aztec.asu.edu

These ruins are the cliff dwellings constructed by the Southern Sinagua, who inhabited the area from approximately 650 C.E. to about 1300 C.E. This site is known for its 3,000-6,000 year-old pictographs. The symbols painted in red are believed mainly to be the work of the Archaic cultures. The animal and human pictographs painted in yellow are believed to be the work of the Sinagua. The charcoal drawings of men on horseback were done in more recent times by the Yavapai or Apache, around the time the Spanish introduced the horse to the New World. There is a $5 entrance fee per car. The ruins are open daily 9:30 A.M. to 4:30 P.M.

Sunsets

Sedona offers many spectacular places to watch the sunset. Airport Mesa offers unobstructed views and visibility up to 70 miles. Take U.S. Highway 89 past the "Y." As you reach the top of the hill, a sign for Sedona Airport will be on your left. Follow the road and find a romantic spot to share the sunset.

Miscellaneous

Chapel of the Holy Cross
780 Chapel Rd.
(520) 282–4069

In 1956, a local architect, inspired by the completion of the New York City's Empire State Building, built this shrine 250-feet high in Sedona's red rock landscape. The chapel is open 9 A.M. to 5 P.M. Monday through Saturday and from 10 A.M. to 5 P.M. on Sunday. Although it does not still function as a working chapel, a Catholic prayer service is held on Mondays at 5 P.M.

Sedona SuperVue Theatre
Oak Creek Factory Outlets,
6615 AZ Hwy. 179
(520) 284–3813

This motion picture offers a "virtual tour" of Sedona, and is shown on a four-story-high screen with digital surround sound. Viewers will take a historical journey and see how this unique region was

> ## Insiders' Tip
> Visitors are asked to refrain from touching the rock art. Oil from your hand can cause deterioration. Please respect the sites, as they are sacred places to Native Americans.

created. There is a show every hour on the hour except for 3 P.M. Admission for adults is $7.50 and $5.00 for children 3 to 11. The theater is located on Arizona Highway 179 at Jacks Canyon Road.

Tlaquepaque Arts and Crafts Village
AZ Hwy. 179, at the Bridge
www.tlaq.com

When visitors come to the arts and crafts village, Tlaquepaque, they encounter more than quaint galleries and shops; they experience a cultural treat as they stroll along cobblestone courtyards and the sycamore trees gently bend down to provide shade from the warm Sedona sun. A landmark since the 1970s, Tlaquepaque has exceptional restaurants, entertaining events, and enchanting galleries and shops. For more about the restaurants in Tlaquepaque, see the Sedona Restaurants section. Tlaquepaque's annual events are referenced in the Sedona Annual Events section. Shops at Tlaquepaque are listed in the Sedona Shopping section. For more information about the galleries, see the Sedona Arts section.

Recreation

Sedona is a favorite spot for visitors and locals alike to enjoy outdoor activities. Situated in the heart of red rock country, Sedona has recreational activities for people of all ages. Surrounded by monolithic rock formations, rugged countryside, and vast open land, outdoor enthusiasts can explore the mysterious area by foot, jeep, horse, mountain bike, or hot air balloon. The mild temperatures and constant sunshine will have you outdoors enjoying the fresh air in no time. This section is full of activities listings, alphabetized under the following headers: Air Service and Charters, Balloon Rides, Camping, Climbing, Fishing, Golf, Hiking, Horseback Riding, Mountain Biking, Parks, Tennis, and Tours.

Air Service and Charters

Arizona Helicopter Adventure
235 Air Terminal Dr.
(520) 282–0904, (800) 282–5141
www.azheli.com

View Sedona's famous red rocks, explore canyons, and visit ancient Indian ruins with Arizona Helicopter Adventures. You will receive an in-flight narrative by a skilled pilot, while enjoying a comfortable ride in a Bell Jet Ranger Helicopter. For information about take-offs and rates, contact Arizona Helicopter Adventure.

Red Rock Biplane Tours
1225 Airport Rd.
(520) 204–5939, (888) 866–7433
www.sedonaairtours.com

Journey through the red rock country of Sedona in a Waco open cockpit biplane. The pilot flies from the rear cockpit while passengers sit in the front cockpit. Contact Red Rock Biplane Tours for more information.

Sky Safari
1225 Airport Rd.
(520) 204–5939, (888) 866–7433
www.sedonaairtours.com

Sky Safari offers fully narrated local tours, charter services, and destination flights to the Grand Canyon, Lake Powell, Monument Valley, and Laughlin, Nevada. The aircrafts can hold three to five passengers plus the pilot. Call Sky Safari for times, different destinations, and current rates.

Balloon Rides

A Sky High Balloon
(520) 204–1395, (800) 551–7597

If you are looking for something a little out of the ordinary, try "Splash and Dash!" Beginning at sunrise, pilots will have passengers floating through the air, before they make a dramatic landing on the water. Hold on! Then you will ascend into the air again and land on a solid surface. A champagne picnic in the forest after the ride is included. Sky High will pick passengers up at their hotel. The cost is $139 per person. Children must be at least four feet tall. Call A Sky High Balloon for more information.

Northern Light Balloon Expeditions
(520) 282–2274, (800) 230–6222
www.sedona.net/fun/balloon

This early morning adventure starts at sunrise and ends with a gourmet picnic. The cost is $135 per person. Children

Insiders' Tip

Sedona temperatures average 10 degrees cooler than Phoenix and 10 degrees warmer than Flagstaff.

must be 42 inches tall to ride in the balloon. Northern Light Balloon Expeditions will pick you up from your hotel. Please call ahead for reservations.

Red Rock Balloon
(520) 284–0040, (800) 258–3754
www.redrockballoons.com

Explore the red rock country by balloon at sunrise. This company flies deeper into red rock country than any other. After the flight, a champagne breakfast is served. Passengers will receive a previously filmed flight video as a souvenir. The cost is $155 per person.

Camping

All designated Forest Service campgrounds in the Sedona area have toilets, picnic tables, fire rings, and are wheelchair accessible. The cost per night for one vehicle is $15. A $5 fee is charged for the second vehicle. There is a $3 fee for visitors who want to picnic in the campgrounds between 10 A.M. and 4 P.M. A $15 fee will be charged to picnickers after 4 P.M.

All campgrounds have spigots for drinking water except for Bootlegger. If you have any questions, contact the Sedona Ranger District, (520) 282–4119, or for reservations call (877) 444–6777.

Bootlegger

This small yet beautiful campground is a good fishing spot nestled among ponderosa pines in Oak Creek. Bootlegger has ten camping sites and RVs and trailers are not allowed. Only one vehicle is allowed per unit. The campground is open April 15 through October 31. If you are coming from Sedona, Bootlegger Campground is 9.1 miles north of U.S. Highway 89A past the Junipine Resort on your left.

Cave Springs

Cave Springs is a secluded campground, ideal for both couples and families. It has eighty sites and is one of the largest campgrounds in the area. Cave Springs allows two cars per unit and RVs and trailers up to 36 feet. This campground does fill up quickly. Call ahead for reservations. Cave Springs is 11.9 miles north of the "Y" intersection in Sedona on U.S. Highway 89A.

Chavez Crossing

Chavez has three sites that can accommodate group campers. Two of the sites can hold 10 to 30 people, while the third site holds up to 50 campers. Walk along the nature trail by the creek and enjoy privacy and seclusion at this campground. Camping fees are $35 at the sites for 10 to 30 campers; a $55 fee is charges for the third site, which holds up to 50 people. The campground is 2.1 miles south of the "Y" intersection on Arizona Highway 179.

Manzanita

This campground is open all year and has nineteen camping sites. One vehicle per site is allowed. RVs up to 24 feet are allowed; trailers are not allowed in this campground. Campers should arrive early; this is a popular place to camp. Visitors will enjoy walking or relaxing by the creek. Campers: beware of poison ivy.

Pineflat East and West

These campgrounds are across the highway from one another and are 12.9 miles north of the "Y" intersection in Sedona on U.S. Highway 89A. Pineflat East visitors can enjoy access to the Cookstove Trail. This shaded campground is open from April 1 to November 15. There are twenty-one sites available and RVs and trailers up to 36 feet are allowed. Reservations are not necessary. Pineflat West has thirty-seven sites and is open from March 1 through November 15. This campground can accommodate RVs and trailers up to 36

feet; two vehicles per site are allowed. Pineflat West has trail access on either side of the creek.

Rustic Camping

Here a few suggestions for campers looking to escape the crowded campgrounds and find seclusion in the forest. This is real camping; there are no amenities available in the National Forest. Camping in dispersed areas of the National Forest is only allowed for fourteen days.

Beaverhead Flat Road

Take Arizona Highway 179 past the Village of Oak Creek for 3 miles. Beaverhead Flat Road or Forest Road 120 is on the right-hand side of the road.

House Mountain

Take Arizona Highway 179 south of the Village of Oak Creek to Beaverhead Flat Road (FR 120). Drive 2 miles on Forest Road 120, which leads directly to House Mountain.

Sycamore Street/Deer Pass Drive

Drive 6 miles west of Sedona on U.S. Highway 89A until you reach Forest Road 525. Take FR 525 north for 2.5 miles to Forest Road 525C. Get out and camp!

Fishing

If you want to fish in Oak Creek Canyon, you must first purchase a fishing license. Fishing licenses can be purchased at Safeway, Bashas', or participating sporting good stores.

Gon' Fishen
30 Kashmir Rd.
(520) 282–0788

Your fishing guide Jim McInnis will take you to secluded fishing holes, provide transportation, lunch, and basic fly-fishing instruction. Equipment can be rented and private fishing lessons are available. Contact Jim for more information and an unforgettable fishing experience.

Rainbow Trout Farm
N. Hwy. 89A, Oak Creek Canyon
(520) 282–5799

Pay $1 and you will be armed with bucket, pole, and net. Be ready to catch some trout. You cannot throw back what you have caught. The fee per fish ranges from $3.99 to $6.95 depending on the size and weight. Rainbow Trout Farm is open seven days a week from 9 A.M. to 5 P.M. year round. A fishing license is not required at the trout farm. Barbecue grills and picnic facilities are available.

Golf

Canyon Mesa Country Club
500 Jacks Canyon Rd.
(520) 284–0036

A private course that is also open to the public, this 9-hole executive course is well-maintained and offers putting and chipping facilities. Greens fees are $15 to walk plus an additional $10 for a cart.

Oak Creek Country Club
690 Bell Rock Rd.
(520) 284–1660, (888) 703–9489

Thirty-two years ago, Robert Trent Jones, Sr. designed this traditional-style 18-hole golf course. Today it is one of the most played courses in the Sedona area. The $75 greens fee includes a cart. Call for tee times.

Sedona Golf Resort
35 Ridge Trail Dr.
(520) 284–9355, (877) 733–9882
www.sedonagolfresort.com

This championship 18-hole course has received more than one four-star rating from *Golf Digest*. The views of the surrounding red rocks makes this an unforgettable golfing experience. Contact the Sedona Golf Resort for tee times and fees.

Hiking

Whether you are looking for wildlife, archaeological sites, or an afternoon walk, Sedona's endless hiking trail choices are bound to please everyone. Don't forget to bring plenty of water and to wear sunscreen.

"Coffee Pot" is a well known rock formation in red rock country. PHOTO: STACEY WITTIG

Allen's Bend Trail
Easy

This tranquil 0.5-mile walk takes you along Oak Creek through an old orchard. The trail provides access to the creek for fishing, swimming, and picnicking. To find the trailhead, go north on U.S. Highway 89A to milepost 376.7. Make a right and park in the lot for Grasshopper Point. There is a $3 fee. This trail is not recommended for horses.

Bell Rock Pathway
Easy

This 3.5-mile long trail is the widest in the state. Members of the local organization Red Rock Pathways helped to build the trail that offers stunning views of Bell Rock and Courthouse Butte.

To reach the Bell Rock Pathway, take Arizona Highway 179 south and just beyond the Sedona Methodist Church; the trailhead is on the east side of the road.

Brins Mesa Trail
Moderate

This trail begins at the edge of town and exposes the hiker to unobstructed views of the red rocks. Bring a map along this 3-mile trail so you can identify Coffee Pot Rock, Wilson Mountain, Chimney Rock, and other rock formations. Take U.S. Highway 89A for 3.1 miles to Dry Creek Road. Turn right on Dry Creek Road and drive for 1.9 miles to unpaved Forest Service Road 152 and turn right. Go 2.4 miles on 152 and to the right for Brins Mesa Trail Forest Service Road 119.

Secret Canyon Trail
Moderate

This 4.2-mile trail climbs from 4,640 feet to 5,300 feet and the first two miles follow an old, flat roadbed. The rest of the trail traverses in and out of the bottom of the canyon and is used by both hikers and equestrians. To access the trailhead, drive on U.S. Highway 89A for 3.1 miles to Dry Creek Road. Turn right on Dry Creek Road and drive 1.9 miles to Forest Service road 152. Make a right on FR 152 and drive northeast for 3.4 miles to the parking area for Secret Canyon Forest Service Road 121.

Horseback Riding

A Day in the West & Sedona Photo Tours
(See Tours for more about Sedona Photo Tours)
(520) 282–4320, (800) 973–3662
www.adayinthewest.com

Step back in time and visit an authentic Western movie town by horseback. A Day in the West provides guided horseback rides and cowboy cookouts with all the fixins'! Contact A Day in the West for reservations and rates.

Sedona Red Rock Tours
(520) 282–6826, (800) 848–7288
www.redrockjeep.com

Experience the "Old West" with Sedona Red Rock Tours. "Legends of Sedona Ranch Trails." Riders will be surrounded by national forest, and view some of Sedona's most stunning red rock formations. Call Sedona Red Rock Tours for reservations and rates. See below for more information about Sedona Red Rock Jeep Tours.

Trail Horse Adventures
(520) 282–7252
www.trailhorseadventures.com

For the complete Western experience, Trail Horse Adventures offers hayrides, sunset rides, cattle drives, and Western entertainment. Call Trail Horse Adventures for corporate and family rates and special events.

Mountain Biking

Peddle your way through the pine forests and the desert landscapes of Sedona. Visitors can rent mountain bikes at Desert Jeep & Bike Rentals, 75 Bell Rock Plaza, Suite #3, (520) 284–1099, and at Sedona Bike & Bean, 6020 Highway 179, (520) 284–0210.

Broken Arrow
Moderate

Broken Arrow provides scenic views, awesome rock formations, and a sink hole. This trail can get a bit tricky (some might say technical) and fluctuates from easy to hard riding terrain. To access the Broken Arrow trail take Arizona Highway 179 south from the "Y" intersection 1.4 miles to Morgan Road, which is on the left. The trailhead is at the end of Morgan Road.

Cathedral Rock
Moderate

This 10.9-mile trail ranges from easy to expert. The clincher of this ride is a swimming hole, a welcome relief for tired and sweaty riders. To access the trail, take

Arizona Highway 179 south from the "Y" intersection for 4 miles until you come to an intersection with Back o' Beyond Road on the right. Take Back o' Beyond Road 0.7 miles to the trailhead on the left.

Deadman's Pass
Easy to Moderate

This 6.4-mile single track takes you through the backcountry north of Sedona. The trail goes mostly downhill through rough, rocky sections. To access the trailhead, take U.S. Highway 89A through West Sedona to Dry Creek Road. At Dry Creek Road make a right and follow the road until it ends at a "Y" intersection. Before the intersection, the road turns into Boynton Pass Road. Turn right on Long Canyon Road at the "Y" intersection. Drive for 0.6 miles; the trailhead is on the left.

Dry Creek Road
Easy

Beginning mountain bike riders will enjoy the smooth forest road and spectacular views, but remember the return trip is uphill. To reach the Dry Creek Road Trailhead, take U.S. Highway 89A through West Sedona and turn right on Dry Creek Road. Dry Creek Road turns into Boynton Pass Road. Bikers will want to head right at the "Y" intersection and park their car here as well.

Parks

Red Rock Crossing/Crescent Moon Ranch
Day Use Area
www.visitsedona.com

Families will enjoy swimming under the towering red cliffs. Picnic tables are available. To access Red Rock Crossing, take W. U.S. Highway 89A to Upper Red Rock Loop Road. Overnight camping is prohibited. There is a $3 fee per vehicle.

Red Rock State Park Nature Center
(520) 282-6907
www.visitsedona.com

The park was founded to preserve the natural habitat of Oak Creek and to provide educational activities for adults and kids. The park also offers hiking trails, picnic facilities, and special programs. Red Rock State Park is located on Lower Red Rock Loop Road off of W. U.S. Highway 89A. There is a $5 entrance fee per vehicle.

Slide Rock State Park
(520) 282-3034
www.visitsedona.com

This natural water slide is one of the most popular parks in Arizona. The park, besides offering relief from the summer heat, has picnic tables, barbecue grills, fishing, and nature trails. Slide Rock State Park is located 8 miles north of Sedona in Oak Creek Canyon. A $5 entrance fee is charged per vehicle.

Tennis

Play a set of outdoor tennis surrounded by the beautiful red rocks of Sedona. These private clubs are also open to the public. Reservations are required and there is a $10 fee to play: Poco Diablo Resort, 1736 Hwy. 179, (520) 282-7333, and Sedona Racquet Club, 100 Racquet Rd., (520) 282-4197.

Posse Grounds Park
Posse Grounds Rd.
(520) 282-7098

Bring the family here to enjoy the playground facilities, have a picnic, or play tennis. This park is located in West Sedona on Posse Grounds Road.

Insiders' Tip
Tune your radio to 1500 for more information about Sedona's parks.

Tours

Blue Feather Tours
P.O. Box 3474
(520) 284–3343, (877) 733–6621
www.azgrandcanyontours.com

Blue Feather Tours will pick you up at your hotel and take you through Oak Creek Canyon and along Historic Route 66. The tour will then introduce you to the beauty of the Painted Desert and stop at a Navajo trading post. The next stop is the Grand Canyon. Passengers will stop at lookout points and walk along the rim. Tours can be personalized to accommodate a group of five or more. Two day excursions to Monument Valley and Canyon de Chelly, and to the Hopi Reservation are available. Call Blue Feather Tours for rates, departure times, and reservations.

Pink Jeep Tours and Ancient Expeditions
204 N. Hwy. 89A
(520) 282–5000, (800) 873–3662
www.pinkjeep.com

Explore the desert country of Sedona in a pink jeep. Take a tour to the ancient Indian ruins with professional and knowledgeable guides. Pink Jeep Tours offers exclusive "world famous" four-wheel drive adventures, customized tours, and special events. Contact Pink Jeep for more information and reservations.

Sedona Adventures 4X4 Tours
(520) 282–3500, (800) 888–9494

Specializing in customized tours of Sedona's canyons and monuments, Sedona Adventures will take you on the off-road experience of your life. Call Sedona Adventures for group rates and reservations.

Sedona City & Scenic Tours
P.O. Box 1635, Sedona, 86339
(520) 282–5400

Tour Sedona by trolley and see famous galleries, shops, and resorts. The tour leaves on the hour across from the Chamber Visitor Center. Tickets for the trolley

Take a Pink Jeep Tour in Sedona and you'll see the landscape from a whole different angle.
PHOTO: PETER PFEIFFER

tour are $7 for adults and $2 for kids 12 and under. Visitors can pick from two tours; the price for both tours is $11.

Sedona Nature Excursions
(520) 282–6735
www.rahelio.com

Embark on a spiritual journey in the Red Rock Country to the world-renowned vortices of Sedona. Your guide will customize your tour to include healing ceremonies, nature walking, or meditation. Please contact Rahelio for more information.

Sedona Photo Tours
252 N. Hwy. 89A
(520) 282–4320, (800) 973–3662
www.adayinthewest.com

Sedona Photo Tours range from "mild to wild" and offer some of the best photographic opportunities. Learn about

Native American customs, geology, and history while experienced guides offer great photography tips. Don't forget your camera!

Sedona Red Rock Jeep Tours
(520) 282–6826, (800) 848–7728

Sedona's renowned cowboy tour company also offers 4x4 Jeep, Jeep-helicopter tours, and special personalized events. Ride along the same trail traveled by General George Crook during the final Apache campaign in 1871–1872. Contact Sedona Red Rock Jeep Tours for more information.

Sedona Vortex Connections
(520) 204–9355, (800) 393–6308

Sedona Vortex Connections will help make your visit to Sedona into a life-changing experience and provide nurturing tours to the renowned vortices. Contact Sedona Vortex Connections for details on tours and rates.

Shopping

Even the most hesitant of shoppers will agree that Sedona is a shopper's paradise. Visitors enjoy strolling through the stores and along cobblestone courtyards as they eye some of the most unique gifts under the sun.

One of the major retail areas is located in Uptown Sedona, on U.S. Highway 89A. Don't be startled by the abundance of souvenir shops. Seek and you shall find, and you will find a little of everything within a convenient walking distance—arts, crafts, jewelry, Western wear, and clothing stores with a "Southwestern" flair.

South of U.S. 89A, below the "Y," on both sides of Arizona Highway 179, you will find bookstores, mineral shops, and clothing boutiques. Hillside Sedona is on AZ 179 and has scenic views, sculpture gardens, boutiques, and Southwestern furnishings. Tlaquepaque Arts and Crafts Village is located at the "Y." Shoppers will enjoy the Spanish Colonial architecture, bending sycamores, and flower-filled courtyards. The major draws in the Village of Oak Creek are the factory outlet stores and a few specialty shops.

Numerous shopping centers, professional plazas, and specialty shops line West U.S. 89A.

We have divided this chapter geographically: Arizona Highway 179 (which includes Hillside Sedona, Tlaquepaque, and Oak Creek). Then we head to Uptown Sedona, and West Sedona.

Arizona Highway 179

The Book Loft
175 AZ Hwy. 179
(520) 282-5173
www.abebooks.com/home/book_loft

Specializing in regional guidebooks, The Book Loft has 10,000 new, used, and rare books. Try their organic coffee by the cup or take a pound of it home with you. The Book Loft is open Sunday through Tuesday 10 A.M. to 6 P.M., 10 A.M. to 7 P.M. on Friday and Saturday; it is closed on Tuesday.

Insiders' Tip

The Book Loft specializes in out-of-print book searches. Visit the bookstore, or call (520) 282-5173 to find your title.

Crystal Castle
313 AZ Hwy. 179
(520) 282–5910, (800) 688–2665
www.crystalcastle.com

Crystal Castle has products to soothe your mind and soul including aromatherapy products, New Age music, bells, chimes, jewelry, rocks, and crystals. Crystal Castle is open 9 A.M. to 7 P.M. daily.

Ramsey's Rocks and Minerals
152 AZ Hwy. 179
(520) 204–2075

Since 1949 Ramsey's has offered a large selection of Arizona gems, crystals from around the world, and quality minerals. Jewelry is custom made by artist Jeffrey Goebel. Ramsey's is open daily 10 A.M. to 6 P.M.

Victorian Cowgirl
204 AZ Hwy. 179
(520) 203–9809
www.easy-finder.com/brochures/vcgirl

For a classic look, Victorian Cowgirl combines the elegance of the Victorian Age and the freedom of the West. Victorian Cowgirl, featuring women's clothing, unique bridal wear, and accessories, is open 10 A.M. to 6 P.M. daily.

Hillside Sedona

Hillside Prints & Framing
671 AZ Hwy. 179
(520) 282–6567

Hillside Prints & Framing has a great selection of prints, posters, and original art of Sedona and the Southwest. After you have picked out your piece, they will happily frame it for you too.

The shop also carries note cards, postcards, and gift items. Hillside Prints & Framing is open 10 A.M. to 6 P.M. daily.

Favorite Clothing Co.
671 AZ Hwy. 179
(520) 204–1920

Featuring contemporary natural fiber clothing, Favorite Clothing also has their own line of handmade batik clothing for women and children. This natural shop also has accessories, jewelry, and gift items. The store is open 10 A.M. to 6 P.M. daily.

Santa Fe Savvy
671 AZ Hwy. 179
(520) 204–9848

Decorate your home with the spirit of the West. Santa Fe Savvy has leather furniture, end tables, bookcases, dressers, and so much more. Santa Fe Savvy is open daily 10 A.M. to 6 P.M.

Sofia's Boutiques
671 AZ Hwy. 179
(520) 282–4499

Sofia's has contemporary, classic, and off-the-wall women's fashions. From evening gowns, to breezy summer dresses, to silk pajamas, Sofia's has it all, even leopard-print items. The boutique is open daily 10 A.M. to 6 P.M.

Steppes
671 AZ Hwy. 179
(520) 204–0606

Get lost in this quaint boutique for hours and discover Brighton leather goods and gifts, women's clothing, and accessories. Steppes is open Monday through Sunday 10 A.M. to 6 P.M.

The Wine Basket
671 AZ Hwy. 179
(520) 203–9411

Immerse yourself in the decadence of the Wine Basket. They have gourmet everything, from chocolates, to pastries, to imported coffee. The Wine Basket has California, New Zealand, French, Chilean, and Italian wines. Specialty baskets can be designed and shipped from the store. The Wine Basket is open Monday through Thursday 10 A.M. to 6 P.M., Saturday 10 A.M. to 9 P.M., Sunday noon to 6 P.M.

Village of Oak Creek

Amanda Jane's Doll Shoppe
70 Bell Rock Plaza
(520) 284–5222

Amanda Jane's Doll Shoppe has over 600 dolls on display in their showroom. They carry dolls by Madame Alexander, Robert Tonner, Lee Middleton, Lloyd Middleton, Annette Himstedt, and others. The shoppe will ship anywhere in the United States. Amanda Jane's is open Monday through Saturday 10:30 A.M. to 5 P.M.

Sedona Bike & Bean
6020 AZ Hwy. 179
(520) 284–0210

Sedona Bike & Bean can outfit you for all your cycling needs, with bike clothing and accessories for men, women, and children.

They also rent mountain bikes for the family (ages eight years and up). Wondering what the Bean part is about? Sedona Bike & Bean has an espresso bar with specialty drinks and snacks. Sedona Bike & Bean is open every day 8 A.M. to 5 P.M.

Oak Creek Factory Stores
6600 AZ Hwy. 179
(520) 284–2150, (888) 545–7227

Oak Creek Factory Stores feature over thirty national store chains. From Bass to Anne Klein to Geoffrey Beene, the stores have a large selection of clothing and home furnishings at discounted prices. The factory stores are open Monday through Saturday 9 A.M. to 7 P.M. and Sunday 10 A.M. to 6 P.M.

Tlaquepaque Arts and Crafts Village

Cocopah
Ste. C101
(520) 282–6404

Cocopah has beads, shells, ethnic pieces, jewelry kits, and jewelry stringing materials. Call for their color bead catalog. Cocopah is open 10 A.M. to 5 P.M. daily.

The Juice & Candy Bar
Ste. F104
(520) 282–5455

The Juice & Candy Bar has fine chocolates, handmade fudge, and fresh squeezed juices. Locals love the Raspberry Rave, Strawburst, and Pink Grapefruit. The store also sells sugar-free candy and ice cream. The Juice & Candy Bar is open daily 10 A.M. to 5 P.M.

Kitchen Wizard
Ste. D101
(520) 282–3905

The Kitchen Wizard has Southwestern spices, condiments, cookbooks, and fun accessories for the home. Kitchen Wizard is open daily 10 A.M. to 6 P.M.

The Melting Pot
Ste. C106
(520) 204–9881

The Melting Pot has candles, candle holders, and accessories. They feature candles and accessories made by local artists. The Melting Pot is open 10 A.M. to 5 P.M. daily.

The Storyteller Bookstore
Ste. #B105
(520) 282–2144

The Storyteller has Southwestern children's books, and hard and soft cover books about Sedona, the Southwest, and Native American tribes. They also have music, hiking maps, and guides. The Storyteller is open daily 10 A.M. to 6 P.M.

> ## Insiders' Tip
> Kitchen Wizard at the Tlaquepaque Arts and Crafts Village has a fresh salsa bar where you can sample a taste before you make your purchase.

Shoppers enjoy the flower-filled courtyards at Tlaquepaque. PHOTO: STACEY WITTIG

Torke Weihnachten Christmas
Ste. A116
(520) 282–2752

Featuring glass pieces and ornaments from Poland and Germany, Torke Weih- nachten also has holiday collectibles and Christmas art from the Southwest. Torke Weihnachten is open Monday through Sunday 10 A.M. to 6 P.M.

Uptown Sedona

Burkhalter Collection
208 N. U.S. Hwy. 89A
(520) 282–7894

This eclectic shop features hand-blown glass pieces and sculptures. They also have kitchen knives and specialty T-shirts. Burkhalter Collection is open daily 10 A.M. to 6 P.M.

Cowboy Corral
219 N. U.S. Hwy. 89A
(520) 282–2040, (800) 457–2279

The Cowboy Corral offers one-stop shop- ping, with Victorian style women's fash- ions, custom-made boots and hats, cowboy music, food, and gift items. Cow- boy Corral is open 10 A.M. to 6 P.M. daily.

Looking West
242 N. U.S. Hwy. 89A
(520) 282–4877 (800) 345–6944

Featuring ladies' fashion with a taste of the Southwest, Looking West has a selec- tion of locally made clothing and acces- sories and is open daily 9 A.M. to 7 P.M.

Richard David for Men
301 N. U.S. Hwy. 89A
(520) 282–6938

Richard David features men's clothing and accessories. Even the most hesitant of male shoppers will like the selection of sportswear, golf wear, and casual outer- wear. Richard David is open 10 A.M. to 5:30 P.M. Monday through Sunday.

Rollies Camera Shop
297 N. U.S. Hwy. 89A
(520) 282–5721
www.rolliescamera.com

Rollies Camera Shop is a full-service shop that specializes in film, accessories, and of course cameras. Ask about their overnight processing policy. Rollies Camera Shop is open from 8:30 A.M. to 5:30 P.M.

Sedona Fudge Company
257 N. U.S. Hwy. 89A
Bashas' Shopping Center,
W. U.S. Hwy. 89A
(520) 282–1044, (520) 282–7747

Calling all sweet tooths! Sedona Fudge Company has homemade fudge in assorted flavors, truffles, toffee, cookies, and more. This candy heaven is open Saturday 9 A.M. to 8 P.M. and Sunday through Friday 9 A.M. to 7 P.M.

The Worm Book & Music Store
207 N. U.S. Hwy. 89A
(520) 282–3471
www.sedonaworm.com

The Worm Book & Music Store specializes in Western, health, and travel books and hard and soft cover fiction. Featuring world, classical, and Native American music, the Worm also has a large children's book section and is open daily 9 A.M. to 8 P.M.

West Sedona

Bob McLean Custom Boots
40 Soldiers Pass
(520) 204–1211

Manufacturing quality handmade Western boots and belts, Bob McLean will measure and fit you in the shop. Customers choose from only the finest leather. The store will ship anywhere in the United States. Store hours are 9 A.M. to 6 P.M. daily.

Canyon Outfitters
2701 W. U.S. Hwy. 89A
(520) 282–5293

Canyon Outfitters will dress and outfit you with quality equipment for your outdoor adventure. They also have a large selection of USGS topo maps, area hiking maps, and books. Canyon Outfitters is open Monday through Friday 9 A.M. to 6 P.M., Saturday 9 A.M. to 5 P.M., and Sunday 11 A.M. to 4 P.M.

Gift Baskets of Sedona
Bashas' Shopping Center, 160 Coffee Pot Dr.
(520) 282–7747

You will find a gift basket for any reason and season here. Baskets are designed especially for you. They will do the shopping or you can shop and they will assemble the basket for you. Or try one of their unique creations, like the "Southwest Basket" with cactus pot holders and prickly pear jelly. The "Get Well" Basket comes with crossword puzzles and fresh

squeezed juices. These baskets make great gifts for the person who has everything. Gift Baskets of Sedona is open 10 A.M. to 6 P.M. Monday through Saturday.

Lightn' Up
1710 W. U.S. Hwy. 89A
(520) 282–7902

For all your cigar needs, Lightn' Up has the finest selection of cigars, pipes, and accessories from around the world. Lightn' Up is open Monday through Saturday 10 A.M. to 6 P.M.

Mexidona
1670 W. U.S. Hwy. 89A
(520) 282–0858

Featuring handcrafted imports, Mexidona has Mexican colonial furniture, home and garden decor, and ethnic and folk art at reasonable prices. Take a piece of the southwest home with you! Mexidona is open 10 A.M. to 5 P.M. Monday through Saturday, noon to 5 P.M. on Sunday.

Sedona Clothing Company and
West Fork Men's
1710 W. U.S. Hwy. 89A
(520) 204–9390

Both men and women can find casual or dressy attire for any occasion. Open 9 A.M. to 6 P.M., Sedona Clothing Company and West Fork Men's will even gift wrap your purchases at no extra charge.

Wayne B. Light Custom Jewelry
3000 W. U.S. Hwy. 89A
(520) 282–2131, (800) 894–2131
www.wayneblight.com

Featuring custom design and traditional jewelry for men and women, this extensive selection includes pendants, rings, earrings, and tie-tacs, all in your choice of precious metals or diamonds. Wayne B. Light is open 10 A.M. to 5:30 P.M. daily.

Nightlife

As a resort town, Sedona hums through the day, but the nights seem quiet under the star-filled sky. Most people like to rest at night so they can tackle the following day's activity-packed itinerary. But there is plenty to do here once the sun goes down.

Live entertainment is everywhere. Solo acts and bands fill the bars. Whether you like to two-step or listen to rock 'n' roll, you can find it almost any night of the week during the high season (from February to April and from September through the end of December). Free dance lessons are given everywhere. Sedona nightclubs hear their Spanish roots and offer Salsa lessons and then they listen to their Western roots and provide two-step and country line dancing.

If dancing isn't up your alley, we have provided quiet and intimate establishments that encourage conversation and provide quality local and regional entertainment.

We have also included Sedona's only two theater companies, which have been well received by locals and visitors. Please call the organization for a listing of performances, dates, and times.

Most resorts have family activities and bars so visitors don't have to leave the grounds. If you are looking for a night out or for a nightcap after dinner, keep in mind Arizona's strict enforcement of DUI laws. If you are pulled over and your blood alcohol level is anywhere between .05% to 1.0%, you may be arrested. Sedona is a small city. It won't take more than 10 to 15 minutes to reach your destination by cab.

Bars and Nightclubs

Casa Rincon and Tapas Cantina
2620 W. U.S. Hwy. 89A
(520) 282–4849

Featuring live entertainment almost every night, Casa Rincon will have you dancing in the aisles or at least in your seat. Local and regional bands perform on Friday and Saturday beginning at 9 P.M. The music entertainment on weekend nights changes regularly. Guests can expect to hear Motown, reggae, and rock 'n' roll. Special entertainment is scheduled for Sunday. Call for an updated schedule of events. Wednesday night is Ladies' Night starting at 5 P.M., with drink specials all evening. For more about the Casa Rincon and Tapas Cantina, see the Sedona Restaurants section.

The Laughing Coyote
U.S. Hwy. 89A
(520) 282–1842

Here the music is as eclectic as the crowd. This is where the locals hang out. Bands play every Wednesday, Friday, Saturday, and Sunday starting at 9 P.M., except for Sunday, when the music starts at 7 P.M. Ladies, come out on Wednesday, this is your night. Drink specials, free pool, and jukebox music start at 7 P.M.

Lizard Head Lounge
2675 W. U.S. Hwy. 89A
(520) 282-1808

Lizard Head Lounge features music, music, and more music. From rock 'n' roll to reggae, to the latest hip-hop, live music happens every Tuesday through Saturday. Lizard Head Lounge is located behind Nationwide UPS in West Sedona and opens daily at 7 P.M.; bands start at 9 P.M.

Oak Creek Brewing Co.
2050 Yavapai Dr.
(520) 204-1300

Get a taste for what the locals drink at Oak Creek Brewing Co. Handcrafted stouts, ales, and seasonal beers are made on the premises. Wine and soft drinks are also served. Look for entertainment almost every night of the week. A full band is featured Friday and Saturday nights beginning at 9 P.M. Dancing is mandatory. Live solo entertainment is every Sunday, Tuesday, and Thursday. Times do fluctuate, so call ahead for exact schedule.

On the Rocks Bar & Grill
Los Abrigados Resort & Spa,
160 Portal Ln.
(520) 204-7849
www.ilxinc.com

Come watch the game on the giant, 10-foot screen, or relax with a glass of Los Abrigados private label wine. On the Rocks Bar & Grill has appetizers and offers a lighter menu for snacking. The bar is open until 1 A.M.. For more about On the Rocks Bar & Grill, see the Sedona Restaurants section.

Orchards Grill Restaurant
254 N. U.S. Hwy. 89A
(520) 282-7200
www.lauberge.com

Visitors will enjoy the quaint bar and casual atmosphere with entertainment every Thursday, Friday, and Saturday. Enjoy live acoustic music from 7 P.M. to 9:30 P.M. Local and regional musicians play here. For more about the Orchards, see the Sedona Restaurants section.

Rainbow's End Steakhouse & Saloon
3235 W. U.S. Hwy. 89A
(520) 282-1593

The Rainbow's End has something for anyone who wants to dance. Learn the latest country swing dance moves every Tuesday night, and every Wednesday night learn how to country line dance. And if country isn't your cup of tea, try Rainbow's End on the weekend when they feature live country, Motown, or classic rock bands. The band starts at 9 P.M. Call for a listing of bands. For more about the Rainbow's End, see the Sedona Restaurants section.

Steak & Sticks
Los Abrigados Resort & Spa,
160 Portal Ln.
(520) 204-7849
www.ilxinc.com

This room has pool, backgammon, and small intimate tables for conversation. The room opens at 11 A.M. The bar is opened from 5 P.M. 'til 1 A.M., and is stocked with fine wine, premium liquors and cordials, and imported beer. For more on Steak & Sticks, see the Sedona Restaurants section.

> **Insiders' Tip**
> Rainbow's End Steakhouse & Saloon has free dance lessons every Tuesday and Wednesday. Lessons begin between 8 and 8:30 P.M.

Theater

Oak Creek Theatre Company
Sedona Arts Center, 15 Art Barn Rd.
(520) 282–3809   www.sedona.net

Sedona's professional theater company performs at the Charles W. Raison Theatre in the Sedona Arts Center. Past performances include *The Dining Room*, *The Glass Menagerie*, and *Turn of the Screw*. Tickets can be purchased at the Sedona Arts Center, or by calling (520) 282–3809. They can also be purchased at the door the day of the performance, or at the Tlaquepaque Arts & Crafts Village Information Booth located on Arizona Highway 179, just south of the "Y."

Sedona Arts Center Community Theatre
15 Art Barn Rd.
(520) 282–3809
www.sedona.net

Sedona's only community theater group performs twice a year in the spring and the fall. Past performances includes *Chicken Man*, an original musical. Tickets can be purchased at Sedona Arts Center, (520) 282–3809, and at the door the day of the performance. Contact Sedona Arts Center for the year's upcoming performances.

Kidstuff

Forget the video games here. Sedona is nature's playground with endless outdoor recreational activities that will appeal to kids from all walks of life.

In this chapter we have searched for fun and entertaining activities that promise to amuse and delight any family member. Whether your kids enjoy hiking, taking nature walks, or swimming in outdoor, pristine pools, Sedona has it.

Fishing along Oak Creek Canyon is a traditional family activity that will never go out of style. Or if a true western adventure is calling, try a guided horseback trip and an authentic cowboy cookout. And if you and your family need to take a break, buy some popcorn and head to the Sedona SuperVue Theatre.

Your kids can learn from Sedona as well. Introduce your child to ancient Indian cultures and tour historic forts and home sites of Sedona's first settlers.

Fishing

Rainbow Trout Farm
N. U.S. Hwy. 89A, Oak Creek Canyon
(520) 282–5799

Plan to spend the day fishing along Oak Creek with the family. Pay $1 and the entire family will be armed with bucket, pole, and net. And after the kids fish to their heart's content, cook the catch of the day right at the farm. Barbeque grills and picnic facilities are available. Rainbow Trout Farm is open seven days a week from 9 A.M. to 5 P.M. year round. For more information about Rainbow Trout Farm, see the Sedona Recreation section.

Insiders' Tip

Visitors can stop almost anywhere along Oak Creek and throw in a fishing line. Watch for signs that warn against trespassing. Please be aware of areas that are restricted to swimmers and are private property.

Hiking

Hiking trails in the Sedona area offer scenic views, a chance to see wildlife, or just a pleasant way to spend the day with your child. The trails are usually dry and exposed to sunlight: don't forget to bring plenty of water and to wear sunscreen.

Allen's Bend Trail
Easy

This easy 0.5-mile walk takes you along Oak Creek through an old orchard. The trail provides access to the creek for fishing, swimming, and picnicking. For more information about the trail, see Sedona Recreation section.

Bell Rock Pathway
Easy

This 3.5-mile long trail offers stunning views of Bell Rock and Courthouse Butte. To reach the Bell Rock Pathway, take AZ Hwy. 179 south just beyond the Sedona Methodist Church. The trailhead is on the east side of the road. For more information about this hike, see the Sedona Recreation section.

Brins Mesa Trail
Moderate

Bring a map (you can get one at the Sedona Chamber of Commerce) along this 3-mile trail so you can identify Coffee Pot Rock, Wilson Mountain, Chimney Rock, and other rock formations. For more information, refer to the Sedona Recreation section.

Horseback Riding

A Day in the West & Sedona Photo Tours
(520) 282–4320, (800) 973–3662
www.adayinthewest.com

What child would not want to visit an authentic Western movie town by horseback, take a guided horseback ride through red rock country, or have a cowboy cookout with all the fixins' under the star filled Sedona sky? Contact A Day in the West for reservations and family rates.

Trail Horse Adventures
(520) 282–7252
www.trailhorseadventures.com

For the complete Western experience, Trail Horse Adventures offers hayrides, sunset rides, cattle drives, and Western entertainment. Call Trail Horse Adventures for family rates and special events.

Parks

Fort Verde Historic Park
(520) 567–3275
www.arizonaguide.com

Fort Verde was the primary base for General Crook's army during the Indian campaigns that were fought in the 1880's. Most of the original buildings stand today, including the officers' quarters and the headquarters building, which is now the fort's museum. The Park is in the town of Camp Verde, 3 miles east of Interstate 17, and is open 8 A.M. to 5 P.M. every day except Christmas. The entrance fee is $2 for adults and $1 for children ages 7 through 13. (For more about Fort Verde Historic Park, please refer to the Sedona Attractions section.)

Posse Grounds Park
Posse Grounds Rd.
(520) 282–7098

Are your kids tired of shopping and browsing through art gallery after art gallery? If they are, bring the family here to enjoy the playground facilities, have a picnic, or play tennis. The park is located in West Sedona.

Red Rock Crossing/Crescent Moon Ranch Day Use Area
www.visitsedona.com

Families will enjoy swimming under the towering red cliffs in the clear waters of Oak Creek. Picnic tables are available. To access Red Rock Crossing, take W. U.S. Highway 89A to Upper Red Rock Loop Road. For more information, see the Sedona Recreation section.

Red Rock State Park
(520) 282–6907

This nature and wildlife preserve is a family oriented park with hiking trails, picnic area, and guided tours. The Visitor Center has daily programs and slide presentations. The entrance fee is $5 and a $1 fee is charged to pedestrians, equestrians, and bicyclists. To preserve and protect the natural environment in the park, dogs, swimming, and camping are prohibited.

For more information about Red Rock State Park, see the Sedona Recreation section.

Insiders' Tip
The Sedona Ranger District provides maps and detailed information about the hiking trails in red rock country. Call the Ranger District, (520) 282-4119, or stop by 250 Brewer Rd., 7:30 A.M. to 4:30 P.M. daily.

Slide Rock State Park
520) 282–3034

This popular recreational site is known for its natural 30-foot waterslide. Plan on spending the day here! The park also has a picnic area, barbecue grills, a nature trail, and fishing. The entrance fee is $5 per vehicle and $1 per person (walking in). Please refer to the Sedona Recreation section for more information.

National Monuments

Montezuma Castle National Monument
(520) 567–3322
www.nps.gov/moca

Montezuma Castle, a well-preserved cliff dwelling, is five stories tall and has 20 rooms. The structure was built by the Sinagua Indians during the twelfth and thirteenth centuries. Early settlers discovered the ancient cliff dwelling and named it after the Aztec king, Montezuma. Junior Ranger Program activity guides are provided upon request. This program is designed to educate children about the prehistoric environment of the ancient pueblo. The monument is open from 8 A.M. to 5 P.M. every day except for Christmas Day. Extended summer hours run from Memorial Day through Labor Day. Children under 16 are admitted free; adults pay $2.

Tuzigoot National Monument
P.O. Box 219
(520) 634–5564
www.nps.gov/tuzi

Tuzigoot Monument was built by the Sinagua Indians in the thirteenth century and the original pueblo had 110 rooms with second and third stories. Junior Ranger Program activities are designed to educate children and develop awareness of the park's prehistoric environment. Junior Activity Guides are distributed upon request only. The monument is open daily except for Christmas. Summer hours are 8 A.M. to 7 P.M. Winter hours are 8 A.M. to 5 P.M.

Other Native American Ruins

Honanki
Sedona Ranger District
(520) 282–3854
www.visionsofheaven.com

The 700-year-old ruins are regarded as a sacred place to two different cultures: the Yavapai and Apache Nations. The walls are covered with well-preserved rock art. Different colored markings differentiate between the inhabitants and the time periods. The site is open 9:30 A.M. to 4:30 P.M. Entrance fee is $5 for adults. Children 16 and under are admitted free. For more about Honanki, see the Sedona Attractions section.

Palatki Ruins
Sedona Ranger District
(520) 282–3854
www.aztec.asu.edu

The Southern Sinagua constructed these cliff dwellings and lived in the area from approximately 650 C.E. to 1300 C.E. This site is known for the well-preserved pictographs that date back 6,000 years. Palatki Ruins are open daily 9:30 A.M. to 4:30 P.M. There is a $5 entrance fee per car. For more information about Palatki, see the Sedona Attractions section.

Swimming Holes

Swimming in the pristine waters of Oak Creek is a wonderful way to spend the day. The swimming holes and wading options are abundant. Don't forget to bring plenty of drinking water and sunscreen, and wearing a hat is always recommended. Visitors can pull off the side of U.S. Highway 89A (just about anywhere). Most of Sedona's parks have access to the creek. If you would rather have facilities to accommodate the family, refer to the Parks section in this chapter.

Grasshopper Point
U.S. Highway 89A

You'll have too much fun jumping off these cliffs into the cool creek water. Or if you want a little more seclusion, rock hop down the creek and you can sit with your feet in the water and enjoy your own personal pool! Grasshopper Point is located between Oak Creek Canyon and Uptown Sedona. The point is well marked so it's not hard to find.

Theater

Sedona SuperVue Theatre
AZ Hwy. 179 and Jacks Canyon Rd.
(Oak Creek Factory Outlets)
(520) 284–3813

Kids will love this adventurous motion picture that offers a "virtual tour" of Sedona. There is a show every hour on the hour except for 3 P.M. Admission is $5 for children ages 3 to 11; adults pay $7.50. For more about the Sedona Super-Vue Theatre, see the Sedona Recreation section.

> **Insiders' Tip**
> Remember: if you pack it in, pack it out. Keep Sedona clean. Don't litter.

The Arts

Art within the community of Sedona comes in various shapes and sizes. It can be found inside galleries, decorative outdoor venues, and in the landscape. Nature has played an artistic role as it has etched the magnificent red rocks with the help of the sand, seas, and wind. Ancient civilizations have left their artistic mark as well in the form of petroglyphs and pictographs. Art is everywhere you look in Sedona. Whether you like to gallery hop, listen to chamber music, or enjoy community theater, the artistic presence is essential to this community's existence.

Sedona was home to Western art legends Joe Beeler and John Hampton as well as internationally acclaimed surrealist artist, Max Ernest, who rented his home to Egyptian-born American sculptor Nassan Gobran. Known for his sculpture "Capricorn," Gobran decided to make Sedona his home and envisioned making Sedona "a center for the arts." In 1961 he saw his dream turn into a reality when land was purchased and proposed as the site for the Sedona Arts Center. This artistic institution was to be a center for national and local art shows. Today the Sedona Arts Center is also dedicated to promoting visual and performing arts for all levels of experience.

Another turning point in the city's history was the birth of one of the most successful and influential art organizations in the United States. Cowboy Artists of America was founded in 1965 in a back booth of what is now the Cowboy Club, a popular eatery in Uptown Sedona.

Today the community enjoys its colorful artistic past while still looking to the future. More than 300 artists call Sedona home. More than 40 art galleries showcase the work of local, regional, and international artists.

The galleries are spread throughout the city, so we have geographically divided the Gallery section into five parts: along Arizona Highway 179, you will find the following divisions: Hillside Sedona, Hozho Center, and Tlaquepaque Arts and Crafts Village. We also list galleries in Oak Creek Canyon and Uptown Sedona.

Sedona is not limited to galleries. The Sedona Arts Center is home to the Oak Creek Theater Company and Sedona Arts Center Community Theatre. The Sedona Chamber Music Society provides year-round concerts around northern Arizona, including the Grand Canyon.

A recent addition to the art community is the Sedona Cultural Park. This outside arena and educational facility will host such Arizona favorites as Arizona Opera, Ballet Arizona, and the Phoenix Symphony. The popular Sedona Jazz on the Rocks has moved its festival to the Cultural Park.

Music and Theater

Oak Creek Theatre Company
Sedona Arts Center, 15 Art Barn Rd.
(520) 282–3809
www.sedona.net

Sedona's professional theatre company was founded in 1997 and has one mission: to bring high quality theatrical presentations to northern Arizona. The company functions in association with the Sedona Arts Center. Past performances include *Turn of the Screw, The Glass Menagerie*, and *The Dining Room*. Tickets can be purchased at Sedona Arts Center or the Tlaquepaque Arts and Crafts Village Information Booth. See Sedona Nightlife section for more information.

Sedona Arts Center
15 Art Barn Rd.
(520) 282–3809, (888) 954–4442
www.sedona.net

The Arts Center is a non-profit membership organization dedicated to the performing and visual arts. Home to the Oak

Creek Theatre Company, Sedona Arts Community Theatre, and an affiliate with Children's Classic Caravan, the Arts Center provides educational programs and activities for all levels of experience. The Gallery Shop displays and sells the work of over 120 local and regional artists. The Exhibition Gallery rotates exhibits by local and regional artists, and sponsors group and juried shows. Contact Sedona Arts Center for a complete schedule of events. See the Sedona Nightlife section for more about Sedona Arts Center Community Theatre.

Newly built Sedona Cultural Park invites nature enthusiasts, art aficionados, and music-lovers year-round. PHOTO: STACEY WITTIG

Sedona Chamber Music Society
P.O. Box 153, Sedona, AZ 86339-0153
(520) 204–2415
www.chambermusicsedona.org

Continuing to gain national and international attention, this is Arizona's only organization that performs chamber music year-round. Enjoy world-class concerts in the beauty of Sedona. Contact the Chamber Music Society for more information.

Sedona Cultural Park
1725 W. Highway 89A
(520) 282–0747, (800) 780–ARTS
www.sedona.net/scp

Encompassing 50 acres in western Sedona, Sedona Cultural Park is an outdoor venue for live entertainment, an educational center for children and adults, and a park preserve. The park offers hiking trails, musical perform-ances, and nature walks all surrounded by the majestic beauty of the red rock country. The Cultural Park is now home to Sedona Jazz on the Rocks, Sedona Arts Festival, and the Flagstaff Symphony Pops Concerts. Contact the Sedona Cultural Park for a schedule of events and more information.

Shakespeare Sedona
(520) 203–4TIX, (800) 780–ARTS

An outdoor celebration of the works of Shakespeare, this festival takes place at Tlaquepaque Arts and Crafts Village and Sedona Cultural Park. Past performances include *A Funny Thing Happened on the Way to the Forum*, *Twelfth Night*, and *Romeo and Juliet*. Tickets can be purchased through the Sedona Cultural Park, 1725 W. U.S. Highway 89A, (520) 282–0747, (800) 780–ARTS. The event runs from the beginning of June through the end of July.

Galleries

Hillside Sedona

Blue-Eyed Bear
671 AZ Hwy. 179
(520) 282–4761   www.blueeyedbear.com

If you are looking for contemporary Native American jewelry, Navajo folk art, and Zuni fetishes designed by the most prominent artists, Blue-Eyed Bear has one of the most extensive collections in Sedona. Open 10 A.M. to 6 P.M. daily, the shop offers elegant Native American jewelry and crafts, quality, and affordability.

The Clay Pigeon
671 AZ Hwy. 179
(520) 282–2845

This gallery is known for setting standards for Southwest contemporary crafts. Specializing in sculpture, ceramics, and jewelry, the Clay Pigeon is also located in Uptown Sedona, 250 N. Highway 89A, (520) 282–2862, and is open daily 10 A.M. to 6 P.M.

Compass Rose Gallery
671 AZ Hwy. 179
(520) 282–7904
www.oldmaps.com

This gallery has an intriguing collection of sixteenth to nineteenth century maps from the world over. Compass Rose has also one of the largest collections of Native American photography, as well as some of Audubon's original etchings and engravings. The gallery is open daily from 10 A.M. to 6 P.M.

Geoffrey Roth LTD.
671 AZ Hwy. 179
(520) 282–9550, (800) 447–7684
www.ghhr.com

Select craftsmen and jewelers have been chosen from across the country and Europe to complement the elegant work of Roth. Geoffrey Roth LTD. carries a fine selection of jewelry, timepieces, accessories, and exotic hardwood creations. Look for the first Geoffrey Roth LTD. located under the bell tower in Tlaquepaque Arts and Crafts Village, Arizona Highway 179. The second gallery is next to Javelina Cantina at the Hillside Marketplace. Both locations are open 10 A.M. to 6 P.M. daily.

Scherer Gallery
671 AZ Hwy. 179
(520) 203–9000

Since 1968, the Scherer Gallery has featured the work of local and internationally acclaimed artists. Some of the more outstanding selections include sculpture, studio art-glass, and photography. The gallery is open Monday through Sunday from 10 A.M. to 6 P.M.

Hozho Center

Lanning Gallery
431 AZ Hwy. 179
(520) 282–6865
www.lanninggallery.com

This contemporary gallery features jewelry, sculpture, paintings, handmade paper, and beautifully designed hand-painted furniture. Lanning Gallery is open 9:30 A.M. to 5:30 P.M. Monday through Saturday and 10 A.M. to 5 P.M. on Sunday.

Turquoise Tortoise Gallery
431 AZ Hwy. 179
(520) 282–2262
www.turqtortsedona.com

Since 1971, Turquoise Tortoise Gallery has assisted both the seasoned collector and the novice buyer in purchasing only exceptional Native American art. The expansive selection will take your breath away. Choose from oil and acrylic paintings, sculpture in bronze and other metals, and custom-made jewelry. The gallery is open from 9:30 A.M. to 5:30 P.M. Monday through Saturday and 10 A.M. to 5 P.M. on Sunday.

Visions Fine Art Gallery
251 AZ Hwy. 179
(520) 203–0022

A unique gallery that focuses on enhancing your quality of life, Visions Fine Art Gallery features spectacular contemporary art that the buyer is bound to fall in love with. Visions Fine Art is open daily 10 A.M. to 6 P.M.

Exposures International Gallery of Fine Art
561 AZ Hwy. 179
(520) 282–1125, (800) 526–7668
www.exposuresfineart.com

Art aficionados will get lost among the largest fine art display in Arizona. Encompassing 20,000 feet, the gallery showcases bronze and stone sculptures, fine art photography, ceramics, and glass. Collectors will drool over the complete works of the area's most prolific artists. The gallery is open from 10 A.M. to 6 P.M. daily.

Art sculptures are found throughtout Sedona.
PHOTO: STACEY WITTIG

Garland's Navajo Rugs
411 AZ Hwy. 179
(520) 282–4070
www.garlandsrugs.com

Garland's offers quality Native American arts and crafts, including hand-carved Hopi Katsina carvings, Navajo sand paintings, Pueblo pottery, handwoven baskets, and the largest selection of Navajo rugs purchased directly from Navajo weavers. These authentic pieces of art include hard-to-find floor rugs and colorful blankets. Garland's is open from 10 A.M. to 5 P.M. Monday through Sunday.

Tlaquepaque Arts and Crafts Village

Aguajito Del Sol
Suite #A103
(520) 282–5258

Since 1973, this gallery has featured watercolors, concrete sculpture, and bronze art for the home, office, and garden. Aguajito Del Sol is open daily 10 A.M. to 6 P.M.

Bearcloud Gallery
Suite #C107
(520) 282–4940

Rod Bearcloud Berry's work is reminiscent of the romantic painters of the 1800s. Each piece captures the connection between Earth and the heavens. The gallery is open 10 A.M. to 5 P.M. daily.

El Prado Galleries, Inc.
Suite #E101
(520) 282–7390, (800) 498–3300
www.elpradogalleries.com

Antique and art lovers will enjoy browsing among this gallery's antique furniture works by nationally acclaimed artists. This gallery features traditional, Western, contemporary, and impressionist paintings, sculpture, and ceramics. El Prado is open daily 9:30 A.M. to 5:30 P.M. Monday through Sunday.

Esteban's
Suite #B103
(520) 282–4686
www.zoniesgalleria.com

Showcasing the work of Southwestern artists, Esteban's will make you feel right at home as you browse in their comfortable atmosphere and find pottery, jewelry, and home decor. Esteban's is open daily 10 A.M. to 5 P.M.

Isadora Handweaving Gallery
Suite #A120
(520) 282–6232

The gallery is a celebration of handcrafted and handwoven garments, accessories, and jewelry. This "wearable art" has the spirit of the Southwest woven into it. Isadora is open daily 10 A.M. to 5 P.M.

Kuivato Glass Gallery
Patio Azul, Suite #B122
520) 282–1212
(800) 282–4312

This gallery sets itself apart from the other galleries in town because it has an exclusive collection of glass art and sculpture by American artists. Kuivato is open 10 A.M. to 5 P.M. Monday through Sunday.

How to Buy Art and Jewelry

As you are browsing through art gallery after art gallery you finally decide you would like to purchase a piece of authentic art or jewelry. Why not? How many times do you come across true Southwestern art?

The actual purchase can be intimidating. But it need not be. The most important rule to remember is that you like what you are buying. If you follow this rule, you're sure to appreciate and enjoy your piece of art for years to come, regardless of whether or not the value increases.

The second step is to learn as much as you can about the artist. Do not feel awkward; a smart consumer is an informed consumer. Ask about the artist's biography and bibliography. Ask for a list of collectors, galleries, or museums who display the artist's work.

Know what is out there. Tour as many galleries as you can. Get a feel for the craftsmanship and quality that is available. Many art aficionados will make return trips to a gallery several times to ask more questions and to just see the piece one more time.

Practice the same shrewd purchasing skills when buying jewelry. The market has a wide range of styles, quality, and pricing. Be sure to ask if a piece is solid gold, silver, or merely plated. Sometimes nickel is used on less expensive items.

If you are interested in a piece of Native American jewelry, ask the name of the jeweler, what tribe he or she is from, and ask to see other pieces created by the artist.

Remember to enjoy the experience. Take the time to research and educate yourself about your possible purchase. This is part of the fun

Oak Creek Canyon

Garland's Indian Jewelry
3953 N. U. S. Hwy. 89A
(520) 282–6632

Tucked beneath the oak trees in the canyon, you'll find Garland's, a gallery featuring Southwestern-style and Native American jewelry, Katsina carvings, pottery, baskets, and paintings. Garland's is open daily from 10 A.M. to 5 P.M.

Hoel's Indian Shop
9589 N. U. S. Hwy. 89A
(520) 282–3925
www.hoels.com

For the past 45 years, Hoel's has been dedicated to selling authentic Native American art. Featuring Pueblo pottery, Hopi Katsina carvings, jewelry, baskets, and Navajo rugs, Hoel's Indian Shop is open daily 9 A.M. to 6 P.M.

Uptown Sedona

Joe Wilcox Fine Arts
300 N. U. S. Hwy. 89A
(520) 282–2548
www.sedbiz.com/wilcoxfinearts/

This fine art gallery proudly represents award-winning artists who work in oils, pastels, and bronze. The gallery is open daily from 9:30 A.M. to 8 P.M.

Jordan Road Gallery
395 Jordan Rd.
(520) 282–5690
www.jordanroadgallery.com

As you enter the Jordan Road Gallery, prepare to view the most eclectic art in the area. The gallery boasts one of the finest collections of fine art, sculpture, paper, and works on canvas in a variety of mediums and diverse subject matter. Jordan Road Gallery is open Monday through Saturday 9:30 A.M. to 5:30 P.M. and noon to 6 P.M. on Sunday.

Zonies Galleria
215 N. U.S. Hwy. 89A
(520) 282–5995
www.zoniesgalleria.com

Showcasing the arts and crafts of Arizona artists, this gallery offers pottery, jewelry, home decor, and kaleidoscopes. Zonies Galleria is open 9:30 A.M. to 6 P.M. daily.

Annual Events

Sedona residents are proud of the caliber of annual events that occur throughout the year, blending their community's diverse culture, strong artistic influence, and taste for fun. Local organizations provide artistic and fund-raising events for the whole family. Many visitors return year after year to partake in the annual festivities.

In this chapter we have provided musical events, duck races, and cultural gatherings from March through December. If you visit Sedona during the months of January and February expect a quiet city.

March

Sedona International Film Festival
(520) 282–0747, (800) 780–ARTS

Featuring American and international independent films, documentaries, animation, shorts, and features, the Sedona International Film Festival is a weekend-long celebration of cinema. The event is usually scheduled for the first weekend in March, but venues vary from year to year so call ahead. The festival honors film personalities and schedules panel discussions and interactive workshops. Contact the film committee for more information.

St. Patrick's Day Parade
(520) 204–2390

Put on your green and get ready as locals line the streets of Uptown Sedona to watch floats, merrymakers, and leprechauns pass by. Contact the Sedona Main Street Program office for parade date and times.

April

Authors Luncheon
(520) 204–1346

In conjunction with the Flagstaff Symphony, this annual luncheon raises money for the symphony and brings local and regional authors to Sedona for book signings and readings. This event does sell out early, call for tickets.

Great Northern Arizona Duck Race
Los Abrigados Resort & Spa, 160 Portal Ln.
(520) 204–2390

This charity fund-raiser is a collaboration between the Sedona Main Street Program and Boys & Girls Club of Sedona. The event is held creek side at Los Abrigados and benefits various adult and children's charities. Please call to adopt a duck or to find out more about this fun and popular event. The Duck Race is usually held the last weekend in April.

May

Sedona Chamber Music Festival
(520) 204–2415

This magical and prestigious event attracts more than 4,000 music lovers and features guest artists and quartets. Performances are scheduled in various locations during one weekend in May. Please call for more information.

June

Sedona Taste
Los Abrigados Resort & Spa,
160 Portal Ln.
(520) 282–7822

Come out and taste fine food and drink at the creek side resort of Los Abrigados. This event benefits the Boys & Girls Club of Sedona. Call for tickets early, as this is a popular event that sells out quickly.

July

Buy the People for the People Auction
L'Auberge de Sedona Resort,
301 L'Auberge Ln.
(520) 282–2834

This charity auction is organized by the Adult Community Center and Sedona Main Street Program. It all happens at the elegant L'Auberge Resort. Local galleries and artists donate work to be auctioned. Call for tickets.

Annual Fourth of July Celebration
Sedona Red Rock High School,
995 Upper Red Rock Loop Rd.
(520) 282–4126

Celebrate the 4th surrounded by the beautiful red rocks of Sedona. Sponsored by the Sedona-Oak Creek Canyon Lions Club, festivities include food, live music, games, and fireworks at Sedona Red Rock High School's athletic field.

September

Fiesta del Tlaquepaque
Tlaquepaque Arts and Crafts Village,
AZ Highway 179
(520) 282–4838
www.tlaq.com

For the past 27 years, the annual Fiesta del Tlaquepaque has brought the courtyard of the arts and crafts village to life with live Mariachi bands and Flamenco dancers performing throughout the day. Taste the food and appreciate the art of the Hispanic and Native American Southwest. Festivities begin at 10 A.M. Admission is free.

Pops at Poco
Poco Diablo 1736 AZ Hwy. 179
(520) 282–6649

This outside event has attracted crowds for the past 15 years. Enjoy the music of the Flagstaff Symphony under the brilliant blue skies of red rock country. Tickets can be purchased at the Sedona Chamber of Commerce, Forest Rd. and U.S. Highway 89A, (520) 282–7722.

Sedona Jazz on the Rocks Festival
Sedona Cultural Park,
1725 W. U.S. Highway 89
(520) 282–0747

Called "the event you'll always remember in a place you'll never forget," Jazz on the Rocks features famed musicians and of course breathtaking scenery and views. Call for more information, dates, and concert schedule.

Sedona Sculpture Walk
(520) 282–3809

Sponsored by Sedona Arts Center, this event brings artists from across the country to display their work. Exhibits are placed throughout the city and range from monumental bronze to small marble or wood sculptures. Call for dates.

October

Verde Valley Concert for the Native American Scholarship Fund
Verde Valley School,
3511 Verde Valley School Rd.
(520) 284–1982

Hosted by Jackson Browne, this outdoor concert is now an Arizona tradition. Each year Jackson Browne and a few of his friends (Bonnie Raitt, Indigo Girls, Keb Mo) entertain music lovers of all ages. Get ready for a day of music and more music. Proceeds benefit the Native American Scholarship fund. Call for dates and tickets.

Insiders' Tip

The Verde Valley Concert is a popular event in the Northland. Buy your tickets in advance and don't forget to wear your sunscreen.

Sedona Arts Festival
Sedona Red Rock High School,
995 Upper Red Rock Loop Rd.
(520) 204–9546

This celebration combines arts and crafts and cuisine from some of Sedona's finest restaurants. Regional musicians provide live entertainment and locals and visitors alike agree that this event is one of the nation's top art festivals.

Carnival de Máscaras
Tlaquepaque Arts and Crafts Village,
AZ Hwy. 179, at the Bridge
(520) 282–4838
www.tlaq.com

The crafts village's cobblestone courtyard fills with live music, colorful decorations, and revelers wearing masks during this event. Proceeds benefit Sedona Cultural Park.

November

Red Rock Fantasy of Lights
Los Abrigados Resort & Spa, 160 Portal Ln.
(520) 282–1777

This holiday extravaganza lights up the town with over one million lights and fifty displays. Bring your family and get a jump start on the holiday season. The Festival begins November 22 and ends January 8.

December

Festival of Lights
Tlaquepaque Arts and Crafts Village
(520) 282–4838   www.tlaq.com

Thousands of luminaries light up the cobblestone courtyards for the month of December. Kick off your holiday season with live music and dancers. This event is usually scheduled for the second weekend of the month. Call for exact date and time.

Daytrips

As you explore the area surrounding Sedona, you will find ghost towns and quaint cities that were once boomtowns at the beginning of the nineteenth century. These communities thrived on the prosperity of the mineral mines and those who sought its wealth. People and businesses—especially saloons and restaurants—prospered until the mines were exhausted and residents moved on to the next town.

As prospectors sought their fortune elsewhere, residents and time worked together and have produced peaceful communities. Not only do these small communities cater to families, but artists from around the country have made their home in this unique region surrounded by natural wonders and rich history.

As you travel from Sedona, whether you are looking for a day jaunt or perhaps a weekend trip, visitors can stroll through historic downtown areas and browse through shops while enjoying the mild climate.

In this chapter, we will introduce you to the ghost town of Jerome and the city of Prescott.

Jerome

The town of Jerome was built on Cleopatra Hill above a copper deposit. Native Americans first came to the area looking for colored stones. The Spanish, in search of gold, followed them. As the United States looked to the uncharted territories of the West, Anglos came to the area and staked the first claims in 1876. By 1883 Sedona was rapidly growing from a tent city to a thriving town riding on its successful copper, gold, and silver mines.

Eventually the arrival of the railroad and then the automobile replaced horses, mules, and burros. Fires were common in the frontier town destroying buildings and businesses time and time again. For nearly twenty years, landslides also plagued the town. Jerome's economic stability depended upon the mines, and when labor unrest and the fluctuation of copper prices had finally taken their toll, the mines were closed in 1953.

After the closure of the mines, the population of Jerome fell from 1,500 to about 50. The Jerome Historical Society guarded the vacant buildings against vandalism. However, the 1960s and 70s brought in new residents and people interested in restoring the town. Today, the population hovers around 550.

Surrounded by Coconino and Prescott National Forests, Jerome offers quaint bed-and-breakfast inns, restaurants, historic attractions, gift shops, and galleries. Contact the Jerome Chamber of Commerce, (520) 634–2900, for more information.

From Sedona, take U.S. Highway 89A west to Jerome, or take Interstate 17 S to the Camp Verde exit. Jerome is approximately 30 minutes from Sedona. The area is well marked and locals are always ready to give directions.

Accommodations in Jerome

The Cottage Inn
747 East Ave., Jerome
(520) 634–0701

Offering two suites, each with a sitting room and private bath, the Cottage Inn is just off the main drag (U.S. Highway 89A) of Jerome. Tucked away in a residential neighborhood, the inn is decorated in the progressive styles of the 30s and 40s. A full American breakfast is served each morning in the main dining room. Call for availability and reservations.

Ghost City Inn
541 Main St.
(520) 634–4678   www.ghostcityinn.com

Originally a boardinghouse, Ghost City

Inn was built in 1898. The building has survived fires and different facades before evolving into a bed-and-breakfast. If a pampered evening is on your agenda look no further. The inn has six rooms, two with private baths. Some of the rooms have verandas that offer breathtaking views of the Verde Valley, Jerome, and, in the distance, the Red Rocks of Sedona. Afternoon tea with homemade cakes and cookies is served at check-in (4 P.M.).

Call for reservations. Rates range from $85 to $125 per night.

The Inn at Jerome
309 Main St.
(520) 634–5094

The eight guest room inn has been restored to its elegant Victorian state, and is now packed with authentic Southwestern antiques. Guests will enjoy relaxing by the fire in the parlor.

Some rooms offer incredible views of the Verde Valley and guests can even see the snow-covered San Francisco Peaks in Flagstaff. Room rates start at $55 and go to $85.

The Jerome Grand Hotel
200 Hill Street
(520) 634–8200, (888) 817–6788
www.jeromegrandhotel.net

Expect the quaintness of a bed-and-breakfast with the privacy and convenience of a hotel. All rooms come with TV and VCR, private bath, and telephone. Therapeutic massages are available by appointment. Jerome's only hotel, the building is the highest in town and promises amazing views. Call for availability and reservations. Standard rooms with queen-size beds are $85. Balcony rooms are $105, and the two-room suite is $185 per night.

Attractions in Jerome

Gold King Mine
1000 Perkinsville Rd., Jerome
(520) 634–0053
www.goldkingmineghosttown1. bizonthe.net

This private museum is a replica of an authentic ghost town and mine. Wander through old cabins and mine shafts, view old cars, trucks, and authentic mining equipment. Visitors will enjoy the daily demonstrations of the antique mining equipment. The Gold King Mine is open 7 days a week, 9 A.M. to 5 P.M. To reach Gold King Mine, take Main Street just past the fire station. There will be signs guiding your way. Admission is $4 for adults and $2 for children 12 and under.

Jerome Historical Society/The Mine Museum
200 Main St.
(520) 634–5477

One of the oldest museums in Arizona, the Mine Museum formed immediately after the mines closed in 1953 to protect the historical buildings of Jerome from vandalism and the elements. A visit to the museum provides insight into the town of Jerome. The museum and gift shop are open 7 days a week 9 A.M. to 4:30 P.M. Admission for adults is $1 and children 12 and under are admitted free. The Mine Museum is located on the corner of Jerome Avenue and Main Street (U.S. 89A).

State Historic Park/Jimmy "Rawhide" Douglas Mansion
100 Douglas Rd.
(520) 634–5381
www.jeromechamber.com

The mansion—once the family home of the owner of the Little Daisy Mine, Jimmy "Rawhide" Douglas—has been converted into a museum and sits on a knoll next to the shaft of the Little Daisy Mine. The Little Daisy Hotel, originally the residence for miners, rests on a hill above the mansion and is now a private residence. The museum is open seven days a week from 8 A.M. to 5 P.M.. Admission for adults is $2.50, $1 for children, and kids 7 and under are admitted free. From Sedona, take U.S. Highway 89A west towards Prescott. Before you reach Prescott, you will see signs for Jerome. The area is well marked. Turn right on Douglas Road. The museum is on this road.

Restaurants in Jerome

Flatiron Cafe
416 Main St.
(520) 634–2733

Choose one of the healthy and delicious breakfast or lunch specialties that will have you back on your feet window shopping in no time. Try a frothy cappuccino or espresso and a gourmet treat to balance out the healthy meal. The Flatiron Cafe is open 8 A.M. to 3 P.M. Monday through Saturday and 8:30 A.M. to 3 P.M. on Sunday.

House of Joy
416 Hull Ave.
(520) 634–5339

Make your reservations months in advance, because House of Joy is open Saturday and Sunday for dinner and you can only dine with reservations. Once the home of a historic brothel, this unique restaurant specializes in continental cuisine with extravagant seafood dishes. The homemade desserts are "to die for."

Jerome Brewery
111 Main St.
(520) 639–8477

Comfortable and inviting, the Jerome Brewery is a local favorite featuring a classic Italian menu with pizza, salads, and sandwiches. Enjoy a game of pool or relax in the upstairs dining room while you savor the views and sip on a handcrafted ale. The brewery is open daily for lunch and dinner 11 A.M. to 9 PM.

Jerome Grille
309 Main St.
(520) 634–5094

Tucked inside the Jerome Inn is this breakfast and lunch stop that locals have decreed a "must." The Grille serves a traditional menu, but adds a few surprises to it. Try the Breakfast Burrito or a crisp salad for lunch. Jerome Grille is open daily 8 A.M. to 4:30 P.M.

Jerome Palace-Haunted Hamburger
410 N. Clark St.
(520) 634–0554

Don't let the casual atmosphere fool you! The Palace has good food from burgers to prime rib to succulent desserts. Indoor and outdoor seating is available. Check out this local "haunt" seven days a week for lunch and dinner from 11 A.M. to 9 P.M.

Shopping in Jerome

Aurum Jewelry
369 Main St.
(520) 634–3330
www.aurumjewelry.com

Since 1984, Aurum has been making jewelry in Jerome. The shop also does custom work with silver and gold, remounting, design, and repairs. Aurum has a collection of ethnic and folk art from Indonesia and the Himalayas. Aurum Jewelry is open daily 10 A.M. to 6 P.M.

The Cactus & Curiosity Shop
329 Main St.
(520) 634–4148

This gift shop is an eclectic blend of figurines, housewares, and cactus. The store has over 100 live cacti for sale and is open daily 10:30 A.M. to 5:30 P.M.

Cheers
111 B Main St.
(520) 634–7988

Cheers has the largest selection of T-shirts, sweatshirts, and hats for men, women, and children. Call for your free T-shirt brochure. Cheers is open daily 10 A.M. to 6 P.M.

Jerome Gallery
240 Hull Ave.
(520) 634–7033

The Jerome Gallery is a fine arts establishment that showcases local and Arizona artists. Specializing in "sand painting" furniture made by Navajo artists who use recycled wood and turn it into handcrafted furniture. The gallery also features Southwestern jewelry, pottery, and home furnishings. Jerome Gallery is open daily 10 A.M. to 6 P.M.

Nellie Bly
136 Main St.
(520) 634–0255
www.nbscopes.com

This unique gallery of kaleidoscopes and art glass features local, national, and international designers and artisans. Nellie Bly also has a large selection of children's scopes and is open daily 10 A.M. to 5:30 P.M.

Rickeldoris Candy
419 Hull Ave.
(520) 639–9013

Attention candy lovers! Rickeldoris Candy has the finest selection of chocolates, old-fashioned and imported candies, and salt-water taffy. Rickeldoris ships anywhere in the United States and is open daily noon to 5:30 P.M.

Skyfire
140 Main St.
(520) 634–8081

Featuring home accessories from handmade furniture, to candles and candle holders, to mirrors, this "gift" shop is a home decorator's dream. Skyfire also sells sculptures and carvings by regional artists. Check out the fine selection of architecture, design, and humor books. Skyfire is open daily from 9:30 A.M. to 6:00 P.M.

Prescott

Arizona's mile-high city was established in 1864. The discovery of gold in the surrounding mountains and the decision to create the Arizona Territories by Abraham Lincoln helped Prescott to grow rapidly, and it quickly become the region's economic center and first territorial capital.

When the town was incorporated on February 27, 1883, residents decided on the name of Prescott, in honor of William Hickling Prescott, a local historian noted for his books about the Aztecs and for his translations of Spanish works.

Whether or not Prescott would remain the capital of Arizona caused many problems within the Arizona Legislatures of 1864-1866. Representatives leaned in favor of Tucson, and in 1867 Tucson was made the capital. Eleven years later (1877), Prescott was chosen again as the state's capital, but only held the title until 1889, when it permanently lost the honor to Phoenix.

Even though Prescott is no longer the state's capital, the city has taken steps to maintain its precious heritage. Some of the most well-preserved examples of nineteenth-century Southwestern American architecture sit within Prescott's city limits.

The city owes its character to the Midwestern and Eastern roots of its residents. With its elegantly restored Victorian homes set among the green lawns and large trees, and the town plaza, with its courthouse surrounded by a park, the architecture reflects the influence of the Eastern American cities rather than the desert towns of the Southwest.

The city has evolved from a territorial capital to a small city with a population of 30,000 that brags about its small town charm. The Courthouse Plaza, or Courthouse Square, is centrally located (the names can be used interchangeably) and has shops, restaurants, and onlookers strolling the streets. Look for arts and crafts shows and other cultural events in the Courthouse Plaza. Contact the Prescott Chamber of Commerce for a complete listing of annual events.

Also along the plaza is Whiskey Row, a well-known street in Arizona. At the turn of the century, Montezuma Avenue boasted 40 saloons. The first was the Kentucky Bar at the corner of Goodwin and Montezuma. The row ended down at the Santa Fe depot at a bar named Depot House. Bars and establishments along the Row will happily share some wild tales of the past with you.

Prescott is set in the central mountains of Arizona and is approximately a one-hour drive from Sedona. From Sedona, visitors can take I-17 S to the exit marked Prescott or take U.S. Hwy. 89 west past Jerome. The city enjoys four mild seasons, and an occasional snowfall to make life a little more interesting.

> ## Insiders' Tip
> Prescott has more than 400 buildings listed on the National Register of Historic Places.

The Prescott National Forest lies between the mountain ranges of Central Arizona. The elevation ranges from 3,000 to 8,000 feet. Outdoor enthusiasts will enjoy the hiking, fishing, and backpacking opportunities. Information and maps can be obtained at the Prescott National Forest, 344 S. Cortez St., (520) 771–4700.

For more information, contact the Prescott Chamber of Commerce and Visitors Center, 117 W. Goodwin, (520) 445–2000, (800) 266–7534.

Accommodations in Prescott

The Cottages at Prescott Country Inn
503 S. Montezuma St.
(520) 445–7991, (888) 757–0015
www.cableone.net\cottages

The intimate cottages include full kitchens and some have living rooms or sitting areas. Each cottage has original art from local artists, antique collectibles, and is decorated in either French/American or English country motifs. A deluxe continental breakfast is brought to your cottage each morning. A Jacuzzi spa room is available by appointment only. The rates range between $49 and $129. Call for reservations.

Hotel St. Michael's
100 S. Montezuma
(520) 776–1999

Located across from the Courthouse building and along legendary Whiskey Row, Hotel St. Michael's is a piece of the Old West. This 100-year-old historic hotel has sixty-nine rooms with phone, TV, private bath, and your stay here includes a complimentary continental breakfast. The hotel has a full-service restaurant serving breakfast, lunch, and dinner. Hotel prices range between $59 and $99.

Pleasant Street Inn Bed & Breakfast
142 S. Pleasant St.
(520) 445–4774, (877) 226–7128
www.cwdesigners.com/pleasantstreet

Step back into time as you enter this luxurious Victorian home. The inn has four rooms, each with a private bath and is only three blocks from Courthouse Plaza. A full breakfast, which includes fruit, muffins or buns, and breakfast entrée, is served at 8:30 A.M. Room rates range from $89 to $135. Call for reservations.

Prescott Pines Inn Bed & Breakfast
901 White Spar Rd.
(520) 445–7270, (800) 541–5374
www.prescottpinesinn.com

The inn has a reputation for its comfortable atmosphere, with a white picket fence and country Victorian elegance. Guest-rooms are located in one of four guesthouses around the main house, and each is non-smoking, has a private bath with tub and shower (unless noted, shower only), private outside entry, queen-

or king-size bed, heat and air conditioning, phone (free local and toll free calls), and color cable TV. Ask about rooms with kitchenettes or full kitchens for longer stays. Guest room rates range from $65 to $109.

Attractions in Prescott

Antelope Hills Golf Course
1 Perkins Dr.
(520) 776–7888

Golf enthusiasts will enjoy the mild weather and 36 holes of golf year-round at this municipal course. The North Course is one of the top public courses in Arizona; the South Course was designed by Gary Panks. Greens fees are $48, including cart.

Sharlot Hall Museum
415 W. Gurley St.
(520) 445–3122
www.sharlot.org

Poet and territorial historian Sharlot M. Hall founded this museum, whose grounds include the original Governor's Mansion, the John C. Fremont House, the William C. Bashford House, restored Fort Misery, the Transportation Exhibits Building, Museum Center, and the Sharlot Hall Building, which features contemporary, Western and Native American artworks. The museum is open Monday through Saturday 10 A.M. to 5 P.M., and Sunday 1 to 5 P.M. There is no entrance fee, but donations are appreciated.

Smoki Museum
147 N. Arizona St.
(520) 445–1230
www.smoki.com

This museum houses an extensive collection of Native American art, artifacts, and archaeological displays. Smoki Museum is open Monday through Saturday 10 A.M. to 4 P.M. and Sunday 1 to 4 P.M. The entrance fee is $4 for adults; seniors 65 and older pay $3; children under 13 years of age are admitted free. The museum is open on Saturday and Sunday only from November 1 to April 15. Winter hours are Saturday, 10 A.M. to 4 P.M., and Sunday 1 P.M. to 4 P.M.

Restaurants in Prescott

Cadillac Bar & Grill
216 W. Gurley St.
(520) 777–0018

Looking for entrees with a seasoned kick? Try the Cadillac Bar & Grill, which specializes in Cajun cuisine. The menu also includes fresh seafood, steaks, and burgers. Look for the live entertainment on Friday and Saturday night from 5 P.M. to 9 P.M. The restaurant is open for lunch and dinner 11 A.M. to 9 P.M. Entree prices range from $6.95 to $23.95.

Caffe St. Michael's
100 S. Montezuma St.
(520) 778–2500

Caffe St. Michael's serves breakfast, lunch, and dinner daily. Try their specialty sandwiches, homemade soups, and chili that will make your eyes water. They also have fresh baked pastries, cakes, and breads. The restaurant is open 8 A.M. to 9 P.M. Menu prices range from $5.95 to $10.95.

Kendall's
113 S. Cortez St.
(520) 778–3658

Take a trip back to the 1950s at Kendall's. Try the old-fashioned soda fountain and their flame-broiled "Build your own Burger Bar." The fresh-cut fries are out of this world. Kendall's is open Monday through Saturday 11 A.M. to 8 P.M., and Sunday 11 A.M. to 6 P.M. Don't forget your poodle skirt.

Prescott Brewery
130 W. Gurley St.
(520) 771–2795

Visitors will enjoy the comfortable atmosphere that caters to Prescott locals and families. The menu has something for everyone, from pub food to Southwestern specialties to veggie dishes. They even have a special menu for the little ones. Handcrafted beers are brewed on-site. Prescott Brewery is open 11 A.M. to 10 P.M. daily. The bar stays open 'til midnight. Menu prices start at $6.95 and go up to $13.95.

The Rose Restaurant
234 S. Cortez St.
(520) 777–8308

For an unforgettable fine dining experience, try the Rose Restaurant. Locals agree that they never tire of the menu. House specialties include the roast duck and double-cut veal chops. A full bar is available and the wine list is extensive. Reservations are recommended. The Rose Restaurant is open Wednesday through Saturday 5 P.M. to 9 P.M. Prices range from $14.95 to $26.95.

Shopping in Prescott
The Galloping Goose
162 S Montezuma St
(520) 778–7600

For a little bit of everything that is Western, the Galloping Goose has Southwestern jewelry, Western wear for men and women, and novelty items for kids and adults. The Goose also has an art gallery in the back of the store, featuring Western paintings and sculpture. The Galloping Goose is open daily 9 A.M. to 6 P.M.

Lavender's Blue
124 S Granite St., Ste. A
(520) 445–2344
www.lavendersblue.com

This gift shop/kid's clothing store has an endless selection of brand-name clothes for newborns and toddlers, women's clothing and accessories, and a great selection of gift items, including candles and cards. Lavender's Blue is open daily 9 A.M. to 6 P.M.

Mountain Christmas of Prescott
130 W. Gurley St #101
(520) 771–2824

Mountain Christmas has holiday decorations as well as collectibles and seasonal gifts. Christmas lovers can enjoy the holiday here any day of the week at any time of the year. Mountain Christmas is open 10 A.M. to 5:30 P.M. Monday through Saturday and 10 A.M. to 4 P.M. on Sunday.

Ogg's Hogan & Maggie Manygoats
111 N Cortez St.
(520) 443–9856

Celebrating the many cultures that make up the Southwest, Ogg's Hogan & Maggie Manygoats feature Mexican furniture and Native American jewelry, crafts, and rugs. They also have a fine selection of Southwestern ladies' clothing and accessories, cowboy gifts, and Old West collectibles. The store is open daily 10 A.M. to 5:30 P.M.

Trinkets
130 W. Gurley St. #104
(520) 445–9116

Trinkets has gifts in every shape and size. This eclectic store has garden fountains, candles, holders, dishes, clocks, pictures, and frames. Trinkets is open from 10 A.M. to 5:30 P.M. Monday through Saturday, and Sunday 10 A.M. to 4 P.M.

We're a Basket Case
415 S. Montezuma (on the alley)
(520) 443–5233

Assemble a gift basket yourself or have a "designer" assemble one for you. There is a gift basket for every occasion—baby baskets, get-well baskets, wedding baskets, and just because baskets. We're a Basket Case can ship anywhere in the United States and to some foreign countries and is open 9 A.M. to 6 P.M. daily.

Insiders' Tip
Locals pronounce the city of Prescott as "Presskitt." Be prepared to be corrected if you pronounce it wrong in front of a local.

Other Activities

Verde Canyon Railroad
300 N. Broadway, Clarkdale, AZ
(520) 639–0010, (800) 293–7245
www.verdecanyonrr.com

The Verde Canyon Railroad travels from Clarkdale to Perkinsville through Arizona's "other Grand Canyon." The train ride features rugged cliffs, dramatic rock faces, and magnificent views of the Verde Canyon. The four-hour round-trip tour travels through a 680-foot manmade tunnel and skirts along the waters of the upper Verde River.

Each season brings surprises; visitors can expect to see the wildflowers and cacti bloom in the spring. During the summer months, passengers will watch black hawks and blue herons soar above the rugged terrain. Passengers will enjoy the fall colors along the Verde River, and the winter months bring bald and golden eagles.

The train schedule fluctuates from season to season. During the month of June, the train runs every day except for Monday and Tuesday. During July and August, the train runs every day except for Monday, Tuesday, and Friday. Trains depart at 1 P.M. and return at approximately 5 P.M. Some days (these days change, call for schedule) two trains are scheduled. On those days, trains depart at 9 A.M. and 2:30 P.M. Starlight Tours are available May through October and depart at 5:30 P.M. and return at approximately 9:30 P.M.

The Verde Canyon Railroad offers special holiday train rides throughout the year. Kids will enjoy the Easter Bunny Express. Celebrate Mother's Day in style with "Throw Mama on the Train." Father's Day would be just another ordinary day without "Throw Papa on the Train." The Haunted Halloween Express promises an evening of chills and thrills. Start your Christmas season with Santa Claus Express every weekend in December.

Allow 40 minutes for the drive from Sedona. Go west on U.S. Highway 89A to Cottonwood. Stay on U.S. 89A to Cottonwood (about 18 miles). U.S. 89A will make a left to Jerome, but do not turn here. Instead, continue straight on Main Street through old town Cottonwood, past Tuzigoot Monument. You will see a large green sign that reads "Train Depot" straight ahead. Continue across the bridge and park in the designated parking area.

Navajo Reservation

Area Overview

The Navajo are the largest Native American tribe in the United States, with a population of about a quarter million people. The Navajo Reservation covers 27,000 square miles in three states—Arizona, New Mexico, and Utah. About 170,000 people live in Diné Bikéyah, or Navajoland. Most of remaining Navajos live in border towns such as Flagstaff and Gallup and in other urban settings like Phoenix.

According to Navajo tradition, the Diyin Diné planned the universe with holy pollen and all spiritual beings and natural forces existed in a mist in complete harmony. A disagreement between Father Sky and Mother Earth ensued, and twelve sacred Diyin Diné (Darkness, Early Dawn, Evening Twilight, Sun, First Talking God, Second Talking God, Turquoise Carrier Boy, One Corn Carrier Girl, White Corn Boy, Yellow Corn Girl, Corn Pollen Boy, and Ripener Girl) preserved the universe by creating a covenant between male and female, with the sun to rule the day and the moon and stars to rule the night. Harmony was restored.

First Man and First Woman emerged and were given a sign from the universe, a mist, within which First Man and First Woman found First Male Talking God with a newborn child, White Shell Woman. She was named Changing Woman at puberty. Changing Woman gave birth to the Hero Twins, Monster Slayer and Born for Water. The twins, with the help of Spider Woman, found out that their father was Sun. The twins overcame many obstacles as they journeyed to meet their father and through those trials, they developed courage. Their father gave them the tools necessary to fight the Challengers of Life. When the Twins returned to earth, they began to slay the Challengers of Life. Only Old Age, Hunger, Poverty, and Sickness remained. Thus began the existence of the Diné on earth.

The Holy People placed the four sacred mountains to protect the area in which the Diné were to live. Sisnaajini or Yoolgaii Dziil (White Shell Mountain) is in the east. This mountain, also called Mt. Blanca, represents male, spring, dawn, and the beginning of life.

The mountain to the south is Tsoodzil or Dootl'izhii (Turquoise Mountain of Strength). This male mountain represents summer, adolescence, and leadership, as well as power and authority over the sky. Also known also as Mt. Taylor, this mountain is near Grants, New Mexico.

Dook'o'oosliid or Diichili Dziil, the Abalone Shell Mountain of Strength, is in the west (near Flagstaff) and is also known as Humphreys Peak. It is a female mountain and represents fall, adulthood, and the physical strength of life.

Dibé Ntsaa or Baashzhinii Dzil is Black Jet Onyx Mountain on the north. Also known as Mt. Hesperus, it is a female mountain that represents old age and harmony. This mountain, near Durango, Colorado, along with the moon, is the ruler of night.

According to archaeologists, the Diné, whom the Spanish called Navajos, came to the Southwest five to seven hundred years ago from northwestern Canada where they were hunters and gatherers. They are an Athapaskan people, related to the Native American tribes of the Northwest Coast and the Apaches.

By the time the Spanish arrived in the mid-sixteenth century, Dinétah, the first Navajo homeland in the Southwest, occupied much of the area that had been abandoned by the ancient Anasazi, or Pueblo peoples. The Diné were seminomadic hunters and gathers, though they may also have grown some maize. They made pottery, wove baskets, and traded with the Pueblo tribes who lived along the Rio Grande. Within a few hundred years of coming to the Southwest, they were planting corn, beans, and squash.

The earliest recorded contact between the Navajo and the Spanish was with the Antonio de Espejo expedition of 1582–1583. According to Spanish accounts, the meeting at the base of Mount Taylor began as a friendly one, but resulted in hostilities. Warfare was the hallmark of relations with the Spanish throughout the seventeenth century. Petroglyphs in Canyon del Muerto in northeastern Arizona record the arrival of Spanish armies in the area. By the early 1600s, the Navajo had acquired horses and iron tools from the Spanish invaders through trade with colonists in New Mexico.

The Navajo helped Acoma Pueblo in its unsuccessful attempt to defend its mesa-top village from Juan de Oñate's army in 1599, and they joined in the Pueblo Revolt of 1680, which succeeded in driving the Spanish out of New Mexico and Arizona. During the subsequent reconquest of the New Mexico Pueblo tribes, some people from those pueblos fled to seek refuge at Navajo strongholds. Refugees from Awatovi on Hopi joined the Navajos at Canyon de Chelly when their village was destroyed. Thus a strong Puebloan influence came to the culture in the Four Corners area for a time, including the herding of sheep and goats, which the Pueblo Indians had learned from the Spanish. Relationships between the Navajos and the Pueblo peoples deteriorated under the pressure of drought and enemy attacks by the Utes, Comanches, and Spanish in the early-eighteenth century, and the Navajo began to migrate toward the south and west to Ramah, the Chuska Mountains, Black Mesa, and the land along the Little Colorado River. They brought with them their thriving herds of sheep, goats, horses, and cattle.

Traditionally, leadership among the Navajo was conferred on respected families from whom a clan na'taanii (leader) and a regional na'taanii were chosen, based on the individual's wisdom, leadership, traditional knowledge, and ability to live in harmony. In addition, each clan group chose a hashkééji naat'ááh, or war leader, and a hózhóóji naat'ááh, or peace leader. The twelve war leaders and twelve peace leaders would meet in a tribal assembly, or naachid, every two to four years.

Narbona was a much-respected headman from the Chuska Mountains. He was able to negotiate a peace treaty with the Spanish in 1819, but when Mexico gained independence from Spain in 1821, hostilities resumed as the New Mexicans raided the Navajo for slaves. Narbona and a Mount Taylor Navajo, Antonio Sandoval, negotiated a peace treaty with the Mexicans. In 1833, they visited all of the Navajo bands, asking them to stop fighting the Mexicans and to return Mexican livestock. The Mexicans, however, did not keep their promise to return Navajo livestock and slaves, so warfare resumed under the leadership of Hastiin Ch'ilhaajinii, whom the Mexicans called Manuelito. In the meantime, Sandoval had joined the Mexicans in attacking other Navajo bands in order to protect his own band who lived near Mt. Taylor.

The United States Army joined the war in the mid-1840s. In 1846, Navajo leaders, including Narbona, Sandoval, Manuelito, Zarcillos Largos and more than 500 other Navajos met to make peace with the Mexicans and Americans. They negotiated the Bear Spring Treaty with Colonel Doniphan, but the Navajo leaders could not speak for all Navajo bands, and so Navajo raids continued. A new and equally unsuccessful treaty was negotiated in 1848.

In 1849, Indian Agent James Calhoun met with Navajos under the leadership of Narbona. Narbona and six other Navajos were killed by the U.S. Army. Narbona had been one of the Navajo leaders who wanted peace, but after his death, Manuelito, who wanted revenge, was the most influential leader, and the bloody conflicts continued. Navajos were routinely taken as slaves by the New Mexicans, a practice that continued even after the Civil War.

Anglo-European settlement put tremendous pressure on the Navajo resources as Mexicans and Anglos usurped Navajo grazing lands for their own sheep. By the late 1850s, hostilities between the Navajos and the U.S. government were ongoing, and war was formally declared by the United States on September 8, 1858. In the meantime, another Navajo warrior and leader, Barboncito, had emerged.

In April of 1860, the Navajo, under the leadership of Manuelito and Barboncito attacked the U.S. Army's Fort Defiance and were barely repulsed. But in September of 1861, a group of Navajo women and children, who had gone to Fort Fauntleroy to collect rations promised them under one of the several U.S.-Navajo treaties, were massacred.

The next year, Brig. General Carleton became the military commander for New Mexico. Having defeated the Mescalero Apaches, he moved against the Navajo, first demanding that they surrender and move to Fort Sumner in New Mexico. His strategy was to force the Navajos to become farmers and live in small towns, where they would, he believed, forget their language and customs. He pursued a scorched-earth policy to force the Navajos to move.

In the winter of 1863-1864, Kit Carson invaded Canyon de Chelly, where Barboncito's band was living, and took 200 prisoners. All through the winter, starving Navajos surrendered at Fort Canby and Fort Wingate. In the winter and early spring of 1864, the U.S. government moved more than 4,000 Navajos from Fort Wingate and Fort Defiance to the banks of the Pecos River, known as Bosque Redondo. The terror and hardship of Long Walk, which covered several hundred miles in sleet, snow, and cold, are still remembered and bitterly recounted. The march was intentionally brutal, since the soldiers' intent was to eradicate the Navajo. By March of the next year, more than 9,000 Navajos were incarcerated at Fort Sumner, though several thousand, some under the leadership of Manuelito and Barboncito, had avoided capture. In August of 1864, Barboncito and a few of his band surrendered at Fort Wingate and Manuelito and twenty-three followers surrendered in 1866.

The rations allotted for the captives were never sufficient, no shelter was provided, and fodder for the animals was inadequate, so the Navajos' livestock starved. Smallpox swept through the camps, killing more than 2,000 Navajos. For four years, the Navajos' crops failed and the prisoners starved and died of disease during an illegal incarceration that began during the administration of President Abraham Lincoln.

By 1868, partly because settlers were disturbed by the presence of Navajos so far east, the U.S. government negotiated the 1868 treaty with the Navajo. Seven Navajo headmen, Delgadito, Barboncito, Manuelito, Largo, Herrero, Armijo, and Torivio met with U.S. Peace Commissioners. Barboncito, as spokesman for the Navajos, argued successfully for the Navajos that they be allowed to return to their land in the Four Corners area rather than be sent to live with other Indians on reservations in Oklahoma, Mississippi, and Florida.

The Navajos were accorded a 3.5-million-acre reservation, an area equal to about ten percent of the land they had occupied before the Long Walk. Several million acres were added to the reservation between 1878 and 1934, but some of those acres, which had been part of the Hopi Reservation, have been returned to the Hopis by U.S. government courts as part of the settlement of the Navajo-Hopi land dispute. The Treaty of 1868 remains the binding agreement between the United States government and the sovereign Navajo Nation.

The Navajos walked home and began the difficult process of rebuilding their homesteads. The U.S. government provided each family with seeds, farm tools, and two sheep, from which they began to rebuild their flocks. The period after the Navajo returned to their land brought in the era of trading posts and the beginning of the tourist trade, as well as the establishment of government boarding schools that children were forced to attend despite many families' strong objections. Off-reservation boarding schools persisted as the main educational opportunity for Navajo children until the 1930s, when some reservation day schools were built.

In the early 1900s, oil was discovered on the reservation, and in 1922 Midwest Oil Refining Company struck oil near Shiprock. In 1923 the U.S. government set up a tribal council of twelve delegates and twelve alternates to lease the oil and gas resources.

Traditionally, the Navajos had conducted their political lives within much smaller units under the authority of a naat'áanii. This first tribal council was completely under the authority of the U.S. government, which had the right to remove any delegate it wished, leaving the council with no defined powers. Nonetheless, the council was able to exert some influence on what the federal government was doing in regard to the Navajo people.

According to the U.S. government, their stock reduction programs of the 1930s and 1940s were the only way to stop soil erosion caused by overgrazing. From the Diné point of view, stock reduction meant destroying their livelihoods—the herds that they had patiently built from the sheep allotted to them under the Treaty of 1868.

The council, which was supposedly the structure by which the Navajos would govern themselves, was powerless to stop the U.S. government's programs. Under the leadership of John Morgan, the Navajos rejected the Indian Reorganization Act of 1934 because in addition to setting up a council and tribal courts, it would authorize the Secretary of the Interior to limit livestock. John Collier, the Commissioner of Indian Affairs, responded with even more punitive enforcement of the program.

In 1938 the secretary set up a new tribal council with seventy-four delegates, a chairman, and a vice-chairman. This council, like the first, had no actual power. Jacob Morgan, one of the men who had led the opposition to the stock reduction program, was voted chairman, but was unable to halt the program. Resistance continued throughout World War II, when finally the livestock numbers were within the government's parameters.

Thirty-six hundred Navajos served in the armed forces during the war, bringing much-needed money to the tribe. The Navajo language was used by some of these servicemen to create a secret code that was never broken by the Japanese. The Navajo Code Talkers have been recognized for their invaluable service in winning the war for the Allies by both the federal government and the Navajo Nation.

After the war, the Indian Claims Commission was set up to compensate Native American tribes for the land that had been taken from them. Norman Littell was hired as attorney for the Navajo, and he began a campaign to assert Navajo rights. The government's termination policy of the mid 1950s, which sought to end the federal government's treaty responsibilities to Native American tribes, actually worked to strengthen the council as the Bureau of Indian Affairs withdrew from the tribe's affairs.

In the late 50s, oil and gas reserves were discovered in the Four Corners area, and revenues from those leases and Littell's legal work to affirm the tribe's sovereignty added to the tribal government's ability to act on behalf of the Navajo. By the end of the decade, the tribe had assumed responsibility for water development, emergency welfare, the building of chapter houses, tribal enterprises, and the court system on the reservation. Littell was fired in 1966 when he failed to win more than a compromise in one decision in the Navajo-Hopi land dispute.

The council decided at the end of the decade to allow the strip mining of Black Mesa for coal to power the generators that would support the development of the new cities of the Southwest. The decision was as controversial here as it was on the Hopi Reservation.

Sheep graze along the highways on the Navajo Reservation, which has an open range. That means it's up to you to look out for sheep, cattle, and horses on the road. PHOTO: TANYA LEE

Visiting the Navajo Nation

Respect the privacy of the residents of Navajoland by not entering houses or hogans uninvited, not knocking on doors, not yelling or throwing things, especially near sacred sites, observing quiet hours between 11 P.M. and 6 A.M., and recognizing that teepees are always used for religious purposes, and therefore, you should not intrude.

Obey all tribal laws and regulations. Do not enter areas that are marked off limits or that you have been told not to enter. Stay on designated trails unless your tour guide says otherwise. Rock climbing and off-trail hiking are not allowed, nor is off-road travel by dune buggies, ATVs, jeeps, or motorcycles.

Do not touch or remove any artifacts, plants, rocks, or animals.

Use trash containers, and do not litter or burn or bury debris.

Alcoholic beverages and firearms are strictly prohibited.

If you want to take photos, ask first, and remember that a gratuity is always appreciated. Photographing for commercial use requires a special permit.

Attend a dance or an event only after you have confirmed that visitors are welcome. If it is a religious event, behave as you would in a church or synagogue. Do not disturb any event by pushing your way to the front or blocking someone's view, and do not ask questions about what is happening.

Do not applaud unless it is clearly acceptable to do so.

If you are asked to leave a private religious event, do so quietly and promptly.

Use permits are required for hiking, camping, and backcountry use. Contact the Navajo Parks & Recreation Department, P.O. Box 9000, Window Rock, AZ 86515; (520) 871–6647/7307; fax (520) 871–6637. For hunting, fishing, trapping, and boating licenses, contact Navajo Fish & Wildlife, P.O. Box 2310, Window Rock, AZ 86515; (520) 871–6451/6452; fax (520) 871–7069.

In the mid 1970s, Exxon signed an agreement with the tribe to mine uranium on reservation lands. The tribal council had signed the agreement though it had inadequate information about the health hazards of mining uranium and the difficulty of restoring the land after the mining. Navajo miners and millers worked without safety gear and took the radioactive dust on their work clothes back to their homes. Despite the passage of the Radiation Exposure Compensation Act, the federal government (which is responsible for overseeing mineral leasing on Native American lands) has still done little to help the miners or their families.

The exploitation of mineral resources is the major revenue-producing enterprise on the Navajo Nation, and while much of the tribe's revenues are derived from mineral leases, most of the profits go to the corporations that hold those leases, and the tribe has never had the capital to extract and process the minerals itself.

Peter MacDonald was elected tribal chairman in 1970, as the movement for Native American nationalism was well underway. His mission was to increase self-determination and sovereignty for the Navajo Nation by increasing economic opportunities and providing children with bicultural, bilingual education. Today schools on the reservation are run by the state school districts, individual communities, or the Bureau of Indian Affairs. High school students sometimes go to school in border towns and live in dormitories there. There is one Navajo-controlled community college with several campuses, and Northern Arizona University runs a number of degree programs on the reservation. In addition, NAU and the other two state universities have begun to focus on recruiting and retaining Native American students.

MacDonald's administration also saw great improvements in health care, law, and politics. By the late 1980s, however, tribal politics had created factionalism that led to a violent confrontation in Window Rock. MacDonald was sentenced to jail for his part in the incident. President Clinton pardoned MacDonald just before he left office in January 2001, following a presidential tradition of granting clemency to some prisoners whose sentences are excessive or otherwise questionable.

The Navajo Nation government was restructured by the Tribal Council in 1989, forming a three-branch—executive, legislative, and judicial—system, and today, the Navajo Nation continues to work toward self-determination and economic development while preserving its cultural heritage. Part of their economic development effort is focused on increasing destination tourism.

Today about 170,000 Navajos live on the reservation. Some are traditional farmers and ranchers living in rural areas without electricity or running water. Others live in the more urban centers of Window Rock (the capital), Shiprock, and Tuba City.

The Navajo Nation Tribal Council meets in Window Rock, and eighty-eight delegates from the 110 chapters, or communities, make the laws and decisions for the people in a representative form of government.

Navajo Nation chapters were established in 1923, along with the tribal council, as units of agricultural administration. They subsequently became community centers for a largely rural, dispersed population. Each chapter elects a president, vice president, and secretary. Chapters hold regular meetings, rather like town halls, to decide on matters of local importance and to meet with their representatives to the Navajo Nation Tribal Council. Tribal programs, such as building or economic development programs, are administered through chapter government.

Most chapters have chapter houses, which provide services and facilities for chapter members. Chapter houses are usually built near recently dug wells or other water sources and therefore can provide facilities for bathing, laundering, and cooking. Chapters also organize community events, such as fairs, rodeos, sports, social dances, clinics, and educational classes.

The Navajo Nation elects a president and a vice president every four years. When the Tribal Council is not in session, twelve standing committees of the Navajo Nation Council carry on the work of the nation. In 1998, the Local Governance Act, giving more authority to the chapters rather than to the central government in Window Rock, was passed. Shonto Chapter became the first to be certified under the act.

The Navajo language is spoken widely, and it is the only language used in Navajo prayers, songs, and religious ceremonies. The number four plays an important part in Navajo philosophy and religion. Traditional medicine men use songs, prayers, and ceremonies to cure illness or protect from harm a person who has been exposed to a dangerous situation or experience. The more than fifty ceremonies that may be used are performed at specified times for particular purposes; they may last from several hours to nine days. The medicine man may also use sandpaintings as part of the ritual.

The Navajo Nation Fair is held in Window Rock and the Western Navajo Fair is held in Tuba City, usually during the second or third weekend of October.

The tribe's newspaper is the *Navajo Times*, started in 1958. The paper's address is Window Rock Mall, AZ Hwy. 254 at Route 12, Window Rock, Navajo Nation, AZ 86515-0310; (520) 871-6641/6642; fax (520) 871-6409. Tribal news is also covered by the *Arizona Republic*, the *Arizona Daily Sun*, the *Gallup Independent*, and the *Navajo-Hopi Observer*. KTNN, 660 AM and KWRK 96.1 FM are the Navajo-English radio stations.

The Navajo Reservation observes Daylight Savings Time, but the Hopi Reservation and the rest of Arizona do not, nor do some private enterprises on the Navajo Reservation.

Navajo Art

Navajo Jewelry

Navajos began to make jewelry around the time of the Long Walk in the mid 1860s. Whether they learned jewelry making at Fort Sumner or before their incarceration is not clear, but Atsidi Sam (Old Smith) is known to have been one of the first Navajos to learn metalworking. He probably learned from one of the itinerant Mexican silversmiths who traveled among Navajo trading silverwork for Navajo livestock. In the late 1800s, John Lorenzo Hubbell hired Mexican smiths to teach silversmithing to Navajos; the trader also provided some of the silver coins that were melted down and fashioned into jewelry.

By the early 1900s many Navajos wore silver bead necklaces and the squash blossom design developed during this period. By this time, the use of United States coins to make jewelry was illegal, and Mexican pesos were not being exported, so Navajo jewelry was created from one-ounce pieces of coin silver. Trading posts often advanced materials and groceries against the jewelry that Navajos would sell there. The jewelers began adding large turquoise stones to their silverwork.

When the railroad was built and the Fred Harvey Company started encouraging tourism in the Southwest in the early twentieth century, a new market for jewelry opened up, but most of this "Route 66" jewelry was of inferior quality, both in material and workmanship. Much of it was mass-produced and machine stamped.

In 1941 the U.S. government established the Navajo Arts and Crafts Guild to promote the manufacture and sale of high-quality, Navajo-made jewelry. After the World War II, the Navajo Tribe took over the guild.

The war brought money to the reservation, and Navajos were able to buy new, more elaborate tools and equipment for making their jewelry. During the post-war period, the tribes of the Southwest began to develop individual styles. Navajo jewelry was typically massive and heavy, set with large stones.

This sterling silver and turquoise bracelet is typical of Navajo jewelry you'll see at many trading posts and stores. PHOTO: TANYA LEE

By the 1970s, Indian jewelry was fashionable, partly because of the hippie movement of the 1960s, and partly because innovators such as Hopi Charles Loloma and Navajo Kenneth Begay had begun to explore imaginative new styles and new techniques during the 1950s. The boom also brought imitators and poor quality jewelry that could be sold to an uneducated public.

By the next decade, much of the authentic, high-quality Navajo jewelry was being sold by museum shops, galleries, and traders, and another period of innovation began.

Today, some fine jewelers use the lost wax method of casting, but most use the more traditional tufa or stonecast method. Navajo jewelers also make stamped jewelry using dies and tools they have themselves created. This stamped method of silver decorating had been developed by observing the way Mexican leatherworkers stamped designs on saddles and bridles.

Channel inlay and mosaic inlay (in which there is no metal between the stones) are popular, as is fabrication, in which pieces of silver are soldered together. Navajos also create squash blossom necklaces in which small turquoise stones are set in individual settings. This kind of work resembles Zuni petit point.

Jewelry with a bumpy surface is probably done using a granulation or granule fusion technique in which tiny pieces of metal are fused onto the piece without solder. Overlay, etching, appliqué, and engraving are other techniques you will see.

Today, much Navajo jewelry includes gemstones such as turquoise, diamonds, malachite, coral, lapis lazuli, and opal, to mention only a few.

Turquoise is a traditional favorite in Navajo jewelry. A stone's color, texture, and design indicate what mine it came from. Natural turquoise is becoming harder to find and more expensive since many U.S. mines have closed down in the last few decades. Most turquoise today is artificially treated. Stabilized turquoise is a lesser grade stone to which plastic resin has been added under high pressure to improve its color and strength. Stabilized turquoise is very difficult to distinguish from the natural stone. Reconstituted turquoise is made from chips of stone that have been glued and subjected to high pressure. Its value is less than that of stabilized turquoise. Poor quality stones can be temporarily improved in appearance by being treated with wax, oil, or polish, but this stone will revert to its previous whitish color within a few weeks. Plastic turquoise "stones" are used in some jewelry.

If you're interested in buying high-quality Navajo jewelry, look in galleries, museums, guilds, and reputable shops to accustom your eye to what fine jewelry looks like. Ask the proprietor to tell you what kinds of stones are incorporated in the pieces that appeal to you. You can also find very good pieces at craft fairs where artists sell their own work.

Navajo Rugs

Weaving is a way of life for many of the 30,000 Navajo women who make rugs today. The art of weaving was taught to the Navajo by Spider Woman, who built a loom according to the instructions of the Holy People.

Traditionally, women raise and herd the sheep that produce the wool for the rugs. They shear the sheep in the spring, a task which must be done with manual, not electric, clippers—usually there is no electricity at the sheep camp, and anyway, electric shears could not get through the grit embedded in the fleece of animals that have grazed outdoors all year.

Once the fleece is removed from the animal, it is combed, or carded, and stickers and burrs are removed by hand. The tools used for this and all other aspects of creating a rug are often made by the weaver herself. The carded wool ends up in a loose roll, ready for the next step.

Spinning is the next task. The weaver uses a spindle made of a long, tapered shaft of wood and a flat round whorl. The roll of wool is attached to the spindle and spun as many times as necessary to create the right thickness and tightness for the kind of yarn being made. Yarn for the warp (the vertical yarns in the weaving) is thinner and tighter than yarn for the weft (the horizontal yarns that create the design).

The yarn is removed from the spindle and wound into a skein, which is then washed in warm, soapy water. The yarn must then be dried by hanging it to set the spin so it does not unravel.

Now the yarn, if it is not going to be used in its natural color of white, brownish-black, gray, or brown, is ready for dying, and the precise color that can be achieved depends on the kinds of plants used, the time of year when they are picked, the part of the plant used, the kind of metal container in which the plant is boiled, and the other elements that are added to the dye bath. Among the many dozens of plants useful for creating the colors in Navajo rugs are rabbitbrush, sagebrush, mistletoe, wild carrot, cliff rose, cedar, oak, wild holly, and lichen. Today weavers may also buy yarn that has already been dyed, or they may use aniline (synthetic) dyes that produce colors similar to natural plant dyes. One of the most interesting purchases you can make while visiting Navajoland is a dye chart, which holds some of the plants used for dying wool and shows you strands of colored yarn dyed with those particular plants.

Navajo women construct their looms from logs or two-by-fours, or they may use two trees or two poles of the hogan. The loom must be square, and it must be sturdy enough to hold the tension of the warp. Warping a large loom may take several hours, and it is traditional to do all of the work at once, without interruptions from children or from attending to other tasks.

A fine Ye'ii weaving graces the wall at the Thunderbird Lodge Gift Shop at Canyon de Chelly. PHOTO: TANYA LEE

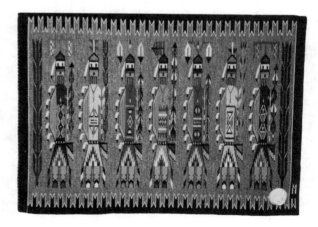

Then the weaving can begin, although the weaver has been planning the design for this particular rug all along. Navajo rugs are woven in a tapestry weave—the weft yarns are woven over and under the warp yarns, which do not show in the finished piece. In addition to the loom, the weaver uses battens, a weaving fork, and shuttles, all of which she may have made herself or which may have been passed down to her by her mother or grandmother.

The weaver may carry the design in her head, or she may draw it out on paper. The weaving will take many hours of physically demanding and mentally challenging work. The rug is not only an object, but also a process, and everything that happens during the weaving is part of the final piece. Some weavers put in a spirit line, a contrasting piece of yarn from the inner portion of the design through the border. This practice, and the prayers associated with weaving, help ensure that the weaver will be able to weave another rug when the one she is working on is finished.

Navajo women have been perfecting the art of weaving for nearly four hundred years. Not so many decades ago, one could purchase a Navajo rug for fifty cents a square foot. Fortunately, that has changed, as the skill and artistry of rug weaving have become recognized and appreciated. Many women support their families with the proceeds from their weaving, and some say that this work, although difficult and demanding, is particularly appealing because it allows them to stay home and care for their families.

From the delicate pastels of Burntwater and Wide Ruins rugs to the vibrant reds and blacks of the Ganado Red and Chief's Blanket, there are dozens of styles of Navajo rugs that you will soon learn to recognize. Some, like Two Grey Hills, are associated with particular geographical areas, and others, such as the Eye Dazzler, with particular time periods. Other styles include pictorials, which show scenes from everyday life, and ye'ii bicheii rugs, which depict ceremonial Navajo dancers.

Every Navajo weaving is a work of art, and every rug is different. Today, many weavers sign their works, and a photograph of the weaver may be attached to the rug at the trading post. While the weavings are called "rugs," often they will be hung on walls rather than placed on the floor.

You will soon learn what style appeals most to you, and this (and what you can afford) will determine what you want to buy, whether you are thinking of purchasing just one rug or starting a collection. You can begin to evaluate the quality of a piece by looking for symmetry, square corners, an even texture to the weaving, and consistent colors in the piece as a whole. Eventually you will want to learn to distinguish between natural dyes and synthetic ones and between commercial yarns and the ones made by the weaver herself.

You can find Navajo rugs at galleries, in museum gift shops, and at upscale shops in Sedona and Phoenix, but you can also find some of the most beautiful ones at the trading posts, such as the Cameron Trading Post, the Tuba City Historic Trading Post, and the Hubbell Trading Post in Ganado, where you might also be fortunate enough to see weavers demonstrating their craft. Some weavers sell their work directly to the public.

Cameron

Cameron, a small chapter of the Navajo Nation, is 52 miles east of Grand Canyon Village on Highway 64 and 54 miles north of Flagstaff on U.S. Highway 89. The Visitors Center, (520) 679-2303, is at the intersection of the two highways.

Going north on U.S. 89 from Flagstaff to Cameron, you will travel through a spectacular cinder-covered landscape of landslides and glacial deposits north of San Francisco Mountain, a once-active volcano. Beginning at about milepost 421 is the Interior

The Little Colorado River cuts through Paleozoic rock as it descends to meet the Colorado River east of the Grand Canyon. PHOTO: TANYA LEE

Valley or Inner Basin of the volcano. While Ice Age glaciers contributed to the formation of the basin, the most important factor in its creation was the collapse of the central part of the volcano when the magma beneath it was released during frequent volcanic eruptions between 2.8 million and 200,000 years ago.

The black cinders along the highway are the youngest in Arizona, deposited when Sunset Crater became active in 1064-1065 C.E.

The colorful rocks further up the road are Triassic dark red sandstone, shale, and mudstone.

Fossil amphibians are found in the Triassic rock formations near Cameron, and reptile footprints can be seen on some of the sandstone ledges. Most of these were made by a four-footed reptile, Chirotherium, and are about the size of human handprints.

In this area you can also see ripples in the sandstone. These result from currents of water that covered the mudflats here during Triassic times. Other evidence, such as

The Bennett Freeze

For more than 30 years, some Navajos around Cameron have lived under the Bennett Freeze, a federal mandate that forbids them to build new houses, make repairs on existing housing, install indoor plumbing, run electrical lines to their homes, or make any improvements without going through a lengthy, and often futile, approval process.

The Freeze was imposed in 1966 by then U.S. Indian Commissioner Robert Bennett on land disputed between the Navajo and Hopi Tribes. Originally the Freeze applied to 1.5 million acres of the 1934 Navajo Reservation. The Hopi Tribe claimed in court that they had sacred and archaeological sites on that land. This land had been part of the 2.5 million acres, only a small portion of their ancestral homelands, set aside for the Hopi in 1882 by President Chester A. Arthur. Bennett imposed the Freeze to prevent further development on the land until the issue of which tribe should control it was decided by the courts.

The order for the Freeze was finalized by the courts in 1972 and was in effect until 1992 when Judge Earl Carroll of the Arizona District Court lifted it. Just three years later, however, the Ninth Circuit Court reinstated the Freeze.

In March of 1997, Judge Carroll lifted the Freeze from 800,000 acres which were no longer in dispute. The action was hailed as a major step forward.

In 1999, a grassroots organization, The Forgotten People, formed to try to get the Freeze lifted from the remaining 700,000 acres. They maintain that for three generations they and their families have suffered extreme hardship. The group succeeded in convincing Congressman J.D. Hayworth of Arizona's Sixth Congressional District and other representatives to introduce a bill into the House to ask Congress to lift the Freeze. The bill failed to make progress that year, and it was introduced again in 2000.

The issue, however, is one that probably will not be resolved by Congress but by the cooperative efforts of the Navajo and Hopi Tribes.

---

circular craters formed by raindrops, suggest that wet and dry times alternated in this region. This notion is consistent with the concept that this area was periodically covered by a western sea that advanced and retreated. The climate was warm and the vegetation that grew here decayed and formed the rich coal deposits of the region during the Cretaceous period.

The Little Colorado River cuts through sold rock at Cameron. The river is usually dry, but during spring snowmelt and after summer thunderstorms, the riverbed has water in it, and flash floods may even occur. From Cameron, the Little Colorado descends 2,000 feet to meet with the Colorado River 30 miles to the northwest.

Cameron Trading Post and Motel
Box 339, Cameron, AZ 86020
(520) 679–2231, (800) 338–7385,
fax (520) 679–2350
www.camerontradingpost.com

One mile north of the intersection of Hwy. 64 and U.S. Highway 89 is the historic Cameron Trading Post, founded in 1916 by Hubert and C.D. Richardson.

The trading post combines modern economic practices and traditional trading post customs—Native Americans sell and trade their arts and crafts items here for merchandise and groceries, and the trading post also accepts credit cards.

Inside the trading post you will find a wide range of arts and crafts created by artisans from many of Arizona's tribes. The store is chock full of Navajo rugs, Acoma, Hopi, Santa Clara, Jemez and Navajo pottery, Tohono O'odham basketry, Navajo stone carving and sandpaintings, Naatsilid pottery, and Navajo, Hopi, and Zuni jewelry. Pendleton blankets, Western-style hats and belts, regional-interest books, and the usual collection of T-shirts and inexpensive souvenirs complete the collection. In the center of the store is a counter selling many flavors of delicious, locally-made fudge. The grocery store/commissary at the back of the building stocks everything from snacks and sodas to nails and 25-pound sacks of Blue Bird flour.

Near the Navajo rugs, look for a small display of rock art. These are small petroglyph-like carvings on sandstone done by local children using nails as their carving implements. All proceeds from the sale of these charming souvenirs goes to benefit the Cameron Youth Project and the Dzil Libei Elementary School, which you passed a few miles back on U.S. 89. The rock art carving project was started by a teacher at the school to buy the children books that they could take home and keep.

The trading post is open daily year-round except for Christmas Day and a half-day on Thanksgiving.

Walk through the trading post to the restaurant, which opened about 15 years ago. A huge sandstone fireplace dominates the back wall of windows overlooking the Little Colorado. A decorated tin ceiling and handmade wooden display cabinets add to the Old West charm. The walls display magnificent basketry, Katsina carvings, and Navajo rugs.

The restaurant serves a varied menu of American, Mexican, and Navajo food, including Navajo tacos, green chili stew, and Navajo stew (beef, carrots, celery, and onions in a thick gravy, served with fry bread). A Navajo taco is a plate-sized piece of Navajo fry bread topped with a spicy combination of ground beef, mild green chili, beans, cheese, lettuce, and tomato. Both locals and tourists come here for breakfast, lunch, and dinner. Reservations are not required, and the restaurant is wheelchair accessible.

Don't leave without ordering Navajo fry bread—a soft, sweet dough rolled thick and deep-fried to a golden brown, served with honey and butter, though some folks prefer to eat it just with salt. You can order it for breakfast, lunch or dinner. It is a treat you won't soon forget!

The motel has sixty-six recently renovated rooms, each with stunning hand-carved and decorated beds, vanities, bureaus, and valances in Southwestern mission style. Smoking and non-smoking rooms are available and two rooms are wheelchair accessible. All rooms have TVs, and most have balconies overlooking a

Some rooms at the Cameron Trading Post Motel overlook this courtyard of terraced gardens.
PHOTO: TANYA LEE

terraced garden oasis. The gardens here were recently restored and the outdoor area has a large barbecue and fountains. Reservations for motel rooms are strongly recommended. Reservations are held until 7 P.M. unless guaranteed with a credit card or full prepayment is received before your arrival date. Cancellation requires a 24-hour notice prior to your arrival date.

For museum-quality artwork, visit the gallery across the parking lot from the trading post. The artwork here is absolutely top quality. Weaving, painting, basketry, jewelry, Hopi Katsina carvings, Apache burden baskets, bronze sculptures, and modern steel and glass furniture share this space with antique Native American beadwork, weaving, and other art. Be sure to ask the salesperson to let you see the second floor of the gallery. If the front door of the gallery is locked, the salesperson is probably showing visitors the second floor. Knock on the door and wait a few minutes, or ask in the trading post for another salesperson to open the first floor for you. The artwork inside the gallery is definitely worth the little extra effort it may take to see it. Even if you cannot afford to buy the magnificent pieces here, the friendly and helpful staff will provide a unique opportunity to learn more about authentic Native American art.

The trading post complex also features a Texaco gas station, telephones, restrooms, a post office, as well as RV sites with full hookups rented at nightly, weekly, and monthly rates. No public restrooms or showers are available at the RV campground.

Tuba City

A plaque on a sandstone monument near the Tuba City Boarding School commemorates Chief Tuba (or Tuve). The monument, erected in 1941, says that Chief Tuba was a Hopi of the water and corn clans. He was born in 1810 and died around 1887. In 1865, he acted as a scout for Kit Carson's U.S. Expedition.

Natural springs attracted Hopi, Navajo, and Paiute Indians to this area for many generations. Mormon missionaries arrived as early as 1859. In 1875, Chief Tuba, having been converted to Mormonism, gave the spring and the land around it on which Tuba City now stands to Mormon pioneers in return for protection from his enemies. The Mormons laid out the city and built their structures using cut stone from nearby sites.

The Mormons, however, could not get clear title to the land and the settlement was taken over by the U.S. Indian Agency in 1903.

Tuba City, with a population of 7,300, is now the administrative and trade center for the Western Navajo Agency. It is 1 mile north of the junction of Arizona Highway 264 to the Hopi mesas and U.S. Highway 160 through Kayenta to Monument Valley. U.S. 160 travels through Mesozoic sedimentary rocks formed in the Triassic and Jurassic periods. Here, as near Cameron, the area was periodically covered with water. The brilliantly colored rock formations all around you are evidence of the ancient floodplains and sand dune deposits.

U.S. 160 climbs steeply from the valley of the Little Colorado onto a platform, the Coconino Plateau, capped by erosion-resistant sandstone. About 4.5 miles east of the U.S. 89 and U.S. 160 junction, a small sign on the north side of the highway between mileposts 316 and 317 directs you to dinosaur tracks embedded forever on the once-muddy flats. The dinosaurs that left these tracks walked on two legs with a stride of about seven feet. Their short front legs were probably used for clasping food.

If you continue north on U.S. 160 from Tuba City toward Tonolea, Black Mesa, which yields high quality coal to fuel the cities of the Southwest, is on your right, rising higher as it moves eastward. Lagoon deposits that document the periodic retreat of a great western sea are near the surface of the mesa. These form the coal deposits being strip-mined today from the top of the mesa.

To strip mine the coal, the trees, grasses, and other plants are removed and the top-soil is pushed away. As much as 180 feet of the overburden is removed next. Overburden is "useless" rock that overlies a mineral deposit. Gigantic shovels loosen and remove the coal. The coal is crushed and taken by belt line, railroad, and slurry pipeline to coal-powered power plants near Page, Arizona and Laughlin, Nevada. These are among the power plants of the Colorado Plateau that fueled the development of the Southwest and that continue to provide energy to cities as far away as Denver and Los Angeles.

After an area is strip-mined, the overburden and topsoil are replaced and the area is reseeded to "restore" it to its original condition. Since the rainfall is scant in this region, it will take many decades for the land to recover its vegetation, which the mining company claims will be more productive for sheep grazing.

This recovery operation, however, does not take into account the emotional damage done to the people who live nearby and must now live with blasting and coal dust or those who were forced to move to make room for the mining operations. Nor does this equation of removal of minerals and land restoration take into account the spiritual damage that the Native peoples of this land say is being done to the earth itself.

Area Overview

Tuba City is the headquarters of the Western Agency of the Navajo Nation. It is governed as one of the 110 Navajo chapters, with a chapter president, vice president, treasurer, and secretary. Chapters elect delegates to send to the Navajo Nation Council in Window Rock. With a population of about 10,000 Tuba City is larger than most other chapters.

There is a small U.S. Public Health Service Hospital in Tuba City, and the city is only about 70 miles from the regional hospital, Flagstaff Medical Center.

Temperatures during the summer range from the high 90s (degrees Fahrenheit) to lows in the mid 50s. During the winter, expect daytime highs of about 50 degrees and overnight lows in the mid to high 20s. The elevation of Tuba City is approximately 5,000 feet and the average precipitation is less than 10 inches a year.

Restaurants

Kate's Cafe $
P.O. Box 95, Tuba City, AZ 86045
(520) 283–6773

Kate's Cafe is a local favorite and you will probably see more Tuba City residents than tourists here. The restaurant is on Edgewater Drive; turn east at the Tuba City Trading Post. Since Tuba City has just renamed all of its streets, people may not immediately know where Edgewater Drive is, but everyone knows where the trading post is located.

This place is so casual that it feels more like an old-time diner than a restaurant. You can get mostly plain American fare here—steaks, chops, pasta, salads, and sandwiches. Favorites are Kate's Club Sandwich and the Baja, a hamburger. Kate's is open for breakfast, lunch, and dinner. Parking is plentiful and reservations are out of the question, but you probably won't have to wait for a table.

This restaurant does not take credit cards, so be sure to have enough cash on hand to pay for your meal. Tuba City has branches of Bank of America, Norwest, and Wells Fargo, all of which have ATMs within a few blocks of Kate's.

Hogan Restaurant $
P.O. Box 247, Tuba City, AZ 86045
(520) 283–5875

When the waiter told me one of this restaurant's most popular meals was New York steak wrapped in fry bread, I thought he was joking—but he wasn't, and it's definitely worth ordering. Other meals enjoyed by the locals include Navajo tacos and vegetarian Navajo tacos. The menu runs the gamut from Mexican to Navajo to American food; an unusual feature is a full salad bar.

The Hogan is open every day for breakfast, lunch, and dinner. The atmosphere is casual and non-smoking. The restaurant is between the Tuba Trading Post and the Tuba City Quality Inn, so there is plenty of parking.

This is a frequent meeting place for locals and visitors, which can sometimes lead to utter confusion. Arizona does not observe Daylight Savings Time. The Navajo Reservation, however, does. But the Hogan Restaurant, like the trading post and the motel, is on a small piece of private property within the reservation, so the restaurant, trading post, and motel are on Mountain Standard Time. If you're in the restaurant at 3 P.M. on a July after-noon, it will be 2 P.M. when you walk across the street to Kate's Restaurant. Fortunately, the Hogan staff has a great sense of humor. When I asked if reservations were accepted, one of them pointed out that I was on a reservation! (The answer to the reservations accepted question is no.)

Szechwan Restaurant $$
160 Hwy. No. 2, Tuba City, AZ 86045
(520) 283–5807

No one's ever heard of Highway 2. This Chinese restaurant is in the Tuba City Shopping Center (also called the Toh Nanees Dizi Shopping Center) next to Bashas' grocery store. The shopping center is one-half mile east of the center of town on Highway 160.

In this modern, casual setting, you may want to try the Mongolian beef dish (shredded onions and beef in a dark sauce, served with steamed or fried rice). Or try the inexpensive lunch buffet served Monday through Friday. This place does a booming take-out business, so it is a favorite with locals and is open all year. No credit cards are accepted and only local checks with a phone number will be honored, so plan to pay with cash.

Motels

Quality Inn $$$
Main Street and Moenave Ave.,
P.O. Box 247, Tuba City, AZ 86045
(520) 283–4545, (800) 644–8383,
fax (520) 283–4144

This 80-room motel has a peaceful, comfortable feel to it. The lobby is decorated with fascinating old photographs and historic descriptions of the area and the people who lived here. Quiet music plays in the background, and on your way to your room, you'll see wall murals by Native artists in the hallways.

The rooms are spacious and well furnished in the Southwest style. All the rooms have full baths, cable TV, and queen-size beds, as well as coffeemakers and air conditioning. Smoking and non-smoking rooms are available and some rooms are wheelchair accessible.

Major credit cards are accepted here. Pets are accepted only in smoking rooms, and the additional fee is $20. There is also a charge for more than two people in a room. A 24-hour advance notice is required for cancellation of reservations, which are recommended, especially around the holidays and during the Western Navajo Fair usually held the second or third weekend of October.

Call the motel to find out about the RV park with full hookups, cable TV, shower, and laundry facilities.

Diné Inn Motel $$$
U.S. Hwy. 160 and Peshlakai Ave.,
P.O. Box 1669, Tuba City, AZ 86045
(520) 283–6107, fax (520) 283–5639

A nicely designed exterior and very basic rooms describe this 15-room motel, which just opened a few months ago. Rooms have full baths, air conditioning, and cable TV.

One room is wheelchair accessible and all rooms are non-smoking. Prepare to pay extra for additional people and pets. Reservations are recommended during the holiday season.

Greyhills Inn $
Greyhills Drive, P.O. Box 160,
Tuba City, AZ 86045
(520) 283–4450, fax (520) 283–4432

If you're traveling on a budget, this is the place to stay. The Greyhills Inn is a training site for high school students who want to get into the hotel management and hospitality industry. Students take courses at Northern Arizona University and in the business department at the high school, then work in the motel to get real-life experience.

One-half mile east on U.S. Highway 160 from the intersection with Arizona Highway 264, the inn offers thirty-two rooms, all non-smoking, and all with shared baths. The wheelchair-accessible rooms have central air conditioning, TVs, and telephones for local calls. Pets are not allowed and the inn takes only Master-Card and Visa. The facility is open year-round except for Christmas Day and New Year's Day. Reservations are recommended, particularly as the school sometimes hosts conferences and then all rooms are booked.

Shopping

Historic Tuba Trading Post
Main Street and Moenave Ave., P.O. Box 247, Tuba City, AZ 86045
(520) 283–4545

One mile north of the junction of U.S. Highway 160 and Arizona Highway 264, this historic trading post dates back to 1880s. The octagonal building was constructed in 1905 and has been remodeled several times and has only recently stopped selling hardware, lumber, groceries, and other trade goods, catering now more to tourists. The trading post, like a traditional hogan, faces east to catch the rising sun.

You can find very high quality, authentic artwork here. Walk into the raised central area to see spectacular Navajo rugs, fine Hopi and Navajo pottery, Zuni, Navajo, and Hopi jewelry, Zuni carvings, superb Hopi Katsina carvings, prayer fans, and basketry. The outer area of the trading post holds Western-style hats and belts, moccasins, books, CDs and cassettes, Pendleton blankets, jackets, and pillows, and the usual collection of inexpensive tourist keepsakes. Particularly endearing are some examples of

The Historic Tuba Trading Post has high-quality art and plenty of souvenirs, as well as friendly, helpful staff. PHOTO: TANYA LEE

Navajo folk art, including teddy bears made of Blue Bird flour sacks and toddler-size dolls made of fabric and clothed in traditional-style dress.

Check at the trading post to find out about upcoming public events on the Navajo and Hopi Reservations. The staff is friendly and very helpful.

The trading post, like the motel and restaurant beside it, are owned by the Bab-bitt Brothers on a small piece of private land on the Navajo Reservation.

Toh Nanees Dizi Shopping Center

This shopping center, one-half mile northeast of U.S. 160 on Arizona Highway 264, has a Bashas' supermarket, movie theater, and a general store. Convenience stores and gas stations abound in Tuba City.

Attractions

The Western Navajo Fair, held the second or third weekend of October, features rodeo, arts and crafts, dance performances, and other entertainment. Call the Tuba Trading Post or the Quality Inn for specific information.

Dinosaur Tracks

For your little boy, these dinosaur tracks might be the high point of your whole vacation. Look for several signs on the right hand side of the road as you travel from the junction of U.S. Highways 89 and 160 toward Tuba City. The road to the dinosaur tracks is 4.5 miles on the left. The beginning of the road is paved, making it easy to recognize.

The tracks are 200 million years old and were left in the muddy flats by a three-toed carnivorous dinosaur, Dilophosaurus, who walked on its hind legs and grasped food with its front legs. A partial fossilized skeleton of the animal is somewhat more impressive than the tracks.

A guide will point out the tracks and skeleton to you, so be sure to have small bills for a tip. A few people will be selling jewelry and petrified wood at the site.

Navajo guide Morris Chee, Jr. shows us a fossilized dinosaur skeleton just outside Tuba City.
PHOTO: TANYA LEE

Hantavirus

Sensationalized international reporting of the occurrence of Hantavirus in the Four Corners area and California has discouraged some travelers from visiting Northern Arizona.

According to the Navajo medicine men, Hantavirus is not a new phenomenon, but one that occurs at irregular intervals depending upon the amount of rainfall in the area. Increased rainfall promotes an increase in the population of rodents, including the deer mice that are the most common carriers of the virus. The traditional healers cite Hantavirus outbreaks in 1919 and 1933.

According to the Indian Health Services and the Navajo Division of Health, people at risk for contracting the disease are families living in houses where rodents have been; suggestions about how to avoid contracting the disease are:

• Seal, air out, and disinfect buildings that have been empty before using them.

• Avoid rodents and their burrows and dens. Air out and disinfect cabins before using them, and pitch tents in areas where you do not see rodent droppings or burrows. Do not camp near woodpiles or garbage dumps. Use tents with floors, or cover the ground where you will be sleeping and sleep on elevated cots if possible. Use bottled, filtered, or chemically disinfected water, and store foods in rodent-proof containers.

• Before cleaning out a building where rodents might have lived, trap the rodents for two or three days and then air out the buildings. Then disinfect the building while wearing rubber gloves, disposable clothes, and shoe covers or clothing you can launder and rubber boots. A dust respirator is recommended. Disinfect all protective gear when you have finished cleaning out the building.

Hantavirus is an airborne virus that is destroyed by sunlight and by disinfectants. It is primarily carried by deer mice, which are four to nine inches long from head to tail and are pale gray to reddish-brown with white fur on their bellies, feet and under their tails. Squirrels, rats, chipmunks, and other kinds of mice may also carry the virus.

In general, common sense should prevail, and all rodents should be avoided, as they may carry Hantavirus or other diseases, such as bubonic plague.

The symptoms of Hantavirus are similar to those of the flu, and include a fever of 101 to 104 degrees Fahrenheit, body aches, chills, and trouble breathing. If you have these symptoms, you should see a doctor immediately.

Little Colorado River Gorge Navajo Tribal Park

Drive 10 miles west of Cameron on Hwy. 64 to reach the Little Colorado River Gorge Navajo Tribal Park. This overlook, maintained by the Navajo Nation, offers a spectacular view of the narrow Little Colorado Gorge, which is cut through Paleozoic rock. The river has only seasonal flow, so you are most likely to see it running during summer monsoon season (July to September) and during spring snowmelt. The overlook area has portajohns and a summer Indian market.

Navajo Arts & Crafts Enterprise
P.O. Box 464, Cameron, AZ 86020
(520) 679–2244, fax (520) 679–2207

Established by the Navajo Nation in 1941 to promote traditional Navajo arts and crafts, the Navajo Arts & Crafts Enterprise at the intersection of U.S. 89 and Hwy. 64 offers high-quality, genuine Navajo arts—rugs, silver and turquoise jewelry, sandpaintings, and pottery—as well as Pendleton blankets, backpacks, pillows and purses, yarn, moccasins, and T-shirts. For the music lover, an extensive collection of cassettes and CDs by Native American artists makes the stop worthwhile. Among the books offered are some out-of-print scholarly texts and anthropological studies reprinted by the University of Arizona's Arizona Books on Request at (800) 426–3797, www.uapress.arizona.edu.

Navajo Arts & Crafts Enterprises has three other stores—in Window Rock at the intersection of Hwy. 264 and Hwy. 12, (520) 871–4090, in Kayenta at Hwy. 160 and Hwy. 163, (520) 697–8611; and in Chinle at Hwy. 191 and Hwy. 7, (520) 674–5338.

Anasazi Inn and Gray Mountain
Trading Post
Box 29100, Gray Mountain, AZ 86016
(520) 679–2214, (800) 678–2214

The Anasazi Inn, 10 miles south of Cameron on U.S. 89, features 112 homey rooms. Convenient to the Grand Canyon and to Wutpaki National Monument and Sunset Crater only 12 miles south, this motel is open year-round and has satellite TV and an outdoor swimming pool. Pets are welcome at an additional charge; reservations (for both you and your pets) are recommended.

The small trading post just across the highway has an abundant selection of souvenirs, maps, T-shirts, and other tourist sundries, as well as a few Navajo rugs and Minnetonka hats and moccasins.

A restaurant adjacent to the trading post has a low-key but spacious dining room with a player piano and Native crafts. Since this restaurant is not on the Navajo Reservation, beer and wine are available. Navajo tacos are the favorite entree for both locals and tourists. The restaurant opens early for breakfast and stays open through a late dinner hour.

Here at Gray Mountain you can also buy gasoline and some groceries, find public telephones, and mail home your purchases at the post office branch in the trading post.

Insiders' Tip

A particularly good map for this area is "Guide to Indian Country of Arizona, Colorado, New Mexico, Utah," published by the Automobile Club of Southern California. The map is widely available in this area, or it may be ordered from Southwest Parks and Monuments Association, P.O. Box 2173, Globe, AZ 85502-2173; (888) 569-SPMA; fax (520) 425-6560; www.spma.org.

Monument Valley

Restaurants
Accommodations
Shopping
Tours
Campgrounds

Your drive northeast from Tuba City to Kayenta will take you through some spectacular landscapes culminating in the exotic spires, pinnacles and buttes of Monument Valley. U.S. Highway 160 east goes through the Mesozoic (63- to 240 million-year-old) rock formations that are so common on the Colorado Plateau.

Climbing out of the valley of the Little Colorado River, the highway reaches a platform of layers of red and orange stream-deposited sandstones and gray and pink wind-deposited Navajo sandstone. About 37 miles north of Tuba City, you can't miss the spectacular rock formations known as Elephant Feet on the north side of the highway. Not far beyond is a pullout where you can stop to take a photograph.

You will pass Tonalea, and to the east is Black Mesa, which records the existence of vast floodplains and advancing and retreating seas. The lagoon deposits of vegetation and animal life lie atop Black Mesa, which supplies the coal deposits being strip-mined by Peabody Coal Company. To the east and south, Black Mesa rises and divides into the finger-shaped mesas of Hopiland.

At Black Mesa's northern end, U.S. 160 runs through the defile that separates the mesa from the Shonto Plateau, where you can see the Triassic and Jurassic rocks that underlie Black Mesa.

At the intersection of U.S. 160 and Arizona Highway 564, look south to see a massive conveyor belt that carries strip-mined coal off Black Mesa. The conveyor belt crosses the highway on an "overpass" and takes the coal to the huge storage towers just north of the highway. From here the coal is loaded onto the train that takes it to Navajo Generating Station in Page, Arizona. About a quarter of the power generated at this power plant is used to pump Central Arizona Project water uphill from the Colorado River in western Arizona to the urban centers of Phoenix and Tucson.

Traveling along Highway 160 you can see the northwestern edge of Black Mesa. PHOTO: TANYA LEE

The power plant created an obnoxious haze over the Grand Canyon, but it was approved before the environmental protection movement of the 1970s. However, in 1991, the Environmental Protection Agency, responding to a lawsuit brought by environmental groups, issued regulations to reduce emissions from the plant. Later, the EPA, Grand Canyon Trust, the Environmental Defense Fund and the power plant settled the suit with an agreement that Navajo Generating Station would, among other conditions, reduce its emissions of sulfur dioxide by 90 percent no later than 1999. These conditions have, indeed, been met.

Just beyond Tsegi, wedges of pink Navajo sandstone to the north of the highway demarcate the edge of the Organ Rock monocline. The 100-square-mile area between Shonto Plateau and Black Mesa theoretically forms the main recharge area for the N-aquifer.

Over thousands of years, rainwater percolates through the porous sandstone until it is trapped by less permeable beds of mud and shale. Since the water cannot flow downward through these layers, it flows horizontally and emerges through seeps and springs. This ancient N-aquifer water not only supplies drinking water to the reservations and feeds seeps and springs, but it is also the water being used to supply the slurry pipeline that carries coal from Black Mesa to the Mohave Generating Plant in Laughlin, Nevada. This is the only coal slurry pipeline in the country. It was built partly because the coal company could buy the N-aquifer water cheaply when it negotiated the original leases with the Hopi and the Navajo Tribes. The quality of the water itself was another reason the slurry pipeline was economically advantageous to the coal company. The water is so pure that it does not gum up the pipeline. Less pure water would make the enterprise much less profitable.

The township of Kayenta is in a fairly level valley created by erosion. The area around Kayenta is dotted with ancient volcanic cores that rise from the landscape behind the mesas like huge sailing ships. Navajo sandstone ascends to the north along the monument upwarp.

North of Kayenta, U.S. 160 climbs through Comb Ridge, threading its way through the "teeth" of the pink Navajo sandstone formation. Beyond the ridge is the same Triassic rock that forms the glorious pastels of the Painted Desert. This rock weathers into crusty badlands. Further on, the surface changes to the hard Shinarump Conglomerate, eroded by water and wind to form a pebbled surface.

Wedges of Navajo sandstone edge the Organ Rock monocline north of Highway 160. PHOTO: TANYA LEE

To the east are the Navajo Buttes, 15- to 20 million-year-old cores of ancient volca-noes. Then the layers of sedimentary rock, steeply tilted at Comb Ridge, level out. The Shinarump Conglomerate overlies a thin layer of red Moenkopi shale, and below that is wind-deposited de Chelly sandstone, Permian age rock formed more than 240 million years ago.

The dramatic formations of Monument Valley have been created over the past fifty-million years, as wind and rain erode the soft de Chelley sandstone that lies under resistant caps of the Shinarump Conglomerate. Once a thousand-foot-high plateau, Monument Valley will eventually disappear, as the bases of the buttes and spires erode further and leave the capstones unsupported. For now, however, this valley is awe-inspiring.

Navajo National Monument: Betatakin and Keet Seel

Navajo National Monument lies nine miles north of U.S. Highway 160 along Arizona Highway 564. This monument was established to protect some of the most spectacular and best-preserved cliff dwellings in the Southwest, Betatakin, Keet Seel, and Inscription House.

These places were, for a brief period at the end of the thirteenth century, home to the descendents of Paleoindians who had probably arrived at least 10,000 years earlier. The earliest inhabitants of the Four Corners area were nomadic hunters who killed large mammals, such as bison, mammoths, and camels. One theory holds that the coming of humans to this continent led directly to the extinction of the large mammals that once roamed here in large numbers. The animals, having evolved in a vast region where they had no natural enemies, had not developed a fear of predators. Since they were not afraid of humans, they were easy targets for groups of Stone Age hunters, despite their formi-dable size. In any case, the large mammals (with the exception of the bison) did disappear from the North American continent many thousands of years ago. The people then began to rely more heavily on wild plants for their diet, while they hunted smaller ani-mals, such as rabbits, birds, mountain sheep, and deer. Archaeologists believe this "Desert Culture" lasted until the first century of the Common Era.

About a thousand years ago, the Basketmaker Culture emerged and lasted until about 700 C.E. This culture is named for the superb baskets the people made (some of which were so finely woven they could be used to carry water). Baskets, made of twigs and grasses using a coiling technique, were also used for cooking and storing food. Artisans today employ a similar technique to make finely decorated baskets from sumac twigs, many of which are sold at various gift shops and trading posts around Kayenta.

The Basketmakers were a nomadic people who used natural cliff overhangs for tem-porary shelter. As they learned to grow corn and squash, they settled for at least part of the year near their fields and built pit houses in which to live. As they developed better agricultural skills, they built small villages of pithouses.

The Pueblo Culture, which followed, dominated this area until about 1300 C.E. by which time the Colorado Plateau was largely abandoned. Today's Hopi people refer to the members of this culture, their ancestors, as the "Hisatsenom." The Navajo call the builders of these magnificent cliff dwellings the "Anasazi," which means "ancient ene-mies" or "ancient ancestors" and until recently archaeologists also used the term. Today they usually refer, instead, to the "Pueblo people."

The Pueblo people were related to and traded with the peoples of cultures to the south, the Hohokam and the Mogollon. They lived in small villages and began to build

The Pueblo peoples of Betatakin and Keet Seel used narrow-leaf yucca to make plaited sandals and baskets, and they may have used the root to make soap, as some Pueblo tribes do today. PHOTO: TANYA LEE

above-ground structures. Though they did not know the sophisticated masonry techniques used by the people who built at Chaco Canyon and Mesa Verde, the builders of Betatakin and Keet Seel constructed cliff dwellings ranging in size from ten to two hundred rooms. As at other cliff-dweller sites, the Pueblo people built their living quarters in alcoves that faced south or southeast to catch the sun's warmth in the winter and to take advantage of the cliff overhangs to provide shade during the summer.

Betatakin, Keet Seel, and Inscription House are located in what is now called the Tsegi Canyon system. Alluvial flats along the bottom of the canyon, which today are mostly eroded away, provided good farmland watered by a high water table in the canyon bottom and flood irrigation. (Even one hundred years ago, Tsegi Canyon was probably much greener than it is today—severe erosion, drought, and overgrazing have taken their toll.) In addition to growing corn, squash and beans (the "Three Sisters" of the Pueblo diet), they kept domesticated turkeys and possibly dogs.

While the tradition of basketmaking continued, pottery was better for some uses, such as storing water and cooking. The Pueblo people used the coil and scrape technique that is still used by Hopi potters. They also made corrugated pottery, leaving some or all of the coils unscraped and incising designs on the outside of the container, which would have made the contents of the pot cook more quickly.

Kayenta area pottery was particularly well made. In addition to the typical Anasazi black-on-white pots, Kayenta potters also made a polychrome pottery that was widely traded.

The cliff dwellings you see at Navajo National Monument today were built, occupied, and abandoned within a brief 50-year period from about 1250-1300 C.E. Did they leave because of drought, erosion, deforestation or other environmental factors? Were they attacked by outsiders? Did their religious and philosophical beliefs tell them it was time to continue their migrations? No one knows for sure.

"Betatakin" is a Navajo word that means "ledge house." The Hopi, who still make annual pilgrimages to this and other sites along their ancestral migration routes, call this place "Kawestima." This spectacular ruin is located in a sandstone alcove near a spring. It is less than a mile away from bottomlands at the mouth of the canyon that would have been perfect for growing crops. Between 1267 and 1269 C.E. few families lived in the alcove. Between 1275 and 1280, the population increased and eventually plateaued. By the end of the century, the people had built more than 100 rooms and at least two above-ground rectangular kivas. East of the main overhang are many petroglyphs, including one that has been identified by the Hopi as a Fire Clan symbol depicting Maasaw. Hopi Fire Clan members still visit this sacred shrine.

The Sandal Trail, which originates at the Visitor Center at Navajo Nation Monument, takes you to an overlook from which you can see Betatakin across the canyon. A telescope is available, but you might want to bring your own binoculars or camera with a telephoto lens to get a good look. The self-guided trail is 1 mile round-trip and quite steep in places. Allow about 45 minutes to go down and come back up. Along the trail, signs identify various plants and explain how the plants were used by ancient dwellers and how the Hopi and Navajo use them today. This trail is not recommended for wheelchairs.

From Memorial Day through Labor Day, Park Service Rangers conduct tours to Betatakin. The five-mile trip takes about five hours and is a very strenuous hike, descending 700 feet into the canyon. The tour, which is free, departs once a day at 8:15 A.M. The number of hikers for each tour is limited to 25. You must carry your own water, and the trip is not recommended for people who have heart or respiratory ailments.

As at all archaeological sites, you are reminded not to touch or remove anything, however insignificant it may seem to you. Also, at Navajo National Monument, you need to remember at all times that the area has been preserved in as natural a state as possible, so falling rocks, flashfloods, and falls are dangers, as are snakes, rodents, and scorpions. Be alert at all times, and hang on to the kids. Pets must be on leashes.

The name "Keet Seel" is derived from a Navajo word that means "remains of square houses." The Hopi call this place Talastima. Construction at the cliff dwelling that you see today on the west side of Keet Seel Canyon started around 1250 C.E. At least two previous groups of people had lived in this sandstone alcove, beginning around 950 C.E., and the new inhabitants used some of the old house beams in their own construction. Between 1272 and 1276, the population grew quickly as more immigrants arrived. Eventually Keet Seel probably housed 125 to 150 people in more than 150 rooms. The population here seems to have been less stable than at Betatakin. Families moved out and others moved in during its brief period of occupation, and archaeologists identify a larger variety of artifacts and building techniques here than at Betatakin. Two features of this ruin indicate a high level of community organization: the construction of a retaining wall running 180 feet across the eastern half of the ruin and the existence of three wide streets that connect different parts of the village. Keet Seel also includes four kivas, each unique, again suggesting that several distinct groups of people built and inhabited this cliff dwelling.

The Betatakin cliff dwelling can be seen from an overlook across the canyon at Navajo National Monument. PHOTO: TANYA LEE

After 1286 C.E., construction at Keet Seel stopped and the village declined as more and more families moved out. Before they left however, they sealed the doorways of many rooms containing jars of corn, and they embedded a large log in masonry above an access ladder to the village. Did they mean to return one day?

You will need a backcountry permit, obtainable at the Visitor Center, to visit Keet Seel, which is open from Memorial Day through Labor Day. Only 20 visitors a day are allowed to visit, and the 8.5-mile trail is a strenuous climb. Once you reach the site, park rangers will escort you on a tour of the ruin. The trip will take you a least a day to complete; hikers may camp for one night in the canyon. Reservations are required for this free tour.

Inscription House, the third cliff-dweller site at this National Monument, is too fragile to allow any visitors at all.

Navajo National Monument has a campground with thirty-one sites for tenting and RV use that is open year-round on a first-come-first-served basis. RVs may not exceed 27 feet in length. Wood and charcoal fires are not allowed at the campground, but campstoves are okay to use. No hookups are available, though the campground does have restrooms, a camper service sink, and running water. Expect cold temperatures and deep snow during the winter. Food and gasoline are available at the Black Mesa Trading Post at the intersection of U.S. Highway 160 and Arizona Highway 564.

The Visitor Center provides exhibits and books, videos and posters for sale, as well as wheelchair-accessible restrooms and public telephones. It is open every day year round except on Thanksgiving, Christmas, and New Years Day. Just behind the Visitor Center is a family home display with a forked-stick Navajo hogan and a sweat lodge.

The Aspen Forest Overlook Trail branches off the Sandal Trail 400 feet from the Visitor Center and descends 300 feet to view an ancient, ice-age aspen and fir forest. You cannot see any ruins from this trail.

Next to the Visitor Center is a Navajo-owned and -operated gift shop, Ledge House, selling Native American arts and crafts. Here you can find Navajo jewelry, rugs, and folk art, Hopi overlay jewelry, Acoma seed jars, and Zuni carvings and jewelry.

Among the most interesting items for sale are ceramic interpretations of ye'ii masks, which are used in healing ceremonies, and for that purpose, made of buckskin. These that are for sale are made of clay, because to make buckskin masks for sale would violate the religious sanctity of the ceremonial masks. This shop also has original paintings by David John. The staff is friendly and happy to share any information you might need about the items they sell. They accept major credit cards, personal checks, and traveler's checks. The address for Ledge House is Navajo National Monument, HC-71 Box 3A, Tonalea, AZ 86044-9704. The phone number is (520) 672-2404.

Navajo National Monument is administered by the National Park Service. For more information, you may contact the superintendent of the site at HC-71 Box 3, Tonalea, AZ 86044-9704; (520) 672-2366/2367 or go to www.nps.gov/nava.

Today, the Tsegi Canyon system is part of the Navajo Reservation. The Athapaskan-speaking ancestors of the Navajo probably arrived on the Colorado Plateau five to seven hundred years ago from the north.

In the sixteenth century, the Spanish arrived, bringing with them sheep, horses, goats, epidemic diseases, and an insatiable need for gold and religious converts. The Pueblo Revolt of 1680 drove the Spanish out of the area, but they returned and again conquered the pueblo tribes (except for most of Hopi) within ten years. Some of the Pueblo peoples (including perhaps refugees from Awatovi) sought shelter with the Navajo living in the remote canyons near what is now Kayenta. These people intermarried, thus some Navajo rightly claim descent from the Pueblo people, or Anasazi.

The scorched-earth policy of the early 1860s sent U.S. military forces to round up the

This view into Tsegi Canyon is a good reason to stay at the Anasazi Inn. PHOTO: TANYA LEE

Navajos for the Long Walk to Bosque Redondo. This effort was not successful in the Kayenta area, and many Navajos here were never captured. The Treaty of 1868 allowed the Navajo to return to a small portion of their traditional homeland, which was set aside as a reservation for them. The Tsegi Canyon system was included in the reservation when it was expanded in 1884.

Kayenta, at an elevation of 5,700 feet, is the Arizona gateway to Monument Valley, 25 miles to the north on AZ Highway 163. Both Black Mesa Mine and Kayenta Mine are located near here, and thus the Peabody Coal Company has been a major employer. Today, however, things are changing. In 1985, after several years of effort on the part of Kayenta business leaders frustrated by the loss of opportunities for economic development because of bureaucratic red tape, the Navajo Nation Tribal Council approved the five-year Kayenta Township Pilot Project, a self-governance program unprecedented in the Navajo Nation since the institution of the Tribal Council in 1923. According to this program, a chapter president and vice president are elected to represent Kayenta's 6,500 people and Kayenta sends one delegate to the Navajo Nation Tribal Council in Window Rock. The township was authorized to pass local ordinances and to impose and collect a sales tax. Kayenta is the first community in Navajoland, and perhaps the first Indian community in the country, with this power.

In addition, the township now operates a solid waste transfer station and is negotiating with a private company to build a juvenile detention center. Eighty families have applied for some of the 230 homes that will soon be built. A women's shelter is set for construction, and they are in the early planning stages for the construction of an administration complex

Kayenta is served by radio stations, television channels and newspapers in Arizona, Utah, and New Mexico, including the tribal newspaper, *The Navajo Times.*

Educational facilities in Kayenta include local primary and middle schools as well as Monument Valley High School, a Bureau of Indian Affairs boarding school. Northern Arizona University in Flagstaff offers undergraduate and graduate programs in Kayenta.

Monument Valley Hospital is located at 4 Rock Door Canyon Drive in Monument Valley, Utah. The phone number is (435) 727-3241, and you can reach the Kayenta

Navajo Code Talkers

The Navajo Code Talkers were instrumental in winning World War II for the Allies. In the spring of 1942, just a few months after Pearl Harbor, a recruiter for the Marines Corps visited Window Rock. He was looking for young Navajo men to join the United States Armed Services. Twenty-nine young men and boys, some of whom exaggerated their ages to enlist, answered their country's call.

During World War I, the Navajo language had been used as a code, and the idea was to try the same strategy for encoding critical military messages during World War II. However, there was some fear that the enemy would be able to figure out what language was being used. So instead, the Navajo Code Talkers, in a military project created by Major General Clayton B. Vogel, Amphibious Force, Pacific Fleet, and Commandant Thomas Holcomb, United States Marine Corps, developed a code based on the Navajo language. The entire code was committed to memory by the young Navajo soldiers. These soldiers would then code, transmit, and decode the messages.

More than 400 Navajo Code Talkers saw military action in the Pacific at Bougainville, New Britain, Kwajalein, Saipan, Guam, Peleliew, Okinawa, and Iwo Jima. The invasion of Iwo Jima was directed entirely by orders communicated by the Navajo Code Talkers. In two days, they transmitted over 800 messages without one error. It is the Code Talkers, more than any other single group, that is credited with the success of this mission.

Some names of the young men who served as Code Talkers are Merrill Sandoval, Dan Akee, Johnny Alfred, John Scott, Mike King, Peter MacDonald (who would later serve as president of the Navajo Nation), Martin Napa, William McCabe, Preston Toledo, Harold Y. Foster, Carl N. Gorman (father of the well-known artist R.C. Gorman), Eugene Roanhorse Crawford, and Mike Kiyaani.

No Code Talker was ever captured by the enemy, but they were sometimes mistaken for the enemy by United States troops because of their physical characteristics. The Marine Corps assigned white bodyguards to protect them.

For more than 20 years, the contribution of the Navajo Code Talkers went unheralded by the free world that owed them so much. In 1969, the information about them was declassified and in 1981, President Ronald Reagan signed a Certificate of Appreciation for their work. August 14, 1982 was declared National Code Talkers Day.

Today, Navajo Code Talkers proudly march in Veterans Day, Memorial Day, and Fourth of July Parades and are honored guests at other events conducted by the Navajo Nation.

The Burger King at the intersection of U.S. 160 and AZ 163 in Kayenta (P.O.Box 1217, U.S. Highway 160, Kayenta, AZ 86033; (520) 697-3170; fax (520) 697-3189) has an extensive exhibit about the Navajo Code Talkers, including World War II memorabilia, news accounts, and a list of the approximately 400 Code Talkers who served during World War II, twelve of whom were killed in action.

Dialysis Facility by calling (520) 674–3674. Contact ambulance services at (520) 697–4101/4102. The number of the Fire Department for non-emergency calls is (520) 697–5600. The Police Department's non-emergency number is (520) 697–5600. In all emergencies, dial 911. The Conoco gas station at the intersection of U.S. Highway 160 and Arizona Highway 163 can do minor car repairs such as fixing tires and oil changes. Their phone number is (520) 697–8338.

During the summer, expect high temperatures in the high 80s and lows in the mid 50s. In winter, highs are in the 50s and lows in the 20s. As always on the Colorado Plateau, the best way to keep warm (or cool) is to bring clothing that can be worn in layers. The difference between day and night temperatures is usually 20 to 30 degrees.

The Kayenta Visitor Center, which has been in operation for about five years, is located on U.S. Highway 160 in the center of town. Here you can get information about Monument Valley and tour companies that offer horseback, jeep, and hiking expeditions in the area. The gift shop offers a wide selection of items, including Navajo, Hopi and Zuni pottery and jewelry, traditional ceremonial wraparound knee-high moccasins, original paintings by David John and others, baskets, sandpaintings, weavings, ye'ii bi chii masks, Navajo folk art, and the usual souvenir items. Check out their extensive collection of books for sale, as well as their CDs and cassette tapes. They also offer magnificent dye and medicinal plant charts. Expect to pay several hundred dollars for the largest ones, which measure roughly two feet by three feet and have dried examples of the actual plants used in dying wool or for healing. The Visitor Center is octagon-shaped with a central courtyard where artisans offer their work for sale directly to the public. The center is open all day, seven days a week. The gift shop accepts Visa and MasterCard, personal checks, and traveler's checks. The mailing address is P.O. Box 545, Kayenta, AZ 86033-0545. The phone number is (520) 697–3572.

The Teeh'indeeh Shopping Center is located in the center of town, with a do-it-yourself car wash, pizza shop, hardware store, general store, variety store, and Bashas' supermarket. You'll also find some fast food restaurants and a Wells Fargo bank nearby.

Restaurants

Reuben Heflin Restaurant at the Hampton Inn $$
U.S. Hwy. 160 at the west end of town
P.O. Box 1217, Kayenta, AZ 86033
(520) 697–3170; fax (520) 697–3189

Located in the lobby of the hotel, the very pleasant Reuben Heflin Restaurant is open for lunch and dinner, serving a range of items from Southwest specialties to New York cheesecake. The Sheepherder's Sandwich, for example, is a delight—roast beef, tomatoes, lettuce and onions served between two pieces of fry bread. They also offer other sandwiches, appetizers, and salads, as well as steak, chicken, and trout dinners. An outdoor patio is open for dining when the weather permits. This hotel complex is the newest in Kayenta and is Navajo-owned and -operated. Credit cards and traveler's checks are accepted; personal checks are not. The restaurant is wheelchair accessible.

Blue Coffee Pot Restaurant $
Intersection of U.S. Hwy. 160 and AZ Hwy. 163
P.O. Box 652, Kayenta, AZ 86033
(520) 697–3396

If you want to find the best place in town to eat as far as the locals are concerned, look for the parking lot with the most cars, which is how I chose the Blue Coffee Pot Restaurant for lunch. The place was indeed patronized mostly by locals, partly because of its reasonable prices, and partly, my friendly waitress told me, because of their special Navajo dishes. Here you can choose between a Navajo taco with chili, meat, beans, lettuce, tomatoes and sour cream and Navajo mutton strips, which are fried mutton strips rolled in a tortilla and served with potato salad. Or try the cold beef and fry bread sandwich, also served with potato salad. On the dinner menu, you'll find steak, roast beef, pork chops, enchiladas, tacos, and barbecue ribs. Daily specials are offered for lunch and dinner. The restaurant is another octagon-shaped building, with casual tables and booths. Several of the walls are glassed, creating a particularly cheerful atmosphere during the day. The restaurant is open for breakfast, lunch and dinner on weekdays. Reservations are not expected and the building is wheelchair accessible. The Blue Coffee Pot accepts only cash.

Amigo Café $
AZ Hwy. 163, a quarter mile from the intersection with U.S. Hwy. 160
P.O. Box 1534, Kayenta, AZ 86033
(520) 697–8448

Don't let the shabby exterior of this place fool you—it is very nice inside and serves the best Mexican food around. Their most popular entrees are the combo plate, chimichangas and the "largest Navajo taco on the reservation." This restaurant is locally owned and the dishes are all made from scratch. Open air dining is available on the patio in good weather. Open Monday through Saturday for breakfast, lunch and dinner, the Amigo Café takes major credit cards and traveler's checks, but not personal checks. The restaurant is wheelchair accessible, though the parking lot is gravel. The restrooms are not accessible. This casual eatery does not accept reservations.

Wagon Wheel Restaurant at Holiday Inn
$$$ Intersection of U.S. Hwy. 160 and AZ Hwy. 163 on the southwest corner
Box 307, Kayenta, AZ 86033
(520) 697–3221; fax (520) 697–3349
hi.monumentvalley@worldnet.att.net

This restaurant offers full menus for breakfast, lunch, and dinner, as well as a breakfast buffet bar and a non-alcoholic beer and wine selection. Decorated in the mission style, it is a comfortable, casual place to dine, and you will see many foreign tourists here. The waitresses wear traditional long velvet Navajo skirts with vests, and they are invariably friendly and pleasant. For breakfast, the menu ranges from biscuits to griddle items to egg dishes. Getting ready for a day of strenuous sightseeing, you'll appreciate the good strong coffee. Lunch and dinner offerings include appetizers, sandwiches, steaks, and a well-stocked salad bar. You can pay with cash, credit cards, or cash, but personal checks are not accepted. If you're staying at the Holiday Inn, kids under 12 eat free. The Holiday Inn complex is wheelchair accessible.

Golden Sands Café $$
AZ Hwy. 163, about one-and-a-half miles from U.S. Hwy. 160, on the left
P.O. Box 458, Kayenta, AZ 86033
(520) 697–3684; fax (520) 697–8615

The Golden Sands Café has been here forever, serving Navajo and American food in a very casual Western-theme atmosphere. Frequented mostly by locals, the restaurant serves hot and cold sandwiches, Navajo tacos, soup, roast beef, chicken and trout dinners, and a dinner omelet. Open seven days a week, the Golden Sands closes in mid-afternoon on weekends. Cash, personal checks, or traveler's checks are accepted; credit cards are not.

Accommodations

Visit the Hogan
AZ Hwy. 163, 20 miles north of the junction with U.S. Hwy. 160 at milepost 415
$ P.O. Box 3136, Kayenta, AZ 86033
(520) 674–4111

For a unique experience that will give you a special understanding of Navajo culture, spend the night in this traditional Navajo hogan. You can bring your own sleeping bag, or rent one here. Groups of up to thirty can be accommodated in the round

Visit the Hogan just outside the entrance to Monument Valley where you'll be welcome for a night or a week. PHOTO: TANYA LEE

hogan constructed of juniper logs and plastered on the outside with mud. For a small, extra fee, you can request a home-made Navajo taco for dinner, but a full breakfast is included in the per person rate. Children are welcome, and are charged at the same rate as adults. Reservations are recommended. Entertainment—a bonfire, powwow, and/or dancers—can be ar-ranged with advance notice. The host stresses that people are welcome to stay as long as they wish and may bring and cook their own food, just as they would if they were camping out. The owners of this enterprise are Agnes Gray and her husband. She is a well-known basketmaker, and you should ask to see her traditional coiled wedding baskets made from sumac. The proprietors also offer horse, jeep, or hiking tours of Monument Valley. The horses are kept on the property, and you will enjoy watching their antics and learning how they are cared for.

Roland's Navajoland Tours and Bed and Breakfast $
AZ Hwy. 163, 0.5 mile north of the junction with U.S. Hwy. 160, on the right
P.O. Box 1542, Kayenta, AZ 86033
(520) 697–3524; (520) 697–3374

This bed-and-breakfast offers not only rooms, but the opportunity to stay in a tee pee for the night. See the listing under Tours in this section.

Hampton Inn $$$
U.S. Hwy. 160 at the west end of town, north side of the highway
P.O. Box 1217, Kayenta, AZ 86033
(520) 697–3170; fax (520) 697–3189

Navajo-owned and -operated, this brand-new, three-story, adobe-style hotel has seventy-three rooms, each with one king or two double beds. A large, comfortable lobby with Southwest-style furniture is separated by a central fireplace from the dining area, where you'll enjoy a free continental breakfast of danish pastries, fruit, cereal, oatmeal, waffles, coffee, and juice. The pleasant, spacious smoking and non-smoking rooms have coffeemakers, cable TVs, phones, computer dataports, hair dryers, clock radios, irons and ironing boards. Standard rooms have a recliner, and king studios have a pull-out couch for extra people. Children under 18 stay for free and there is a small charge for more than two adults in a room. Four first-floor handicapped rooms are available, two of which have roll-in showers. An outside heated pool is open from May through October, and a two-and-a-half acre Navajo cultural center including exhibits and displays adjoins the hotel grounds. Major credit cards and traveler's checks are accepted; pets are allowed.

Holiday Inn $$$$$
Intersection of U.S. Hwy. 160 and AZ
Hwy.163 on the southwest corner
Box 307, Kayenta, AZ 86033
(520) 697–3221; fax (520) 697–3349
hi.monumentvalley@worldnet.att.net

A comfortable reception area greets you at this 163-room, two-story motel operated by Ocean Properties, Inc. Children under 12 stay and eat for free. There is an additional charge for more than two adults in a room. The motel features well-appointed rooms with cable TV, in-room movies, coffeemakers, irons, ironing boards and hair dryers. An outdoor swimming pool and a fitness room with cardiovascular and weight training equipment will help get you in shape for horseback riding in Monument Valley. Some rooms are wheelchair accessible. Credit cards and traveler's checks are accepted; pets are not allowed. In the lobby of the motel is the Little Mesa Gift Shop, offering authentic Native American jewelry and souvenir items. Be sure to ask which items are hand-made and which are machine-produced. The Wagon Wheel Restaurant provides room service.

Best Western Wetherill Inn $$$
1.5 miles north on AZ Hwy. 163
P.O. Box 175, Kayenta, AZ 86033
(520) 697–3231; fax (520) 697–3233
www.bestwestern.com/wetherillinn;
wetherill@gouldings.com

You'll find TVs, coffeemakers, phones, irons, ironing boards, and alarm clocks in each of this motel's fifty-four rooms; and the indoor swimming pool is open year-round. Smoking and non-smoking rooms are available, but wheelchair-accessible rooms are not. A gift shop in the lobby offers Navajo jewelry and rugs, a large selection of concho belts, Zuni jewelry, books, cassettes, and CDs. All major credit cards and traveler's checks are accepted here. The Golden Sands Restaurant is adjacent.

Shonto Trading Post

If you're eager for a small adventure, take Arizona Highway 98 north off U.S. Highway 160 toward Shonto. Six miles down the road, turn right at the sign for Shonto. Go four more miles, turn right at the sign for Shonto Trading Post, and get ready for a hair-raising, sharply vertical drive down a gravel road and across Shonto Wash, where the trading post, established in 1919, is located. The cottonwoods and palo verde trees at the bottom of the wash are beautiful, and Shonto gives you a sense of why communities were (and are) located where they are. While the trading post is mostly a convenience store, you will also find gasoline, a public phone, and a Laundromat here. Unless you have a four-wheel drive vehicle and know how to drive over very slick, steep roads, do not attempt this half-mile-long journey into the canyon in wet weather, as you are likely to end up in the wash in very uncomfortable circumstances.

Shonto Trading Post is open six days a week with shorter hours on Saturdays. It is closed Sundays. The mailing address is P.O. Box 7713, Shonto, AZ 86054 and the phone number is (520) 672–2320.

Anasazi Inn $$$
U.S. Hwy. 160 in Tsegi,
overlooking Tsegi Canyon
P.O. Box 1543, Kayenta, AZ 86033
(520) 697–3793; fax (520) 697–8249

Fifty-six small, basic rooms have coffeemakers, cable TV, hair dryers, irons and ironing boards, but no phones. The coffee shop serves breakfast, lunch and dinner and is open 24 hours a day in the summer season from April to mid October. A public phone can be found just outside. Children under 6 stay free at the motel. The office has a small gift shop with tourist necessities, snacks and T-shirts. Pets stay for an additional $10 non-refundable fee. Some rooms are non-smoking, and some are wheelchair accessible. All major credit cards are accepted; personal checks are not.

Shopping

Kayenta Trading Company at the
Hampton Inn
U.S. Hwy. 160 at the west end of town,
north side of the highway
P.O. Box 1217, Kayenta, AZ 86033
(520) 697–3170; fax (520) 697–3189

This gift shop in the lobby of the Hampton Inn is packed full of unique and interesting items, some of which you won't see anywhere else. The paintings and assemblages by 82-year-old Navajo elder Mammie Deschillie are charming and unusual—most Navajo folk art is expressed in painted woodcarvings, of which this shop also has a particularly good selection. The store carries carvings by Carlos Begay, whose vibrant paintings are very well known in northern Arizona. Here you'll also find Southwestern-style jackets, skirts, shirts, coats and shawls. Fine-quality Navajo jewelry and concho belts, Hopi and Acoma pottery, handwoven baskets, and Zuni carvings are for sale. And there is no shortage of the books, guides, tapes, and souvenir keepsakes you would expect to see in a shop geared for tourists. Open every day from very early morning till late evening, Kayena Trading Company accepts credit cards and traveler's checks, but no personal checks.

Navajo Arts & Crafts Enterprise
U.S. Hwy. 160 just north of the junction
with AZ Hwy. 163
P.O. Box 1770, Kayenta, AZ 86033
(520) 697–8611, fax (520) 697–3369

The Navajo Arts & Crafts Enterprise was established by the Navajo Nation in 1941 to promote traditional Navajo arts and crafts. The Enterprise's four shops offer high-quality, genuine Navajo arts—rugs, silver and turquoise jewelry, folk art carvings, sandpaintings, original watercolors and pottery, as well as Pendleton items, weaving and jewelry-making supplies, and T-shirts. You'll also find a collection of cassettes and CDs by Native American artists. This store is open Monday through Saturday. Traveler's checks, credit cards, and personal checks are welcome. Navajo Arts & Crafts Enterprises has three other stores—in Window Rock, Cameron, and Chinle.

Historic Kayenta Trading Post
Just past the Wetherill Inn on AZ Hwy.
163; left at the sign for the Trading Post
P.O. Box 1220, Kayenta, AZ 86033
(520) 697–3541

This store is worth a stop just to see an example of the evolution of trading posts. Here, as you would expect, you can buy groceries, fresh meat and produce, auto supplies, axes, shovels, oats for your horse, paper goods, and coffee. What you might not expect is a Radio Shack—you can buy a car stereo, order a computer, and sign up for internet access and cellular phone service! A small selection of Native American arts and crafts is next to the Western Union desk, where you can also buy a hunting license and check out the community bulletin board. There is a public phone out front and restrooms in the back. The Trading Post is open seven days a week.

Tours

You've seen Monument Valley many times in movies such as *Stagecoach, How the West Was Won,* and *Back to the Future 3,* and in dozens of television commercials, mostly for pickups and four-wheel drive vehicles. But nothing compares to experiencing these magnificent natural rock formations up close. Bring your camera and binoculars, at least. And if you've been wanting to try your hand at painting or drawing, this is a great place to begin.

The Visitor Center is located four miles off AZ Highway 163. As you turn off the highway, you may want to stop at the twenty-or-so stalls where people are selling souvenir-quality jewelry and pottery. There is a $3 per person fee to enter Monument Valley Navajo Tribal Park, which is charged before you reach the parking lot. The small restaurant at the Visitor Center is

The natural beauty of Monument Valley is not limited to just the rock formations. PHOTO: GARRET ROSENBLATT

open for breakfast and lunch. The park and Valley Drive (described below) are closed Christmas Day. This is the only place in the park where drinking water is available.

You can explore Monument Valley on your own. A 17-mile unpaved road loops through the park and you can drive this self-guided tour route in most passenger cars. Vehicles with very low clearances and those over 21 feet long are not recommended. Markers along the way identify the formations for you. The drive takes about one-and-a-half hours.

The loop road will take you past the Mittens and Merrick Butte. According to legend, the Holy People left behind the mittens, the tallest of which towers over 1000 feet. Merrick Butte is said to hide a silver mine discovered in the 1800s by the prospector for whom the butte is named.

Elephant Butte, which you will see next, is 778 feet high, and, obviously, looks like an elephant.

At the formation called the Three Sisters, go straight ahead. The road becomes one way here, and you'll be going the wrong way if you turn left. Before you turn, look right to see John Ford Point and Mitchell Mesa. The former is named for that director's early Westerns, many of which starred John Wayne.

Camel Butte was named by early settlers and traders John Wetherill and Harry Goulding. The camel's hump is on the right.

The Hub is a wagon-wheel shaped formation that includes Rain God Mesa, which once had four springs that were used by Navajo medicine men for healing ceremonies.

Next is a 400-foot-high red rock formation called the Totem Pole, which resembles the totem poles carved by the Indians of the Northwest Pacific. The formation called Yei-Bi-Chei looks like one of the Navajo holy figures. You also see these figures on Navajo weavings and in sandpaintings.

Sand Springs is a water source for livestock.

The name Artist Point is self-explanatory. To the right is Spearhead Mesa, and Cly Butte, 598 feet high, is on its right.

Next you will see North Window, and then the Thumb, a formation in the shape of a thumb pointing up. Return to the Visitor Center by turning right and following the road to the intersection, where you take another right.

While you can drive this road in your own vehicle, pamphlet or tour book in hand, there's a lot to be said for taking a tour with a Navajo guide. For example, one guide explained to me that latecomers to this sacred valley bestowed names upon these spectacular rock formations. The names do not convey the meaning or spiritual importance of this place to the people who have lived here for hundreds of years. He told me that he has been guiding tours for more than a decade, each time thinking and learning about the significance of Monument Valley. To him, the Mittens and Merrick Butte represent a human. Merrick Butte is the person's face. The Mittens are his arms reaching out for a hug. Another advantage of taking a tour is that more of the valley is open to tourists with guides than to those exploring on their own.

Several tour guides for jeep tours, horseback riding, and hiking have booths in the parking lot at the Visitors Center. If you haven't reserved your tour in advance (which is recommended during the summer and for longer tours), prices at the parking lot booths for shorter excursions seem to depend partly on how busy things are that day. You may be able to negotiate. Remember that gratuities are not included in the price of any of the tours.

Roland's Navajoland Tours
One-half mile on the right going north on AZ Hwy. 163
P.O. Box 1542, Kayenta, AZ 86033
(520) 697–3374; fax (520) 697–3374

Navajo-owned and -operated, Rolands' Navajoland Tours offers one- to four-hour tours in open air 4x4 vehicles or buses. The shortest tour includes Mitten View, Merrick Butte, Elephant Butte, Camel Butte, Raingod Mesa, John Ford Point, and North Window. The two-hour tour adds Moccasin Arch, Big Hogan, Ear of the Wind, Echo Cave Ruins, Thunderbird Mesa, Profile of Navajo, and various petroglyph sites. In three hours you can also see Sam's Eye, and on a four-hour tour you'll be treated to a Navajo rug-weaving demonstration, a visit to a traditional hogan, and an afternoon or evening cookout including steak, beans, corn on the cob, salad, fry bread, juice, and coffee, or, if you prefer, Navajo tacos and Navajo beef sandwiches. For the four-hour tour only, there is a 15-passenger minimum. Roland can also take you on private, custom half-day, whole-day, sunset, sunrise, and overnight camping tours.

Special tours for photographers and hiking tours (four person minimum) are also available. Children under 5 years old travel free. Cash and traveler's checks, but not credit cards, are accepted.

Roland's has a small bed-and-breakfast on the premises. Four wheelchair accessible rooms with queen beds are available, or you can spend the night in a teepee! Rates are charged per person for the rooms and per teepee. Both options include a continental breakfast with cereal, juice, toast, pastry, coffee, and milk. Walk-ins are welcome for both the tours and the bed-and-breakfast, but reservations are recommended in the summer. Roland's also offers location scout services for filmmakers, commercials, photographers, and documentary films.

Bill Crawley Tours
P.O. Box 187, Kayenta, AZ 86033
(520) 697–3463/3734; fax (520) 697–8553
www.crawleytours.com;
crawley@crawleytours.com

Bill Crawley has had 40 years' experience providing Navajo-guided half-day, full-day, and sunset tours of Monument

Bill Crawley Tours offers several tours through Monument Valley. In the background are the Mittens.

PHOTO: BILL CRAWLEY TOURS

wheelchair facilities are available. There is no minimum age, but parents must provide a car seat if the child requires one, and children of all ages are charged at the regular rate. Reservations may be made a day ahead of time, but shorter notice is fine. No deposit is required. Crawley Tours accepts cash, traveler's checks, and personal checks drawn on U.S. banks. Inquire about group rates.

This company also offers custom adventure tours to Hunt's Mesa on the southern side of Monument Valley and to Mystery Valley, where travelers will see magnificent natural rock arches, such as Spiderweb Arch, and Puebloan Indian ruins dating back nearly a thousand years. Four-by-four safaris with overnight camping (gear and equipment provided) include guides who will do all the cooking.

Crawley's Film Service offers production help for films and commercials, such as obtaining federal, state, and tribal permits, scouting locations, building sets, supplying livestock, providing equipment rentals, and restoring the site after the shoot.

Valley. Tours leave from Kayenta or your guide can meet your tour bus or airplane at any nearby location. A morning tour of the valley leaves at 8:30 A.M. and an afternoon tour leaves at 2:30 P.M. The sunset tour leaves three-and-a-half hours before sunset. Other tours leave throughout the day, and private tours leave at your convenience.

You'll enjoy your trip in comfortable backcountry vehicles, ranging from eight-passenger vans to 29-passenger minibuses. Crawley Tours' Navajo guides are well versed in their own culture, as well as in geological and historical information. All tours make numerous photo stops and even amateurs are assured great pictures. You may also arrange to visit a hogan and see a weaving demonstration.

The company can provide lunch; special diets require 24 hours notice. No

Sacred Monument Tours
P.O. Box 360530,
Monument Valley, UT 84536
(435) 727–3218; fax (435) 727–3355;
cell (520) 691–6199
www.sacredtoursmv.com;
www.monumentvalley.net;
smtours@monumentvalley.net

Professional guides will take you or your group through Tsebii nidzisgai or "the valley within the rocks" in a 1998 Jeep Wrangler or a 1998 Chevy Suburban for a one-hour to an overnight tour. Jeep tours, which leave all day from the Visitors Center, take you along the 17-mile loop road, and into the backcountry to see natural arches, Puebloan ruins, and petroglyphs, or to Mystery Valley, depending on how much time you have. On the longer tours, you'll have time to explore small side canyons and take short hikes. The Red Earth Tour is three hours in the late afternoon or early morning, particularly good times for photography. Teardrop Drive is a two-hour adventure during which you'll visit Puebloan ruins and an ancient lookout over Mystery Valley. The 17-mile Loop Tour stops at five scenic points and a hogan. The Mystery Valley Tour takes three hours and includes walking trails to ruins, petroglyphs, and arches. Bring your camera, sunglasses, sandwiches, and cool drinks, and don't forget your water and sunscreen.

One of the best ways to understand this land is to hike it. Sacred Monument Tours offers the Teardrop Trail Walk (two-and-a-half hours), the Hunt's Mesa Trek (a strenuous four-hour hike to the top of Hunt's Mesa, overnight camping, and a four-hour sunrise hike back), and the Mitchell Mesa Day Hike (four-and-a-half hours), a selection of treks for anyone with the time and stamina to see Monument Valley the way its first inhabitants did. The serious adventurer will choose the Navajo Mountain Expedition, a six-day, 65-mile guided trek to the base of Navajo Mountain, or Naatsis'aan. A shuttle will take you back to Kayenta..

My favorite way to see this land is on horseback. Sacred Monument Tours offers trail rides ranging from one hour to overnight. The Mitten Tour is two hours; The Mystery Valley Trail Ride is an all-day adventure; and the Overnight Trail Ride is a six-hour tour of Monument Valley, a stay in a traditional hogan, dinner, breakfast and storytelling. Sleeping bags and other necessities are provided.

Credit cards, traveler's checks, and cash are accepted. You may make your reservations ahead of time for the longer tours, including private educational tours; for shorter trips, stop at the yellow booth in the parking lot at the Visitors Center. Group rates are available.

Ed Black's Monument Valley Trail Rides, Inc.
P.O. Box 310155, Mexican Hat, UT 84531
(435) 739–4285
www.cas-biz.com/valleyhorseback

Ed Black's offers a 90-minute horseback ride to the Mittens, a Full Moonlight Trailride (90 minutes when there is a full moon), Magnificent Sunrise and Sunset Tours by special arrangement, and an All Day Tour lasting six to seven hours. Custom trips for five to twenty riders during the summer include a two- to three-hour ride to Saddle Rock and an overnight camping experience (gear, breakfast and dinner included). Ed Black's Stable is located one-half mile north of the Visitors Center. The operation also has a booth in the Visitors Center parking lot.

Daniel's Guided Vehicle Tours
P.O. Box 360153,
Monument Valley, UT 84536
(435) 727–3227, (800) 596–8427;
fax (435) 727–3363
www.members.aol.com/tourmonument;
danielstours@aol.com

Daniel's Tours, Navajo-owned and -operated, offers 28-mile loop guided tour to restricted areas. You'll see the rock formations of Monument Valley, natural arches, Puebloan ruins and petroglyphs as well as visiting Susie Yazzie's hogan, where she

Insiders' Tip

If you do not have time to visit Canyon de Chelly, the next destination we suggest on the Navajo Nation, the quickest route back to Flagstaff is to take U.S. Highway 160 west to U.S. Highway 89 south, which will take you right to the center of town.

will share the details of Navajo rug weaving with you. Tour the Valley in open-air vehicles for one hour or all day. Lunch can be arranged for an additional fee. Private, commercial, photography, and overnight tours can also be arranged. You can schedule ahead of time or visit Daniel's booth in the parking lot. Cash and traveler's checks are accepted; credit cards are not.

Black's Hiking, Jeep Tours, and Trail Ride
P.O. Box 310393, Mexican Hat, UT 84531
(435) 739–4226

Roy Black's guided tours originate at the Visitors Center. The one-hour vehicle tour does the 17-mile loop, and the two-hour tour takes you on the 28-mile loop to some restricted areas. Sunrise and sunset tours, as well as half-day and full-day tours, are also available.

You might also want to try a day hike to Hunt's Mesa or Mitchell Mesa, an overnight hike to Hunt's Mesa and Douglas Mesa, or a trail ride of one-half to seven hours. Children are welcome on trail rides, but they must be over four feet tall and able to ride their own horse. Bus groups are welcome. Credit cards and personal checks are accepted.

Campgrounds

Mittenview Campground
Monument Valley Navajo Tribal Park
P.O. Box 360289,
Monument Valley, UT 84536
(520) 727–3353/3287

Mittenview Campground is open year-round on a first-come-first-served basis.

Each of the 99 fee sites has a table, ramada, trash barrel, and barbecue grill. Restrooms, pay showers, and a filling and dump station are open during the summer. No hookups are available, and campers are allowed to stay a maximum of 14 days. Register at the Visitors Center.

There are spectacular pinnacles in Monument Valley. This is one of the "Mittens." PHOTO: TANYA LEE

Canyon de Chelly

You come to these sandstone canyonlands at the beginning of the third millennium of the Common Era, but you might have come at the beginning of the fifth millennium before the Common Era. Then you would not have traveled by car, or bus, or plane, or even by horseback, but on foot. You would not have stopped at a motel for the night, but you would have constructed a temporary shelter of brush for a night or a few nights. You would not have gone out to breakfast at the Holiday Inn, but you would have known this 20-mile long canyon so well that finding a breakfast of nuts or berries would have been easy.

Even if you had come here seven thousand years ago, though, this magnificent canyon would look pretty much the way it does today, with its sheer sandstone cliff walls rising from 30 feet at the west end of the canyon to 1,000 feet at the east end. Chinle (CHIN lee) Wash, part of the drainage system of the Chuska Mountains to the east, would run in the winter and spring and during summer monsoon rains. Rock overhangs would provide shelter from winter rain, wind, and snow and summer sun.

The sandstone rock of these canyons formed during the age of the dinosaurs as flat-lying wind-deposited layers of sand. These layers rose as part of the Defiance anticline two to three million years ago. The meandering streams draining the Chuska Mountains flowed west, cutting Canyon de Chelly (d'SHAY), Canyon del Muerto and the other canyons of this system as the land rose.

The caprock, along which you drive on the rim drives described below, is Shinarump Conglomerate—sand and pebbles deposited by streams during Triassic times (205 to 240 million years ago). In the conglomerate, small potholes collect rainwater and tiny plants and animals grow for a few hours or a few days. These living forms create an acidic environment and that acid eats away at the calcium carbonate that holds the conglomerate together. Desert winds then blow away small grains of sand, eventually leaving a pebbly surface.

Below the conglomerate is the peach-colored rock known as the de Chelly sandstone, which formed in Permian times 200 million years ago. Over thousands of millennia, moisture collected in the recesses in the sandstone and weakened the rock walls during alternate periods of freezing and warming. Slabs and sheets of the rock wall fell away (and continue to fall). Canyon de Chelly sandstone is dense, and it erodes to form large, arching alcoves. In time these recesses became deep enough for people to construct the cliff dwellings you see here.

The dark stains on the sandstone walls are formed by manganese and iron oxides. For many centuries, inhabitants of these canyons used smaller rocks to peck through this desert varnish and create the rock art known as petroglyphs.

The early people who came here were hunters and gatherers. They probably made their way through the canyons at certain times of year, collecting useful plants and hunting rabbit, deer, antelope, and some larger mammals. There is no evidence that they lived here on a permanent basis, or that they took advantage of the rock alcoves for more than a few nights' shelter.

During the Archaic Period, which lasted from about 2500 to 200 B.C.E., small groups of people settled here for longer periods of time, probably for a season or so. They hunted animals and gathered plants on both the canyon floors and the canyon rims. The steep

The Hogan

As you explore Canyon de Chelly or drive across the Navajo Reservation, you will undoubtedly see many examples of the traditional Navajo house, the hogan. In Navajo, the hooghan is "the home place."

There are several types of hogans; all are one-room, more or less circular buildings. They are heated by a stove or fireplace in the center. A stovepipe or a hole in the center of the roof lets smoke out of the hogan. Hogans have one door, facing east, and no windows.

The styles of hogans were given to the Navajo by Talking God when First Man and First Woman emerged into this world. The hogan itself is more than a place to live—it is a symbolic map of the universe, and each detail of its construction is specified. Every element is an analog to some feature or aspect of the world outside the hogan.

The original hogan was the forked-pole style, which Talking God fashioned from forked poles made of white shell, turquoise, abalone, and obsidian. In this style, three of the four main poles are forked and these interlock to make the framework to support the entry, which is the east pole. Then the vertical sides, made of poles that lean inward, are added, forming a conical structure, which is then covered with damp earth. This is the "male" hogan.

Talking God also gave the Navajo the "female" hogan, a round structure made by stacking logs horizontally in a pattern that diminishes as it rises, forming a building that is almost a hemisphere, chinked with bark and covered with damp earth to keep out wind, snow, and rain. By the late 1800s, another form evolved because steel axes made it possible to notch the logs and make a building with vertical sides and a domed roof. Often these hogans are six- or eight-sided structures.

Hogans were traditionally made of juniper logs, but now they are also made from stone masonry, cinderblock, 2x4s, and other materials, depending on what is available.

trails they used to get from the bottom of the canyon to the rim can still be seen. The earliest petroglyphs date from this period.

The period from about 200 B.C.E. to 750 C.E. in this area is called the Basketmaker Period. During this time people made important changes in the way they used the canyon. These were the people who learned to farm the canyon floors and upland mesas, growing corn, which came from the south, as well as beans and squash. Probably these people lived in extended family groups and were able to produce surplus food, necessitating the invention of some way to store that food so that rodents and insects could not contaminate it. They also collected wild plants and hunted rodents, deer, and antelope. Toward the end of the Basketmaker Period, around 600 C.E., these ancient Pueblo people began to make ceramic pots for cooking, food storage, and carrying water, and they built pit houses and storage rooms in the canyon's rock shelters. The earliest circular structures, which may have been used for public ceremonies involving several settlements, also date from this period.

Archaeologists date the Pueblo Period from 750 to 1300 C.E., and in Canyon de Chelly, this period is well documented. The Pueblo people began to build larger aboveground masonry villages and the use of the rock shelters declined somewhat from about

Each hogan is usually home to one family, and hogans may be grouped together to form homesteads based on matrilineal relationships. The family's possessions are stored along the walls, and bedding is put away each day to create an open area in the center of the hogan.

Even when a family lives in a Western-style home, they may build a hogan for ceremonial purposes, such as births, weddings, girls' initiations, and healing. During a healing ceremony, which may last for several days, men sit on the south side of the hogan, women on the north, and the healer on the west side. When a death occurs in a hogan, especially an unexpected death, the body is removed through a hole made in the wall, and the hogan is then abandoned or burned.

As a visitor to Navajoland, remember that hogans are private family living quarters, so you should not disturb the residents or take photographs. Next to the Tuba City Trading Post, there is a "display" hogan that you may enter.

This abandoned hogan was constructed of notched logs with a corbelled roof.

PHOTO: TANYA LEE

You can see this fork-stick hogan at the Visitors Center at Navajo National Monument.

PHOTO: TANYA LEE

1000 to 1250 B.C.E. Around the middle of the thirteenth century, though, the construction of cliff dwellings became extremely important. Growing populations and environmental pressures, including climatic changes and severe droughts, may have impelled the people to devise or import new ways to organize their lives and new building technologies. Social organization and religious practices may have become even more complex during this period.

But by the beginning of the fourteenth century, the cliff dwellings of Canyon de Chelly—in fact, the villages of most of northeastern Arizona—were abandoned. Whether climatic changes, disease, conflict among villages, or religious and philosophical ideas were the cause, the ancient peoples of northeastern Arizona moved south and west to establish the pueblo villages along the Little Colorado River and on Black Mesa. For four centuries, no one made a permanent home in these canyons. In the mid 1700s the Navajo arrived from the north and the east, pushed from the Four Corners area by the Spanish intruders. The Navajo farmed the canyon floor, growing corn, peaches, and other crops, and raised horses and sheep. By the late 1700s, though, Canyon de Chelly had become one of the battlegrounds of the struggle between the Navajo and the Spanish colonists, aided by other Native American tribes.

Canyon de Chelly (a name derived from the Spanish corruption of the Navajo word Tsegi, pronounced "SAY-ih") became a refuge for Navajo and others fleeing Spanish, then Mexican, and finally American, raiding parties. The complex of smaller canyons provided defensible hiding places that could be stocked with food and water.

But by the late 1850s, the United States had declared war on the Navajo people. In 1862, Brig. General Carleton moved against the Navajo, demanding that they surrender and move to Fort Sumner in New Mexico. His scorched-earth policy brought widespread hunger and hardship. In the winter of 1863–1864 Kit Carson invaded the eastern end of Canyon de Chelly, and moved westward toward the canyon mouth, pushing the cold and hungry Navajo ahead of him. Carson took 200 prisoners, and came back the next spring to destroy the remaining Navajo hogans, crops, and sheep. In the winter and early spring of 1864, the U.S. government forced more than 9,000 Navajos to walk 300 miles from Fort Wingate and Fort Defiance to the banks of the Pecos River, known as Bosque Redondo. Many died on the Long Walk and those too weak to continue were killed or simply left to perish on the trail. For four years, the Navajo suffered from starvation, cold, disease, loneliness, and demoralization until finally the United States government decided that the "experiment" to turn the Navajo into pueblo villagers had failed and was costing too much money. In 1868, the Navajos negotiated a treaty with the United States that allowed the 4,000 survivors of the Long Walk and subsequent imprisonment to return to a small part of their homeland. Barboncito, a Navajo leader from Canyon de Chelly, was instrumental in negotiating the treaty and in convincing the government that the Navajo would be sent home, not to other reservations in Oklahoma and Florida. The boundaries of the 1868 Navajo Reservation were drawn with Canyon de Chelly at its center.

After the Navajos returned from Fort Sumner, government food distribution centers evolved into trading posts, which became important influences in Navajo life. The Indians exchanged rugs, jewelry, and other crafts for food staples and iron tools. Two trading posts were established near Canyon de Chelly by Lorenzo Hubbell (see close-up). Camille Garcia's trading post, established in the early 1900s, lasted until the 1960s and is now represented by the restaurant and shop at the Holiday Inn in Chinle. Samuel Day's trading post, built in 1902, is now part of the Thunderbird Lodge complex.

Today, Navajo families continue to farm and raise sheep and horses in this spectacular canyon with its rich history that has such a tremendous physical and spiritual influence on the Navajo people.

Area Overview

In 1931, President Herbert Hoover created the 84,000-acre Canyon de Chelly National Monument. Owned by the Navajo Nation but managed by the National Park Service, Canyon de Chelly National Monument is one of the few national monuments that does not charge an entrance fee.

The town of Chinle, just outside the western end of the canyon is a Navajo Nation chapter that sends three delegates to the Navajo Nation Council. Chinle Agency is one of the five Bureau of Indian Affairs jurisdictions for the Navajo Reservation. Chinle is considered one of the major growth centers for Navajo and one area of likely development is increased tourism. Like the rest of Apache County, Chinle is a designated Enterprise Zone.

Temperatures during the winter average around 50 degrees Fahrenheit during the day and in the low 20s at night. During the summer, highs are in the high 80s and lows in the 50s.

You'll find a large array of convenience stores, gas stations, grocery stores, and Laundromats in this town, which has a population of about 8,500. The Tseyi' Shopping Center on Highway 191 has a Wells Fargo bank, a Bashas' supermarket, a United States Post Office, a pizza joint, and a general store. You'll have no trouble finding fast food restaurants along Highway 191.

The Chinle area is served by two weekly newspapers, *The Navajo Times* and the *Navajo-Hopi Observer*, two radio stations, and cable TV.

It's feeding time and this horse is headed home. You'll often see small herds of horses or cows roaming around the town of Chinle.
PHOTO: TANYA LEE

Diné College is 24 miles east in Tsaile. The phone number of this two-year tribal community college is (520) 674–3319. Both the community college and Northern Arizona University in Flagstaff offer college courses in Chinle.

The Navajo Police Department in Chinle can be reached at 911 in emergencies or at (520) 674–2111 for non-emergency situations. If you need help, you can also call the park rangers at (520) 674–5500, ext. 270. After hours only, call them at (520) 674–5523/5524. The hospital's phone number is (520) 674–7001.

Getting Here, Getting Around

You can reach Chinle by taking Highway 191 south from Monument Valley. You can also take Highway 264 out of Tuba City and drive east across the Hopi Reservation. Take Highway 191 north about 35 miles east of Keams Canyon. If you're coming directly from Flagstaff, go east on Route 66 (also U.S. Highway 89 north) past the Flagstaff Mall and turn right on the Townsend-Winona Road. About eight miles down the road, turn left at the sign for Leupp (pronounced "loop"), which puts you on Highway 15. Take Highway 15 (which becomes Highway 191) north until you reach Chinle at the intersection of Highways 191 and 7. Here you will see signs for the Canyon de Chelly National Monument, Thunderbird Lodge, and the Holiday Inn.

Restaurants

Garcia's Restaurant $$
P.O. Box 1889, Indian Route 7
Chinle, AZ 86503
(520) 674–5000; fax (520) 674–8264
www.holiday-inn.com/chinle-garcia;
holidayinncdc@cybertrails.com

Located at the Holiday Inn—Canyon de Chelly, just two miles from the intersection with Highway 191, this casual restaurant in a mission-style building offers a pleasant dining experience with professional service, whether you're here for breakfast, lunch, or dinner. Classic cookery with a Southwestern flair describes the menu here. The produce, meat, and fish are always fresh and top quality. For lunch, salads, burgers, sandwiches, and local specialties are offered, and we can highly recommend the Veggie Quesadilla listed under Lighter Fare on the last page. The whole wheat tortillas were full of fresh vegetables and low-fat cheese. The lunch size serving was enough for two meals. At dinner, sirloin steaks, ribs, chicken, salads, and burgers make for a varied menu. Because the restaurant is on the Navajo Reservation, no alcoholic beverages are served, though there is a selection of non-alcoholic beers and wines. The restaurant is open year-round, is wheelchair accessible, and accepts major credit cards. Reservations are recommended for dinner. There is plenty of parking in the motel parking lot.

Thunderbird Cafeteria $
P.O. Box 58, Chinle, AZ 86503
(520) 674–5841, (800) 679–2473;
fax (520) 674–5844
www.tbirdlodge.com;
tbirdlodge@cybertrails.com
Located 0.5 mile south of the Visitor Center on the South Rim Drive, this place really is a cafeteria offering simple breakfasts, burgers, chili dogs, fish and fries, fresh fruit, and salads.

The central part of this building was constructed in 1902 by Samuel Day as a trading post. One important function of trading posts at the turn of the century was that they pawned jewelry for people when they needed cash. Day's large vault, where he stored these valuable items, is now a picture gallery. The trading post closed in 1969 and the building was later converted to a restaurant and expanded. Open from very early in the morning into the evening, large comfortable booths, varied artwork on the walls, and friendly staff more or less compensate for the unexciting food. Some of the wall displays are contemporary Navajo weavings, reconstructions of hunting weapons and other tools, and genuine antiques, and all of it is for sale. The cafeteria accepts major credit cards, but no personal checks. It is wheelchair accessible, and of course, it is the most convenient restaurant if you are staying at Thunderbird Lodge or booking one of their motorized tours of the canyon.

Junction Restaurant $$
Route 7, Box 295, Chinle, AZ 86503
(520) 674–8443
This is a popular stop for tour bus groups, serving such favorites as Navajo sandwiches made with shredded beef, Navajo beef stew and fry bread, Navajo tacos, steaks, salads, and sandwiches. The restaurant is open for breakfast, lunch, and dinner seven days a week. Reservations are not needed, except for large groups. The Junction also offers set menus for tour groups. Major credit cards are accepted, and the restaurant is wheelchair accessible.

Accommodations

Holiday Inn—Canyon de Chelly
$$$ • P.O. Box 1889, Chinle, AZ 86503
(520) 674–5000; fax (520) 674–8264
www.holiday-inn.com/chinle-garcia;
holidayinncdc@cybertrails.com
Located 2 miles from the intersection of Highways 191 and 7, this is the newest and nicest motel in Chinle, with pleasant landscaping and well-maintained grounds. Built in 1992, the motel has 108 rooms with TVs, phones, irons and ironing boards, hair dryers, and coffeemakers. The outdoor heated pool is open from May through October, depending on the weather. Smoking and non-smoking rooms are available, and some rooms are wheelchair accessible. The hotel is part of the complex that includes Garcia's Restaurant and a gift shop where you can also book private and group jeep tours, making it a convenient refuge from a day of strenuous horseback riding, jeep touring, hiking, or driving. The staff is invariably helpful. Single and double rooms go for the same price and children under 19 stay free. There is an extra charge for more than two adults in a room. Pets are not allowed.

Thunderbird Lodge $$$$ P.O. Box 58, Chinle, AZ 86503
(520) 674–5841, (800) 679–2473; fax (520) 674–5844
www.tbirdlodge.com;
tbirdlodge@cybertrails.com

Located just 0.5 mile south of the Visitor Center on the South Rim Drive, Thunderbird Lodge is part of the Canyon de Chelly National Monument complex run by the park service, and the only lodging within the national monument itself. The cafeteria, started when Samuel Day's trading post went out of business, was the first building, and over the succeeding seventy years groups of motel rooms have been added in this bucolic setting shaded by huge cottonwood trees. All seventy-three rooms are in single-story buildings, and they all have small porches. The rooms have mission-style décor, color TVs, air conditioning, and phones. The lodge is completely non-smoking, pets are not allowed, and each person in the room after the first (including children) incurs a small additional charge. Credit cards are accepted, and some rooms are wheelchair accessible. Reservations are strongly suggested, especially from May through October.

Best Western-Canyon de Chelly Inn $$$
P.O. Box 295, Chinle, AZ 86503
(520) 674–5875; fax (520) 674–3715
www.grandcanyondechelly.com;
bwcdc@cybertrails.com

Located three miles west of the Visitor Center on Route 7, this 106-room inn has an indoor heated pool and both smoking and non-smoking rooms. Expect to pay an extra charge for more than two adults; children under 12 stay free. Some rooms are wheelchair accessible. The rooms have TVs, coffeemakers, phones, and hair dryers. From 10 P.M. to 6 A.M. security patrols check the parking lots as this is a place vendors often stay. Major credit cards are accepted, but pets are not. The motel lobby has a small gift shop with tourist items and some Navajo weavings and jewelry. If you are not certain whether an item is authentic Indian-made work, be sure to ask.

Campgrounds

Cottonwood Campground
Canyon de Chelly National Monument,
P.O. Box 588, Chinle, AZ 86053
(520) 674–5501 or 674–5510

Cottonwood Campground is maintained by the National Park Service and is just southwest of the Visitor Center next to Thunderbird Lodge. Except for groups of 15 to 50 tent campers, no reservations are accepted and sites are allotted on a first-come first-served basis year-round, so arrive early in the summer. The campground welcomes both tents and RVs. Ninety-six sites are available with rest-rooms. There is a dump station with water, but no showers or hookups are available.

Spider Rock RV Park
P.O. Box 2509, Chinle, AZ 86503
(520) 674–8261

Located 10 miles east of the Visitor Center on the South Rim Drive, this campground is run by the Navajo. No water or electricity are available here, but you can buy bottled water and lanterns. The Chapter House in Chinle has showers that you may use for a fee.

Shopping

Navajo Arts & Crafts Enterprise
P.O. Box 608, Chinle AZ 86503
(520) 674–5338; fax (520) 674–5339

Established by the Navajo Nation in 1941 to promote traditional Navajo arts and crafts, the Navajo Arts & Crafts Enterprise at the intersection of Highways 191 and 7 offers high-quality, genuine Navajo arts—rugs, silver and turquoise jewelry, sandpaintings, and pottery, as well as

These wooden carved and painted figures are wonderfully expresive examples of Navajo folk art. PHOTO: TANYA LEE

Katsinas especially, by what tribe), what kind of metal is used, and what stones are incorporated in the piece. Ask the salesperson to help you distinguish between handmade, traditionally-fired pots and hand-painted greenware. This shop is also a good place to book group and private jeep tours of the canyon. The shop closes in December for the off-season and reopens in March. Credit cards are accepted.

Pendleton blankets, backpacks, pillows, purses, yarn, moccasins, and T-shirts. For the music lover, an extensive collection of cassettes and CDs by Native American artists makes the stop worthwhile. Among the books offered are some out-of-print scholarly texts and anthropological studies reprinted by the University of Arizona's Arizona Books on Request at (800) 426–3797, www.uapress.arizona.edu.

Navajo Arts & Crafts Enterprises has three other stores in Cameron, Kayenta, and Window Rock.

Holiday Inn-Canyon de Chelly Gift Shop
P.O. Box 1889, Chinle, AZ 86503
(520) 674–5000; fax (520) 674–8264
www.holiday-inn.com/chinle-garcia;
holidayinncdc@cybertrails.com

In addition to a great selection of T-shirts (some of which have designs I have not seen elsewhere), Tony Hillerman novels, snacks, tourist pottery, Pendleton items, and other souvenirs, this gift shop, just two miles from the intersection of Highways 191 and 7, carries a lot of jewelry. Most of the jewelry is Navajo, but some is Zuni and Hopi. The buyer here features the work of some very well-known artists. Ask for help when selecting your jewelry, pottery, and Katsina carving purchases to ascertain whether what you are considering is Indian made (and in the case of

Thunderbird Lodge Gift Shop
P.O. Box 58, Chinle, AZ 86503
(520) 674–5841, (800) 679–2473;
fax (520) 674–5844
www.tbirdlodge.com;
tbirdlodge@cybertrails.com

From beautiful Navajo weavings to the dyed weft yarn and neutral warp yarn from which they are woven, this shop—located just 0.5 mile south of the Visitor Center on the South Rim Drive—offers a wonderful selection of rugs, Zuni and Navajo jewelry, pottery, and souvenir items, such as T-shirts, books, maps, moccasins, and tapes and CDs. The good Navajo rugs and the Hopi Katsina carvings have a room of their own (which they share with some charming Navajo folk art), and the strictly tourist items are separated from the handmade Indian items and clearly labeled to avoid any confusion about what you are buying. The shop also offers sandpaintings and reconstructions of early weapons, shields, and other interesting items. If you're touring the canyon by jeep, truck, or horseback, be sure to stop here to pick up a hat, sunscreen, and water if you've forgotten them. Open year round, the shop accepts major credit cards and personal checks with identification. In the front of the shop is the counter where you can book the canyon tours offered at Thunderbird Lodge.

Hubbell Trading Post National Historic Site

On your way to or from Canyon de Chelly, make sure to take an hour or two to stop at the Hubbell Trading Post National Historic Site in Ganado.

Trading posts had a significant influence on the life of the Navajos after they returned from Fort Sumner in 1868. Often started as distribution sites for the food promised by the United States to the Indians to help them as they reestablished their fields, orchards, and herds, trading posts eventually became important meeting places for families who lived in small extended family groups, shopping centers to obtain staple foods, tools, fabrics, and other manufactured goods, and venues for selling arts and crafts to traders who sold them to tourists.

John Lorenzo Hubbell, son of a Connecticut Yankee father and a Spanish mother, started trading in Ganado in 1876. Pictures of the exterior of the trading post from the turn of the century show pretty much the same building you can see today, sandstone masonry with vigas (poles used as horizontal roof supports, often seen in Santa Fe–style houses).

The inside of the building is not much changed either. The main room holds trade goods, which now include sodas and snacks as well as fabric, saddles, tools, Minnetonka moccasins, Pendleton blankets, and Blue Bird flour. Further inside to the left is the rug room, with superb examples of many traditional and modern patterns. You will be encouraged to spread out the rugs you like on the floor. Among these might be a red, white, tan, and black geometric Ganado Red, a style that Hubbell helped to encourage Navajo women to weave because he thought it was a style tourists would be likely to buy—and he was right. Most rugs will have a card that tells the artist's name, the area from which she comes, and the price of the rug. A photograph of the weaver might also be attached. Ask the salesperson to help you identify the differences among the rugs, and to find out if there is any leeway in the marked price. (There probably is.)

The middle room has jewelry (including some incredible concho belts), fine Hopi Katsina carvings, pottery, basketry, and the usual tourist souvenirs. The trading post carries items from many Southwest tribes, including Navajo, Hopi, Zuni, Acoma, Tohono O'odham, and Apache.

The Hubbell Trading Post Historic Site also includes a Visitors Center that is open seven days a week year round except January 1, Thanksgiving, and December 25. The National Park Service staff are friendly and helpful, and weavers or other artists may be giving demonstrations. Photos may be allowed, but ask first. The Visitors Center is a good place to shop for books, tapes, and maps.

Tours of the Hubbell home behind the trading post are offered daily, conducted by park rangers, or you can get a booklet for a self-guided tour. The Hubbell Homestead also includes a barn, a warehouse, a guest hogan, and a chicken coop, all of which are open to the public. You can find public restrooms, a drinking fountain, and picnic tables near the Visitors Center. No camping facilities or motels are available in Ganado, but Chinle is not far away.

To get to the Trading Post from Chinle, take 191 south and turn east toward Ganado at the intersection of Highway 264. Coming from the Hopi Reservation, you'll be on Highway 264, so just continue past 191 about five miles. From Flagstaff, you will be on 191 north. Turn east at the junction with Highway 264. Signs clearly direct you to the Trading Post, just across the Ganado Wash.

For more information on this historic site, write Hubbell Trading Post Historic Site, P.O. Box 150, Ganado, AZ 86505 or call (520) 755–3475. You can also visit the website at www.nps.gov/hutr.

Exploring the Canyons

You may explore the canyons by driving along the south or north rim, hiking down White House Trail, taking a horseback or jeep tour, or hiking into the canyons. All activities except the rim drives and the White House Trail hike require that you be escorted by an authorized Navajo or National Park Service guide.

The Rim Drives

Both rim drives start from the National Park Service Visitor Center. The center, open every day except December 25, has a small museum, offers an extensive collection of books for sale, and shows a 22-minute video, *Canyon Voices*, to introduce you to the canyons. Ask here about ranger-led activities such as Hogan Talks, Campfire Programs, and other special programs.

The rim drives are spectacular at any time of day as the colors of the sandstone walls of the canyons change as the sunlight hits them from different angles.

The South Rim Drive

The South Rim Drive takes you along the southern rim of Canyon de Chelly. The drive is approximately 37 miles round-trip and offers seven overlooks, three of which are wheelchair accessible. The drive is at an elevation of 5,500 feet at the Visitor Center and rises to about 7,000 feet at Spider Rock Overlook.

At Tunnel Canyon Overlook, the canyon walls are 275 feet high. A sign will alert you not to proceed further without a guide. This overlook is wheelchair accessible.

From Tsegi Overlook, you can see some of the Navajo agricultural lands at the bottom of the canyon, which are farmed during the summer months. Horses and sheep graze here as well. If you look across the road, you will see sand dunes. Millions of years ago, the De Chelly Sandstone formed from dunes like these.

Travelling east to Junction Overlook, you can see First Ruin across the canyon to your left. This small ruin was occupied about a thousand years ago. Looking straight ahead across the canyon, you can see Junction Ruin where Canyon de Chelly and Canyon del Muerto meet. You will notice that most of the cliff dwellings are on the north side of the canyon, offering a southern (and therefore sunnier and warmer) exposure during the winter months. Junction Ruin is also small, consisting of fifteen rooms and one kiva.

White House Overlook is a "must" stop. White House Ruin once was home to more than a dozen families, with cliff dwellings in the canyon wall and pueblo buildings on the canyon floor. At the height of its occupancy about 800 years ago, this ruin probably once had eighty rooms and four kivas, though only about sixty rooms remain. You can hike to White House Ruin beginning about 150 yards to the right of the rim. The trail is 2.5 miles round-trip and drops about 550 feet to the canyon floor. This is a moderately difficult hike, and plenty of water, good hiking shoes, sunscreen, and a hat are absolutely required. Plan on spending about two hours on this trail. Pit toilets are available at the bottom of the canyon. Temperatures may be extreme during the summer and the winter. You are requested not to disturb any of the natural or archaeological features you may encounter, and not to bother the Navajos for whom this canyon is home. Pets are not allowed on the trail. The overlook, but not the trail, is wheelchair accessible.

Sliding House sits on a narrow ledge across from the overlook. Retaining walls kept the houses from sliding down into the canyon below. This ruin of about fifty rooms and three kivas was built and occupied from the beginning of the tenth century to the middle of the thirteenth century C.E.

Face Rock Overlook has a viewfinder through which you can see four small ruins.

Look to the far right to see Face Rock, which tells Spider Woman the names of naughty children.

Spider Rock Overlook is the highest point on the South Rim drive at about 7,000 feet. The canyon floor is 1,000 feet below. The 800-foot sandstone spire at the meeting of Canyon de Chelly and Monument Canyon is Spider Rock, the home of Spider Woman, who taught Navajo women how to weave. Black Rock, just to the left of and a little above Spider Rock, is a volcanic plug, the core of an ancient volcano, about 70 million years old. The Chuska Mountains are on the horizon.

Return to the Visitor Center along the same road that you followed to get here.

The North Rim Drive

This drive takes you along the north rim of Canyon Del Muerto. There are four overlooks, none of which are wheelchair accessible. The 35 mile round-trip from the Visitor Center will take you about two hours.

Some nine hundred years ago, the Pueblo people built Ledge Ruin 100 feet above the canyon floor. No archaeological excavations have been done

Spider Rock in Canyon de Chelly is home of Spider Woman, who taught weaving to the Navajo. The 800-foot high spire can also be viewed from Spider Rock Overlook along the rim of Canyon de Chelly.
PHOTO: TANYA LEE

here, but surface remains of ceramics suggest that this site of at least twenty-nine rooms and two kivas was occupied from about 1050 to 1275 C.E. From this overlook you can also see Round Corner Ruin on your left high above the floor of the canyon. It appears to be a single kiva connected to Ledge Ruin by a toe and handhold trail, but its purpose and the reason for its location remain a mystery.

From Antelope House Ruin Overlook, you can see Antelope House on the left and Navajo Fortress on the right. The first ruin is named for an extraordinary painting of an antelope to the left of the ruin, which may date to the mid-nineteenth century and may have been done by a renowned Navajo artist named Dibe Yazhi. A pit house under the surface construction here dates back to 700 C.E., and the site has been occupied more or less continuously since then. A twelfth century circular central plaza distinguishes this from other known sites in the area. The ruin also has circular kivas and a multistory pueblo of at least eighty rooms. Like so many other sites in this region, Antelope House was abandoned near the end of the thirteenth century.

A high redstone butte across the canyon, Navajo Fortress, provided a defensible position for the Navajo defending themselves from Spanish, American, and other Native American enemies beginning around the end of the eighteenth century. Log poles, which were pulled up behind the refugees, provided the only access to the butte. Navajo Fortress provided temporary refuge for the Navajos during the Americans' slash and burn attack on the people in the mid 1860s. But eventually most of the Navajos who sought refuge here surrendered for lack of food, water, and shelter and were forced on the Long Walk to Bosque Redondo, where they were imprisoned until the Treaty of 1868 allowed them to return to their homeland.

Mummy Cave Ruin is one of the largest ancient Pueblo ruins in Canyon del Muerto. In Navajo, its name means "house under the rock," and archaeological research indicates that this site was occupied from about 300 to 1300 C.E. The eastern cave contains about fifty rooms and four kivas, while the western cave had about twenty rooms. The most recent architecture here is in the Mesa Verde style, and scientists speculate that these seven rooms and a three-story fortress were built by refugees or migrants from Mesa Verde in what is now Colorado. It was probably the last site occupied before the abandonment of the canyon in the late-thirteenth century.

The name Massacre Cave suggests a terrible history, and that is in fact what happened here. Antonio de Narbona led a military force into Canyon de Chelly in 1805 to force the Navajos to accept Spanish settlement on Navajo land. When he arrived, most of the men were out hunting. The women, children, and elders saw the soldiers coming and took refuge in a cave high on the canyon wall, but Narbona's troops attacked from the rim and the bullets ricocheted off the walls of the cave, killing 115 women, children and old people. Almost three dozen more were captured.

Yucca Cave Viewpoint allows you to see a small site probably occupied by late Basketmaker and early Pueblo peoples.

While experiencing the canyons from the rim, there are a few important things to remember. The first is that the canyons are sheer vertical walls as much as 1,000 feet deep. Stay on established trails and remember that the walls at the overlooks are there for your protection. Keep control of your children and pets. A fall from the rim would cause serious injury and quite possibly death.

Keep your eyes open for snakes and stinging insects. Look before you step or put your hands on the rocks and don't put your hands anywhere you cannot see into. Cultural artifacts, natural features, animals, and plants are all protected by federal and Navajo law. Do not remove or disturb anything.

Horseback Tours

Justin's Horse Rental
P.O. Box 881, Chinle, AZ 86503
(520) 674–5678

One of our favorite ways to see Canyon de Chelly is on horseback. Two companies, one at either end of the canyon, offer guided horseback tours.

Justin's Horse Rental is located at the mouth of the canyon; you will see signs on your way to Thunderbird Lodge. The tours start at the shallow end of the canyon and as you go further, the canyon walls become higher. Riding in the spring may take you along Chinle Wash when there is water running. In the summer, the canyon bottom will be sandy and your guide may let you run the horses!

Visitors pay both for the horse they are renting and for the services of a guide, who must be hired to escort you (partly to protect the canyon and the people who live there, and partly to protect you from hazards such as quicksand). Horses and guide must be reserved for a minimum of two hours, and a guide can be responsible for only six riders. Larger groups need additional guides. The shortest ride (two to two-and-a-half hours round-trip) takes you to Antelope House. The longest one-day ride is eight to nine hours and takes you to Mummy Cave. This is a one-way ride; the horses are trailered and you drive the other way. Rides of in-between lengths are available, and overnights can be arranged. The company provides horses, guides, dinner, and breakfast. You

A treat not to be missed is a horseback ride down into Canyon de Chelly. Here riders catch sight of a white stallion grazing along the bottom of the canyon. PHOTO: TANYA LEE

bring your own sleeping bags, tents, and lunch.

For the spring and summer months, you need to make your reservations here one to two months in advance. It's slower during the winter, but reservations are still a good idea. You should call a few days before your reserved trip to confirm. Only cash and traveler's checks are accepted, and remember to tip your guide.

Totsonii Ranch
P.O. Box 434, Chinle, AZ 86503
(520) 755–6209

At the other end of Canyon de Chelly, 1.25 miles beyond the end of the pavement of the South Rim Drive, you'll find Totsonii Ranch.

This ride starts at the deep end of the canyon, and the descent from the rim to the canyon floor is along a narrow, rocky, steep trail. Since I am somewhat afraid of heights, it was a challenge, but you can always get off and walk your horse down the steepest parts, and it's always good to remind yourself that the horse wants to fall even less than you do, and it has made this trip dozens if not hundreds of times. Along the trail we occasionally caught sight of two horses, one a beautiful white stallion, that were grazing in the canyon. They were not wild horses, but here, as on the rest of the Navajo Reservation, livestock graze on open range.

Once you reach the bottom of the canyon, you are very close to Spider Rock, which is even more magnificent from the bottom of the canyon than from the rim. Your guide will point out petroglyphs and other interesting features. Feel free to ask questions, as guides are happy to share aspects of Navajo history and culture. Again, reservations are strongly recommended, and tipping is appreciated.

Motorized Tours

De Chelly Unimog Group Tours
P.O. Box 976, Chinle, AZ 86503.
(520) 674–1044,
(520) 674–5433 (reservations)

De Chelly Unimog Group Tours is the only Navajo-owned motorized tour company at Canyon de Chelly. Leon Skyhorse Thomas is an authorized guide who will take you on a half-day tour to Antelope House Ruin and White House Ruin in an open, four-wheel drive vehicle. Other sites on this tour include Kokopelli Cave,

Petroglyph Rock, First Ruin, Junction Ruin, Ceremonial Cave, and Ledge Ruin. The three-hour tours leave in the morning and the afternoon from the Holiday Inn parking lot, and they are limited to twelve passengers each. Children 12 and under get special rates, and babies under one year of age must have car seats. De Chelly Tours also offers private jeep tours. You can arrange your tour through the gift shop at the Holiday Inn or you can contact the company directly.

Thunderbird Lodge
P.O. Box 548, Chinle, AZ 86503
(520) 674–5841, (800) 679–2473;
fax (520) 674–5844
tbirdlodge@cybertrails.com

Thunderbird Lodge, operated by the National Park Service, offers all day, half-day, and private tours with experienced Navajo guides. Their 6x6 open-air jeeps hold up to 24 passengers. The all-day tour is a 60-mile round-trip through Canyon del Muerto to Mummy Cave and through Canyon de Chelly to Spider Rock. The tour leaves Thunderbird Lodge at 9 A.M. and returns at about 5 P.M. (Remember that the Navajo Reservation observes daylight savings time from April through October.) Lunch is provided. This tour operates from spring, when the water in the canyons is sufficiently low, into the late fall, depending on the weather.

The half-day tour lasts about three-and-a-half hours and takes you into the lower parts of Canyon de Chelly and Canyon del Muerto. Tours leave the lodge at 9 A.M. and 2 P.M. during the spring through fall season. In the winter (November through March), plan to leave at 9 A.M. or 1 P.M..

Private tours are also available. You may buy your tickets for these tours at the gift shop at Thunderbird Lodge, or you may make your reservations in advance (particularly recommended for private tours).

Hiking Tours

Tsegi Guide Association
P.O. Box 1903, Chinle, AZ 86503
(520) 674–5500

At the Visitor Center at the entrance to the national monument, you can hire a guide for a minimum three-hour hike of the canyon or an overnight camping excursion. You can make your plans when you arrive, but for large groups and for overnight hiking/camping trips, you should call in advance. Remember that except for White House Ruin Trail, unescorted hiking in the canyon is forbidden. Each guide can take up to fifteen people. A park ranger at the Visitor Center will help you get the necessary permit.

Canyon Hiking Service
P.O. Box 2832, Chinle, AZ 86503
(520) 674–1767

This service offers various hiking options, including nighttime hikes into the canyon. You can find them 0.25 mile north of Thunderbird Lodge.

Coconino National Forest

Hiking
Mountain Biking
Campgrounds
Plateau Country/
    Mormon Lake
Other Lake Areas

Featuring some of the highest mountains in the state, the Coconino National Forest is a fascinating blend of alpine tundra, coniferous forest, and high desert. Encompassing 1.8 million acres, Coconino Forest is the world's largest contiguous ponderosa pine forest.

In this chapter, we explore the forest's Volcanic Highlands area, which includes the San Francisco Peaks, and the Plateau Country area, with its rolling terrain that extends from the foot of the Peaks and is home to Arizona's largest natural lake. Outdoor recreational activities abound, with endless hiking, mountain biking, fishing, boating, and relaxing options. Please note that tent and RV camping are available at dozens of sites within the National Forest. These sites offer few amenities and are often primitive, although drinking water is available. The fee to camp is between $8 and $10. Unless otherwise posted, eight people are allowed to camp at each site. For more information, contact the Coconino National Forest, 2323 E. Greenlaw Lane, (520) 527–3600. Or visit their website, www. fs.fed.us/r3/coconino.

Hiking

Volcanic Highlands/The San Francisco Peaks

The following trails are found within the San Francisco Peaks area. For more information, contact the Peaks Ranger Station, 5705 N. U.S. Highway 89, (520) 526–0866.

Fat Man's Loop
Easy

Head east on Route 66 (which turns into U.S. Highway 89) to the Peaks Ranger Station. As you pass the Flagstaff Mall on your right, you will see a sign for the "Mt. Elden Trailhead." The parking lot for the trail is on the north side of the street. As you begin the hike you will pass through a pole fence. Follow the trail until it splits. The trail is clearly marked; choose between Fat Man's Loop and Elden Lookout. You can access this easy two-mile loop from either trail. Fat Man's Loop has a more gradual ascent. Along the route there are a number of fascinating rock formations, and hikers can view the Flagstaff suburbs and surrounding countryside. Estimated hiking time is one hour.

Lookout Trail
Difficult

The Fat Man's Loop Trail provides access to the Elden Lookout Trail. When the trail splits, you will stay to the left. The

Insiders' Tip

At 12,663 feet, Humphreys Peak is the highest mountain in Arizona. The peaks are sacred to the area's Native people. Please leave the area as you found it.

trails are clearly marked for Elden Lookout and Fat Man's Loop. As you reach the top of the loop, follow the sign for Elden Lookout and continue up the mountain for two miles and climb 2, 000 feet to the summit of Mt. Elden. This hike provides great views, and offers an introduction to the diverse flora and fauna of the area with shrubs and smaller trees usually found at lower altitudes. This hike is six miles round-trip and takes approximately four hours.

Oldham Trail
Moderate

This trail is part of a developed trail system around the Mt. Elden and Dry Lakes area of Flagstaff. Take San Francisco Street north and turn right on Forest Avenue (which turns into Cedar Avenue). At the top of Cedar Avenue turn left on Gemini. The trail begins at the fence in the rear of Buffalo Park. Just follow the main graveled path that cuts straight through the park, not the exercise route. This 5.5-mile route traverses fields, cliffs, and pine forest and takes approximately four hours.

Arizona Snowbowl

Humphreys Trail
Difficult

Take Humphreys Street north to U.S. Highway 180. Follow U.S. 180 for 7 miles until you reach Snowbowl Road. Take Snowbowl Road for 7 miles until you reach the first parking lot on the left. The trail begins at the far end of the lot. The first few miles of the trail are dark, filled with fir, spruce, and aspen trees. As you ascend, the forest opens up to a small meadow. At 3.75 miles the footing is rocky and not very good. At 4 miles you can see into the Inner Basin of the Peaks and enjoy the magnificent views. The top of the trail is above timberline and windy and cold. Bring plenty of water and food on this hike. You will climb from 9,500 feet to 12,663 feet, the highest point in Arizona. Be wary of the effects of the change of altitude, bring plenty of water and food, and rest often. This is a 9-mile hike; plan to hike for at least six hours.

Kachina Trail
Moderate

As you follow Snowbowl Road, turn right into the parking lot. The trail begins at the end of this lot. This 6-mile trail (one way) begins in aspen and fir and is a must during the fall when the leaves are chang-

ing. This is a gradual hike that traverses meadows, aspen forests, and wildflower fields. But remember what goes down must come up. Allow for plenty of time to climb back to the trailhead.

Weatherford Trail
Difficult

This 12-mile round-trip trail climbs through a scenic canyon on the southeast side of the San Francisco Peaks. Along the trail, you will find an ammunition can chained to a log. Inside is a logbook where you can add your own entry and see who has been there before you. At the end of the trail is a pond (during wet seasons). This is a great place to see wildlife. To access the Weatherford Trail, go north on Humphreys Street to U.S. Highway 180. Take U.S. 180 to Snowbowl Road and turn right (7.3 miles). Follow Snow Bowl Road to the 9.7-mile point, where you will see an unpaved road, FR 522, that heads to the right. Follow Fr 522 to the fork in the road at 9.8 miles. Take the left fork and drive for 13.7 miles. You will see a parking lot at the end of the road. Park in the lot; you will see a road behind the parking lot. There is a trail sign. Believe it or not, this is the easiest way to hike to the top of the San Francisco Peaks.

Lava River Cave: A Natural Museum

This museum is like no other museum. There isn't a front door you can walk through; the entrance is a hole in the ground that you must crawl through. The cave appears today as it did shortly after its formation almost 700,000 years ago. Molten rock from a volcanic eruption in Hart Prairie cooled and solidified in only a few brief moments.

Historians believe the Lava River Cave was discovered in 1915 and that Flagstaff residents visited the cave to collect ice to use for refrigeration.

The cave contains a variety of lava flow features. "Flow ripples" can be found further inside the cave. These ripples give the appearance of a flowing river. "Splash-downs" are hardened rocks that fell into the lava flow and froze. "Long cracks" can be found in the floor, ceiling, and walls. These "cooling cracks" formed as the lava cooled and hardened. Icicle-like formations formed after the floor and ceiling hardened. Experts believe hot gas shot through the cave, remelting the floor and ceiling. "Lavasicles" are drips of remelted lava that form and quickly harden.

The "lava tube" is the longest cave of its kind in Arizona. The temperature in the cave during the summertime is about 42 F.

You will need to dress properly, wear sturdy shoes, and bring two to three flashlights; the only natural light inside the cave comes from the entrance. Unfortunately, the Lava River Cave was defaced by graffiti in the past, but it has recently been cleaned up. Help preserve the Lava River Cave for all to enjoy. Visitors are asked to report any damage to the Park Service. Please do not build fires inside the caves. If you see litter you can help by packing it out with you.

To get to the Lava Cave take Humphreys Street to U.S. Highway 180. Drive north on U.S. 180 for 9 miles and turn left on FR 245. Follow the road for 3 miles to FR 171 and turn south 1 mile to where FR 171A turns left. You will only be a short distance from the entrance of the Lava River Cave.

Mountain Biking

Novice and advanced riders will enjoy the single track trails, grand scenery, and gratification of a hard but fun workout through some of Arizona's prettiest places.

Dry Lake Hills
Difficult

This ride might sound a bit confusing, but what a fun ride! The trail starts at the Schultz Creek parking area. It climbs, rolls, and descends all in 9.3 miles. Dry Lake Hills bypasses and traverses other trails in the Mt. Elden/Dry Lake trail system. Begin with a climb up Rocky Ridge Trail and head toward Elden Lookout Road. Follow the Lookout Road until you reach the steep Lower Brookbank Trail up to Dry Lake Hills. Then head over to Little Gnarly Trail and head back down to Schultz Creek Trail and back to the parking area. To get to the Dry Lake Trailhead, take U.S. Highway 180 north. At milepost 218.6 you will see a sign for Schultz Pass; take a right. Follow the road until the pavement ends, go through the gate, and take a short, steep right down into a parking area. A sign marking the trailhead says Rocky Ridge Trail.

Fisher Point
Easy

This is an easy 7.2-mile single track for the novice rider. The trail takes you to a cave at the entrance to the isolated and quiet Walnut Canyon. Bring along a picnic and enjoy the scenery. To start the ride, take Butler Avenue east. At Lone Tree Road there is a stoplight, head south on Lone Tree or make a right. Follow Lone Tree Road under the freeway. When the road makes a sharp right, go straight on the dirt road and follow it until the trail splits after the first mile. (You can go either way because it rejoins a mile later.) The trail splits again another mile later. Stick with the trail that goes to the right; it takes you right to Fisher Point. You will return the way you came. This ride could take two hours; the time does not include lounging.

Flagstaff Nordic Ski Center
Easy to Moderate
We know it reads Nordic Ski Center, but after the snow has melted and the tracks have dried, the Nordic Center has free, paved trails without any difficult climbs. Bikers will enjoy the views of the San Francisco Peaks, and the peacefulness of the surrounding aspen groves. Take U.S. Highway 180 north of Flagstaff past the Arizona Snowbowl about 8 miles. The Nordic Center is on the right hand side of U.S. 180. You will see the sign. Don't worry you can't miss it.

Waterline Road
Moderate
This ride has a steep climb, but allows access to the same superb views of the Peaks. The ideal time for this ride is between May and October. Head north on U.S. Highway 89A to Lockett Meadow Road at mile post 431.2. Take the 4.5-mile road up to Lockett Meadow, where you will find plenty of places to park. Follow the trail up to the "cabins." At the cabins, turn right. Now it will be a pleasant ride to Abineau Canyon. This excursion totals 14 miles. The hardest part is the 1 mile up to the cabins. Plan on this being an all-day adventure, and bring plenty of water and snacks!

Campgrounds

Bonito Campground
Peaks Ranger Station, 5075 N. Hwy. 89, Flagstaff, AZ 86004
(520) 526–0866
Bonito Campground is named for the Bonito Lava Flow that covered the area about 900 years ago. The Sunset Crater National Monument is located just beyond the boundaries of the campground. Also nearby is Wupatki National Monument. Both Sunset Crater and Wupatki have visitor centers featuring self-guided tours. The forty-four campsites include tables, fire rings and cooking grills, drinking water, and toilets. To access the campground, drive 12 miles northeast of Flagstaff on U.S. 89. Turn east (right) on FR 545 and drive 2 miles to Bonito Campground. The campground is open from May 1st to the end of September. There is a $10 per vehicle per night fee (single family), and a $5 fee per vehicle for day use. (Prices are subject to change.)

Please note that tents, motor homes, and trailers under 22 feet are permitted. There are no utility hookups.

Little Elden Springs Horse Camp
Peaks Ranger Station,
5075 N. U.S. Hwy. 89
(520) 526–0866
At the base of Mt. Elden, this campground is designed especially for horse lovers. Each of the fourteen sites allows easy access for trucks and horse trailers. Riding trails are accessible from the campground. Little Elden has water, picnic tables, restrooms, and hitching rails. Larger sites can accommodate vehicles up to 35 feet. There is a $12 per night/campsite fee, and a $4 per vehicle day use fee. To access the campground, drive 5 miles northeast of Flagstaff on U.S. Highway 89. Turn west (left) on FR 556 and drive 2 miles. Make a right onto FR 556A and follow this road into the campground.

The Plateau Country/Mormon Lake

Home to the area's largest natural lake, the Plateau Country is made up of open meadows, rolling hills, and endless prairies. A large population of elk and antelope graze the open land, while bald eagles and osprey also make their homes here. This is a year-round destination for hikers, boaters, anglers, and cross-country skiers. For more information, contact Mormon Lake Ranger District, 4373 S. Lake Mary Rd., (520) 774–1147.

Hikes

Lakeview Trail #132
Moderate

Follow Lake Mary Road 23 miles (MP 323.6.) Turn right onto Mormon Lake Road. At 28 miles, you will see a sign for Lakeview Trail. Turn right here and follow the gravel road and signs to the 28.2 mile sign near the restrooms at the campground. A sign marking the trail will be to your left as you enter the Double Springs Campground. Most of the two-mile hike weaves through ponderosa pine, oak, and aspen. For a majority of the hike you will not understand why the trail is named Lakeview, but as you reach the lava cliff at the top, the views of the Mormon Lake are unobstructed and plentiful. Depending on the amount of moisture the area has received, the lake might be full or it might be a grassy pasture with a small body of water at its center. This moderately easy hike will take a little over an hour to complete if you walk fast, but why bother? Enjoy the view!

Ledges Trail #138
Easy

This easy, one-mile trail connects with the Mormon Mountain Trail and takes you through a pine forest to a basalt cliff with great scenic views of Mormon Lake. You will encounter ledges for which the trail is named along the way. This is an excellent place to observe wildlife; you may spot elk or mule deer by the lakeside. To access the Ledges Trail, follow Lake Mary Road to the 23 mile mark (MP 323.6.) Turn right onto Mormon Lake Rd., you will see a sign marked "Dairy Springs Amphitheater." Turn right here and follow the gravel road to the 27 mile marker; there is a large sign at the parking lot marking the trailhead. Ledges and Mormon Mountain Trails begin at Dairy Springs Campground.

Mormon Mountain Trail #58
Moderate

A popular trail for cross-country skiers, Mormon Mountain Trail also connects with the Ledges Trail. Follow the white triangles to reach the top of the mountain. The three-mile trail climbs through aspen, fir, and spruce. Before you reach the top of the mountain, you will pass through an old growth forest that has been logged. Various places along the trail offer views of Mormon Lake, tree covered hills, and open meadows below. (See Ledges Trail for directions.)

Boating/Fishing

For fishing (and hunting) information, contact Arizona State Game and Fish, 3500 S. Lake Mary Road, (520) 774–5045.

Lake Mary Fishing Boat Rentals
480 Lake Mary Rd.
(520) 774–1742

Whether you like to canoe, row, or drive a 14-foot fishing boat, this rental shop has the watercraft for you. All boats can be used at any lake within a 35-mile radius of this rental shop. The shop is open from 7 A.M. to 7 P.M. May through September. Buy your bait or rent your fishing poles here.

Other Lake Areas

Ashurst Lake

Twenty miles southeast of Flagstaff, Ashurst Lake is stocked regularly with rainbow and brook trout. In addition to fishing, the lake is popular with paddlers, windsurfers, and boaters. A boat ramp is available; boat motors are limited to 8 horsepower or less. Locals and visitors enjoy the panoramic views, sightseeing, biking, photography opportunities, and picnicking in the area.

Ashurst Lake and Forked Pine Campgrounds

Ashurt Lake Campground offers forty sites nestled between FH 3 and East FR 82. The campground has drinking water and toilets. Forked Pine, with twenty-four sites, is located right next to Ashurst Lake Campground on East FR 82. Both campgrounds have picnic tables, fire rings, and cooking grills.

Lower Lake Mary

The smaller of Flagstaff's twin lakes, Lower Lake Mary is nonexistent during dry spells. When it does have water, anglers are lined up at the banks ready to catch northern pike and catfish. Whether the lake has water or not, it is still an ideal location to fly a kite, have a picnic, and just relax. A boat ramp is available; boat motors are restricted to eight horsepower or less. To get to the lake, drive 8 miles south on Lake Mary Road. A day use parking lot is on the west side of the road.

Marshall Lake

Marshall Lake is a marshy body of water bursting with wildlife. At sunset an elk might wander through the muddy meadow, or you may spot a bald eagle soaring above. This lake is a valuable wildlife habitat managed by the Arizona Game and Fish Department and Ducks Unlimited. The northwest side of the lake is closed to vehicles. The lake is open in early May and closes in mid October. To get to Marshall Lake, drive 9 miles on Lake Mary Road. Turn left on FR 128 and drive 3 miles to the lake. The last mile is unpaved and may be impassable due to mud or snow.

Mormon Lake

When Mormon Lake is full it can be an excellent place to fish, boat, and windsurf. Watch hawks, ospreys, cranes, and an occasional bald eagle in their natural habitat. Picnic, hike, or kick back by the edge of the lake. Dairy Springs and Double Springs National Forest Campgrounds are located nearby. A country store, restaurant, and service station are in close proximity to the lake.

Dairy Springs and Double Springs Campgrounds

Twenty-seven camping sites are available at each campground, along with drinking water, tables, fire rings, and cooking grills. RVs up to 35 feet are allowed. Dairy Springs and Double Springs are 24 miles southeast of Flagstaff at FR 90. Drive south from Flagstaff 20 miles on Forest Highway 3 (Lake Mary Road) to Forest Road 90. Turn west on FR 90 and drive 3.5 miles to Dairy Springs Campground or 4.6 miles to Double Springs. Both campgrounds are open from May 1st to the end of September.

Upper Lake Mary

The Arizona Game and Fish Department stocks this long narrow lake with northern pike, channel cat, walleye, crappie, and some trout. Upper Lake Mary is the twin lake of Lower Lake Mary and is the primary source of drinking water for the city of Flagstaff. The lake is popular with water skiers and boaters. There are two paved boat ramps at the parking area near the dam and an additional ramp at the Lake Mary Narrows Recreation Area. Boat camping is permitted only on the south shore of the lake. Camping and campfires are permitted only in Lakeview Campground. Drive 12 miles on Lake Mary Road (Forest Highway 3) to reach the lake. Swimming is allowed but not recommended.

Lakeview/Pine Grove Campgrounds

This campground allows for easy access to Upper Lake Mary and is located near FH 3 (Lake Mary Road). Lake View Campground is surrounded by a grassy hillside and offers thirty camping sites and allows RVs up to 26 feet. Pine Grove is bordered by open meadows and has forty-six single-unit sites. Both campgrounds have tables, fire rings, cooking grills, and drinking water. Fees for Lake View are $8 per vehicle per night (single family), and $4 per vehicle for day use. The cost to camp at Pine Grove is $10 per vehicle per night (single family), and $5 per vehicle for day use.

To reach the campgrounds, drive 16 miles south from Flagstaff on Forest Highway 3 (Lake Mary Road) to Lakeview, and 19 miles to Pine Grove. Campers can access both campgrounds from a short turn off of Forest Highway 3.

Contemporary Hopi Katsina carvings (front and back shown) are created from one piece of cottonwood root. PHOTO: TANYA LEE

Hopi Reservation

The Hopi Reservation in northeastern Arizona today occupies about 1.5 million acres, a small portion of the Hopis' ancestral homeland. More than 11,000 Hopis, divided into about thirty clans, now live on and around three sandstone mesas rising hundreds of feet above the plateau floor at elevations of 5,000 to 6,000 feet. Second Mesa is about 90 miles northeast of Flagstaff.

The twelve Hopi villages are built on First, Second, and Third Mesas (named from east to west) and the lands surrounding them, with Moenkopi—culturally and historically part of Third Mesa—just across Moenkopi Wash from Tuba City.

Hopi is a Uto-Aztecan language. Still spoken exclusively by many elders, the language is being aggressively preserved by the Hopi through language classes for students and the recent publication of a Hopi dictionary.

The Hopi people, according to their own accounts, came into this, the Fourth World, from below ground, climbing up through a *sipapu* somewhere in the Grand Canyon at some time in the past. The Fourth World, like those before it, will end catastrophically, but how much we will suffer when the Fourth World is destroyed will be determined by how we behave now.

The Hopi are the descendents of the "Hisatsenom," who lived on the Colorado Plateau more than a millennium ago. The term "Hisatsenom" refers to the people others call the Anasazi or the Pueblo people. They were the builders of many of the pueblo and cliff dweller monuments whose remains we see today, such as those at Mesa Verde in Colorado, Canyon de Chelly in Arizona, and Chaco Canyon in New Mexico. The earliest Hopi villages on the mesas are contemporary with some of these ancestral cliff dwellings.

Hopi history recalls that only after the people completed their migrations in the four directions were they allowed by Massau, the caretaker of this world, to settle on the three mesas they now inhabit. They were given three things: a gourd of water, a planting stick, and an ear of corn with which to survive. In return, the Hopis agreed to act as stewards of this sacred land. An account of the founding of the Hopi villages and the different clans and ceremonies associated with them is detailed in *Truth of a Hopi: Stories Relating to the Origin, Myths and Clan Histories of the Hopi* by Edmund Nequatewa. Hopi is a matrilineal society organized by clans. A person's clan membership prescribes his or her obligations within the society.

Insiders' Tip

The average daytime temperatures in the winter are in the mid 40s; overnight lows average about 18 degrees Fahrenheit. In the summer, daytime temperatures are in the mid to high 80s, and nighttime lows are in the low 20s. Spring and fall temperatures are cool to warm during the day and cool to cold at night.

In such arid country (only about 10 inches of rain fall a year), the Hopi became highly skilled dry farmers and developed a ceremonial cycle tied to the land on which they lived and thrived. Today, they grow corn, fruit trees, squash, beans, melons, and gourds. They are also fine artists, making overlay silver jewelry, decorated coiled pots, Katsina carvings, and weavings of unsurpassed quality. Hopis today are also educators, environmentalists, doctors, lawyers, geologists, hydrologists, historians, and members of many other professions.

The Hopi and the Spanish

The first European record of contact with the Hopi documents the visits of Pedro de Tovar and Fray Juan Padilla, members of Francesco Vázquez de Coronado's expedition in 1540. Hopi, however, knew about the Spanish before this time. Information, as well as material culture, followed the trade routes from as far south as Central America. And Hopi prophecy told of a bahana, a white brother, who would come to them from the east as a savior.

But the Spanish had come instead in search of the mythical seven golden cities of Cibola. They called the Hopi "Tusayan," and believed that they were a hostile and warlike tribe. Coronado sent 20 soldiers with Tovar and Padilla to "explore" the Hopi mesas. This group probably visited the village of Awat'ovi, but their records do not show if they went to any of the other Hopi villages.

Soon thereafter a party led by Garcia Lopez de Cárdenas was sent from Zuni Pueblo in the south to find a great river in the vicinity of Hopi (presumably the Colorado River). He reported that the Hopi were ruled by an assembly of old men and that their priests told the people how to live. He estimated that Zuni and Hopi together had a population of 3,000 to 4,000 people, counting only adult males. Based on that estimate, there may have been about 8,000 Hopi in the middle of the sixteenth century. Whiteley (see Selected Readings), however, notes that this number should not be assumed to be an accurate estimate of the pre-colonial Hopi population. A smallpox epidemic in 1520-1524, the first of many, had decimated the Native populations of the Southwest.

In 1598, the Spanish sent Don Juan de Onate to "conquer" the Hopi for the Spanish crown, but the Hopi did not then, or ever, submit to any outside authority.

Three Franciscan priests arrived in the village of Awat'ovi in the late-sixteenth century and built the first of three Catholic missions; the other two were established in the villages of Shongopavi and Oraibi. The friars tried to prevent the Hopis from following their religion by closing down kivas and forbidding religious dances. They demanded tribute in the form of food, and the Spanish records tell of brutality and torture of the people by the padres.

The Hopis received from the Spanish horses, sheep, burros, and cattle, as well as some Old World fruits and vegetables. The addition of foods high in animal fat to the diet of a mostly vegetarian people has taken its toll—diabetes is a serious health threat among the Hopi, as it is among other Native American tribes.

During the Pueblo Revolt of 1680, the Hopi joined the Rio Grande pueblo tribes and rose up against the Spanish, destroying churches and killing several priests. It was after the Pueblo Revolt that the villages of First and Second Mesa moved to the mesa tops to defend themselves against further Spanish invasions.

Pueblo tribes in what is now New Mexico were reconquered in 1692 and the Spanish visited Awat'ovi, Walpi, Mishognovi, and Songoopavi, but Spain never gained military dominance over the Hopi, in part because of the Hopis' ability to negotiate without surrendering to foreigners. Awat'ovi on Antelope Mesa was the only Hopi village to tolerate missionaries, and that village was destroyed in the early-eighteenth century by Hopis from other villages in protest.

The Hopi sent diplomats, as representatives of their sovereign nation, to offer to make a peace treaty with the Spanish, but Spain summarily rejected the offer.

Attempts by the Spanish to conquer Walpi in 1716 and 1724 failed. Missionaries tried unsuccessfully to convert residents of the six Hopi villages, Walpi, Oraibi, Mishongnovi and Songoopavi, Shipaulovi and Tewa, in 1744 and 1745. The last two villages had been founded after the 1680 Pueblo Revolt.

In 1775, the Spanish made a further major attempt when Father Silvestre de Escalante visited Walpi, Sichomovi, and Tewa on First Mesa, Mishongovi, Shipaulovi and Shongopavi on Second Mesa, and Oraibi on Third Mesa, but this missionary failed to convert anyone.

In July of 1776, while the Declaration of Independence was being signed in Philadelphia, Franciscan priest Francisco Garcés visited the village of Oraibi. The village responded by formally asserting its own independence.

The Hopi were under the authority of Mexico from 1821 to 1846, but the Mexican government never attempted to govern villages so far away from their base of power. They did, however, raid Hopi villages to capture children, who were sold as servants for rich Mexican families.

During the Spanish and Mexican periods, the Hopi were continually threatened by other tribes, particularly the Navajo, who had migrated from the north and east. These seminomadic herders needed grazing land for their animals—the same land that the agricultural Hopi needed for farming. The Hopis sought help from the Mexican government to protect their lands, but Mexico was either not willing or not able to provide that help.

The Hopi and the Anglo-Americans

The first Anglo-American visitors to the Hopi arrived in the 1820s. They included Bill Williams (see the chapter on Williams) who may have lived among the Hopi, though no written record of this exists. However, a party of trappers from Rocky Mountain Fur Company did invade the gardens at Oraibi in 1834, massacring fifteen to twenty Hopis who objected to this raid.

The 1848 Treaty of Guadalupe de Hidalgo ceded the Southwest from Mexico to the United States at the end of the Mexican War. This treaty is an important document in Hopi history because it recognized the Hopi and other pueblo tribes as citizens with full rights. The pueblo tribes, with sophisticated systems of government, agriculture, arts and crafts, and complex religious beliefs, were distinguished from the warring tribes of the Southwest. The treaty also demarcated a specific Hopi land base and promised to protect the Hopi from the Navajo who were encroaching on Hopi land.

The first meeting between the Hopi and the United States government occurred in 1850 when some Hopis visited the Superintendent of Indian Affairs James S. Calhoun in Santa Fe, New Mexico to try to determine the government's intentions toward them and to ask for military protection against the Navajo. In 1852, the Hopi initiated contact with President Millard Fillmore via a messenger who carried ritual objects as gifts. The Hopi offered friendship and communication. Oral histories also recall in the early 1850s another smallpox epidemic caused widespread death. The epidemic was followed by a severe drought. The population of Oraibi was reduced to 200.

In 1858 Mormon missionaries, who believed American Indians to be Lamanites, one of the lost tribes of Israel, arrived on Hopi. Mormons apparently treated Hopis with more respect than other Anglo-Americans, and the Hopi distinguished them by calling the Mormons by a different name from the one that referred to all other Anglo-Americans. The Mormons left four missionaries, but they stayed only a few weeks. Other

Visiting the Hopi Reservation

Most villages have an office where you should check in when you arrive to find out if visitors are welcome at that time.

Disruption of shrines or removal of any artifacts is strictly prohibited, and all archaeological sites are protected by federal and Hopi law.

Overnight camping is limited to two nights at designated campgrounds only. Non-Hopis must have the permission of the village leader to stay in the village for any length of time.

Photographing, sketching, painting, and video and audio recording in the villages are never allowed.

Most ceremonial dances are closed to non-Indians. Social dances and Butterfly Dances held from late August through November, mostly on weekends, are often open to visitors. Precise dates are not known until a few weeks in advance. If you are not sure whether non-Indians are welcome at a dance or ceremonial, ask. Should you be privileged to be invited to a ceremonial dance, you need to remember that you are a guest and are expected to behave appropriately and sensibly. You should wear neat clothing. Women are asked to wear clothing that completely covers them, and men should wear pants and shirts. Hats and umbrellas are discouraged. You should not discuss the event while it is happening, nor should you follow the dancers when they leave the plaza. Choose a place from which to observe and stay there; do not move around the plaza or the village. As a guest, you are also expected to contribute to the event with positive thoughts and prayers to strengthen and benefit all the forms and things in the world.

No alcohol or illegal drugs are permitted on the Hopi Reservation.

Mormon missionaries came, and in 1862 some Hopis went to Salt Lake City and met with Brigham Young.

The ongoing conflict with the Navajo ended for a brief period in the mid 1860s when thousands of Navajo were forced on the Long Walk, which they still remember vividly today, and imprisoned at Bosque Redondo, New Mexico until 1868. The decade also brought famine and another smallpox epidemic to the Hopi.

The 1868 Navajo treaty with the federal government allowed them to return to northwestern New Mexico and northeastern Arizona to live on a 3.5 million-acre reservation there. The Navajos, however, moved westward, again intruding on land to which the Hopi had ancestral claims.

Tuuvi, a Hopi from Oraibi, and his wife, Katsinmana, visited Utah around 1870 and converted to Mormonism. Tuuvi welcomed Mormon settlement of the Moenkopi area west of Third Mesa in 1875 as a means to protect the Hopi from enemy incursions. A year later the Mormons moved a little further west and founded Tuba City. Not many Hopis converted to the Mormon faith, however, and Tuuvi was treated as an outcast. In 1903 the U.S. government forced the Anglo Mormons out of Tuba City, since they had settled on land already allocated to the Indians

On December 16, 1882 President Chester Arthur created by executive order a 2.5 million acre reservation for the "Moqui and other such Indians as the Secretary of the Interior saw fit to settle thereon." This may have discouraged some Anglo settlement in the area, but it had no effect on other tribes encroaching on Hopi land.

The Navajos continued to occupy lands outside the original boundaries of their 1868 reservation, and the federal government expanded the area allotted to the Navajos fourteen times between 1868 and 1934. This expansion of Navajo lands decreased the Hopi land base.

The federal government built a school at Keams Canyon in 1887 and the late-nineteenth century saw increasing pressure on the Hopi to let the federal government educate their children. Some parents and thirty Hopi religious leaders were captured and imprisoned at Alcatraz for keeping their children at home. They did not accept the U.S. mandate to send their children to government schools—they wanted to educate Hopi children themselves in order to keep the Hopi way of life vibrant.

In the early-twentieth century, a disagreement among the Hopi at Oraibi about how to deal with the federal government, its agents, and particularly the educational system it wanted to impose on Hopi children led some of the Hopi families to leave Oraibi and form the new village of Hotevilla (see Old Oraibi below). These families acted under the leadership of Yukioma, the first to have been taken to Alcatraz.

More government day schools were built, and military force was used by the government to make the children of more traditional families attend the schools.

Despite their exemption from military service because of their pacifist religious beliefs, many young Hopi men joined the armed services because they saw it as an opportunity to learn a vocation. During World War I, one tenth of the Hopi Tribe served in the army, but it was not until 1924 that Congress declared Hopis to be citizens of the United States, and not until mid-century that they were allowed to vote in the State of Arizona.

In 1935, the U.S. government mandated a tribal government on Hopi to act as one body for the Hopi villages, which prior to this time had been largely autonomous. The government needed a body that it could authorize to sign leases for the mining of valuable minerals on Hopi lands (see the chapter on the Colorado Plateau), and was not worried that only a minority of Hopis voted to accept the new Tribal Council. Disagreement as to what legitimate authority the Tribal Council wields on Hopi continues to this day.

The Council disbanded in 1940 and was reestablished in 1951 in part because the federal government told the Hopi that they must do so in order to file a claim for compensation with the Indian Land Claims Commission. Attorney John Boyden represented the Hopi Tribe in this matter as well as in the negotiations for mining leases. Traditional leaders from Hotevilla and Songoopavi protested against filing a claim because they thought, rightly, that the commission was another strategy by whites to take Hopi land. They wrote letters to Presidents Truman and Eisenhower stating their views, and the Village of Shungopavi filed its own claim to get back its land from the federal government. It was at this point that the attorney for the tribe, who was under pressure from the Bureau of Indian Affairs to get the Hopi claim filed, explained that it was not within the power of the Land Claims Commission to give back land to any Native American tribe. All the commission could do was to financially compensate tribes for land that had been taken. The government would thereby, in its own view, have clear title to that land.

The stock reduction program of the forties divided the Navajo and Hopi Reservations into grazing districts. This served to restrict the Hopi Reservation to the 630,000 acres known as District Six because this was the only district administered by the Hopi Agency; the other grazing districts were administered by Navajo agencies. By 1953, most of the Hopi Reservation outside of District Six was occupied by Navajos. The Hopi faced the possibility of losing a total of almost two million acres of their 1882 reservation to the much larger Navajo Tribe.

In 1958, the attorney for the Hopi Tribal Council helped craft a bill to clarify the language in the 1882 executive order that established a reservation for the "Moqui and other such Indians as the Secretary of the Interior saw fit to settle thereon." The bill was passed and Congress thereby authorized the creation of a three-judge panel to determine who those "other such Indians" were and what interest they had in the land set aside by the executive order. John Boyden argued on behalf of the Hopi that all of the 1882 reservation should belong to the Hopi Tribe, while attorneys for the Navajo Tribe argued that they were the other Indians referred to in the executive order. Why else had the government built roads and schools for the Navajos on that land?

In the 1960s, Hopi coal and water resources were leased to a mining company. The mining leases generate income that supports the Tribal Council, which determines how the money will be spent in the villages. The Navajos also signed leases for mining of coal on the part of Black Mesa they owned.

The dispute over land between the Navajo and Hopi continued and the Federal Court in 1962 ruled that because the Secretary of the Interior had not acted to remove Navajos from Hopi lands, the Navajo had acquired squatter rights to that land, which constituted nearly one half of the 1882 Hopi Reservation. Hopi and Navajo were to share this land, almost one million acres, which became known as the Joint Use Area.

By 1974, it became clear that the 1962 solution was not working, and Congress determined that the Joint Use Area would have to be partitioned—part would be given to the Navajo for their exclusive use and part to the Hopi. Hopis living on land allotted to the Navajo would have to move, as would Navajos living on land assigned to the Hopi. As part of the 1974 settlement, the Navajo were allotted a quarter million acres to relocate those who would have to move. In 1980, Congress allotted an additional 150,000 acres for Navajo relocatees.

The twenty-six Hopi families living on Navajo land moved, and many Navajo families moved off the Hopi land. However, further court cases ensued when the Navajos challenged the settlement act on religious grounds. Proposed settlements, which would have had the Hopi agree to cede land in exchange for monetary payment were rejected by the Hopi, who had already lost half of their 1882 reservation. After many proposals and counter-proposals, the Hopi Tribal Council offered an Accommodation Agreement to the Navajo families who remained on Hopi land and refused to move.

Under the Accommodation Agreement, Navajo families who signed the agreement were given a 75-year lease, which allows them to remain on Hopi land under the jurisdiction of the Hopi Tribe. Most of the Navajo families remaining on the Hopi Partitioned Land either signed the agreement or moved prior to the February 1, 2000 deadline. The Hopi received reparations from the federal government, part of which they used to purchase ranches near the reservation as a way of regaining some of their Tutsqua, or ancient homeland.

The dispute over tribal land in Northern Arizona has long been of concern to the United Nations. In 1998, a Special Rapporteur from the UN visited the Hopi Partitioned Lands to talk to the Navajos who refused to move or sign the Accommodation Agreement. A Hopi delegation who wanted to talk to the UN representative was refused access to him by some of the "supporters" of the Navajos. In the summer of 2000, a Hopi delegation went to the United Nations to present their perspective and concerns.

Hopi Ceremonies and Tribal Government

Hopis observe a complex ceremonial calendar divided into two parts: a secular year and a religious year. The secular calendar begins at the end of the purification rituals commonly known as the Bean Dance and usually continues through the end of September. Religious activities generally take place from November through the end of December. The calendar has never been accurately understood or described by non-Hopis.

Many religious activities are carried out in the kivas, ceremonial rooms accessed by a ladder leading down into the kiva from its roof. Ancient kivas can be seen at Chaco Canyon, but kivas in the villages are not open to the public. Each village has its own schedule of religious ceremonies. Ceremonial dances are held in the village's plaza. These are usually closed to outsiders, but tourists may enjoy the Butterfly or social dances held in the late summer and early fall. Usually the date for a particular dance is announced only a few weeks or days before the event.

Katsinas, of which there are perhaps 400 (though some of these no longer dance in the village ceremonies), are supernatural beings. They are represented by masked dancers when they live in the villages between Powamu and Home Dance. They are also depicted by wood carvings that are available for visitors to purchase.

Cradle dolls are the first Katsina carvings given to baby girls. PHOTO: TANYA LEE

The Hopi Tribe is governed by an elected chairman, vice chairman, and tribal council.

The listings below go from east to west, which makes sense if you leave the South Rim of the Grand Canyon and take AZ Highway 64 to Cameron, then onto Tuba City. From there you travel north to Kayenta and Monument Valley, and then south to Canyon de Chelly and the Hopi Reservation. However, you can also take AZ Highway 264 out of Tuba City and go across the Hopi Reservation from west to east, then head for Canyon de Chelly and do the loop back to Tuba City. In that case, read this section starting at the end.

Keams Canyon

Keams Canyon is not a Hopi village, but rather a U.S. government administrative center situated at the mouth of the canyon named after Thomas Keams, who established a trading post there in 1875. The Public Health Service Hospital is here; call (520) 738-2211. Doctors, nurses, and medical technicians are available all day every day.

Keams Canyon Shopping Center
US Hwy. 264

Located in Keams Canyon on the north side of the road, this shopping center includes a café and gallery, a convenience store, a grocery store, a Laundromat, a garage, and a 76 gas station. The motel at Keams Canyon is closed.

The garage does repairs on all domestic and some foreign cars and is open five days a week, though emergency towing and wrecker service is available 24 hours a day 7 days a week. You can reach them by calling (520) 738-5555 during regular business hours. The 24-hour tow service can be reached at (520) 738-2298, or try Nate Navasie's answering machine at (520) 738-5445. He says to ignore the outgoing message, which says he's never there, and leave a message telling him what you need. The cell phone number for one of the two truck drivers is (520) 674-6944, though cell phone service on Hopi is sporadic at best. The Hopi Police department is also very helpful in case of car emergencies. Their number is (520) 738-2233. The garage takes credit cards, traveler's checks, and cashiers checks, but no personal checks. The guys at the station said to be sure to mention that they are "friendly, good-looking, and single."

First and Second Mesas

First Mesa

First Mesa is 15 miles west of Keams Canyon on U.S. Highway 264. The three villages of Walpi, Sichomovi, and Tewa on top of the mesa are governed by a traditional form of Hopi government of which the Kikmongwi is the head. Leaders of various religious societies help him to govern the villages. If you need more information on First Mesa villages, contact the Community Development Office at (520) 737-2670.

Polacca

This settlement at the base of First Mesa stretches for about a mile along the highway. If you are planning to visit the top of the mesa and have a large vehicle, such as an RV, plan to park in Polacca. The Polacca M is a convenience store with phones, a Bank of America ATM, but no restrooms.

Tewa

Tewa is on top of First Mesa and can be accessed by passenger vehicle along a one-mile, steep paved road; larger vehicles should park in Polacca. The village was settled by refugees from a pueblo town on the Rio Grande in the early 1700s. The refugees were fleeing from the Spanish after unsuccessful revolt. Hopi leaders allowed them to stay on First Mesa in exchange for protecting the path to the mesa top. The Tewa have their own language and ceremonies.

Sichomovi

Sichomovi was built in the mid 1600s by the people of Walpi. It is located in the middle of the mesa top between Tewa and Walpi.

Walpi

First Mesa narrows to 15 feet then widens at the village of Walpi, founded in about 900 C.E. When Pedro de Tovar visited Walpi in 1540, as many as two thousand Hopis may have lived there.

Walking tours of the villages atop First Mesa begin at Punsi Hall Visitors Center in Sichomovi or at the tourist building at the Walpi parking lot. Tours, which take place during daytime hours every day, are led by a Hopi guide who will share information on the history, life, and traditions of the Hopi people. There is a nominal fee, and it is a good idea to call in advance for current information. The First Mesa Consolidated Villages Tourism Program can be reached at (520) 737-2262. This is the only Hopi village that offers guided tours.

Visitor guidelines, which apply not only to First Mesa villages but to all Hopi

Insiders' Tip

From Second Mesa, you can take a shortcut to Canyon de Chelly. Turn north off AZ Hwy. 264 beside the Cultural Center and head for the Pinon Trading Post, then go 42 miles east. However, 14 miles of the road is not paved, so you should not attempt this route in wet weather.

land, forbid photography, sketching, painting, videotaping, or tape recording. Visitors must also be careful not to approach shrines, prayer feathers, or kivas. Unescorted touring of First Mesa is not allowed, and visitors are asked to stay on the trails the guide will show you.

Artists may be selling their Katsina carvings and polychrome pottery on First Mesa. Signs around the villages indicate which houses to approach if you're looking for art to buy. Here you may be able to speak with the artist directly about the piece you wish to purchase. It is always fascinating to ask the artist to explain the meaning of the symbolic images on a piece of carving, pottery, or jewelry. When you buy directly from the artist, prices are sometimes negotiable.

Second Mesa

AZ Highways 264 and 87 meet at the foot of Second Mesa, 10 miles west of First Mesa. There is a post office at the intersection on the south side of AZ Highway 264. Second Mesa artists are renowned for their Katsina carvings, silver overlay jewelry, and coiled baskets.

Price Code

Restaurants		Accommodations	
$	less than $20	$	$40-$60
$$	$21-$35	$$	$61-$75
$$$	$36-$60	$$$	$76-100
$$$$	$61+	$$$$	$101-125
		$$$$$	$125+

Alph Secakuku
AZ Hwy. 264
P.O. Box 697, Second Mesa, AZ 86043
(520) 737–2222, fax (520) 737–2223
www.hopifinearts.com;
hopiarts@infomagic.com

Set back on the south side of the road (just east of LKD's Diner), Hopi Fine Arts carries the work of "as many local artists as possible." The owner works directly with the artists, and custom orders are welcome. A special treat is watching a silversmith while he creates some of the fine silver overlay pieces that are for sale. He is on the premises every day. Here you will also find Katsina carvings, pottery, baskets, and plaques (flat, plate-size basketry). An item carried here that we have never before seen is a series of three small connected pots. The form is based on items found by the potter, a descendent of Nampeyo, among her grandfather's possessions. The gallery also carries a small selection of Navajo, Santa Domingo, and Zuni jewelry. Open seven days a week including holidays, the shop accepts credit cards and personal checks.

LKD's Diner $
AZ Hwy. 264,
P.O. Box 693, Second Mesa, AZ 86043
(520) 737–2717

For a down-to-earth eating experience in a very casual setting, try this diner, where you are sure to see more locals than tourists. Located between Hopi Fine Arts and the post office on the south side of the road, LKD's Diner is open Monday through Saturday for lunch and dinner. The diner serves burgers, sandwiches, chili beans with fry bread, chicken nuggets, and Hopi tacos and tostadas. There is a restroom (for customers only) and a phone, as well as the post office next door. The diner accepts only cash. Be sure while you're here to visit Hopi Fine Arts, just east of the diner.

Hopi Pottery

Hopi pottery has a long and venerable history, dating back at least to the black-on-white pots produced by the Pueblo peoples. After the arrival of the Spanish, Hopi pottery declined in quality and the art was nearly lost. In the late 1800s, Nampeyo, a woman from the village of Tewa on First Mesa, revived pottery-making by copying the techniques, colors, and designs she found on ancient pots.

Today Hopi pottery is made by quarrying clay from traditional sources and preparing it to the proper consistency by kneading. The potter shapes the base of the vessel by hand and then builds up the form by adding coils of clay around the base and pinching them in place.

Once the bowl or other form is shaped, the potter scrapes it with a gourd rind to get rid of the coil and pinch marks. Then the piece is dried in the sun. When the pot is "leather hard," the potter scrapes the surface again, this time with a pottery sherd or something similar to make sure the walls are thin enough and that all of the walls have the same thickness. Then it is hand-polished with a small stone. The potter decorates the piece using natural slips and other natural paints applied with a strip of yucca pine or a commercial paintbrush.

Often Hopi pots are decorated in black and red, each color having a brownish tint. The black is made by crushing hematite (a black mineral) and mixing it with the juice of a plant. The red is made from limonite clay, to which a small amount of water is added after the clay has been crushed into dust-size pieces. When the design is dry, the pottery is dried around a fire of sheep dung and juniper wood. When the pots (several are fired together) are ready, a grate is put over the fire and topped with pieces of broken pottery. On this pile, the pots are placed upside down. Sherds of broken pottery are placed over the pots, and these pottery pieces are topped with more sheep or goat dung. The whole pile bursts into flame and the pots are fired until the ashes of the fire are nearly cool. Hopi pots are fired in an oxidizing atmosphere, and the temperature of the kiln is usually less than 850 degrees Celsius.

Hopi pottery was traditionally made by women, with the art passed down from mother or grandmother to child, but now some men also make pottery. Most often the pot will be smooth and beige to red in color with rust red and dark brown painted designs, though recently pottery with etched designed and textured surfaces is being made, and some pots may not be painted. You may also encounter decorated white Hopi pots.

Once you have seen some examples of Hopi pottery, you will easily be able to distinguish it from pottery made by other pueblo tribes. The quality of a piece is evaluated by the symmetry and beauty of its form, the consistent thickness of its walls, and the detail, appropriateness, and application of its decoration. Usually potters decorate the pot without any preliminary drawing on the item, and each one is a unique work of art. Executing a fine design without error (for errors cannot be corrected) is a task requiring consummate skill and many years of practice.

Bowls like this one show the artistry of contemporary Hopi pottery. PHOTO: TANYA LEE

Honani Crafts Gallery
AZ Hwy. 264
P.O. Box 221, Second Mesa, AZ 86043
(520) 737–2238

Located on the north side of AZ Highway 264, Honani Crafts Gallery's hallmark item is their spectacular gold on silver jewelry. Owned by King Honanie, this small gallery welcomes custom orders for items such as wedding rings. Also ask to see the fine inlay jewelry and the gold on silver rings with semi-precious stones such as sapphire, green turquoise, and amethyst. The acrylic paintings by artist Bill Dixon are one-of-a-kind. Among the other artists whose work you will find here are Willis Humeyestewa, Phil Sekaquaptewa, Art Honanie, Terrance Lomayestewa, and Hale Kaye. The gallery is open year-round, seven days a week, including holidays. Credit cards, personal checks, and travelers checks are good here.

Phil & Hil's Emporium $
In Songoopavi Village, off AZ Hwy. 264
P. O. Box 290, Second Mesa, AZ 86043
(520) 734–9278; fax (520) 734–9278

This place is off the beaten track and known only to locals. Take the road into Shungopavi. Where the paved road ends and the village really begins, the gravel road forks. In the fork you'll see a new cinderblock building with no windows. Go around to the other side to find the entrance to this tiny restaurant/convenience store which does a booming business in Hopi tacos and tostadas, hot wings, fries, burgers, pizza, nachos, snowcones, snacks, and the best ice cream on Hopi. They do a great take-out business, but there is also a small sit-down counter and a couple of booths if you'd rather eat there. Open for lunch through a late dinner hour, the restaurant, which began as a candy stand and is now putting up a new building, is open seven days a week, including holidays. Personal checks are accepted, but credit cards are not. Shungopavi was one of the first villages in the area. For more information about the village, contact the Community Development Office at (520) 734–2262.

Other Second Mesa villages are Sipaulovi and Mishongnovi. The Sipaulovi Community Development Office's number is (520) 734–2570. To reach the Mishongnovi Community Development Office call (520) 737–2520. You can reach these villages by driving a short paved road which climbs steeply from the north side of AZ Highway 264, one-half mile west of intersection with AZ Highway 87 or by the paved road about 0.25 mile east of the Cultural Center. Mishongnovi is the village to the east. Its people are charged with protection of the Corn Rock Shrine.

Tsakurshovi
AZ Hwy. 264
PO Box 234, Second Mesa, AZ 86043
(520) 734–2478

One-and-a-half miles east of the Cultural Center, on the north side of AZ Highway 264, Tsakurshovi is the home of the "Don't Worry. Be Hopi." T-shirt. This tiny shop is crammed with interesting merchandize and staffed by friendly and helpful people who will not only give you directions to where you're going next but will suggest places to go and books to read. (They carry many of the books listed in our Media chapter.) Half the shop is devoted to art for visitors to purchase, including a huge selection of traditional style Katsina carvings, jewelry, and many Second and Third Mesa-style baskets. One of the people minding the store recently was an old-style Katsina carver, Wallace Hyeoma, whose work was for sale in the shop (and who is included in *Traditional Katsina Carvers* listed in the Media section). Other carvers whose work is sold here include Bert Tenakhongya, Philbert Honanie, Manuel Chavarria, Clark Tenakhongya. You're very likely to meet Hopis here because the other half of the store sells ceremonial items for dances such as turtle shells, deer hooves, furs, skins, shell bandoliers, gourds for making rattles,

Hopi textiles, and moccasins, as well as cottonwood root for Katsina carvings and mineral pigments. It's "the place where all the Hopis shop," according to the staff. You'll also find Plains Indian beadwork, a large selection of Zuni fetishes, and Navajo and Santa Domingo pottery— "a little of everyone's work." Personal, traveler's, and cashier's checks are accepted, but not credit cards. The shop is open seven days a week, except for Thanksgiving and Christmas.

Iskasokpu
On the north side of AZ Hwy. 264
P.O. Box 329, Second Mesa, AZ 86043
(520) 734–9353/9361; fax (520) 734–9370
iskasokpu@earthlink.net

Featuring Hopi silver overlay and gold on silver jewelry, Navajo and Zuni jewelry, baskets, Hopi-Tewa pots, and Katsina carvings, this shop also sells silver jewelry-making supplies. The word iskasokpu means "the spring where the coyote burped." The story of the spring's name, according to a handout at the shop is this: A coyote was traveling toward Shungopavi when he came to a spring on the south side of the village. There he found a turtle, which he decided to eat, but the turtle retreated back into its shell every time the coyote tried to take a bite. He gave up and went to the spring for a drink. He saw something very scary in the spring, so he hightailed it out of there. He came to another spring, Gostutbalvi, but the scary thing was there too. Finally he reached the spring just below the shop's location at the edge of the mesa. This time he was so thirsty that he drank from the spring despite the scary thing. He drank a lot of water and let out a huge burp. The coyote did not know that when he had tried to eat the turtle, he had hurt his mouth. The scary thing he kept seeing in the water was only his own reflection. This is how the spring (and later the shop) got its name.

Hopi Silver Art & Crafts
South side of AZ Hwy. 264
P.O. Box 726, Second Mesa, AZ 86043
(520) 734–6695

This shop, owned by Weaver and Alberta Selina, has its own silverworkers who are there on weekdays. Visitors are invited to watch them as they work. The shop specializes in Hopi silver overlay and gold over silver, but also carries pottery, Katsina carvings, and some Navajo and Zuni jewelry. The owner sells T-shirts he designed himself. The hours vary, but usually the shop is open seven days a week. Credit cards are welcome.

Hopi Cultural Center Restaurant and Inn
P.O. Box 67, AZ Highway 264,
Second Mesa, AZ 86043
(520) 734–2401, fax (520) 734–6651
www.hopionline.com;
hopiculturalcenter@hotmail.com

Being at the "Center of the Universe," as the Cultural Center claims to be, must be something like being in the eye of a hurricane because this pueblo-style motel is tranquil and comfortable, not to mention the most convenient for visiting all of the Hopi villages and arts and crafts stores. The thirty-three non-smoking rooms ($$$) have coffeemakers, TVs, and air conditioners. A $5 charge applies for each of more than two adults in a room, and pets require a $50 deposit. Major credit cards are accepted. Reservations are mandatory in the summer and recommended the rest of the year. Some rooms are wheelchair accessible. The front desk has a selection of T-shirts and books for sale.

Whether you're staying at the motel or just visiting Hopi for the day, you shouldn't

Insiders' Tip
AZ Highway 264 is paved, but the driveways and parking lots of the shops and galleries are gravel. The Cultural Center Restaurant and Inn on Second Mesa seem to be the only wheelchair accessible stops on Hopi. It is also the only motel.

miss the restaurant ($) at the Cultural Center. The white stucco, open-beamed interior is furnished with hand-carved chairs, booths, and valances showing traditional Hopi designs, and the establishment is staffed entirely by Hopis. The restaurant serves both American and Hopi dishes. For breakfast, try the sakwaviqaviki (blue corn cakes), piki (a thin round piece of corn bread rolled into a cylinder), or blue corn fry bread. For lunch or dinner, the tsili'öngava (pinto beans and ground beef in a red chili sauce with fry bread) or the nöqkwivi (traditional Hopi stew with hominy, lamb, red chilis, and fry bread) are good choices. Or try the Hopi taco, which the friendly staff admits with a smile, is pretty much the same as a Navajo taco.

If you don't feel like trying something new, you can order from a selection of burgers, salads, and sandwiches, or try one of the weekday specials. The casual restaurant is open year-round seven days a week and you'll probably see as many local people as tourists eating here. It is wheelchair accessible. Reservations are recommended for large groups. You need to be aware that while breakfast, lunch, and dinner are served here, the restaurant closes earlier in the evening than you might expect. Call to find out what the hours are at the time of year you will be visiting.

The Cultural Center also has a museum with a very well-stocked bookstore and T-shirt inventory. There is a nominal entrance fee for the museum (but not the museum shop).

Hopi Arts & Crafts Silvercraft Cooperative Guild
Just west of the Cultural Center on AZ Hwy. 264
P.O. Box 37, Second Mesa, AZ 86043
(520) 734–2463; fax (520) 734–6647

This gallery carries Hopi overlay jewelry and other authentic Hopi arts and crafts. At the guild, young silversmiths are trained at no charge by experienced Hopi silversmiths who donate their services, but there is nothing amateurish about the work offered for sale here—money clips, bolos, earrings, pendants, necklaces, and other items. You can also see displays about some of the semi-precious stones used in silverwork, including turquoise, coral, and lapis, as well as some jewelry-making supplies. In addition to selling work by its members, the guild offers its marketing services to artists in all of the Hopi villages.

Third Mesa

Kykotsmovi

Founded in the late 1800s near a spring at the base of Third Mesa, Kykotsmovi is now the Headquarters for the Hopi Tribe, P.O. Box 123, Kykotsmovi, AZ 86039; (520) 734–2441. The Office of Public Relations is one mile south of AZ Highway 264. Third Mesa artists are known for Katsina carvings, weaving, silver overlay jewelry, and wicker baskets. The number of the Community Development Office for Kykotsmovi is (520) 734–2474.

Gentle Rain Designs
South side of AZ Hwy. 264
P.O. Box 35, Kykotsmovi, AZ 86039
(520) 734–9535; fax (520) 734–9539
hopifound@aol.com

Located approximately one-half mile before Kykotsmovi on the south side of AZ Highway 264, this is a unique shop, first because it supports the non-profit Hopi Foundation, and second because it offers locally made Native-designed and produced clothing and accessories. Most of the jackets and other items are made of fleece, which is produced from recycled plastic bottles. The jackets come in several styles and lengths with colorful Southwest-style designs. Fleece is also used to make hats, pillows, and purses. In addition, the shop carries a selection of Hopi jewelry, carving, and pottery. The cradle dolls are particularly well-executed with detailed and carefully carved designs. Cradle dolls are flat Katsina carvings about six inches tall. They are the first Katsina carving to be given to little girls, and I couldn't resist buying one for each of my granddaughters. One of the Hopi Foundation's most ambitious projects has been the establishment of a Hopi radio station, which broadcasts Native American and other news all across the reservation, mostly in the Hopi language. The station not only provides a much-needed service to elders who speak only Hopi, but also helps youngsters learn the language. The project has been in the works for over ten years. Among other projects is the implementation of an educational scholarship fund, the retrieval and return of sacred objects to Hopi villages, the restoration of an ancient clan house, the establishment of a solar electric enterprise to bring electricity to rural homes, the publication of a children's book by local children, and the revival of the traditional art of rock quarrying. Credit cards are accepted at the shop, which is open seven days a week, except on major holidays.

Native-designed and produced jackets are sold at Gentle Rain Designs for the benefit of the Hopi Foundation. PHOTO: TANYA LEE

Kykotsmovi Village Store
In the center of the village, between Indian Route 2 and AZ Hwy. 264
P.O. Box 655, Kykotsmovi, AZ 86039
(520) 734–2456

You may not think you need to know about a village store, but you do. Here you can get groceries, fresh meat, and produce, baby supplies such as formula and diapers, gasoline, basic automotive supplies, and money orders. You can also send (or receive) money via Western Union, use the restroom, and make a phone call. Major credit cards are accepted. The store is open every day except holidays, which is helpful, because the next closest places for such items are fifty miles in either direction.

Calnimptewa's Galleria
South side of AZ Hwy. 264,
P.O. Box 37, Kykotsmovi, AZ 86039
(520) 734–2406

Located about four miles west of the Kykotsmovi turnoff on the south side of the highway, this gallery is locally owned and is a good place to get information on Cecil Calnimptewa, though you will not find his work here as most of his pieces are spoken for before he even carves them. But you will find a spacious, artful display of silver overlay jewelry, Katsina carvings, baskets, pottery, sash belts, and paintings all produced by local artists. The collection also includes some Navajo silver and turquoise jewelry, Navajo rugs, and Zuni jewelry. MasterCard and Visa are accepted, and the shop is open every day in the summer, but closed Sundays and open shorter hours on Saturdays in the winter.

Old Oraibi

Old Oraibi was for a long time the largest and most important Hopi village, at least according to outsiders. People have lived at Old Oraibi since at least 1150 C.E., making it the oldest continuously inhabited settlement in North America.

In 1906, "Hostiles" (that is, hostile to the federal government) left this village

Hopi Overlay Silver

The Hopi learned silversmithing from their neighbors, the Zuni and the Navajo, about a hundred years ago. At first, they made jewelry primarily for use by other Hopis, and their work was similar to that of their teachers. Therefore, much pre-1940 Hopi silver jewelry was (and is) identified as Navajo.

The silver for early jewelry was derived from coins, which were melted down, formed into ingots, and then hammered into sheets, or the molten silver was cast in molds. Some pieces incorporated turquoise inlay or turquoise stones in settings.

Mary Russell Ferrell Colton, who, with her husband, founded the Museum of Northern Arizona, was a major influence in the development of Native American arts and crafts throughout the region. In 1939 she wrote a letter to some twenty Hopi silversmiths making some very important points. The first was that even as early as the 1930s, the artwork of the Native peoples of the Southwest was being imitated and machine made by non-Indians. Since buyers were not sufficiently sophisticated to be able to tell the difference between genuine and imitation work, this served to keep the prices of the authentic pieces low. She suggested that Hopi silversmiths have their work stamped by the government's arts and crafts board to guarantee its authenticity. Her second point was that Hopi silver was difficult to distinguish from other Indian silver, and Hopis should develop their own distinctive style. And her third point was that the museum would help Hopis design a few pieces to show what she meant by making the work different from that of other tribes.

However, Hopi silversmithing was affected greatly by World War II as many Hopi men served in the armed forces. Since others had to do their work in the villages, few people had time to pursue silver work. After the war, silversmithing classes for veterans were set up under the G.I. Bill and many Hopis took the classes. It was in the late forties and early fifties that the style known as Hopi overlay silver jewelry developed. This is the highly sophisticated, superbly designed work that the tourist will see in the shops on Hopi and in galleries around the world.

The Hopi artist begins creating an overlay piece by tracing one of his designs onto a sheet of silver from a template. Then small holes are punched into the parts to be cut out and a tiny saw blade is inserted. The design is very carefully cut out, then the piece of silver with the cut-out design is soldered onto a piece of solid silver. After the pieces are joined and cooled, the artist uses chisels to make a texture in the bottom piece of silver where it shows through the cut-out design. The bottom piece of silver is trimmed into the shape necessary to make a belt buckle, pendant, concho belt, or bracelet and the piece is hammered into its final shape. The finding is soldered on and the whole piece is blanched in an acid to get rid of any discolorations from heating. Liver of sulfur is put on the interior of the design to oxidize the silver and create the black interior of the cut-outs. Finally, the piece is cleaned and polished.

Many Hopi artists now hallmark their jewelry with a stamp on the back with the silversmith's personal mark, which is often related to the artist's clan. Dictionaries of hallmarks are available for the collector. But the problem of imitations still remains. Buyers should examine many pieces of work to develop their ability to discern authentic work from fake, and they should buy only from reputable shops and galleries, or directly from the artist.

shop and walk through the village to avoid stirring up dust driving your vehicle. The shop has a selection of silver overlay jewelry, Katsina carvings, and Dawa wall plaques, as well as a display of some large storage pots from the 1800s. The shop is open every day, so you can stop here to get information on what is happening in the village. The mailing address of the shop is P.O. Drawer 193, Kykotsmovi, AZ 86039.

Picnic areas are located on the north side of AZ Hwy. 264 just east of Oraibi and just east of Kykotsmovi on Oraibi Wash.

Monongya Gallery
South side of AZ Hwy. 264
P.O. Box 287, Old Oraibi, AZ 86039
(520) 734–2344/2544, fax (520) 734–2388

Located on the south side of AZ Hwy. 264 between Kykotsmovi and Old Oraibi, this is probably the largest gallery on Hopi, so you won't want to miss it. The main room houses a large selection of Hopi arts— silver overlay and gold on silver jewelry, Katsina carvings, decorated coiled pottery, sash belt weavings, plaques, and painted gourd rattles. The room to the right is reserved for Navajo, Zuni, and Acoma pottery, Navajo and Zuni jewelry, Navajo sandpaintings, Zuni fetishes, and paintings. All of the souvenir items— T-shirts and sweatshirts, Pendleton blankets, jackets, books, mugs, and other items with Hopi and Southwestern designs—are in the room to the left. The gallery is open seven days a week except major holidays. Credit cards are accepted.

after losing a pushing contest with the "Friendlies." The "Hostiles" established the village of Hotevilla, four miles to the west.

The issue was forcible education of Hopi children by the U.S. government. An Old Oraibi leader, Lololoma, had visited Washington D.C. and decided that such an education would benefit the children and the Hopis in general. A more conservative group, headed by Lomahongyoma, strongly disagreed. Eventually a group of parents, including Lomahongyoma, were imprisoned at Alcatraz by federal authorities for refusing to send their children to the government school in Keams Canyon. Fifty-three men served ninety days in jail, while their children were forcibly removed to the boarding school.

About 150 of the roughly 450 people who left Old Oraibi went back to the village in 1907, but then left in 1909 to form the village of Bacavi.

A ruin near Old Oraibi is the remains of a church built in 1901 by Mennonite missionary H.R. Voth, who was in Oraibi from 1893 to 1902. He became privy to, and divulged, many Hopi religious secrets. Lightning has struck the church twice, the first time in 1942. No one is allowed to visit the site.

Old Oraibi is two miles west of Kykotsmovi. You are requested to park next to Hamana So-o's Arts and Crafts

Hotevilla

Hotevilla, founded in 1906 under the leadership of Yokioma after the split from Old Oraibi, is a traditional village known as an agricultural center and has been called the "Peach Capital of the World." You will notice the terraced gardens along the mesa slopes. It is also the only village that is totally self-sufficient in terms of energy production, relying on high-tech solar power. The village is west of Old Oraibi on AZ Highway 264. Check at the Cultural Center on Second Mesa to find out about

Monongya Gallery is one of many on Hopi where you will find high-quality authentic art.

late summer and early fall Butterfly and other social dances that you might attend. Contact the Hotevilla Community Development Office at (520) 734–2420.

Bacavi

The founders of Bacavi were also on the losing side of the 1906 split. Some 150 people returned to Old Oraibi after the split, but the situation was untenable, so in 1909 they moved to Bacavi Spring on the opposite side of highway from Hotevilla. Brian Honyouti—the contemporary leader in Hopi Katsina carving, whose work is in collections around the world—lives in Bacavi. His brother Ronald is a well-known carver as well, and his brother Rick creates custom-designed carved furniture with Hopi motifs. For more information, contact the Community Development Office at (520) 734–2404.

Moenkopi

The two villages, Upper Moenkopi and Lower Moenkopi, are two miles east of Tuba City on AZ Highway 264. Prehistoric pueblo villages sited here date back before 1300 C.E., when they were abandoned. This village was founded by Mormons in the 1870s. The Mormons constructed woolen mill in 1879, but the Hopis refused to work there.

The name "Moenkopi" means "The Place of the Running Water," referring to the numerous springs that created the successful farming community that flourished here until quite recently. Residents have been saying for years that the Peabody Coal Company's removal of water from the Navajo Aquifer to slurry coal to a Laughlin, Nevada power plant is causing the seeps and springs to dry up. People in Moencopi, who once drank water from the pristine aquifer underlying the Hopi and the western Navajo Reservations, now are forced to buy bottled water.

The Black Mesa Trust has recently been organized to investigate Black Mesa coal and water operations. The trust argues that the 1983 water model developed by the U.S. Geological Survey (USGS) to study the Navajo Aquifer and to assess how domestic and Peabody pumping affect the aquifer may have been misapplied and that therefore conclusions drawn from the model are probably incorrect. According to a 1997 report, the coal company is being allowed to pump 4,000 acre feet of water from an aquifer that recharges at a rate of only 2,500 to 3,500 acre feet per year.

The group also argues that the U.S. government's Office of Surface Mining, which oversees operations at the Peabody Coal Company's mines on Black Mesa, failed to take into account traditional wisdom (as opposed to Western science) to evaluate the effects of pumping water from the 35,000-year-old aquifer.

An October 2000 report by the Natural Resources Defense Council, "Drawdown: Groundwater Mining on Black Mesa" affirms that the Interior Department's Office of Surface Mining Reclamation and Enforcement's own criteria for determining if material damage to the aquifer has occurred have been exceeded. The report is available at www.nrdc.org. For more information about Black Mesa Trust, call (520) 734–9255 or (480) 421–2377. For more information about Moenkopi, contact the Community Development Office at (520) 283–8051.

Tours

Left-Handed Hunter Tour Co.
P.O. Box 434, Second Mesa, AZ 86043
(520) 734–2567
lhhunter58@hotmail.com

Left-Handed Hunter Tour Co. is Hopi-owned and -operated. Gary Tso, a Hopi/Navajo from Second Mesa, will guide you through ancient villages, introduce you to traditional and contemporary artists, and take you to a spectacular site where you will see more than 15,000 petroglyphs, all the while sharing Hopi history and culture with you. Tso lives on Hopiland, and he is a traditional Katsina carver and experienced interpreter of the Hopi culture. Lunch, transportation, and entry fees are part of this all-inclusive package of "private cultural and archaeological tours deep into Hopiland."

Williams

In 1880 the rough-and-ready railroad construction town of Williams boasted a population of 500 people. Today more than a million visitors a year stop in this small town (population 3,000) on their way to the Grand Canyon, only 65 miles to the north. Williams is a town that seems never to have left the era when Route 66 was the road to adventure. You'll find quaint, restored shop fronts, a 50s soda fountain, and a B&B that was once a bordello, to name just a few of the attractions here. A short drive from town takes you to high-country lakes, oak and aspen forests, designated wilderness areas, and cliff dwellings such as those at Walnut Canyon.

The area south of the Grand Canyon has been populated for more than 7,000 years. Nomadic hunters and gathers lived here from 9,000 to 1,500 B.C.E., although little evidence of their sojourn through this area has been found. The period from about 800 to 1150 C.E. is well documented by archaeologists. These were agricultural people who made pottery and lived in pit houses. The Williams area was inhabited mostly by the people of the Cohonina culture and the Anasazi, or Pueblo people, who arrived about 700 C.E. and left about 500 years later. The Hopi people, who now live on three mesas to the northeast of Williams, are the descendents of the Pueblo people.

A little later, about 1350 C.E., other groups arrived in the region, including the Havasupai, the Hualapai, and the Yavapai. A hundred or so years after that, the Navajo arrived from the east.

Spaniards explored the area beginning around 1540, but not until the United States won the Southwest from Mexico in 1848 did non-Indian people begin to explore and settle the area in large numbers. In the 1850s, American explorers followed the same trade routes of the ancient peoples that the Spanish had found three centuries earlier.

In the late 1850s, Lieutenant Edward Fitzgerald Beale's expeditionary Camel Corps built the Beale Wagon Trail, one of the most important routes for immigrants from the East to California. He too followed the trails first blazed as trade routes by the original inhabitants of this land. The Beale Road was more or less the route followed by the 1882 transcontinental Atlantic and Pacific Railroad and later by the Mother Road, Route 66. Today, you can hike or horseback ride along part of the original road, which runs parallel to and north of Interstate 40.

The first non-Indian settlers in the Williams area were sheepherders, who arrived in the mid 1870s.

The Williams town site was established in 1879, and named for "Bill" Williams, an early-nineteenth century beaver trapper who worked the Rocky Mountains and the canyons of the Mogollon Rim of Northern Arizona. He was one of the few who survived the harsh life of the trapper. Some believe he was killed in 1849 in southern Colorado by Ute Indians at the ripe old age of sixty-two.

Insiders' Tip

William's elevation is 6,800 feet. The average summer temperatures are in the low 80s with cool evenings in the mid 50s. Winters are cold, especially at night, and occasional heavy winter snowstorms hit the area. The humidity is usually fairly low.

The transcontinental Atlantic and Pacific Railroad began construction in the Flagstaff-Williams area in about 1880. A construction camp was set up at the foot of Bill Williams Mountain to prepare the route and find the materials, especially timber, for building the railroad. At that time, tracklayers and graders were paid $2.25 a day, spikers and iron men $2.50 a day, and stonecutters $5.

Chinese were recruited from California to help lay the rail, and some stayed and opened businesses in Flagstaff and Williams. Williams was also reputedly home to several opium dens during this period. In the summer and fall of 1881, Wilson & Haskell built a sawmill near Bill Williams Mountain and produced ties for the railroad and other lumber products.

Other industries suited to this environment were cattle and sheep ranching. Before the railroad, sheep were raised only for wool. After the railroad arrived, mutton and lamb could be shipped to hungry cities in the East and West.

The railhead reached Williams Sept. 1, 1882 and like all the other towns that had at one time been at the end of the railroad as it moved from east to west, Williams was now a town of gambling halls, dance hall girls, and scoundrels. The local newspaper's pages were filled with stories of shootings, lynchings, vendettas, and other crimes. One story in 1882 reported that George Rich, Deputy Sheriff of Williams, resigned—he was suspected of being one of the men who had robbed a Williams liquor store.

The five Babbitt brothers arrived in the area in 1886, just a few weeks after a fire had leveled Flagstaff. They began cattle ranching, then opened a building materials business and general store, forming the Babbitt Brothers Trading Company in 1889. Soon they added other businesses and trading posts throughout Northern Arizona to their enterprise.

The first school in Williams was built in 1882, but in July 1884 fire leveled this town too. The town quickly recovered, and by the mid to late 1880s, grand balls where women wore the most fashionable dresses of the period were held in Williams and Flagstaff and reported in some detail in the newspaper.

In August of 1888, a major train accident sent the engine and five coaches of a train over a 100-foot embankment, causing several injuries.

During this period, Williams was part of Yavapai County. Then in 1888, the towns of Northern Arizona lobbied for the creation of a new county. Williams was briefly considered as the county seat. The bill to create the new county passed, but it was vetoed by the Arizona Territorial Governor. The issue was the tax revenues that would be lost by Yavapai County if it were split into two counties. The bill finally passed and was signed by the governor in 1891. Flagstaff was chosen as county seat by a vote of 429 to 97. (Some folks in Williams even voted for Flagstaff.)

In the 1890s copper was discovered north of Williams and a rail line to the mines, financed by Eastern capitalists, was built to transport the ore 45 miles from the Anita mines. The mining boom lasted less than a decade before it went bust in 1899. The Atchison Topeka & Santa Fe Railroad took over the railway built for the mines and extended it to the Grand Canyon. Prior to this, the only way for tourists to visit the Canyon was by taking a backbreaking eight-hour stagecoach ride. Now they could ride the train for $3.95. The first trainload of tourists reached the Canyon in the fall of 1901. Williams took that opportunity to declare itself "The Gateway to the Grand Canyon."

Tourism increased when Route 66 went through Williams beginning in 1926. This was a lifesaver for the town because by the mid-twentieth century, the forests were logged out and the livestock industry was becoming less profitable. Williams would need to rely more and more on tourism for its economy.

In 1968 the railroad to the Grand Canyon stopped operating. More people were now visiting the Grand Canyon by car and it was no longer profitable to run the train back

Route 66

Perhaps nothing has so captured the post-war American imagination as Route 66-fast cars, open spaces, and unlimited freedom and adventure.

Designated Route 66 in 1926, the 2,448 mile Mother Road linking Chicago and Los Angeles was completely paved in 1938. During the Depression, the road took desperate families from the Midwest's Dust Bowl to the golden opportunities of Southern California. This is the trip described in John Steinbeck's *Grapes of Wrath*.

After World War II, America started making cars again, which had been impossible during the war because the necessary raw materials were needed for building military vehicles. Americans wanted big cars, and gasoline was so cheap that gas stations offered incentives for people to buy it. Route 66 was made even more popular by the 1946 Bobby Troup song, "Get Your Kicks on Route 66," which has been recorded by artists as different as Perry Como and the Rolling Stones.

By the early 1950s, America's lust for adventure on the open road had outstripped the capacity of the two-lane byways through the small towns of the West and Southwest—Gallup and Holbrook, Winslow, Flagstaff, and Williams. Partly to make life easier for travelers, and partly to make sure that the country's road system was adequate for moving military personnel and equipment, America began a massive highway construction project, building interstates linking all major cities. The 1960s TV series *Route 66* depicted an era that was fast disappearing.

Most of the section of Route 66 that came through New Mexico and Northern Arizona was replaced by Interstate 40, a limited access road that bypassed the towns and cities that had relied on Route 66 to bring tourists—and tourist dollars. Williams, in 1984, became the last town on Route 66 to be bypassed by I-40.

Some sections of the old road, however, still exist. The main street through Williams, Bill Williams Avenue, and the main street through downtown Flagstaff, Santa Fe Avenue, have been redesignated as historic Route 66. Some other stretches of the road are still accessible.

Put some 50s tunes on the CD player and begin in downtown Williams. Go east on I-40 to the Pittman Valley exit. Turn left after the exit, go over the highway, and turn right onto Route 66. Follow the road to the forest boundary where the historic portion of 66 ends. From Flagstaff, access this portion of the road from the Bellemont exit off I-40. This paved and gravel surfaced stretch of road is about 22 miles one way and is accessible by passenger cars year-round. Round-trip driving time is one to one-and-a-half hours.

and forth from Williams. In 1984, the new Interstate 40 bypassed Williams. The section of Route 66 that went right through the middle of town no longer existed, and Williams began to decline as tourists simply drove on by.

The Grand Canyon Railway reopened in 1989 due to the courageous (and costly) efforts of Max and Thelma Biegert. Thanks to the refurbished Grand Canyon Railway and the efforts of the town's restauranteurs and shop owners, Williams is once again a main entry point for visitors to all of Northern Arizona—and to the Grand Canyon in particular. It will undoubtedly become even more important as a gateway to the Canyon when the new transportation system is completed at the Canyon in 2004 and cars are no longer allowed along the Canyon rim.

The mountain near the town is also named after Bill Williams. The mountain itself is a cluster of volcanic spires surrounded by twelve volcanic domes and some lava flows. The mountain is about four million years old. Since the volcanoes in this area erupted first in the west, Sitgreaves Mountain is about 2.5 million years old, and Kendrick Peak about 2 million. The eruptions of San Francisco Mountain occurred from about 2.8 million years to 200,000 years ago. San Francisco Mountain is often referred to as the San Francisco Peaks. Native American tribes in the area have their own names for these mountains, which are sacred to them. Sunset Crater, the most recent active volcano of the San Francisco Volcanic Field, began erupting in 1064 C.E. and continued to be active for about 200 years.

Restaurants

Max and Thelma's Restaurant $$
123 N. Grand Canyon Blvd.,
Williams, AZ 86046
(520) 635–8970, (800) THE–TRAIN
www.thetrain.com

Have breakfast, lunch, or dinner at Max and Thelma's, adjacent to the Williams Depot and Fray Marcos Hotel. Children will enjoy the model electric train of the Grand Canyon Railway that circles this railroad theme steakhouse/buffet. Tourists can begin the day with an all-you-can-eat breakfast buffet, including eggs, pancakes, omelets, and more. Lunchtime also features an all-you-can-eat buffet. For dinner, a barbecue buffet will fill you up, or try an entree from the menu. Favorites are steak, salmon, and ribs. A full-service bar may help you relax after a day of sightseeing. Open every day year-round except Christmas, Max and Thelma's is wheelchair accessible and there is plenty of parking. When you've finished your meal, visit the large gift shop for your souvenir purchases. Major credit cards accepted.

Twister's Soda Fountain $
417 E. Route 66, Williams, AZ 86046
(520) 635–0266
www.route66place.com

Were you a teenager in the fifties? Then this is an opportunity to revisit those days of poodle skirts and sock hops. The soda fountain features fifties treats—old-fashioned cream sodas, shakes and malts, root beer floats, and cherry cokes. Ice cream delectables are made with Dreyer's ice cream. You can also try the burgers, hot dogs, generous sandwiches, fries, and chili dogs while listening to hits from the days when Route 66 was the main road across the country. Open seven days a week, with a continental breakfast and light lunch and dinner menus, Twisters accepts credit cards but no out-of-town checks.

Pine Country Restaurant $
107 North Grand Canyon Blvd.,
Williams, AZ 86046
(520) 635–9718; fax (520) 635–4568

This is where the locals eat, mostly because of the gorgeous pies and home-style cooking. A family-style restaurant with checked tablecloths and bentwood chairs, as well as a few booths, the restaurant serves basic home cooking—burgers, sandwiches, and full chicken and steak dinners, some of which you might feel obliged to taste before moving on to the seven-inch-high pies with beautiful flaky crusts. You won't have trouble parking—a city parking lot is just across the street. Reservations are a good idea here because the place can fill to overflowing very quickly as people enjoy this comfortable, fun setting. Open seven days for breakfast, lunch, and dinner, the eatery accepts credit cards and personal checks and is wheelchair accessible.

Pancho McGillicuddy's Mexican Cantina $
141 Railroad Avenue, Williams, AZ 86046
(520) 635–4150

It's worth having a meal here just to experience the elegance of eating in this

Steve and Mary Fordell of Minnesota recommend the "Route 66" Beer Float at Twister's. PHOTO: TANYA LEE

107-year-old historic building with 15-foot-high arched windows and a painted tin ceiling. The walls of the restaurant area are decorated with charming hand-painted murals in Mexican designs. Everything here is good and the menu includes fajitas, enchiladas, chili relenos, and fish tacos. A city parking lot across the street and wheelchair accessibility make this an easy and convenient stop whether you're just driving through or staying for a few days in Williams. During the summer, the restaurant serves lunch and dinner and you may dine on the open patio. In the winter, they're open for

dinner only. It's within walking distance of many of Williams' motels, a good thing because Pancho's serves thirty types of tequila and is famous for its margaritas. Credit cards are welcome.

Peak Confection $
221 W. Railroad Ave.,
Williams, AZ 86046
(520) 635–0772;
fax (520) 635–1281
smithnme@gateway.com

Okay, so you've had lunch or dinner and you're looking for dessert or something tasty to take along on the next part of your trip. Try the absolutely scrumptious homemade fudge and other candies here at Peak Confection on Historic Route 66. Some products are sugar-free, and ice cream, hot fudge sundaes, and gift baskets are available. The shop is open all day Tuesdays through Saturdays, with shortened hours on Sundays; it is closed Mondays. Park on the street or in the nearby city parking lot. Owner and candy-maker Barbara Brunsing will accept personal checks and credit cards.

Motels and Hotels

Fray Marcos Hotel $$$$
235 N. Grand Canyon Blvd.,
Williams, AZ 86046
(520) 635–4010, (800) THE–TRAIN,
fax (520) 635–2180
www.thetrain.com

Adjacent to the Grand Canyon Railway Depot, the very plush Fray Marcos Hotel offers a turn-of-the-century atmosphere and modern amenities, including air-conditioning, hair dryers, and TVs. The 196 rooms (some non-smoking) are decorated in the Southwest style, and the lobby is graced by genuine Remington sculptures and original oil paintings by Kenny McKenna. A flagstone fireplace in the lobby and an authentic nineteenth-

century handcrafted bar in Spenser's Lounge, which serves drinks, pizza and appetizers, add to the atmosphere of old-time luxury. You can also enjoy the heated indoor swimming pool, a hot tub, and the fitness room. Max and Thelma's Restaurant is next door, and historic downtown Williams is just a few blocks away.

The hotel, like the depot, was originally completed in 1908; it was one of the Harvey Houses built by the Santa Fe Railroad to make rail travel more civilized. This building, similar in style to the original, was finished in 1995. Staying here entitles you to a discount on Grand Canyon Railway trips and packages. The hotel has eight wheelchair-accessible rooms. An extra $10 per person is charged for more than two adults in a room, with a maximum of four adults per room. Children under 18 stay free.

Quality Inn Mountain Ranch $$$
6701 Mountain Ranch Road,
Williams, AZ 86046
(520) 635–2693, (800) 228–5151,
fax (520) 635–4188
www.mountainranchresort.com

If you want a quiet haven as your starting point for exploring Williams and the Grand Canyon area, this 73-room motel is perfect. Set back in the cool pines and away from the railroad tracks, it is just seven miles east of Williams. Rooms have air-conditioning, TVs, hair dryers, and coffeemakers. In good weather, you can enjoy the swimming pool and whirlpool, tennis, basketball, and a putting green. For the children, an inviting lawn is a wonderful place to play after long hours in the car. Non-smoking rooms are available, and the motel is wheelchair accessible. There is a $10 charge for each extra person over age 12 in the room. Pets are allowed with a $20 non-refundable fee; major credit cards are accepted. The restaurant has a view of the San Francisco Peaks and serves breakfast (included in the room rate) and dinner. This motel is also the headquarters for Mountain Ranch Stables (see Recreation).

The Red Garter Bed and Bakery $$$
137 W. Railway Ave., Williams, AZ 86046
(520) 635–1484, (800) 328–1484
www.redgarter.com

Originally an 1897 bordello, this bed-and-breakfast in the middle of the downtown historic district has four non-smoking rooms, three of which accommodate two adults each and one of which accommodates four. The rooms, which are kept quite simple, have queen beds, private baths, and color TVs, but no phones. Children over the age of 8 are welcome. The continental-plus breakfast comprises items from the on-site bakery, including bagels, cinnamon buns, and strudels. Fresh fruit, juice, and coffee are also served. None of the rooms are wheelchair accessible. Ask owner John Holst to tell you about the building's colorful history—from bordello to flophouse to barbecue joint to warehouse. He has a scrapbook that he'll be happy to share, and be sure to ask about the two-story outhouse. He may also be willing to tell you about the ghosts that guests and employees have reported seeing on the premises. Major credit cards are accepted, and reservations are recommended.

Route 66 Inn $
128 E. Route 66, Williams, AZ 86046
(520) 635–4791, (888) 786–6956;
fax (520) 635–4993
www.thegrandcanyon.com/route66inn;
rt66inn@aol.com

Within walking distance of everything in town, this 20-unit inn is housed in a historic 1930s three-story building. Some rooms are family units with three beds, a refrigerator, and a microwave. All rooms have color TV with HBO, air-conditioning, and phones (local calls are free). You can hook up your laptop to the Internet using a phone line in the office. From April though September, the room rate includes a continental breakfast. Staying here entitles you to a 15% discount at Pancho's and discounts on package train, helicopter, and other tours arranged through the inn. The hosts will be happy to make your travel arrangements for you or to help you plan your trip. You can also take advantage of FedEx and UPS service at the inn, and there is a small gift shop. Non-smoking rooms are available, but wheelchair-accessible rooms are not. A $5 charge applies to extra people in the room, and pets require a $5 non-refundable fee.

> ## Insiders' Tip
> The Williams Health Care Center at 301 S. 7th Street, (520) 635-4441, is open 12 hours a day, and the regional hospital, Flagstaff Medical Center, is only 45 miles away

Shopping

The Route 66 Gift Shop
417 E. Route 66,
Williams, AZ 86046
(520) 635–0266;
fax (520) 635–2089
www.route66place.com

Since this large souvenir gift shop is attached to Twister's Soda Fountain, this is a one-stop mecca for the Route 66 enthusiast. The large gift shop has everything you can imagine (and some you probably can't) related to Route 66, from T-shirts to key chains to mugs. You should also check out the selection of Western wear and Minnetonka moccasins.

Neither kids nor adults will be able to resist these life-size carvings at the Dusty Bunch Gallery. PHOTO: TANYA LEE

Dusty Bunch Gallery
517 E. Route 66, Williams, AZ 86046
(520) 635–5332

The whimsical life-size carvings of Old West cowboys and Indians make this a place your kids won't let you drive by. The painted wood carvings are done by Kowalski and Sons, who also create wood bears in all sizes. Owner Linda Odijk carries a full complement of souvenirs for your gift shopping. Her Navajo jewelry and Zuni fetishes are purchased directly from Native American artists. The shop is open seven days a week in summer and six days in winter. Summer hours run into the late evenings so that people on day tours out of Williams will have a chance to shop here. You can pay for your purchases with a major credit card, traveler's checks, or personal checks up to $100.

Attractions

Grand Canyon Railway
Williams Depot, Williams, AZ 86046
(520) 773–1976, (800) THE–TRAIN,
international callers use (520) 773–1976
www.thetrain.com

For the adventure of a lifetime, board the Grand Canyon Railway at the historic 1908 Williams Depot (take exit 163 off Interstate 40 and drive one-half mile south) and ride the train to the Grand Canyon. A vintage steam or diesel engine pulls the old iron horse through valleys, pine forests, high desert plains, and small canyons. As the piercing whistle blows and you leave the depot at 10 A.M., you'll have a view of the majestic San Francisco Peaks. Be sure to get to the depot early—you won't want to miss the Wild West shootout at the depot before the train departs. On the two-and-a-quarter hour ride, uniformed conductors show you old-fashioned courtesy, and costumed strolling musicians will entertain you with country tunes.

The train takes you right to the 1910 Grand Canyon Depot on the South Rim, just steps away from the El Tovar hotel. You'll have more than three hours to explore the South Rim of the Grand Canyon on your own. Be sure not to miss the El Tovar, Hopi House, and Bright Angel Lodge's restaurant at Grand Canyon Village.

The railway also offers escorted motorcoach rim tours to some of the most popular scenic overlooks to give you a more encompassing look at one of the most visited natural wonders of the world. See

Mohave Point, Pima Point, the Abyss, and Hermits Rest. Fred Harvey Company offers three different motorcoach tours, all of which include lunch.

At 3:30, the train whistle will blow and you'll begin your return journey. An Old West train robbery, complete with bad-men armed with blazing pistols, will make you think you're riding the train through the territory a century ago when the first train from Williams pulled out of the station in 1901.

You'll arrive at 5:45 in time to visit the gift shop and free railway museum back at the Williams Depot. Passengers may also stay overnight at the Canyon and return to Williams the next day, and one-way tickets for the train are available.

The railway offers several classes of service for your trip. Coach Class puts you in an authentic 1923 Harriman railroad car with reversible seats so you and your friends can sit facing each other. Coach Class cars seat eighty-eight passengers; each car has its own restroom. Club Class gives you the additional benefit of being able to order drinks at an old-fashioned, fully-stocked mahogany bar in your railroad car, which seats fifty-eight. Coffee and pastries are served in the morning. First Class service will find you in a comfortable recliner. Fruit, pastries, coffee, and juice are served in the morning, and on the return journey, you will be served appetizers and champagne. Other alcoholic beverages are also available. The Deluxe Observation Class passengers enjoy all the amenities of First Class from an upper-level enclosed glass dome from which to view the scenery. Children over 11 years old are welcome. Finally, the Luxury Parlor Car gives you all the advantages of Observation Class, but in an elegant coach with an open-air rear platform, perfect for taking pictures. Some cars can be reserved in advance for groups and special events. Wheelchair access to the train and rim tours is limited, so be sure to inquire in advance. The Grand Canyon Railway operates every day except Christmas Eve and Christmas Day.

A variety of one- to four-night package tours is also available, including one designed specially for guests 55 and older. A one-day tour from Las Vegas includes round-trip airfare, the train ride, a motorcoach tour of the rim, and lunch. Call or write for details and prices. Amtrak has partnered with Grand Canyon Railway to make rail travel to the Canyon an easy option now that the Southwest Chief stops in Williams. Call (800) USA—RAIL for information on Amtrak service.

Kaibab Plateau Scenic Byway

This is AZ Highway 67, 44 miles of meadows, pine forests, and gorgeous aspens, which are particularly magnificent in the autumn. Be sure to bring your camera—this is known as the most beautiful stretch of road in the state. The highway begins at Jacob Lake north of the Grand Canyon and takes you to the North Rim of the Grand Canyon.

Belly up to the bar with an old-time cowboy aboard the Grand Canyon Railroad. PHOTO: COURTESY OF THE GRAND CANYON RAILROAD

Annual Events

Join trappers right out of the nineteenth century at this festival of black powder shoots, trading, and 1800s crafts at Buckskinner Park in south Williams. Throughout Memorial Day Weekend, trappers show off their expertise with flintlock and caplock rifles and pistols, and traders sell small leather pouches, old-style clothing, beads, guns, knives, tomahawks, blankets, and fur hats.

Some of today's buckskinners make rifles and pistols in the spring and summer and return to their traplines in the winter. Others follow the rendezvous circuit as traders. They use the same equipment when they are trapping in the winter as they do at the rendezvous, camping in teepees and four-pole lodges in the park.

The festival is a step back to a time when the Rocky Mountain Fur Trade Company held an annual rendezvous for mountain men each year from 1825 to 1840. Mountain men were trappers who used steel leg-hold traps to catch beavers, which were valuable for their pelts. Trapping was a tough life; only a few of the trappers survived the era of the rendezvous. Many are buried in unmarked graves. The fate of others is completely unknown—they just didn't show up for next rendezvous.

The first annual Rocky Mountain rendezvous was held in 1825 when General William Ashley of the Rocky Mountain Fur Company resupplied his trappers in the summer of 1825 on Randavouze Creek in southwestern Wyoming. During these days of socializing and boozing, trappers would compete to see who was best at throwing tomahawks and knives. These events were even more exciting than they would have been anyway because large sums of money were riding on the outcome as onlookers made their bets.

The men were called buckskinners because of the clothing the mountain trappers typically wore: breeches and hunting shirts made of buckskin, wide-brimmed hats, and leather belts and moccasins. In winter they added heavy fur coats, hats, and mittens, as well as a heavy wool blanket. The Hudson Bay four-point blanket had four stripes, which indicated the number of beaver pelts it cost.

Trappers sold their beaver pelts at the rendezvous for trade items. They usually left the rendezvous with little to show for their year's work—a new outfit, supplies for the next year, and a hangover. They traded for whiskey, which was diluted by half with creek water. To this they added a half plug of tobacco, two tablespoons of cayenne pepper, and a tablespoon of gunpowder. Today's version of trade whiskey is made with grain alcohol half diluted with water and spiked with molasses and cayenne pepper.

Free trappers (in contrast to trappers hired directly by trading companies) usually wintered with Indian tribes and often married Indian women. When the bottom fell out of the beaver pelt trade around 1840, some trappers became guides and hunters for the wagon trains that crossed the mountains to Oregon beginning in the early 1840s.

Today's Buckskinners recreate this legendary time by dressing in period clothing, living in teepees or primitive shelters, shooting muzzleloading black powder rifles and pistols, and throwing tomahawks and knives in friendly competition. Some who attend rendezvous days are still trappers, but most are hunters and outdoorsmen. In the early 1990s, about 150 trappers were licensed by the Arizona Game and Fish Department to trap beaver, fox, coyote, bobcat, raccoon, ringtail, and badger.

This family weekend is too good to miss. It is full of unusual and fun events. In addition to the activities in the park staged by the mountain men, all ages can enjoy downtown events—a parade, arts and crafts, food vendors, street entertainment, and a dance.

The Bill Williams Mountain Men also make an annual trail ride between the city of Williams and Phoenix and have ridden in five U.S. Presidential inaugural parades in Washington, D.C.

For more information, contact the Williams-Grand Canyon Chamber of Commerce, P.O. Box 235, Williams, AZ 86046-0235; (520) 635-4061

Small Town 4th of July

This Fourth of July celebration includes an old-fashioned parade, outdoor entertainment, an ice cream social, barbecue, and a craft fair in downtown historic Williams. After dark, you'll be treated to a spectacular show of fireworks with Bill Williams Mountain as the backdrop.

Cowpunchers Reunion Rodeo

Real working cowboys get together for this big rodeo held the first weekend in August at the Rodeo Grounds. Call (520) 635-9526 for more information.

Labor Day PRCA Rodeo

Spend Labor Day weekend in Williams at this rodeo featuring top professional rodeo cowboys. This big-time rodeo includes bull riding, barrel racing, bucking broncos, and all the other traditional rodeo events. Watch the rodeo parade on Saturday, and join in the barn dancing later in the day.

Mountain Village Holiday

A million Christmas lights adorn this small mountain town from Thanksgiving through New Year's Day, with a Parade of Lights on the second Saturday in December. Hayrides, craft sales, arts shows, and shopping make this a good time to visit Williams.

Kidstuff

Grand Canyon Deer Farm
6752 E. Deer Farm Road,
Williams, AZ 86046
(520) 635-4073, (800) 926-DEER,
fax (520) 635-2357   www.deerfarm.com

Take exit 171 off Interstate 40 (eight miles east of town) and follow the signs to reach this petting and feeding zoo that is a long-time favorite with local children. Kids can visit many varieties of deer, wallabees, llamas, coatimundi, antelope, and a buffalo. They are most likely to see the babies during fawning season, May through July. A large gift shop sells T-shirts, souvenirs, and gifts. Hours vary according to season, but the deer farm is open year-round, except for Thanksgiving and Christmas. Major credit cards are accepted. Children under two are admitted free, and children's entry fees apply to kids 3-13.

Recreation

Elephant Rock Golf Course
(520) 635-4936; pro shop (520) 635-4936
www.thegrandcanyon/golf

This 18-hole, par 72 municipal golf course is a mile west of town near exit 161 off Interstate 40. After exiting the highway, take a right and drive 1.5 miles; the golf course will be on your right. The championship tees are 6,700 yards with a rating of 70.8 and a slope of 128. Middle tees are 6,076 yards with a rating of 67.7 and a slope of 119. Front tees are 5,432 yards; the rating is 69.2 and the slope 127. You will also be able to practice on the driving range and the putting and chipping greens. The pro shop offers club rentals, balls, clothing, bags, and other accessories. Golf carts are available. Tee times may be reserved up to a week in advance. Visa and MasterCard are accepted. The golf course is open from early March to December, but these dates may vary depending on the weather.

Williams Ski Area
Bill Williams Mountain,
Williams, AZ 86046
(520) 635-9330

A poma lift that reaches 8,150 feet takes you to five main runs for beginner, intermediate, and advanced skiers. Adventuresome skiers are also allowed to make their own trails through the trees. Beginners may want to use the rope lift. A day lodge serves snacks, and the ski school offers complete equipment rentals for downhill and cross-country skiing and snowboarding. Kids will enjoy the indoor child play area. Four miles south of town, the ski area is open every day during the season except Wednesday. A defined ski season is a little difficult to determine these days. Usually Williams could count on enough snow for skiing from mid December through mid April. But the last years of the nineties produced very little snow all winter, so be sure to call ahead to find out if the ski area is open. For ski reports call the ski area itself or the Williams Chamber of Commerce at (520) 635-4061.

Mountain Ranch Stables
Quality Inn Mountain Ranch,
P.O. Box 781, Williams, AZ 86046
(520) 635-0706 or 635-2693,
fax (520) 635-4188

One of the best ways to get a sense of the West is to take a horseback trail ride through the beautiful Kaibab National Forest. This stable maintains about 25 horses, so they have suitable mounts for almost anyone. Most rides are one or two hours, but longer rides can be arranged, or enjoy a hayride and cookout with cowboy singing. Take exit 171 off Interstate 40, seven miles east of Williams. The same proprietors also operate Stable in the Pines, 100 Circle Pine Road, Williams, AZ 86046, (520) 635-2626 or (800) 732-0537. Both stables are open April through September or longer, depending on weather.

Kaibab National Forest

In 1934, the Tusayan National Forest and Forest Service land north of Grand Canyon were combined to form the

Insiders' Tip

The Williams Visitors Center is at 200 W. Railroad Avenue, Williams, AZ 86046. The phone numbers are (520) 635-4061, 635-4207, fax (520) 635-1417. The center is open seven days a week year round.

Kaibab National Forest, one of the six national forests in Arizona.

This forest borders both the North and South Rims of the Grand Canyon and covers 1.5 million acres at elevations from 5,500 to 10,418 feet (at the top of Kendrick Peak). At higher elevations, the forest is mostly ponderosa pine with alpine meadows and mixed conifers. At lower elevations, expect to see mostly juniper and piñon.

Travel is restricted to foot and horseback only in the 115,000 acres of wilderness areas, including Saddle Mountain Wilderness and Kanab Creek Wilderness on the north rim of the Grand Canyon and Kendrick Peak Wilderness and parts of Sycamore Canyon Wilderness near Williams.

Photographers and nature lovers will enjoy seeing the wildlife of the forest, which includes mule deer, elk, pronghorn antelope, and black bear, as well as smaller animals, reptiles, and birds, such as bald eagles, other raptors, and marsh birds. One animal, the Kaibab squirrel, is found only on the Kaibab Plateau. You can distinguish it from the Abert squirrel by its dark body and white tail. The best time to see the wildlife is from the beginning of May through the beginning of November when the roads are open.

The natural and cultural resources of the forest are protected and regulated by the stewardship of Forest Service rangers who administer rules on ranching, lumbering, and homesteading, build lookouts to fight fires, and build and maintain trails and roads into the forest.

For more information about the forest, contact Kaibab National Forest, 800 S. 6th Street, Williams, AZ 86046; (520) 635–8200; TTY (520) 635–8222. The Williams/Forest Service Visitor Center is located at 200 W. Railroad Ave., Williams, AZ 86046; (520) 635–4061, (800) 863–0546; www.fs.fed.us/r3/kai. The Kaibab Plateau Visitor Center, open during the summer, is at the intersection of Highways 64 and 67 in Jacob Lake. The voice/TTY phone is (520) 643–7298.

Beale Wagon Road

The Beale Road crosses the Williams Ranger District from east to west north of Interstate 40. The road's hiking and horseback riding trails are accessible at Laws Spring about 20 miles northeast of Williams.

Laws Spring is a water hole where you will see rock carvings inscribed by members of the 1858 Beale Expedition as well as petroglyphs left by Indian travelers, and you can walk to a small section of the original Beale Road. Travel on Beale Road by motorized vehicle is prohibited. To get to Laws Spring from Williams, take AZ 64 about 5 miles to Spring Valley Road (FR 141). Turn right and drive 7 miles to FR 730. Turn left and go 3 miles to FR 115. Turn left and continue 1.5 miles to FR 2030. Follow the sign to the parking area. Laws Spring is a short walk. FR 115 and FR 2030 are not suitable for passenger cars, only for high-clearance vehicles, such as 4x4s or pickup trucks. You can get information on other access points to the Beale Wagon Road and maps at the Forest Service office in Williams.

Hiking and Camping

Dozens of trails around Williams will keep the intrepid hiker busy. They will take you through forests, canyons, meadows, parks, and historic sites. Difficulty varies from quite easy to quite strenuous, especially at these altitudes (6,800 to over 10,000 feet). For a detailed description of over 30 hikes in and around Williams, pick up a copy of *Williams Guidebook* by Richard and Sherry Magnum [Flagstaff, Arizona: Hexagon Press, 1998].

Seven developed campgrounds on the Kaibab National Forest offer tables, drinking water, pit toilets, and fire grates. Reservations are not needed, and campsites are allocated on a first-come, first-served basis. Most are open only during the summer. Backcountry camping is allowed throughout most of the forest.

For more hiking and camping information, contact the Kaibab National Forest at (520) 635–4061 or (800) 863–0546, 742 South Clover Road, Williams, AZ 86046, or visit their website: www.fs.fed.us/r3/kai.

Insiders' Tip

Amtrak has partnered with Grand Canyon Railway to make rail travel to the Canyon an easy option now that the Southwest Chief stops in Williams. Call (800) USA-RAIL for information on Amtrak service.

Circle Pines KOA
1000 Circle Pines Road,
Williams, AZ 86046
(520) 635–4545, (800) 732–0537,
(800) KOA-9379
www.koa.com

Nestled in the tall pines, this well-equipped campground has thirty tent sites and 120 pull-through RV sites, as well as cabins. Take a mini-vacation right here and enjoy horseback riding, hayrides, an indoor heated swimming pool, and two spas. For the basics, Circle Pines KOA offers flush toilets, a laundry, hot showers in a tiled bathroom, a grocery store, and a gift shop. Kids will stay entertained with the playground and miniature golf course. The campground offers a van tour of the Grand Canyon and a free shuttle to the Grand Canyon Railway. Don't forget to ask for your discount coupon for the railroad. Take exit 167 off Interstate 40 to 1000 Circle Pines Road. Major credit cards are accepted, and the campground is open year-round.

Red Lake Arizona Campground
8850 N. Highway 64, Williams, AZ 86046
(520) 635–9122, (800) 581–4753,
fax (520) 635–5321
redlake@infomagic.com

Red Lake, 10 miles north of Williams, was settled in 1896 and served as a camp for Chinese laborers working on the railroad to the Grand Canyon. This four-acre accommodation is much more than a campground, offering an independent hostel, twelve tent sites, a deli, and a gift shop. The hostel has European-style dormitories that hold up to four people in each room as well as private rooms. Everyone shares the common room with a TV, refrigerator, microwave, and free coffee. Guests make and strip their own beds. Tenters and hostel guests share the bath house, which has separate toilet and shower facilities for men and women. Groups should call for special rates. The gift shop features leather jackets and tourist souvenirs as well as signed Native American jewelry, pottery, rugs, blankets, and concho belts. The campground is open year-round, and reservations are strongly recommended. Pets are not allowed in rooms but are welcome at the tent sites. The proprietors will be happy to make reservations for you for air tours, helicopter rides, and river running. Major credit cards are accepted. To reach the campground, take AZ Highway 64 north off Interstate 40. Go 8.2 miles and the facility will be on your right.

Media and Selected Readings

Arizona Daily Sun
1751 S. Thompson St., Flagstaff, AZ 86001
(520) 774–4545
www.azdailysun.com

The Arizona Daily Sun prints 13,500 newspapers each day and 16,000 on Saturday and Sunday. A special Wednesday edition is printed for the Navajo and Hopi Reservations and a mid-week extra is printed for Flagstaff (on Wednesday.) The mid-week extra has classified ads, Dear Abby, and an entertainment section. The Sunday edition includes a Sun Dial TV Guide.

Flagstaff Live!/Mountain Living Magazine
111 W. Birch St., Flagstaff, AZ 86001
(520) 779–1877
www.flaglive.com

Flagstaff Live! is a weekly arts and entertainment free magazine that comes out every Thursday. Special features include "Live!Wire," a section for community announcements. "Pulse," a daily calendar section is separated by the following categories: Interesting & Educational, Kids & Families, Performances, Music, Sedona, and Sports & Outdoor events. The "Hot Picks" page highlights musical, theatrical, and interesting happenings around the northland. *Flagstaff Live!* prints 7,500 copies a week and distributes them to 195 bases around northern Arizona.

Mountain Living Magazine, a free monthly publication, circulates 7,000 copies per month. An estimated 3,300 are mailed to homes in Flagstaff. The magazine is also available at 200 bases around northern Arizona. *Mountain Living Magazine* focuses on Flagstaff's business and community issues.

Red Rock News
298 Van Deren St.
(520) 282–795

Sedona's biweekly newspaper is printed every Wednesday and Friday. An estimated 8,000 newspapers are printed each week.

Sedona Magazine
271 Van Deren St.
(520) 282–9022
www.searchsearch.com

This quarterly magazine focuses on the city and lifestyle of Sedona and 25,000 copies are printed and distributed nationally. You can find a complimentary copy in Sedona area hotels and resorts. The magazine is also available on newsstands across the country. This publisher also comes out with an annual Visitors Guide. You can find the free *Sedona Visitors Guide* in Phoenix, Scottsdale, and Sedona.

Selected Readings

Colorado Plateau

David Roberts,. *In Search of the Old Ones: Exploring the Anasazi World of the Southwest* [New York: Simon and Schuster, 1996].

Edward Abbey, *Desert Solitaire: A Season in the Wilderness* [New York, Simon and Schuster, 1968]

Halka Chronic, *Roadside Geology of Arizona* [Missoula, Mountain Press Publishing Company, 1983]

Charles Wilkinson, *Fire on the Plateau: Conflict and Endurance in the American Southwest* [Washington, D.C.: Island Press/Shearwater Books, 1999]

Geology

Wendell A. Duffield, *Volcanoes of Northern Arizona: Sleeping Giants of the Grand Canyon Region.* Photographs by Michael Collier. [Grand Canyon, Arizona: Grand Canyon Association, 1997].

Grand Canyon

Adkinson, Ron. *Hiking Grand Canyon National Park* [Helena, Montana: Falcon Publishing, Inc., 1997].

Grattan, Virginia L. *Mary Colter: Builder Upon the Red Earth* [Grand Canyon, Arizona: Grand Canyon Natural History Association, 1992].

Hagerty, Donald J., *Beyond the Visible Terrain: The Art of Ed Mell* [Flagstaff, Arizona: Northland Publishing, 1996].

Hughes, J. Donald, *In the House of Stone and Light: Introduction to the Human History of Grand Canyon* [Grand Canyon, Arizona: Grand Canyon Natural History Association, 1985].

Lloyd, Harvey, photographer. *Sacred Lands of the Southwest* [New York: The Monacelli Press, 1995].

Suran, William C. *The Kolb Brothers of Grand Canyon* [Grand Canyon, Arizona: Grand Canyon Natural History Association, 1991].

Hopi

Day, Jonathan S. *Traditional Hopi Katsinas: A New Generation of Carvers* [Flagstaff, Arizona: Northland Publishing, 2000].

James, Harry C. *Pages from Hopi History* [Tucson, Arizona: University of Arizona Press, 1974].

Nequatewa, Edmund. *Truth of a Hopi: Stories Relating to the Origin, Myths, and Clan Histories of the Hopi* [Flagstaff, AZ: Northland Press (in cooperation with the Museum of Northern Arizona), 1967].

Page, Jake and Susanne. *Hopi* [New York: Harry N. Abrams, Inc., 1986].

Secakuku, Alph H. *Following the Sun and Moon: Hopi Kachina Tradition.* Landscape photography by Owen Seumptewa. Object photography by Craig Smith. [Flagstaff, Arizona: Northland Publishing in cooperation with the Heard Museum, 1995].

Whiteley, Peter M. *Deliberate Acts: Changing Hopi Culture Through the Oraibi Split* [Tucson, Arizona: University of Arizona Press, 1988].

Wright, Margaret Nickelson. *Hopi Silver: The History and Hallmarks of Hopi Silversmithing* [Flagstaff, Arizona: Northland Publishing, 1982].

Plateau, a quarterly magazine published by the Museum of Northern Arizona Press, Route 4, Box 720, Flagstaff, AZ 86001. The magazine is free to museum members.

Navajo

Bennett, Noël and Tiana Bighorse. *Navajo Weaving Way: The Path from Fleece to Rug.* Photographs by John Running. [Loveland, Colorado: Interweave Press, 1997].

Feher-Elston, Catherine. *Children of Sacred Ground: America's Last Indian War* [Flagstaff, Arizona: Northland Publishing, 1988].

Hedlund, Ann Lane, *"Contemporary Navajo Weaving: Thoughts That Count."* Plateau Magazine, Vol. 65, No. 1 [Flagstaff, Arizona: Museum of Northern Arizona, 1994].

Johnson, Broderick H., ed. *Navajo Stories of the Long Walk Period* [Tsaile, Navajo Nation, Arizona: Navajo Community College Press, 1973].

Kawano, Kenji. *Warriors: Navajo Code Talkers* [Flagstaff, Arizona: Northland Publishing, 1990].

Navajo Nation Government, Fourth Edition, 1998, published by Navajo Government Development Office, P.O. Box 220, Window Rock, AZ 86515-0220; (520) 871-7241/7161.

Sundberg, Lawrence D. *Dinétah: An Early History of the Navajo People* [Santa Fe, New Mexico, 1995].

Zolbrod, Paul G. *Diné bahane': The Navajo Creation Story* [Albuquerque: University of New Mexico Press, 1984].

Index

About the Authors

Tanya H. Lee

Writer and artist Tanya H. Lee first visited the enchanted land of the Colorado Plateau almost two decades ago. A few years later, she and her husband, Garret Rosenblatt, bought some land east of Flagstaff, built a house, and relocated from Cambridge, Massachusetts. A barn, two horses, and innumerable cats later, she is still exploring the many facets—geological, historical, and cultural—of this unique area.

Ms. Lee earned her Bachelors degree at Tufts University and her Masters at the Harvard Graduate School of Education. She has been a freelance writer for many years, first working on textbooks and teachers' manuals for instruction in elementary school reading and language arts, then moving on to journalism and magazine writing. In the early eighties, she revived her childhood love of art and began to create her own mixed media assemblages, which have been shown in several galleries in Massachusetts and Arizona.

Her job as Managing Editor of the *Navajo-Hopi Observer* published in Flagstaff allowed her to pursue her long-standing interest in the Native cultures of northern Arizona and the Grand Canyon. She has traveled widely on the Navajo and Hopi Reservations and developed a working knowledge of the peoples' histories and current concerns, which she shares with readers of the *Insiders' Guide to the Grand Canyon,* along with detailed information about where to go and what to see to make your visit a memorable one.

Kerri Quinn

Kerri Quinn was born in New York City and lived on the east coast until the age of twenty. She had always been intrigued by the landscape and people of the West and moved to Phoenix, Arizona. After spending a few years traveling around the Southwest and through Montana and Wyoming, Kerri came to Flagstaff, Arizona to finish her Bachelors degree in English and Spanish at Northern Arizona University.

After completing her degree, Kerri left Flagstaff to live in Spain and to continue her studies in Spanish. Upon her return to the United States, she felt the same pull of the West and returned to Flagstaff. She has lived here for the past eight years, and has worked as a Spanish teacher, and is currently a marketing coordinator for a local publishing company.

Since the age of eleven, Kerri has wanted to be a writer. She currently writes for *Flagstaff Live!, SWEAT Magazine, Arizona Daily Sun,* and also writes stories for children.